Seeds of Hate

D1396693

WITHDRAWN

3 3503 00104 5958

Seeds of Hate

How America's Flawed Middle East Policy Ignited the Jihad

Lawrence Pintak

State Library OF Ohio

SEO Library Center
40780 SR 821 * Caldwell, OH 43724

Pluto ▐▛▐▜ Press

LONDON • STERLING, VIRGINIA

This edition first published 2003 by Pluto Press
345 Archway Road, London N6 5AA
and 22883 Quicksilver Drive, Sterling, VA 20166-2012, USA

www.plutobooks.com

Copyright © Lawrence Pintak 2003

Excerpts from *Wall Street Journal* reprinted with permission
© Dow Jones & Company, Inc. 1982
All Rights Reserved.

Lyrics to "Goodnight Saigon" used by permission. Words and music by Billy Joel.
© 1981, 1982 Joel Songs. All Rights Controlled and Administered by SBIC Blackwood
Music Inc. All Rights Reserved.
International Copyright Secured.

The right Lawrence Pintak to be identified as the author of
this work has been asserted by him in accordance with the Copyright,
Designs and Patents Act 1988.

British Library Cataloguing in Publication Data
A catalogue record for this book is available from the British Library

ISBN 0 7453 2044 9 hardback
ISBN 0 7453 2043 0 paperback

Library of Congress Cataloging in Publication Data
Pintak, Lawrence.
  Seeds of hate : how America's flawed Middle East policy ignited the jihad /
Lawrence Pintak.
     p. cm.
Rev. and updated ed. of: Beirut lives. 1987.
Includes bibliographical references.
   ISBN 0–7453–2044–9 — ISBN 0–7453–2043–0 (pbk.)
   1. Lebanon—History—Israeli intervention, 1982–1984. 2.Lebanon—History—Civil
War, 1975–1990. 3. Middle East—Foreign relations—United States. 4. United
States—Foreign relations—Middle East. 5. Terrorism—Middle East. I. Title.
   DS87.53 .P565 2003
   327.7305692'09'045—dc21

                                                              2003007465

10   9   8   7   6   5   4   3   2   1

Designed and produced for Pluto Press by
Chase Publishing Services, Sidmouth, EX10 9QG, England
Typeset from disk by Stanford DTP Services, Towcester, England
Printed and bound in Canada by Transcontinental Printing

Contents

For the violence done to Lebanon shall sweep over you, the havoc done to its beasts shall break your own spirit, because of bloodshed and violence done to the land, to the city, and all its inhabitants.

—Habakkuk 2:17
Old Testament

To Indira: Dakini, partner, eternal love.
Restless, searching
I wandered through time.
Incomplete.
Not knowing why.
Finding you (again), I found myself.

And to Annya, Shantara and Justin, who give meaning to it all.

Preface

"The images that inhabit the television screen each night are violent, bloody. The babble of broken English is incomprehensible. Airplanes are blown up. Embassies are bombed. People with strange names and strange clothes are killing Americans, and it's hard to understand exactly why.

"Shi'ites, Palestinians, Soldiers of God and Revolutionary Cells. In the daily march of the world's horrors, it all becomes a blur."

I wrote those words in 1988 for the preface to the first edition of this book. Tragically, they are just as true today. The only difference is that now there is no corner of the world where Americans – or other Westerners – are truly safe.

A few days after the September 11 attacks, I was a guest on a National Public Radio program that was part of the white noise of analysis trying to answer the plaintive question rising like a moan from the American body politic: Why do they hate us?

"When you were based in Beirut," the host asked, "did you ever, in your wildest dreams, think this kind of thing could happen in the U.S.?"

He appeared genuinely shocked when I answered with a simple yes. The only surprise, I told him, was that it had not happened sooner.

In a world where terror has become part of the fabric of life, a place in which even schoolchildren recognize Osama bin Laden's face, the name *Beirut* continues to strike a special chord. It ranks beside *Iran* and *al-Qaeda* as a synonym for terror. And so it should. For it was in the soil of Lebanon that the seeds of the hatred that stalks America were first planted; seeds of hate that were then fertilized by the detritus of a flawed U.S. foreign policy that alienated our friends and lent succor to our enemies.

America's brief encounter with Lebanon lasted less than two years. But it was long enough to show the world that a handful of men and women with a few hundred pounds of explosives and a willingness to give their lives could bring a superpower to its knees.

It was in Lebanon that America told Muslim civilians it would protect them, then watched them die. It was in Lebanon that supposedly neutral U.S. forces fired in anger on Muslim forces for the first time since World War II. It was amid the Crusader fortresses of Lebanon that American "peacekeepers" sided with the Christians and their Israeli allies against the forces of Islam, reopening a thousand-year-old wound.

It has become almost a cliché to say that "everything changed" on September 11, 2001. Those who have witnessed the evolution of Islamic terror know the *real* watershed occurred April 18, 1983. On that day, a young Lebanese Muslim named Muhammed Hassuna drove a pickup truck carrying the equivalent of 2,000 pounds of TNT into the lobby of the U.S. embassy in Beirut. With that act of martyrdom was launched a deadly new kind of modern warfare that would set Islam and the West on a collision course, engulf the world in fear, and define the post-Cold War era.

The moment those embassy walls collapsed, everything changed. We just didn't know it at the time.

From August 1982 through the final pullout in February 1984, Americans watched helplessly as U.S. marines died in a country where their government said they did not have an enemy. "Why do those people hate us?" Americans first asked back then. "What have we done to them?" When the Lebanese started killing our boys, the folks at home had a hard time understanding why. It was all too confusing; everybody over there seemed to have a gun and it seemed like they were all aimed at us. Two decades later, the echoes of those first suicide bombs still resonate; so, too, does the plaintive question, "Why?"

In the months after the Marines' humiliating pullout, many Americans – especially those in the Reagan administration – tried to put it all behind them. Our involvement, they said, was an ugly chapter best forgotten. But wishing didn't make it so.

The Beirut experience left America's foreign policy in a shambles, its credibility in tatters and the national psyche scarred. The shock waves from Beirut are today being felt from Baltimore to Bali as the anti-Western terror born in the slums of Lebanon has ignited a worldwide jihad that includes in its ranks individuals from every stratum of Muslim society.

There are no simple explanations for the rise of what the West has come to call Islamic fundamentalism: the failure of Arab nationalism, a backlash against the spread of American culture, and the absence of political rights in much of the Islamic world are just some of the contributing factors.

The web sites and communiqués of Islamic militant groups cite specific reasons for their acts. These include the Afghan and Iraqi conflicts, the presence of U.S. troops near the Muslim holy cities (now reduced as a result), American support for Israel and a host of other grievances. But while such issues may drive the generals of the terror movement, not every would-be *jihadi* abhors American culture or gives a damn whether Saddam Hussein lived or died. What binds the foot-soldiers of the jihad – these Lebanese, Egyptians, Algerians, Palestinians, Yemenis, Pakistanis,

Filipinos, and Muslims from scores of other countries – is their hopelessness, their frustration, and their jealousy of a civilization that has so much, yet seems to care so little; their resentment of a country that talks of justice and equality, yet picks and chooses who deserves those rights; their alienation in the face of a superpower that flaunts its brawn.

It was Iran's Shi'ite revolution – and its takeover of the U.S. embassy in Tehran – that gave hope to radical Islamists across the Muslim world. It was on the battlefields of Afghanistan that many leaders of what became the Sunni terror networks learned their trade. But it was in Beirut that modern Islamic terror exposed America's Achilles' heel. That seminal moment in history will haunt America for years to come.

"In the past, when the Marines were in Beirut, we screamed, 'Death to America!'" Hassan Nasrallah, leader of Lebanon's Hizbullah movement, declared on the eve of the U.S. invasion of Iraq. "Today, when the region is being filled with hundreds of thousands of American soldiers, 'Death to America!' was, is and will stay our slogan."[1]

Ronald Reagan defeated Communism. But the seeds of hate he planted in Beirut have spawned a new confrontation that is, in many ways, even more frightening and unpredictable than his worst Cold War nightmares.

L.P.
May 1, 2003
Princeton, MA

Section I

Fertile Ground

1

The Lebanese Jigsaw

If we are there to keep peace, we are far too few. ...
If we are there to die, then we are far too many.
—Representative Sam M. Gibbons (D-FL)[1]

The parking lot had become a morgue. Unrecognizable pieces of what had once been United States marines lay on stretchers lined up on the rubble-strewn tarmac. There was no time for the niceties of body bags or blankets. Those would come later. The living took priority now; God only knew how many were still buried under there.

Scores of marines, some in the red gym shorts they slept in, others wearing camouflage pants and T-shirts, scrambled over the smoking wreckage, prying at the broken concrete with shovels, picks, and their bare hands, desperately trying to reach the buddies they could hear pleading for help below. Italian peacekeepers, Lebanese troops, and teenagers clad in the white aprons of the local rescue squads, toiled beside them. As the survivors were dug out, stretcher-bearers rushed them to hastily set up first aid stations or waiting ambulances.

The roof of the four-story Battalion Landing Team (BLT) headquarters now stood at eye level. The phenomenal force of the blast had literally lifted the building from its foundation, sheared off concrete columns 15 feet around, blown out the lower walls, and caused the structure to collapse onto itself.

The wail of sirens was deafening. Ambulances raced in and out of the compound, some heading for local hospitals, others for helicopters waiting to shuttle the wounded out to hospital facilities aboard the USS *Iwo Jima* offshore. The only medical officer on the beach and most of the hospital corpsmen had been in the BLT. They were dead or wounded. The battalion aid station had been in the basement. It was buried under tons of debris. The surviving medics and ordinary marines frantically applied first aid to the wounded waiting to be loaded onto ambulances, treating the worst

3

cases first, putting to one side those whose injuries were not going to kill them immediately and those who were beyond help.

Jumpy marines, some fighting back tears, took up positions along the fence facing the road that flanked the wrecked building. Eyes shifting nervously over the crowds of Lebanese soldiers and rescue workers who rushed past their posts, it was clear the American boys didn't know who or what they were guarding against. Some of the ambulances were from the militias they had been fighting for months. Whose side were they on now? Later, there would be intelligence reports that the rescue teams had been infiltrated by more terrorists. No one was ever sure if the stories were true. How could the marines tell who among the scores of Arabs was "good" and who was "bad"?

Other marines, trucked in from units on the airport perimeter, stood in stunned silence, awed by the scale of the destruction. When the explosion had first crashed through their dreams, they had assumed that they were under artillery bombardment. They could deal with that. But this ...

Four miles away, the French were digging out their own. The bomb at the Drakker Building had gone off within seconds of the one that hit the Marines. It had been smaller, but so was the building. Unlike the Americans, who were confined to the airport compound, the French were responsible for a wide area of residential Beirut, so their men were scattered at smaller, neighborhood outposts. Fifty-eight French soldiers died when the suicide bomber detonated his load at the entrance to their quarters. The Lebanese civilians who shared the apartment building with them perished, too. One man who lived there survived by a fluke. He had gone out that morning to catch some fish for a friend's Sunday lunch. When he heard the explosion, he quickly returned. His wife and children were gone.

The sound of the explosions woke much of Beirut that quiet Sunday dawn. On the sixth floor of the Commodore Hotel, at least five miles from the Marine compound, I was shaken awake as the building trembled and windows rattled. A groggy glance at the alarm clock revealed the ungodly hour: 6:20.

There comes a time when car bombs begin to lose their fascination. For me, that time had long since passed. Any evening might bring the echo of two, three, or four resounding blasts in the night. Most were the work of local protection rackets or the result of petty feuds. Nothing worth passing on to the American television viewer, whose excitement threshold had been raised in direct proportion to the ability of the people of the Middle East to inflict increasingly horrendous violence on each other.

Most blasts would result in a few injuries or maybe one or two dead. "A little girl was killed, nothing to worry about," someone would report as they came into the hotel, and everyone would relax. In Beirut, cynicism took root quickly. At one time, we would run out with the cameras every time something went bang in the night (or day). But in the weeks before October 23, 1983, so many things had been going bang, with so little return for us, that we had become more selective in what we pursued. It was that or never sleep.

So it was difficult to be enthusiastic about the idea of getting out of bed at 6:20 on an otherwise quiet Sunday morning to go chase some silly noise. I let my head flop back onto the pillow and debated the idea of going back to sleep. It was tempting. The explosion had been loud, louder than anything I had heard in a while, but then it was probably close by. Maybe Lucy Spiegel, my producer, or one of the half dozen camera crews we had on hand would go and check it out on their own. But what if it hadn't woken Lucy? And if the crews didn't get the call, each would probably figure I had phoned someone else. Ah, I told myself, it was probably just somebody blowing up a grocery store again. But then someone had set off a remote control bomb as a Marine patrol had passed a few days before...

I reached for the phone and rang cameraman Dave Green. He had heard the explosion, too, and was already awake.

In the car moments later, the pillar of smoke led us like a beacon to the French blast. As we raced along behind ambulances and fire trucks toward the smoking pyre, it never occurred to us that this was just a sideshow. The main event lay four miles away.

Dozens of French soldiers were carefully climbing over the wreckage. Others stood watching, unsure where to start. Muffled cries for help could be heard from below. Soldiers crowded around one spot. An outstretched hand reach up through the rubble, gripping that of a comrade on the surface as if clinging to life itself.

Some French officers, calm and deliberate, conferred over how to proceed with the search, while others issued orders to the troops.

"How many men are inside?" I asked one officer. "Many," he said, shaking his head gravely. "Too many."

The American television networks spend vast amounts of money pouring people and equipment into foreign stories, but success or failure often ends up resting in the hands of the local drivers. That morning was to be no different. With the videocassette containing the first ten minutes of Green's footage of the French disaster, I hurried back to the hotel to get the tape on the road to the satellite station and send more crews out to the French bombing. As I came in the door and tossed the tape to Lucy, Ayad Harake, one of our best drivers, rushed up.

"They blow the Marines," he shouted.

No, I assured him. It was the French.

"No," he insisted, "the Marines."

"Ayad, I just came from there. It was the French."

He was angry now. It was tough dealing with these thick foreigners.

"The Marines, too. They blow the Marines, too," he said, grabbing me by the shoulders.

I jumped into Ayad's car with Sami Awad and Hassan Harake, our Lebanese camera team, to check out his story. I was convinced we were on a wild-goose chase.

My skepticism ended on the airport road. The thick, gray plume of smoke could be seen a mile away. As we got closer, a cold, empty feeling settled in the pit of my stomach.

In big explosions, where buildings are destroyed, the area immediately around is carpeted in dust and bits of debris. A half-mile away from the Marine compound, the road looked as if it was covered with a layer of fresh snow. As we approached the first Marine positions, still more than 100 yards from the main compound, the car bounced over chunks of cement littering our path. This was a big one.

The wind shifted, blowing the smoke toward us, obstructing our view. I strained to see what had been wrecked, looking for the four-story Battalion Landing Team headquarters to use as a point of reference. The sudden realization was like hitting a brick wall. The BLT was gone.

In a disaster on the scale of the morning of October 23, 1983, the adrenaline takes over. Emotions are sealed off. The door to that part of the brain crashes shut. The mind becomes like a camera. It registers images. It accepts facts. It assesses scale. It notes the human tragedy, but it does so on a mechanical level.

It's almost like watching television. You are caught up in what's going on, but somehow it doesn't directly affect you.

For soldier, rescue worker or reporter, the process is crucial to the ability to function. If the enormity of the horror breaks through at the time, you become useless. The human reaction can come later. If it does not, the emotions have become cauterized. It is time to find another line of work.

From the chaos of the scene at Beirut airport that fateful Sunday morning, individual images linger:

A black marine, his face caked with cement dust, reaching back to pull up a pair of red gym shorts to cover his exposed rear end even as the stretcher that held him was lifted from a gap in the rubble. There was a huge lump on his forehead. Beneath it, his eyes showed wide and frightened. Ignoring fellow marines who were trying to get him to lie down and relax, he propped himself up by his elbows and surveyed the scene in disbelief as they carried him away.

A helicopter pilot, helmet visor obscuring his face, kneeling as if in benediction beside a single stretcher in the empty runway, imparting a few works of encouragement or prayer to a wounded buddy before the flight out to the ships.

The thousand-yard stare on the face of a young marine as he sat in the shade of a water tank to take it all in.

The gaunt, gray face of Major Robert Jordan, the Marine spokesman. Stopping in front of Sami and Hassan, he pushed his helmet back, gazed directly into the camera lens as if it was not even there, and in a voice heavy with unspeakable sorrow, whispered "Sami" in recognition, shook his head as if trying to make himself believe it had all really happened, then wandered off. There was nothing more to say.

Twelve thousand pounds of explosives. FBI investigators would later report that they had never seen an explosion so devastating. British troops in their bunkers a few miles away saw a huge mushroom cloud rise over the Marine compound and thought the Americans had been nuked.

Instead, one man driving a yellow Mercedes truck had taken the lives of 241 U.S. military personnel. Not since D Day on Iwo Jima had so many marines died on a single day.

It wasn't as if the Americans hadn't been warned. The rubble of the U.S. Embassy stood just three miles away. Six months before, it too had been ravaged by a suicide bomber. Sixty-three people had been killed. Security at the new, temporary embassy in a complex of buildings on the seafront corniche had been beefed up, but the lesson had apparently been lost on the Marine brass, who were preoccupied with the political mission to "show the flag" imposed on them by the White House. The Marine compound was protected by the usual barbed wire and guardposts, but, tragically, not enough to deter a suicide bomber.

Blowing up diplomats was one thing, but the attitude among Marine officers seemed to be: "It can't happen to us." After all, Marines knew all about wars.

But they didn't know all about Lebanese wars.

You can't tell the players without a scorecard, so before coming over from the States, Marine units heading for Lebanon were shown a movie that gave them a thumbnail sketch of the country where some of them would soon die. It showed clips of children playing and fighters fighting. The marines saw the Shi'ites and Palestinians they would meet in the shantytowns around the airport, the Druzes of the mountains (they were the guys in the funny baggy pants), and all the rest. Only there was no narration, and the chaplains who led the discussion groups did not really know much more about it all than what they had read.

Nobody ever told the marines who the enemy was. A lot of the young leathernecks decided they were fighting Communists. That was just fine with Ronald Reagan. He thought so, too.

If the Marines were having a hard time figuring out who the bad guys were, they were not alone. In the autumn of 1983, there were at least 25 separate militias operating in Lebanon. They ranged from powerful armies such as Yasser Arafat's wing of the PLO to gangs of thugs that set off a car bomb killing scores of innocents and then disappeared back into the woodwork.

You name the political complexion, it was there: right wing, left wing, pro-Khomeini, pro-Nasser, pro-Begin. Some groups were brought and paid for by foreign governments, others were willing to alter their political stripes as the market required. Alliances changed as fast as dollars at the money stalls on Hamra Street. The joke about the left-leaning, Israeli-backed, pro-Syrian, Islamic fundamentalist Christian militiaman was only just beyond the realm of the possible.

Splinter group bred splinter group. Any band of a dozen thugs could find a sponsor, come up with a nifty name, and go out and kill people. The politically and religiously committed, too, split into tinier and tinier factions for ever more obscure reasons. Even the experts sometimes ended up baffled.

"I have all the intelligence resources of our organization at my disposal," Ghassan Siblani, a top official of the Shi'ite Amal (Hope) militia, once replied when asked about the Shi'ite splinter groups. "I know the sheikhs [religious elders], I have an extensive network of contracts, relatives, and acquaintances to draw on, and even I have no idea who some of these groups are."

The biggest factions, the Shi'ite Amal and the Druze Progressive Socialist Party (PSP) on the Muslim side and the Christian Lebanese Forces (Phalangists), were, in broad terms, working for clearly defined political goals: the Muslims were demanding more power and the Christians were trying to prevent them from getting it. But they, too, operated at the whim of others.

"Nobody is free in Lebanon. Nobody at all," Walid Jumblatt was firmly convinced. As warlord of the Druzes, a breakaway Muslim sect, he was in a good position to know. "Even the president is not free. Everybody does rely on somebody else; a foreign power."

Since civil war erupted in 1975, the feuds of the Middle East had been fought on the streets of Beirut. If a government wanted to make a point without itself going to war, it commissioned a battle in Beirut or hired an assassin to knock off one of its enemies there. The going price for a hit was about $500, but plenty of people were prepared to do it a lot more cheaply.

The Syrian Socialist Party battled the Iraqi Baathists (just to confuse the issue, there were also Syrian Baathists) one day and Christian Phalangists the next. The Syrian-backed Shi'ite Amal militia clashed with Syrian-backed Palestinians. The Jordanian chargé was kidnapped; the Saudi consul disappeared; Libyan and Turkish diplomats were assassinated; the Iraqi embassy was blown up; the Saudi embassy was stormed and burned.

One night in February 1984, the Pakistani ambassador barely escaped death when a sniper on a nearby rooftop fired at him as he sat reading a book in his room at the Commodore Hotel. The ambassador came from a strict Islamic nation. He had refused to flee with the rest of the diplomatic corps when Muslim militiamen took control of West Beirut a few days before. "It is my duty as a Muslim, and the representative of a Muslim country, to stay," he insisted. Even he couldn't figure out why someone would want to shoot him. By the summer of that year, only one Muslim ambassador, the envoy from North Yemen, was left in Beirut, and he was living in Christian East Beirut.

The naive who tried to find logical explanations for everything that went on in Lebanon quickly gave up.

If violence could be bought, so too could peace. After each round of fighting, the checkbooks would come out. Sometimes Syria would foot the bill, but more often than not, Saudi Arabia would open its ample purse. Swiss bank accounts would be fortified, arms stockpiles replenished. And the Lebanese would have a few weeks, or perhaps a few months, but more often only a few hours, of relative calm. A Lebanese cease-fire was nothing more than a chance to reload.

At the end of 1983 someone came up with the figure that there had been 179 formal cease-fires – the kind arranged by politicians – since the war began in 1975. Then there were the informal truces worked out by the fighters on the ground. Both kinds often collapsed as quickly as they were arranged. Some days there were so many cease-fires that it became impossible to keep track. "What's this, the fourth or fifth?" a reporter on deadline would shout to his colleagues. "Where have you been? It's number nine," was often the reply. In the time it took to go to the bathroom, a truce could be announced and collapse.

In Lebanon, peace was a relative term. Militiamen might still be firing rocket-propelled grenades and mortar rounds at each other, but that didn't count. "The cease-fire is holding," Beirut Radio would confidently proclaim, then go on to detail continued clashes in a half dozen neighborhoods.

That was just the usual menu, not important. Lebanon had so many cease-fires that it had a cease-fire committee – representatives of warring militias who sat in a dingy basement room in the ruins of the battered race track, smack in the middle of the mid-city battlefield. Their job was to make sure the local squabbles that inevitably broke out on the uneasy fronts didn't escalate, or at least not unless their political bosses wanted them to. But inevitably the violence would come again. It always had.

"Strengthen," said he, "the arms of activity; never turn back after a victory, without destroying to the end; spare the females, but as to everything else, such as murdering, plundering, burning, be sure to do all this and continue your prayers and confessions, for this is holy war."[2]

They were the words of the Greek Catholic archbishop of Zahle in Lebanon's Bekaa Valley. It was a call to do battle against the Druzes. The date: October 1841. The rallying cry might just as easily have been issued in October 1983 when Christians and Druzes were locked in war in the Chouf mountains; October 1984, when they were fighting in the Kharroub region; October 1985, when the conflict had moved further south...

Col. Charles Churchill, a nineteenth-century chronicler, reported that more than 3,000 people died in the violence of 1841. Lebanese government figures put the death toll in 1983 at 3,240.

Churchill's work, *The Druzes and the Maronites*, should have been required reading in the Reagan White House. Some 140 years before the United States arrived to try to sort things out, another Jumblatt was bristling against the Christians (Walid Jumblatt's top aid was Marwan Hamadeh; his ancestor's right-hand man was Ali Hamadeh), Muslim foreigners (the Turks) were stirring up trouble, a European fleet stood off the coast, Western envoys shuttled between Beirut and Damascus, and French troops who had been sent ashore to keep the peace watched impotently as the blood flowed.

To say the casualties of 1983 died in the "Lebanese War" would be misleading. To say Lebanon was even a country would be to distort the meaning of the word.

There were at least four readily definable conflicts, not counting a score of localized quarrels, going on inside Lebanon in late 1983 as the Marines scrambled to figure out whom they were fighting and why.

There was not one Lebanon, but at least six. The country was a patchwork quilt sewn together with dissolving thread. This tiny nation, smaller than the state of Connecticut, contained 90,000 troops from 16 countries. Together, Israel and Syria controlled three-quarters of Lebanon's soil.

Northern and eastern Lebanon was Syria in all but name. Syrian troops occupied the region; they were the law. Lebanese soldiers in the area did nothing without Syria's okay, nor did the local warlords or politicians (often one and the same) make a move without considering Syria's response. Life in the region gravitated toward the Syrian capital, Damascus, which was easier (and safer) to reach than Beirut. Many families straddled the border, with branches in Tripoli, Damascus and Aleppo. Some who carried Lebanese identity cards still considered themselves Syrian. For what, in fact, was a Lebanese? For centuries, the people of this region had been Syrians. Until Britain and France redrew the boundaries of the Middle East at the end of World War I, "Greater Syria," a loose geographic term for the area under Ottoman rule, comprised modern-day Syria, Israel, the Sinai Peninsula in the south, the Tigris and Euphrates rivers of Iraq in the east, Lebanon's Mediterranean coast in the west, and the Taurus Mountains of Turkey in the north. "Lebanon" was nothing more than Mount Lebanon, the Christian and Druze heartland (the word Lebanon literally means "the White," an apparent reference to the snow that cloaks the summit most of the year). The Sunni-dominated cities of the coast (Tripoli, Beirut, Sidon and Tyre), as well as South Lebanon and the Bekaa Valley, with their large Shi'ite populations, were all part of Greater Syria.

Helping the Syrians of the 1980s rule the area of Lebanon they occupied was a grab bag of leftist militias that sometimes cooperated, sometimes fought each other. Travelers could never be sure who controlled what. Sometimes the militias themselves didn't seem too certain. Take, for example, the glowering militiaman encountered at a checkpoint outside Tripoli. He wore a red star on his beret, an armband embossed with the Soviet hammer and sickle, and the words "U.S. Marines" over the pocket of his camouflage fatigues.

Although the Syrians dominated northern and eastern Lebanon, they were not the only foreigners there with guns. Far from it. Just before the cinder-block sprawl of the Nahr el-Bared Palestinian refugee camp outside Tripoli, you hit the first PLO guerrillas. Dirty teenagers with even dirtier black-and-white *keffiah* scarves draped around their necks, they scanned each car as it pulled up, ever vigilant for Israeli or Arab enemies.

Until the Israelis expelled Arafat and his men from Lebanon in the summer of 1982, as many as 12,000 Palestinian guerrillas roamed the country. After the PLO evacuation of Beirut, thousands of guerrillas remained in the Syrian-controlled Bekaa Valley, northern Lebanon, and the port of Tripoli, while others quickly began slipping back in, starting again the cycle that had led to the outbreak of the civil war in the mid 1970s.

Adding to the foreign mix was a band of more than 1,000 Iranian Revolutionary Guards, who had ostensibly come to help fight the Israelis and stayed to coordinate terrorist operations from their lair in the ancient

Bekaa Valley city of Baalbek, and a small team of Libyan advisors accompanying one of the PLO splinter groups. There were also periodic reports of Soviet advisors with Syrian troops in the Bekaa.

At the other end of the country, South Lebanon belonged to Israel. The Israelis had assumed control of the area in June 1982, when they rolled across the border in their drive on Beirut. Local Lebanese politicians still took care of the nuts and bolts of running the towns, but Israel called the shots. Its soliders controlled the roads, established the curfews, and decided who would be locked up without trial in the huge Ansar detention camp, which sometimes held several thousand prisoners.

In this, the Israelis were assisted by the South Lebanon Army (SLA), which was a Christian-run militia they had helped establish, and the Palestinian Home Guard, made up of members considered sellouts by the majority of Palestinians in the camps.

The Marines and their French, Italian, and British colleagues were not the only foreign troops trying to bring peace to the country. In South Lebanon, 6,000 members of the United Nations Force in Lebanon (UNIFIL) sat contemplating their ineffectual role. The volunteers, from countries as varied as Norway and Fiji, had been sent to stand between Israel and the PLO. Now they stood on the sidelines. The SLA openly defied the blue-bereted peacekeepers, driving through UNIFIL checkpoints brandishing guns; the Israelis had rolled right over them during the 1982 invasion. In the absence of anything else, UNIFIL contented itself with a watchdog role, keeping track of alleged violations of the rights of Lebanese citizens by Israel and its local allies – not that such reports had any effect.

Meanwhile, sandwiched between – and under – the foreign armies, the Lebanese continued to pursue vendettas and nurture hatreds centuries old.

"We are a small island of civilization in a hostile Middle East," explained Christian militia leader Bechir Gemayel as he showed visitors around his military headquarters in 1981. "We stand for Western, Christian values. They [the Muslims] are animals."

If the Maronite Christians had a superiority complex, the French had helped create it. Many in France had a soft spot for the Maronites, in whose veins, both sides liked to believe, ran the blood of the French Crusaders who had established fortified Christian enclaves like Tyre and Sidon along the Levantine coast. After decades of flirting with the Maronites, providing succor and protection during their recurring wars with the Druzes in the 1800s, the French made the Maronites masters of an expanded Lebanon at the end of World War I.

As it chopped up the Turkish Empire with the help of the British, France decided it would do its old friends in Lebanon a favor by giving them their own country. Not incidentally, the move gave France a new, easily dominated sphere of influence. The Arabs to the east wanted historic Syria united under a single Arab ruler, something Britain had promised through the great Arabist T.E. Lawrence in return for help defeating the Turks. But then, Britain had also promised Palestine to the Jews. You couldn't please everybody. But France was determined to please its Christian friends.

By the end of World War I, the Maronites and Druzes had reached an accommodation and were living in relative peace in Mount Lebanon. If that enclave had been declared independent, Lebanon's troubles might have been avoided. Instead, the French added the region south from Beirut to what is now Israel, the fertile Bekaa Valley in the east, and the Akkar plains in the north to create Greater Lebanon. The Muslims who dominated those regions were loyal to Syria. Many supported the concept of an Arab homeland. They were angry that they had been betrayed.

An artificial nation was created against its own will. The day the state of Lebanon was born was the day its destruction began.

During the postwar period, France ruled Lebanon under a League of Nations mandate and blatantly favored its Maronite friends. In those years, the system was imposed that would form the basis for Muslim anger. The president of the republic, it was decreed, would be a Maronite Christian, the prime minister a Sunni Muslim, and the speaker of the assembly a Shi'ite Muslim. Seats in Parliament were distributed according to a ratio of six Christian seats for every five Muslim seats, designed to ensure Christian dominance. The same ratio applied to civil service jobs. For every five Muslims in the bureaucracy, there had to be six Christians. Even outside the government, the Christians controlled the levers of power. The commander of the army, the head of the central bank, each key post from that of president of the bar association to head of the Olympic committee ended up in Christian hands.

But there was nothing on paper that said so. In classic Lebanese fashion, the distribution of government power was part of a deal made on the side.

The Christians believed this system was essential to their existence. They were convinced that if they let down their guard or loosened their grip on power, they would be wiped out like the Armenians in Turkey or subjugated like the Coptic Christians of Egypt. The slaughter of 11,000 Christians by the Druzes in the battles of 1860 was the red flag they waved whenever anyone argued otherwise.

The ratio that gave them control was based on the 1932 census, which found an overall Christian majority and showed the Maronites, at 30 percent of the population, to be the largest single religious group. That was the last census the Christians would allow. Their numbers were already dropping as many Christians were emigrating to Europe, the United States, and Latin America, while the number of Muslims was increasing at breakneck speed.

By the early 1970s, the balance had shifted. Bolstered by the arrival of the guerrillas of the PLO, who had been driven out of Jordan in the Black September uprising, the Muslims set out to take by force what the Christians refused to give up.

In the ensuing conflict, Beirut was torn apart.

2
West Beirut: A City in Chaos

Pity the nation divided into fragments, each deeming itself
a nation...

—Khalil Gibran[1]

It's three o'clock on Hamra Street, the Fifth Avenue of West Beirut. Sidewalk cafes are full. Old men sit hunched over backgammon boards, the plastic disks clicking loudly as the players slap them into place. Cups containing the dregs of Turkish coffee are strewn everywhere. At another table, two smartly dressed women nibble pastry and trade gossip. Elegant businessmen with camel hair coats slung over their shoulders, Italian-style, parade past, mingling with young thugs in designer jeans, pistol butts jutting from the waistbands. Down the block, smiling merchants beckon passersby toward carts heaped with juicy red tomatoes, crisp fresh lettuce, and shiny apples hard up against gourmet shops crammed with Iranian caviar, Scottish smoked salmon, and French champagne. Lining the sidewalks are the shopkeepers who have had their stores blown out from under them and have now set up on the street. Rusted old Mercedes are draped with the latest Paris fashions, car trunks have been transformed into display cases jammed with Chanel No. 5, boxes of Gucci loafers are piled on the ground.

A man with no legs drags himself into the sidewalk cafe. The stumps are old and callused, a sign that the violence that claimed the limbs probably came early in the war. He steadies himself with one arm; with the other, he pulls a sheaf of lottery tickets from his top pocket and waves it toward the women. This is how he makes his living, a few cents profit from each chance. At first the women ignore him. Then, when his shouting starts to annoy them, the more heavily made up of the two shoos him away, the gold of her bracelets jingling in his face. He looks up hopefully toward the other tables but has no more luck. Giving up, he slips the tickets into his mouth, stiffens both arms, and swings his legless torso off in search of better action somewhere else.

At midafternoon, the noise on Hamra Street can be deafening. The steady roar of generators toiling to make up for the city's incessant power cuts, the scratchy blare of Arabic music from broken speakers on the cassette vendors' carts, the shouts of the sidewalk hawkers, the endless cacophony of car horns.

The crash of the first shell slices through the noise. For a split second, the street seems to go silent as Hamra freezes, the senses of a thousand shoppers and merchants and beggars zeroing in on the blast. Then, chaos. Like ants whose nest has been disturbed, Beirutis run in all directions. The old men slam shut the backgammon boards and duck for cover; the women drop their pastries, slap a few Lebanese pounds on the table, and head for the nearest doorway; the cripple huddles behind a telephone pole seeking protection. For him, the pounding feet of the frightened crowds are a more immediate danger than the shells. As shoppers flee, the heavy metal shutters on the storefronts come rolling down, money changers scoop up their neat stacks of bills and abandon their stalls, and sidewalk merchants heave armfuls of goods into the trunks and back seats of waiting cars.

In minutes, Hamra Street is deserted.

But half an hour later, soon after the shelling stops, the shutters are pulled open, the Guccis and perfumes are again laid out, and the beggar is back at work. For those who have survived, life goes on.

Violence was a daily occurrence, bloodshed a way of life. The shopkeepers and their customers had long since adapted. Since 1975, West Beirut had been the most successful sustained experiment in anarchy the world had ever seen.

The Lebanese civil war was probably inevitable. It is doubtful that the Christian minority could have held on to power indefinitely without a fight. But if the Muslims and Christians had had any chance of avoiding conflict, it died with the arrival of the Palestinians in 1970. That was the year of Black September, the year King Hussein of Jordan unleashed his Bedouin army against the PLO to wrest back control of his country.

In the bloody conflict, the PLO was driven from Jordan.[2] Thousands of Palestinian fighters were forced back across the border into Syria, which had supported their battle against the Hashemite monarch. The Damascus regime, fearful its erstwhile allies would try to establish a state within a state on Syrian soil as they had done in Jordan, quickly bundled the *fedayeen* (fighters) into trucks and shipped them to Lebanon. The Beirut government was given no choice.

These were not the first Palestinians to reach Lebanon. Tens of thousands had been living in the camps around Beirut, Sidon and Tripoli since the

Arab–Israeli war of 1948. But the arrival of the new wave of PLO fighters, with their families in tow, would have a dramatic effect on the Lebanese balance of power.

Both in number and muscle, the Palestinians beefed up the Muslim ranks. If the Muslims did not already constitute a majority of the population, the Palestinians certainly pushed them over the line. More important were the guns they brought. Predominantly made up of adherents of the mainstream Sunni branch of Islam, the PLO was a natural ally for the Lebanese Sunnis in their quest for power.

PLO *fedayeen* were soon probing the government's strength. By the early 1970s, the Palestinians had already extended their influence outside the camps, both militarily and economically. PLO financiers were buying up property and establishing or taking over scores of businesses, while the fighters were steadily expanding their turf, all to the chagrin of the Christians.

By 1975, Christian leaders were demanding the PLO's expulsion, but Arafat and his men had dug in to stay. As both sides prepared for war, Pierre Gemayel, head of the largest Christian militia, was the target of an assassination attempt. The Christians retaliated with an attack on a bus carrying Palestinian civilians, and the powder was ignited.

All-out war erupted in a series of clashes, battles and massacres; Christians in West Beirut fled to the East, while Muslims and Palestinians in East Beirut sought safety in the West. Tens of thousands were killed. Neighborhoods were gutted. The Lebanese Armed Forces (LAF) disintegrated and Beirut was split down the middle.

The conflict raged well into 1976, then settled down to a slow simmer that periodically boiled over. Both sides realized that the other could not be defeated outright, so between intermittent battles, they each set about ruling what was theirs.

In the years leading up to 1982, the PLO and Syrian troops controlled West Beirut. Under their tutelage, the city became a center for the arms and drug trade, terrorist training and questionable financial dealings. The Palestinians ran the biggest rackets, but plenty was left over for the local factions to divvy up. The economy flourished. Millions of dollars passed daily through Lebanon's untraceable bank accounts. A lot of people were dying, but a lot of others were getting rich.

The removal of Arafat and his Syrian allies as a result of the 1982 Israeli invasion brought the reconstituted LAF into West Beirut, but it also opened the way for the rise of the community whose name would come to haunt the West: the Shi'ites. Through the long years of civil war, the Shi'ites were bit players. The conflict pitted the Sunnis and their Palestinian allies against the Christians in a struggle for power. The Shi'ites were handy to have around (the more Muslim guns the better), but the Sunni leadership had not taken up arms to better the Shi'ites' lot. Traditionally, the Shi'ites were the peasant farmers in South Lebanon and the Bekaa, and if the Sunnis had their way, peasants they would remain.

The Shi'ites and Sunnis had been rivals since the dawn of Islam. They disagreed over the line of descent of religious authority from the Prophet Muhammed and each group had its own interpretation of Islamic law. But in Lebanon, the differences between the two main branches of Islam ran far deeper.

Lebanon's civil war was not just a religious conflict. It was an economic struggle of rich against poor, a political struggle of conservatives against liberals, an ideological clash that pitted Lebanese nationalists against Arab nationalists, and a feudal struggle of dynastic warlord against dynastic warlord. The permutations and combinations of the conflict's many layers were endless. And all the players had guns.

By West Beirut standards, the Sunnis were the *haves* – the traders, businessmen and landlords. The Shi'ites were the *have nots* – the laborers, auto mechanics and beggars. West Beirut belonged to the Sunnis (though some Christians, who had fled to East Beirut, still owned property in the Western half of the city). The Shi'ites, refugees from their traditional homeland in South Lebanon, were squatters.

While the Sunnis wanted more influence, they had worked hand-in-hand with the Christians to keep the 950,000 Shi'ites – whose sheer numbers were a threat to both groups – under heel. Adding to the tension was the fact that the PLO, which had oppressed the Shi'ites in South Lebanon, was seen as a protector of the Sunnis.

As the Palestinians had created the so-called Fatahland in South Lebanon (named for Arafat's Fatah wing of the PLO), establishing bases among the farms and orchards from which they could launch attacks against Israel, the Shi'ites endured not only Israeli retaliation but also heavy-handed PLO rule. Many fled to Beirut, joining Palestinian refugees in the grime-encrusted shantytowns that had grown up around the airport on the southern edge of the city; places with names like Borg al-Barajne and Ouzai. Hundreds of thousands of them lived in the winding lanes of rough cinder block houses that were never quite finished. Somebody was always adding another floor to accommodate more children or more relatives from the South.

In the Belt of Misery, as the area was known, water came from communal faucets, electricity was stolen from the tangle of overhead wires, and sewage ran in the streets. Yet the Christian government never lifted a hand to help.

All the while, the Shi'ites were biding their time. Their interests were watched over by the Amal (Hope) militia and its leader Nabih Berri. This private army had grown out of a grassroots movement founded in the late 1970s by the Imam Musa Sadr, an Iranian-born cleric. Musa Sadr, who disappeared (and was presumably killed) in Libya in 1979, created the Amal Movement both as a counter to the PLO and as a vehicle to help his people climb up from the bottom of the socioeconomic pile.

Through the years of Palestinian rule, Amal contented itself with sheltering the Shi'ite community from the more overt abuses. At times it accepted training from the PLO, at others it clashed with the guerrillas. All the while, Amal waited patiently.

When the Israeli army rolled across the border in 1982, Berri sent out the word: Amal would not oppose the invaders. Shi'ite militiamen were told to lay down their weapons. The Amal chief would let the Israelis do what he could not: Drive out the Palestinians.

Two months later, when Arafat and his men were forced to board ships for the distant corners of the Arab world, Amal was there to pick up the arms the PLO left behind. Their arsenals thus fortified, the Shi'ites were ready to act. Soon they would emerge as the main force in West Beirut. Power would be theirs; old scores would be settled.

Sometimes allies, sometimes enemies of both the Sunnis and the Shi'ites were the Druzes, a mountain sect that had split from mainstream Islam in the eleventh century. Walid Jumblatt publicly supported Shi'ite aspiration but privately rued the day Amal had been given its first gun.

"I told Kamal Jumblatt [Walid's father] what we had to do back in the '70s: wipe out the Shi'ites." The speaker, Marwan Hamadeh, was a top aide to Walid Jumblatt who had also served his boss's father before he was assassinated. He was sitting at a chrome and glass conference table in his modern West Beirut office calmly discussing mass murder. "I told him we had to strike. Kill men, women and children. That would have stopped the rest from coming up from the south. But he would not listen. Kamal said it wouldn't look good to the outside world."

There was exasperation in his voice. He couldn't understand why anyone would reject such sage advice. "I keep telling Walid to do the same thing. We need another Sabra and Chatilla here," he said with conviction, referring to the 1982 slaughter of hundreds of Palestinians and Shi'ites in Beirut's refugee camps by Christian militiamen deployed under the watchful eye of Israeli troops. "If he let our boys strike without warning against the Shi'ites, in a few hours we could have a massacre they would never recover from."

It was an attitude that kept the violence boiling.

Street battles might break out, armed robberies take place and shelling erupt, but worst of all were the car bombs. These roving massacres were forever lying in wait.

The stretcher is turning red, the sheet drenched in blood. Frantic rescue workers scream at each other as they trip over chunks of concrete in their scramble for the ambulance. But the struggle is in vain. The young boy dies on the way to the hospital.

The car bomb had been parked in a lot behind a building. Although the open breezeway under the structure had diffused the blast, sections of concrete from the floors above hang down. Someone has been crushed, one bystander says, another has died. Reporters weave their way through the wreckage trying to find someone in charge, as local gunmen shove back the crowds. Getting answers in such chaos is never easy; the versions of two witnesses are rarely the same. Everyone is always angry, upset, confused.

This time, the bomber seems to have been confused, too. When the local militia boss is located, he says no one of importance lives in the building. But a controversial religious leader does have an office just across the street. The driver of the car bomb was apparently given bad directions.

Attack, retaliation. Retaliation, attack. The cycle was endless. Blind terror was the usual goal. Let one side strike, the other struck back. Each atrocity had to be worse than the one before.

He stands atop the wreckage holding the baby's ravaged body high above his head. His anguished scream penetrates the sirens and shouts. "*Lesh Allah, lesh?*" the father cries. Why God, why? The answer lies with the men digging out the other bodies. Their car bombs against "the enemy" provoked this attack. Ten people are dead, 84 wounded. A nine-story apartment house has been leveled. But don't worry, the gunmen assure all who will listen, we will get revenge.

There was no pattern, no logic you could plot. A militia office one week, a church the next. Nor was the motive always readily apparent. It could be political, religious, or connected with Beirut's lucrative protection rackets.

During one period in late 1983, a different barbershop or beauty salon was blown up each night. A hairdressers' mafia? Or perhaps the work of some deranged bald person.

From inside the flaming shop comes the sound of smaller explosions. Nervous Lebanese Army soldiers flinch. The bursting liquor bottles sound like gunfire. Everyone is worried about the same thing: a second blast. The great fear at all bombings is that the people who placed the device might have planted another, set to go off after the rescue work starts. It is an extremely effective technique. The thought clearly preys on the minds of the soldiers. Their faces are grim in the eerie red glow of the flames and flashing emergency beacons. As firemen pour water onto the blaze, troops try to cordon off the street, angrily pushing the inevitable crowd back into the shadows, swinging rifle butts at reporters who try to break through.

Suddenly, television lights illuminate a figure hanging from a window. The fire is spreading and residents of the apartments above are trapped. Firemen shout for them to go to the roof and climb across to the next building, but the din of sirens and screams drowns out their words. Finally, most of the people understand, but one man is left behind. Rescue workers will find his body later. Smoke inhalation will be listed as the official reason for his death, but the real cause is mindless terror.

Smith's Supermarket was the target; an innocent who had nothing to do with the shop is dead. Was the market chosen because Patrick Smith is a foreigner (and Christian, at that)? Is it because of his large American clientele or the liquor he sold? Or did he just fail to pay off the right group?

The Smith's bomb was just one of six that echoed through the empty streets of West Beirut on the night of December 28, 1983. There was a lot of broken glass and shattered hopes at the others, but no more clue to the reason why. The two grocery stores, the hair salons and the lingerie shop had little in common.

"My brother and I are Armenians. I have nothing to do with these wars," cried one of the grocers. "I get along with everybody. The people of the neighborhood love us." The metal shutters of his store had been torn like paper by the blast, the meager stock destroyed.

The Palestinian who ran the other grocery store didn't understand either, though he knew that all Lebanese factions viewed his people with scorn. With the PLO gone, Palestinians were now fair game. The Muslim owner of the lingerie shop was confused as well. "I have nothing to do with politics. I'm a merchant. Why do they do this?" At the beauty parlor, the burglar alarm screamed in protest as the owner swept up glass, muttering to himself.

Later, the radio announced that there had been a sixth bomb. It blew up a car in an empty parking lot. Perhaps this bomb never arrived where its masters intended it to go.

The aim that night had been to wreck property. The bombers waited until a few minutes after the 8:00 p.m. curfew to set off the first blast. Whatever their motive, it was a nice change. Crowds were the usual target; success was measured in gallons of blood.

You were helpless. There was no way to protect yourself. You couldn't avoid the cars, they lined every street. Any one of them might have been loaded with a few hundred pounds of TNT or maybe just enough to destroy one shop. Sometimes a few bags of nails were thrown in, for added effect. Walking to work or to the store, I would search for the obvious signs: the old vehicle that looked like nobody wanted it, the Mercedes that was all banged up. But I knew I was fooling myself; Beirut was full of banged-up Mercedes, full of cars that could carry death. Sometimes I looked for the IDs Lebanese drivers had taken to putting on the dashboard. By offering proof that the car belonged to somebody, the owner hoped to prevent the Lebanese Army from getting suspicious and blowing up the vehicle in a controlled explosion. But there was nothing to stop a car bomber from putting a stolen ID in the windshield of his car.

So, like everyone else, I walked and hoped, half expecting each car I passed to erupt in flames, vaguely relieved when it did not, vaguely embarrassed that I thought it might. Until the morning I opened the paper and read that one car had exploded 20 minutes after I had walked by.

"For anyone who has lived in Beirut," said psychologist Richard Day of the American University of Beirut (AUB), "their view of the world around them will never be the same again."

When a West Beiruti walked into a new place, he immediately took stock. The process was subtle, hidden. Did the room face west (the sea) or east (the Christian artillery)? How many floors were above (to absorb the impact of shells)? Where were the stairs (one never took an elevator to the shelter during shelling)? An outsider at a dinner party, for example, was inevitably awed at how little notice most Beirutis gave to the sounds of the night. A burst of automatic weapons fire, the crash of a shell, the rumble of a convoy of tanks, and no one even looked up. On the surface, Beirutis paid as much attention to those noises as a New Yorker paid to the din of traffic.

But the sounds *had* registered in the mind of each person present. Each had mentally evaluated the threat. Was it a sustained burst of automatic weapons fire, which usually signaled someone firing for the fun of it, or the patternless chatter of rounds that might mark a street battle? Was it the dull thud of outgoing mortar rounds or the sharper crack of an incoming shell? If it was incoming, how close? Am I near a window or protected by a wall? As they ran through the mental checklist, the conversation rarely missed a beat.

The discussion usually turned to the noises outside only if they were perceived as a direct threat. The group then compared opinions of the danger. The host was the resident expert. Every Beiruti knew intimately the sounds of his or her own neighborhood. The host might be able to calm guests or send them to the basement shelter.

One person who lived on a hill knew that the sounds of shelling from the mid-city battleground were much louder in his apartment than in many other sections of the city. Although guests were frequently startled at first, he could reassure them that they were safe. Another man lived in a seafront neighborhood where two militias regularly clashed. He knew that the fighting rarely extended beyond a certain street. He also knew that once the battle crossed that street, it was time to panic.

Intramural squabbling was not allowed to get in the way of the real business of West Beirut: making money. The *Daily Star* newspaper reported one morning that the owners of everything from apartment buildings to beach clubs were being questioned by "finance committee" members from local militias as to why they were not paying their monthly "contributions." The "opening bid," according to the paper, was $1,500.[3]

The following day, Walid Jumblatt's Progressive Socialist Party (PSP) denied that it was demanding protection money. The spokesman did confirm, however, that each year the party asked "comrades and friends" for their support in the PSP's "ten year long patriotic and national battle against fascism and hegemony."[4]

With so many factions in the city, and so many freelancers with guns, the problem became whom to pay off.

"I only pay the big groups – Amal, PSP, Mourabitoun," explained the manager of a West Beirut hotel. "I depend on them to keep the other groups away."

But with the economy collapsing, sometimes it was necessary to stand up to these larger groups – to a point.

"Amal came in here one day demanding [about $8,000]. I threw them out. I told them to bring their boss," the hotel manager recalled. "When he came, I told him he could have the hotel. I said, 'Look, ten percent of my rooms are filled. I'm already losing money every day. Most of my staff are Shi'ites. I am keeping them employed even though I don't need them right now. If you want more money it's better you take over the hotel. If I'm forced out of business because of all these demands for money, is Amal going to support these people's families?"

"What did they say?" I asked the manager.

"They said they would settle for [$800]."

"What did you do?"

"I gave it to them," he said with a chuckle. "I'm Lebanese. I know when the bargaining is over."

As the situation deteriorated in late 1983, soliciting "donations" became a popular pastime.

The red PSP flag hangs limply from a pole stuck in a trash can, which forms the basis of the roadblock a few hundred yards from a government ministry. Beside it, an unshaven fighter cradles an armful of PSP newspapers. The charge: one Lebanese pound. No overt threats are made. He doesn't need them. On the surface, the vendor is no different from dozens of other newspaper sellers who hang out on busy street corners. Except, of course, for the guns. In the shade on the other side of the street, three of his comrades, T-shirts emblazoned with the slightly disheveled visage of the late Kamal Jumblatt, lounge by a wall, their AKs leaning against the bare concrete beside them. Each car pays willingly. No one is silly enough to say they've already read enough newspapers for today.

A few miles away, a group of Amal gunmen have set up shop next to the gutted shell of Mar Mikael (St. Michael's) Church on the so-called Green Line, the demarcation between East and West Beirut. As each car reaches the western side of the Galerie Semain crossing, the militiamen step forwards soliciting contributions for charity. The cause: the families of South Lebanon's Shi'ite suicide bombers.

A lot of people were paying protection money, but there wasn't a lot of protection. As the economy collapsed, armed robbery because a popular occupation. Break-ins by gunmen wielding automatic weapons led some families to install heavy steel bombproof doors on their apartments. Most people stayed home at night, but there was no safety during the day either. Cars were stolen almost daily on crowded streets and anyone who resisted was shot. When an Austrian diplomat was killed in the parking lot of his building, it was at first assumed that the incident was political. In fact, the diplomat had simply made the mistake of refusing a thief's demand for his car keys.

Those who owned valuable autos left them at home, hidden beneath tarpaulins.

The flip side of all this was that cars in Beirut were probably the cheapest in the world. You could buy a Mercedes 280 SL for a few thousand dollars. It was "hot," of course, but that was no problem. The dealer could tell you which area of the country to avoid so you didn't run into the original owner.

Individuals weren't the only ones who had to worry about car thefts. Two different groups of gunmen walked into the Lebanese Red Cross compound one day and got into a fight over who was going to steal the organization's last ambulance. "We threw out the keys and said, 'Yallah [let's go], you decide,'" Red Cross worker Wassim Ghalayini recalled. All of the organization's other vehicles had already been stolen. The volunteers ended up transporting the wounded in their own cars. Militiamen even raided a Red

Cross field hospital set up near the front line. "This was a hospital for them and they still took everything," Ghalayini added, incredulously.

The police weren't doing much to help. They probably had the easiest job in Beirut: sit around, drink coffee, maybe stand in the middle of the road and watch cars going the wrong way up a one-way street. Or perhaps tie up traffic by stopping a friend's car to chat. The job was dangerous only if they did something stupid – like arrest someone. Criminals in Beirut tended to have friends with guns.

The story of Ali Bekhch was typical. Shortly after he was arrested, six gunmen surrounded the police station and began firing into the air, demanding his release. "When we realized the shooting was serious," a police spokesman told the *Daily Star*, "one of our men, Sergeant Ali Nasser, went outside with Bekhch to calm them down. But they immediately shot the sergeant and fled, taking Bekhch with them."[5]

The periodic Lebanese Army deployments in West Beirut, designed to try to restore order, were always greeted with a sigh of relief by the police.

From the *Daily Star*: "Six policemen were seen strolling down El Nabeh Street, singing and joking. 'We are free at last,' one of them said. 'This is why we are so happy. We were sick of being stuck in this zone with no one to protect us.'"[6]

I could hear the shooting in the lobby of the Commodore Hotel from my room upstairs. The sound of gunfire outside was by no means unusual, but inside the hotel? I glanced out the window. Residents of the building across the street crowded onto their balconies, looking down into the hotel lobby. Something was definitely up.

Antoine DeMaximi, a small, wiry soundman from one of our French freelance crews, knocked on my door. "Don't go downstairs," he said excitedly. "There are militiamen in the lobby and they are shooting. You are American. Maybe they come for you. Lock the door." This was February 1984. Americans weren't the most popular people in town. We were all worried about a car bomb hitting the hotel (the Commodore had the largest concentration of Americans outside the embassy compound), but the thought of gunmen invading the building had not really occurred to us. Journalists still got along well with most of the militias. The kidnapping phase had yet to begin in earnest.

The hotel switchboard didn't answer the first time I dialed. There was nothing unusual about that. I succeeded on the second try.

"There is nothing to worry about, Mr. Larry," the operator assured me. "There are some men here shooting someone, but it's all right. He is not a foreigner."

"Is it over?"

"Not quite. It should only be a few more minutes."

The operator was alone at the front desk. The rest of the staff and the foreign reporters who had been hanging out at the bar were huddled in the back of the dining room.

"This is a personal matter. You foreigners are safe," the leader of the seven gunmen had told them as they were herded out of range.

Their target was a local drug dealer. They wanted him to go with them. He had a better idea and clung firmly to his barstool. Pistol whipping, kicking and beating did not change his mind.

"Kill me if you want, but I will not come with you," he shouted in Arabic. A silly thing to say in Beirut. They shot him in the side. Then they shot him in the leg and left him in a lump. After the gunmen were gone, Fouad Saleh, the dapper hotel manager, had the staff help the pusher into a taxi that would take him to the hospital. Wounded thugs lying around the bar were bad for business.

The pool of blood was still standing in the middle of the lobby when the "crack" Squad 16 police unit arrived 15 minutes after the danger had passed.

"He was a very bad man," explained the captain as his men took up poses around the lobby. "He did very many bad things. You don't worry; it had nothing to do with you foreigners. My men are here to protect you now."

My Dalmatian, Shendy – who had the run of the hotel – was no more impressed than the rest of us. She cornered one of the "crack" commandos on the stairs and refused to let him move. Shendy knew the house rules: no weapons allowed.

The police spent the next 24 hours standing around the hotel making people nervous with their rifles, then disappeared.

The guns stayed locked away behind the desk at the Commodore that night, but they were always there if needed. Unable to depend on the police or the Lebanese Army, businessmen had learned to look out for themselves.

"There's nobody to protect you," complained Walid Noshe, a dealer in crystal and silver dishes. "You just have to have the guns in the shop and have some people in the shop who know how to use all these guns. You have to be a warrior and at the same time a businessman. This way you don't get threats. Try to be a businessman only and I don't know what could happen."

"We are a peaceful people," the Lebanese repeated that until they almost believed it. The phrase should be chiseled on every tombstone of every grave. "If the foreign powers would only leave us alone. It's all because of the —— [Israelis, Syrians, Americans; pick one of the above or insert your own]. If they would let us solve our own problems, we could end this war."

By the spring of 1984, the foreign troops had left Beirut. But the Lebanese were still killing each other, and they were still refusing to accept the blame.

Advertisement in a Beirut newspaper: "It isn't the size of the man in the fight, it's the size of the fight in the man. Our best wishes for a New Year in a Lebanon of love and faith." The ad, placed by the Publirzk Marketing Group, covered six columns and was printed in three languages.

The scene is almost biblical. In the early morning stillness, rowboats of the type used for centuries along the Mediterranean coast glide gracefully across the mirrored surface of the sea. Then, like some fierce sea god rising from the depths, a pillar of water erupts yards from the boats, accompanied by a thunderous clap. Beirut's fishermen are gathering their morning catch. Since they live in one giant ammunition dump, it is far easier to toss a handful of dynamite into the water and scoop up the stunned fish as they float to the surface than to go through all the trouble of dragging a net.

That was the way most mornings started along the city's seafront. The hunters usually came out shortly after the fishermen. Those residents who lived adjacent to vacant lots were forever chasing off ten-year-old boys who prowled the neighborhoods with pellet rifles and shotguns in search of prey. Anything that moved was killed. The fact that the boys often fired onto people's balconies was of no interest to them. Older hunters in Lebanon's hills and fields usually carried automatic weapons, which were much more effective than shotguns or rifles. Militiamen, too, enjoyed the birds. They were great for target practice. Rare was the pleasant twittering of a robin or wren. An Israeli bird-watcher who served as an artillery officer in Lebanon estimated that one Druze hunter alone had killed 500,000 birds in 45 years stalking the fields. A Dutch ornithologist estimated that there were 400,000 hunters in the country and no bird-watchers.

Each year during the great pelican migration from North Africa to Europe the antiaircraft guns erupted and thousands of birds were shot out of the sky.

European nature lovers were enraged about the pelican slaughter. One West German woman wrote to Beirut's *Monday Morning* magazine demanding that the Lebanese government do something about it. The publication checked with the minister responsible, who replied that when the government got the Lebanese to stop killing other Lebanese, he would worry about them killing birds.

Anyone who ever tried to cash a check or buy a plane ticket in Lebanon had a feel for the country's basic problem: each individual was out only for himself. There was no such thing as a line. Everyone pushed to the front. No one else counted. No one else had rights.

Everyone demanded special treatment. They wanted to elbow the other person out of the way or, better yet, have someone else do it for them. The Lebanese were a people blowing smoke – figuratively and literally – into the faces of everyone around them.

They wielded their cars like they wielded their weapons: foot down on the gas, everyone out of the way. They would park in the middle of the street to buy a pack of cigarettes and drive the wrong way up one-way streets to avoid going a block out of their way. Face-to-face with a car going in the proper direction, many would tie up traffic for a half-hour rather than give in and back up – unless the other guy pulled out a gun. Fender benders sometimes ended up in murder.

The Lebanese brought that same lack of regard for other human beings to their wars. Blanket shelling of civilians and sniping at innocent citizens were all justified as long as their side got ahead. Everyone had been hurt in some way by the war and everyone wanted to get even.

"After all these years of war, revenge is all we know," said one young woman studying at AUB. The revenge killings had gone on for so long, so many people had been murdered, that no one knew who was ahead anymore.

Ali was a Shi'ite from a village in the southern Bekaa Valley, not far from Mount Hermon. When he was young, he was sent to Canada to live with relatives and get his education. While he was away, his father, a village *mukhtar* (headman) who was running for Parliament, was assassinated. A rival family was suspected of carrying out the murder.

"When I went back to the village, they were all expecting me to avenge my father. They wanted me to kill somebody, an eye for an eye and all that." Ali was a gentle, soft-spoken AUB graduate. He was more interested in writing papers on alternate political systems for a resurrected Lebanon than in committing murder. "I don't go in for that. I'm very sorry my Dad's dead, but I'm not going to start killing people. They think I'm weak because of it."

He checked around a bit to try to determine who had ordered the slaying, then stopped. "It's not safe to ask too many questions. I'm not looking for revenge, but they will assume that I am. From what people tell me, the people responsible are sitting in Parliament."

Ali's attitude was unusual. Few Lebanese were willing to turn the other cheek when their honor was challenged.

The gunfire was right in front of my apartment – two or three single shots, then a woman's scream. Hassan, the concierge, was standing up for his honor.

You couldn't find a sweeter, more pleasant man than Hassan. He would do any job, run any errand, and, most amazingly, rarely accepted a tip. But the Druze bodyguards who protected Khalid Jumblatt, an aide and relative of Walid Jumblatt, who lived in the building, did find something wrong with Hassan: He was a Shi'ite. Like so many hundreds of thousands of his people, he had been driven from his home in South Lebanon by years of war.

The story of the shots I had heard was a bit convoluted. Pieced together from the guards, drivers and Hassan himself, it went something like this: A few days before the shooting, one of the usual guards came to work high on hashish. Khalid Jumblatt ordered the guard and his companions to leave and replaced them with another team of militiamen.

The next day, the replacements were still on duty. They were bored and began to harass Hassan, insulting him and his religion. Finally, the concierge decided he had had enough. He grabbed one of the untended AK-47 automatic weapons the guards always left lying around and shot one of the Druzes in the leg and another in the side. Miraculously, no one shot Hassan.

Khalid Jumblatt appeared downstairs before the incident could go any further, dressed down the replacement guards and apologized to Hassan. Jumblatt ordered the regular team back on the job and told them that Hassan was a good man who "should be treated like us."

A few days later, Hassan disappeared. He was never heard from again.

Sometimes you could ignore the violence; turn up the stereo to drown out the noise of the firefights or sleep through the shelling. Other times the artillery duels became the Lebanese equivalent of Chinese water torture. Your senses hung in tatters waiting in anticipation for the crash of the next round, calculating distances as explosions walked closer, waiting for the one that would send you heading for the basement – or get you before you could move.

Those of us who were foreign reporters or diplomats were usually kept going by the knowledge that we were in Lebanon for a limited period of time. Beat the odds for a few years and you moved on to a safer assignment somewhere else. For the Lebanese, there was no such light at the end of the tunnel. Many of them relied on fate to get through each day.

"*Inshallah.*" Allah willing. The phrase punctuated every conversation: "See you tomorrow, *Inshallah.*" "Things will get better, *Inshallah.*" "The ceasefire will hold, *Inshallah.*" Some people truly believed it was all in God's hands. For others, it was just a way of expressing their fatalism.

"Somehow, that combination of, 'It isn't so bad,' and 'If fate means it to happen, it's going to happen,' allows people to open their shops, study, go to work, all of the things that amaze people about this place when they come and look at it themselves," AUB psychologist Richard Day noted in 1984.

But not everyone could be so stoic. Ten years of war had rubbed nerves raw.

At a West Beirut dinner party, an elegantly dressed Lebanese woman is out on the balcony drinking with a group of friends. A couple of shells land in the distance. She leaps up and instinctively dives for the living room. No one else moves. A few seconds later, she realizes there was no real danger. Embarrassed, she tries to make her panicked reflex seem nonchalant. She adjusts the low-cut back of her cashmere sweater as if to say, "Gee, isn't it warm in here?" and sheepishly walks back outside. Everyone pretends not to have noticed. It's not polite.

"I think it's unique in human history to have this long a period of time of trauma after trauma after trauma with no end in sight," said Day, who spent his years at AUB studying the psychological effect of the war. "I liken the situation to a steel mill where the heat is very hot and the effect on metal is either to make it much stronger or to break it. Lebanon in my mind has been a kind of pressure cooker in which people have found out very important things about themselves. And one of the effects has been to devastate a number of people."

After each new outrage, the shock eventually wore off. Since 1975, the Lebanese had been adjusting to new levels of horror every day.

Your sense of proportion became skewed. The insane was transformed into the accepted and eventually the normal. You were in a constant state of physical and mental adjustment.

When I first arrived in Lebanon, street battles were a major cause for concern. I soon learned to view them as nothing more than an inconvenience. If you ran into one, you just went a few blocks out of your way to get around it. If you were caught in the middle of one, you simply sat tight inside a building. Unless you did something stupid, like standing in front of a window, there was little danger. Automatic weapons fire doesn't penetrate walls.

When car bombs came along, people started to miss the street clashes. At least with those, you knew where the danger came from. But we grew to accept the car bomb threat, too, as normal. Shelling was far more deadly than street fighting, but we learned to live with it: Stay off the top floor of buildings and away from the windows. It rarely lasted long or covered more than a few square blocks.

The Israeli invasion put violence into a whole new league. Car bombs paled in the face of 1,000-pound bombs. Then the new, improved car bombs were introduced with the Iraqi and U.S. embassy bombings. That form of violence was even more awesome and unpredictable. When blanket shelling of civilian residential areas became a regular occurrence in 1984, Beirutis spoke almost longingly of the Israeli siege. "In those days it was Hell in the southern suburbs, but at least around Hamra it wasn't too bad."

No matter how bad things were, they could always get worse. Your apartment was wrecked? At least your family was safe. You son was wounded? At least he wasn't killed. Lose your wife? At least the kids are okay. No matter what your woes, things could always get blacker.

John Zeini stands in the charred ruins of his restaurant. A pool of blackened water laps at his feet as workmen try to sweep away the worst of it. Smugglers Inn was a favorite hangout for West Beirut intellectuals. The Zeinis tossed a good salad, the peppered steak was passable and there was always good conversation back by the bar.

That's where the bomb hit. Someone placed it in the alley by the rear window. John's brother was pouring drinks when it went off. Now he is dead. So, too, is one of the customers who had just sat down to eat. Bits of shredded lettuce mixed in with splintered wood are all that's left of the salad bar. The old hanging scale is bent and useless, discarded on a sooty pile of broken dishes, tables and chairs.

The refrigerator is about all they can salvage. John Zeini watches as it is lifted onto a truck.

"Have you had other threats or problems?" he is gently asked.

"No. We were kidnapped. No problem. Looted. It's all right." The blank expression, the flat voice, speak volumes.

"And you had a bomb outside," he is reminded.

"Yes, three weeks ago."

Another horror has been endured and filed away.

"I think as with many things, you become sort of saturated and you get used to it on one level," said Gail Wolfe, an American psychology professor at Beirut University College, "yet it's taking its toll."

Reporters and diplomats often didn't realize how much it was affecting them until they took a break from Lebanon. It would then become obvious that normal people did not instinctively start when they heard a bang or duck when a plane went over.

The Lebanese did not have nervous breakdowns on the streets of Beirut. They did have them quietly in their own homes. Suicides occurred, but there was nothing to indicate that they were much more prevalent in Beirut than anywhere else. In a city where you could get shot walking down the wrong street, there was no need to take your own life. Formal studies, because of the nature of the country, were few. Psychiatrists were not deluged with a flood of people cracking up. Families in Lebanon were close-knit. The mentally ill spilled their troubles to relatives, not on the psychiatrist's couch.

For those who kept it pent up, the trouble often took physical forms: ulcers, heart disease, skin disorders, hypochondria – all stress-related disorders. Not surprisingly, insomnia was a common complaint. So too was the inability to concentrate.

Drug dependence became widespread. Virtually any kind of pharmaceutical could be bought over the counter without a prescription. Powerful sedatives were the most popular. People ate Valium like candy. Fighters needed its calming effect on the front lines, businessmen needed it to help them face each day, students needed it to get through classes. The hard stuff was there, too. Morphine and heroin were readily available on the black market, but their use was limited. Hashish, one of Lebanon's biggest crops, was everywhere.

Many psychiatrists feared the worst was yet to come. Years of dealing with massive doses of stress had buried the neuroses deep. "People here must constantly cope with stress. They live with it. It consumes so much energy that once the stress is removed, they run the risk of collapse," warned Nizar Halabi, director of the Islamic Hospital.

"People have had incredible trauma that has surpassed what Vietnam veterans may have gone through, [they experience it] at younger ages, at more impressionable ages," added Day. "We can guess there are going to be long-term effects that are going to have to be dealt with. We look forward to the day when we can have post-traumatic stress disorders. So far, we can't get past the day when we have to deal with trauma."

And even if the war ended, the Lebanese would probably still be doomed to have no peace.

"They have grown accustomed to violence," explained Dr. Nizar Azouri, a Christian who treated patients in East Beirut. "Death accompanies every day, so to be aggressive, to be violent, becomes something natural. [The Lebanese] have been unchained. They are simply driven by their instincts, so [in the future] we will have to deal with people who were called some time ago the psychopaths."

Life in Beirut was an emotional roller coaster. In the morning, the city might be alive with hope. All the ministers had turned up for a cabinet meeting (a momentous occasion) or some minor Syrian functionary had spoken of the need for Lebanese unity. "The end is in sight! Peace is at hand!" A people drowning together grasp for the tiniest bit of flotsam. By afternoon, hope usually lay shattered amid the wreckage of a car bomb or shell. Endemic depression was the result.

At the Swiss Bakery, a patisserie just off Hamra Street run by a European couple who have been in Lebanon for decades, a customer is studying a case crammed with rich chocolate cakes and fresh fruit pies, trying to decide what he wants. "It all looks so good," he tells the Lebanese woman behind the counter.

"We have to have some good things when everything is so bad," she replies glumly.

Ask someone, "How are you doing today?" and it was unlikely you would hear, "Just great!" The more common responses: "I'm surviving," or "I'm alive, what more can I ask?"

At a party, the discussion turns inevitably to the war. "How long can this go on?" a woman asks, the question repeated a thousand times a day. "As long as they want," someone replies.

The quest for reassurance was an obsession. Anyone with the slightest bit of extra insight into the situation – politician, diplomat, journalist – was pounced upon for predictions. "Will it get better?" was a question people asked again and again. When told by the person they had cornered that he or she didn't know either, they would often answer their own question. "It *has* to get better," they would say, trying to convince themselves. "We're all so tired. It can't go on like this. It's been too many years."

And they never really believed that the foreigners didn't know more than they were saying. To the Lebanese, everything was a conspiracy. In many minds, Reagan and Brezhnev sat huddled over maps of Beirut ordering aides to set a bomb off on this corner or provoke a clash on that street. Diplomats, reporters and assorted politicos were, of course, privy to those presidential chats.

One way of coping with the violence was to make believe it was not there.

Saturday morning in West Beirut: A shell explodes in the distance. Screams of panic can be heard from a nearby apartment building as frightened mothers scoop up children from exposed balconies. Doors slam as they race for the basement. On a tennis court a few yards away, players in spotless white outfits continue their volley, not missing a stroke.

Few waking moments passed when the Lebanese did not, at least fleetingly, think of the war. It occupied their dreams (and nightmares), too. Rare was the conversation that did not contain some reference to it. Yet they were reluctant to refer to the conflict by name. It was as if they were keeping some great secret. Their discussions were in code. They spoke of "the Events," as in "the Events of 1975–76" or "the September Events," when talking about the various rounds of civil war. "The Situation" referred to the mess the country was in at any given moment.

"It's a kind of protection, a way of not having to ultimately face the ugly reality of bombing, shelling and death," psychologist Gail Wolfe concluded. "Only [we] all know what it really means."

Announcers on the country's eight radio stations, each representing a different faction, developed a special language to help people stay alive. Traffic reports told Beirutis which streets were safe, not which ones were backed up with cars. Weather reports checked the temperature of the street, not the air: "How is it out today?" (Is there any fighting?) "It's heating up." (The clashes are spreading.)

Richard Day divided those who remained in Lebanon into two classes, "Thrivers" and "Survivors." Those who merely existed were the Survivors. They didn't "filter enough out," allowing fear and anger to dominate their lives. They ran to the shelters each time there was shelling, they cringed when a plane passed overhead, they suffered the most from stress-related diseases. The Thrivers were those who threw themselves into the breach. For them, the challenge was to overcome the war.

"To me, one of the most amazing things about the Lebanon story is these groups of people that have been able not only to continue, but to accomplish incredible things in the midst of a situation that has been at times incredibly insane," Day marveled.

"I couldn't possibly sit in a basement somewhere every time there was shelling. My God, I would crack up," said Margot Moussi of the Lebanese Red Cross. Instead, when the artillery opened up, Moussi climbed into an ambulance and drove into the heart of the fighting. She and the other young men and women of the Red Cross and a half dozen other rescue teams were the classic Thrivers.

"Of course we are afraid," admitted Iyad Ramadan, another Red Cross volunteer on duty outside the emergency room at the AUB hospital one day. "But I would rather die in the street trying to save others than be killed cowering in my house. The only other thing I could have done is to become a fighter," he said, glancing at a group of militiamen helping a wounded colleague out of a car. "That's not for me."

Both were AUB students, both were trying to juggle their education and the war.

"I have to leave here in a little while and take a final [exam]," said Moussi with an ironic smile. "Imagine it, we've been on duty for the past 24 hours because of last night's shelling." She pointed to the bloodstains on the bright orange jumpsuit worn by all the Red Cross volunteers. "Try concentrating on an exam after this."

"One thing this job does," confirmed Wassim Ghalayini, the leader of the Red Cross team, "is make you realize how far you can push yourself and how much one person can accomplish."

An old 1950s cabaret movie is in the videotape player. The little boy is dancing in front of the screen. When it's time for bed, he goes reluctantly to his room, then begins screaming hysterically.

"It's like this every night," Rosanne Khalaf apologizes as she gets up from the dinner table. "He's terrified. He wakes up in the middle of the night screaming. It's terrible. I feel so helpless. Anything can set him off. He used to get hysterical when there was thunder. We explained it was just a storm. Now when there's shelling, he calls it 'rain without water.' We can't leave him alone at night anymore. It's just not fair to him."

A little while later, two-year-old Ramsi is curled up asleep on a blanket on the living room floor, near the security of his parents and their guests.

It was the children that the conflict was affecting most. Kids ten years old had never known life without war. By the time they reached adolescence, most Lebanese had already lost friends and family members to violence.

Three little boys are playing in the dirt at the end of a street. They put sticks that are supposed to be houses in the sand. "Brrm, brrm," one of them says, stopping his toy car in front of a make-believe house. He pulls something out of his pocket and pushes it under the car, then steps back a few feet just before the sharp explosion of a firecracker sends the car spiraling through the air.

The boys are playing a new game: car bomb.

Death was very real to Lebanese children almost from the day they began to understand the world around them. Kids five or six years old talked about what they would do "if" they grew up. They quickly learned that dying of old age in their country was considered an accomplishment. News that an acquaintance was killed by a heart attack, not a bullet, was always greeted with a degree of surprise. "Druze Leader Dies of Natural Causes," a magazine headline would report. Anywhere else it would have been, "Druze Leader Dies."

Children learned to expect the worst. As Dr. Nizar Azouri put it, "The fear is transmitted by the environment."

The Muslim holy month of Ramadan provided one of the many excuses for the Lebanese to fire their guns. The last night, when the long fast ended, was the worst. The explosions began when the voices of the *muezzins* broadcast from the mosques proclaiming that the fast was over and the feast had begun. AK-47s quickly took up the refrain – guns on one street announcing the news, those on the next tapping out a reply. The crash of rocket-propelled grenades played percussion. Rat-tat rat-tat-tat. Dozens of guns around the neighborhood would take up the familiar pattern, melting into a rhythm worthy of the bass track for a heavy metal band.

The four-year-old girl was asleep when the racket began. Awakened by the noise, she walked out of her bedroom and curled up with her blanket on the hall floor. Her mother found her there and patiently explained that there was no need to worry, the gunfire was just part of the celebration and would not harm her.

With the wisdom of one who had been through it all, she looked up at her mother and said earnestly, "Mommy, I don't want to die. If you want to sleep in your bed and maybe be killed, that's okay. But I don't want to die. I'm sleeping here."

"Our children have lost their childhoods, and that's very sad," said child researcher Imam Khalife, who worked in a nursery at Beirut University College.[7]

Many of the psychological problems of adults were also seen in Lebanon's children. "Kids are having a hard time concentrating in their schools. Kids are getting aggressive with each other and the teachers are very concerned about that. Kids are getting withdrawn. A whole variety of symptoms are coming up," psychologist Richard Day discovered. "They are the least defended psychologically. They have not had the time to build up defense mechanisms."

"My daughter is becoming badly behaved, generally making herself a nuisance," complained Lena Aouad, the wife of a hairdresser, as she sat on a friend's balcony one evening. "But how can I discipline her? During the week we have to stay in my parents' house because of the fighting. She doesn't have her toys; she doesn't get to sleep in her own bed. She spends half her time in a basement shelter. How can I get angry or punish her?"

Children who never wet the bed suddenly started. Otherwise-calm kids became jumpy. Independent children grew unnaturally attached to a parent and refused to leave his or her side. One girl hid behind her refrigerator whenever there was shelling. An eight-year-old boy at the Islamic Orphanage who lost his parents in an Israeli bombing raid often pounded his head against the wall and threw fits. Orphanage officials weren't sure whether he was epileptic or had brain damage from the time he was trapped under the rubble of a bombed building. A businessman told of the time that his ten-year-old daughter suffered from diarrhea for two weeks. When he took her for a checkup, the doctor said there was nothing physically wrong with her. It was nerves. The girl was put on tranquilizers and the diarrhea stopped.

A common complaint among Lebanese children was ear trouble. It was caused by the explosions. While infants lay in their cribs, vibrations from bombs and shelling permanently damaged their eardrums.

Sunni Muslim politician Tammam Salam was a tall, effusive man whose shiny bald head set him apart in any crowd. His father, Saeb Salam, was one of the old guard Lebanese politicians who had ruled the country since its inception. Like the heirs of Lebanon's other political dynasties, Tammam was following in his father's footsteps. He saw it as his job to try to save Lebanon for the next generation. But as he sat in his office in May 1984 discussing the country's future, he confessed that he had recently begun to think it might already be too late.

"My wife and children have been in Europe for the last few months. I send them there when the fighting is bad. My wife called me the other day and told me she had asked our youngest girl, who's four, whether she misses her daddy. She shook her head and said, 'No.' 'But how can you not miss your wonderful daddy who plays with you and loves you so much?' my wife asked. My daughter just shrugged.

"'Do you miss your grandfather?' she asked. 'No,' my daughter said. 'But your grandfather loves you so much and takes you on his lap. Don't you miss him?' my wife asked. My daughter just shook her head no again. My wife couldn't understand what was wrong.

"Then, a few minutes later, my daughter burst into tears. 'I love my daddy and grandfather so much,' she cried. 'I miss them so much, but I don't want to go back there [to Lebanon] ever again.'"

Schools offered children no protection. The *Daily Star* ran this story on its front page: "A 12-year-old boy was killed [and] 15 others were wounded at the Annunciation School in [Christian] East Beirut when a 120mm mortar landed in the school's playground while the school children were on their morning break."[8]

"I don't think I shall go to school [again]," one of the wounded, 12-year-old Paul Yazbeck, was quoted as saying. "It's too dangerous."

After the incident, the Student Council of the Phalangists, the main Christian rightist party, issued a statement warning that "the attacker should understand that we will continue to stand up to him even if it were [sic] with the breasts of our children and innocent students."

It was that kind of thinking which groomed another generation for war.

3
East Beirut:
Shelling and Champagne

The sense of self-complacent security, and even of superiority, which the Christians ... entertained, and their haughty and arrogant defiance of all authority ... would have been vastly pleasant and desirable for them, if it could have lasted; and the idea of its not lasting, of course never once entered their protector's mind.

—Col. Charles Churchill[1]

Bechir Gemayel stared unseeing toward his enemies in West Beirut. The 50-foot-high painting towered over the traffic of the Green Line's Museum crossing point just as the assassinated warlord had towered over his co-religionists in life. The poster of Gemayel – dressed in a jacket and tie, with eyes that were not quite focused set in a beefy face – looked like an oversized yearbook snapshot of an all-American class president who would later be killed in Vietnam, gazing toward a future he would never know.

The Savior. The Butcher. Bechir Gemayel had a reputation as both. The Great White Hope of the Christians, he united East Beirut under a single flag and honed a unified military machine designed to cement the Christians' position of political dominance. The route he took to get there was stained with blood. The corpses of allies and enemies alike littered his path.

The Christian enclave had long been ruled by a troika of families: The Gemayels, the Chamouns and the Franjiehs. Each consisted of an aging patriarch who had once served as Lebanon's President and sons who were being groomed for power. Bechir Gemayel did not intend to share. Tony Franjieh was his main rival for the presidency. On the morning of June 13, 1978, Gemayel's men made sure Franjieh would never pose a threat. A force of 100 Phalangists attacked the lightly defended stone walls of the Franjieh summer palace at Ehden. Scarcely 15 minutes later, 34 people lay dead, among them, still in their bloodstained bedclothes, Tony, his wife and their three-year-old daughter. Even the dog had been shot.

The Chamouns, the other powerful Christian family, were next. As many as 150 people died, half of them innocent bystanders, as the Chamouns' private army was cornered and decimated in a lightning 1980 raid that left the bloody bodies of bathers floating face down in pools at luxury hotels on Chamoun turf.

Even Amin Gemayel was not spared his younger brother's quest for power. Christian folklore had it that the Gemayels had divided up the duties. Father Pierre, founder of the dynasty, was the godfather, watching over the family's fortunes from on high. Tough Bechir was the fighter, leading the Christian forces to battle. Urbane Amin was the professional, supervising the family businesses and preparing to inherit the political mantle. But Bechir wanted it all.

In 1981, with his brother in Europe on a business trip, Bechir quietly disarmed Amin's own militia. Bechir's Lebanese Forces (LF), a private army of 5,000 regulars, was now the only military force in East Beirut, aside from the largely ineffective and ineffectual Lebanese Army, which was led by Christian officers sympathetic to Bechir's aims. The LF had started during the civil war as a united command of the various Christian militias. The Phalange was its large component. Now the Phalange had fed on the other components and grown to become the LF with Bechir Gemayel at its head.

Gemayel had the platform he needed. Israel provided the rest. The first direct contacts between the Christian leadership and Israel had come in 1976. Israeli assistance had helped the Christians get through the civil war. By the early 1980s, the flow of Israeli weapons to the Christians was brisk. Some Phalangist militiamen were drilling in Israel, while others were taught by Israeli trainers on Lebanese soil. During the Christian confrontation with Syria in the spring and summer of 1981, Israeli advisors were with the Phalangists in the mountains above Zahle, the main Christian town in the predominantly Muslim Bekaa Valley. When Israel invaded Lebanon in June 1982, Israeli Defense Minister Ariel Sharon and his aides envisioned it as a joint operation with the Christians. They expected the Phalange to fight alongside Israeli troops and were deeply disappointed and scornful when they did not. "Toy soldiers" was what Israeli soldiers began calling the Christians.

Yet Bechir Gemayel held back. If the Israelis were going to fight his battles for him, the Christian strongman saw no reason to get his hands dirty. LF militiamen fought a few skirmishes against the PLO, but Gemayel steadfastly rejected Sharon's urging that *his* men, not the Israelis, should take on the bloody job of cleaning out West Beirut street by street.

It wasn't just men that Gemayel was worried about losing. By standing aloof from the carnage, the militia chief hoped to avoid further alienating the Muslims. After all, he had an election to think about. The ultimate prize, the presidency of Lebanon, was at stake.

On August 23, 1982, Gemayel and his backers got their wish: Bechir was elected president of Lebanon. Just how much it cost the LF no one was saying, but one estimate put the payoff to the Speaker of Parliament alone at $10 million. Although Lebanon was a democracy, the election of Bechir Gemayel was something short of democratic. In Lebanon, Parliament elected the president, not the people. Because of the war, the last parliamentary election had been held in 1972. Some members of Parliament were dead; others were old and infirm. Few represented the new Muslim militias that had arrived on the scene since the previous vote. Those who did were trapped in West Beirut by the Israeli siege. And Bechir Gemayel's name was the only one on the ballot.

"The candidate of Israeli tanks," as Druze leader Walid Jumblatt called him, had achieved his goal. East Beirut erupted in an orgy of celebration. Christian militiamen careened through the streets firing thousands of rounds of ammunition into the sky.

That night, the homes of two members of Parliament who had boycotted the vote were bombed and another was burned down. It all sounded uncannily similar to another election about which Col. Charles Churchill had reported a century before: "Where bribery failed to work its way, threats and blows, and every species of personal indignity were dealt out to and heaped upon the unhappy Christians, to compel them to vote. ... Several died from the effects of the barbarous bastinado to which they were subjected."[2]

Sheltered behind the respectability of his new title, Gemayel was disdainful of those who brought up his ruthless past. "Here we are elected in a very democratic region in a very democratic way, so I'm not impressed by all that," he snapped at reporters on the steps of the Presidential Palace when asked how he expected to unite the Lebanese, given what people were saying about him.

Resigning themselves to the inevitable, some Muslim politicians tried to put the best face on things. Perhaps Gemayel *was* the man who would grant equality to the Muslims. Perhaps, like Nixon and the Chinese, they reasoned, he would have the rightist credentials needed to compromise with the left. Desperate for a ray of hope after the black days of the Israeli siege of West Beirut, ordinary Muslims seized on that thought.

But just when some Muslims had begun to convince themselves that Bechir Gemayel might be their savior, too, he was dead. The blast that

killed him tore through the LF headquarters in the Ashrafieh neighborhood of East Beirut. Gemayel's violent past had caught up with him just 23
days after he was elected. The scion of the Gemayel family had not even
taken office yet. A Christian with known Syrian ties was arrested for
planting the bomb. The LF blamed Syria and the PLO for its leader's murder,
but plenty of other people had a reason to see him dead. One Machiavellian
version even had Israel behind the blast. Two weeks before the bombing,
at a meeting with Menachim Begin at the border town of Nahariya, Bechir
had enraged the Israeli prime minister by summarily rejecting his plan for
a quick peace treaty between the two countries. Bechir knew such a deal
would kill any chance of a rapprochement with Syria. He would stick to his
father's policy of sitting firmly on the fence in the Arab–Israeli conflict.
After all the years of Israeli support for the Christians, and the very fact that
it was their invasion that had propelled Bechir to the presidency, Begin
felt betrayed.

The tiny world over which Bechir Gemayel had reigned was only about
20 miles long. For the bulk of Christians, the northern boundary was the
Barbara checkpoint. There, the Christian militia took its cut. Private cars
were usually waved through, but each truckload of goods heading for Beirut
was required to pay a toll. Although the government did not tax locally
produced goods, the militia did, which was one reason the Phalangists had
money and the government did not.

Barbara was the gateway to Marounistan, the name diplomats and foreign
reporters gave the Maronite Christian enclave. Not far beyond Barbara was
"The Mountain," Mount Lebanon, where the Maronite Christians had
ruled for centuries.

The differences among the various Islamic sects leave many Westerners
confused. Lebanon is a continuing reminder that over the centuries,
Christians, too, have had a hard time agreeing on just what it is they believe
in. Ten separate versions of Christianity are still practiced there: Maronite,
Syrian Orthodox, Syrian Catholic, Greek Orthodox, Greek Catholic,
Armenian Orthodox, Armenian Catholic, Chaldean, Assyrian (Nestorian),
and Roman Catholic. God forbid they should all get along. At one time or
another, the major sects had all fought one another.

The Maronites arrived in what is now Lebanon sometime in the eighth
century, fleeing persecution in Syria. In the Middle East back then, there
were few roads and no form of quick communication. Whole communities
existed with little contact with the outside world. As the teachings of
Christianity slowly spread, each community interpreted God's word in a
different way. The Maronites, who took their name from a one-eyed hermit
monk of the fourth century, followed the teachings of the Monothelites,

who believe Christ had two natures but a single will. That heresy brought them into conflict with the Orthodox Church of the ruling Byzantines. Eventually, they were forced to seek sanctuary farther west.

By the sixteenth century, they had settled into the safety of the mountainous spine that runs along the Mediterranean coast and generally remained aloof from outside events. Technically, they fell under the control of the Ottoman Empire when it rose to power, but as long as the Maronite rulers paid their taxes, they were generally left alone.

The Maronites grew fiercely independent. Nourished by French missionaries, they turned their backs on the Arab world and looked to Europe for inspiration. By the 1970s, French was the preferred language of the Maronites. They used it to set themselves apart from the Muslims. The Arabic of many in the Maronite elite was purposefully basic.

"We are Phoenicians, not Arabs," was the familiar refrain. By claiming descent from the ancient traders of the Mediterranean or the Crusading knights of Europe, rather than some vague tribe that emerged from the deserts to the east, the Maronites could justify their insistence that their society was not the western edge of the Arab world, but the eastern edge of the Western world.

The crux of the Maronite argument was that they were better than the rest of the Lebanese: more intelligent, better educated, and, most importantly, Western. They wanted with all their hearts to be Europeans and acted as if wishing would make it so.

Amin Gemayel inherited the presidency from his brother in September 1982, but he did not inherit his prestige. The Maronites considered Amin a Milquetoast in comparison to Bechir, but at least he carried the Gemayel name. Most important to a country that needed unity more than anything else, he was acceptable to the Muslims. Whereas Bechir's election was riven with dissent, Amin won Parliament's unanimous endorsement. That did nothing to raise his prestige among Bechir's fighters, who already regarded him with scorn and weren't about to take orders from him. The LF continued as the undisputed rulers of East Beirut, as they would throughout Amin's presidency.

Amin's relationship with the LF was complex. As a Gemayel, he ranked just below his father in the hierarchy of the Phalangist party, the key component of the LF alliance. As long as Bechir was alive, the militia was the equivalent of the family's private army, doing the bidding of the Gemayels. With the death of the younger brother, the fighters began to distance themselves from the politicians. Sheikh Pierre still had the last word, but even his authority could not prevent the growing tension between the two wings.

Cynics argued that the danger inherent in a head-to-head confrontation with the militia wasn't the only reason Amin didn't try to strip the LF of its power. There was also the huge financial operation, which he had helped to create. A lot of money was being made in East Beirut.

The House of the Future was Amin Gemayel's pride and joy. A futuristic bunker perched on a hill not far from one of the illegal ports that provided the money to build it, the structure was the nerve center of the Phalangist economic empire. In 1981, after an interview in which he outlined his view of how to solve the country's problems (a federal state with each sect controlling its own affairs), Gemayel took me downstairs to see his "baby."

The IBM mainframe computer stood in a sanitized cocoon behind glass walls. Attractive young girls pecked away at keyboards, sweaters over their shoulders to protect against the air-conditioned chill.

"See this?" Gemayel asked enthusiastically, proffering a printout he had torn from the computer. "It tells us everything about this person – where he lives, how much he makes, how many children he has, how much property he owns. We're just beginning to gather this data in the computer, but when we're done, we will have all the information we need about all the individuals and businesses in our area right at our fingertips."

Of course, it would never be misused, the future president assured me in a soft voice that dripped with sincerity. It was all for the good of the party and the people. Determining a family's equitable tax level, for example, became far easier.

Keeping track of the family budget at the House of the Future didn't occupy Gemayel full-time. He also ran several enterprises of his own, one of them an insurance company – called, simply, "Protection" – that provided security guards to private companies. The rates were high, but it was the kind of offer few businessmen could refuse.

Three years after my visit with Gemayel, Cyril Bustros leaned back in his leather armchair, unbuttoned the jacket of an expensive Italian-tailored suit, and chuckled at the notion that his visitor had not heard his name before. In the outer office was a computer terminal linked to the House of the Future. It gave the tall, graying man behind the desk access to all the information Amin Gemayel had foreseen. In his hands lay command of a vast financial empire estimated to rake in upwards of $100 million a year.

Bustros was chairman of the Joint Financial Committee of the LF. Put simply, his job was to provide the money to run the Maronite enclave. The militia was the first priority. The organization had to pay 2,000 full-time fighters and thousands more that were called up in time of war, as well as to train every high school student in Marounistan how to handle a gun. Then there were the bills for weapons and equipment (Israel and the LF's black market supporters demanded cash), treatment of wounded militiamen, and compensation for the families of those who were killed.

Financing the private army was not Bustros's only job. He had to keep solvent an entire shadow government. In West Beirut, anarchy ruled the streets. In Christian East Beirut, bands of foreign workers swept them. While the Phalangist police kept order, specialized committees were overseeing road maintenance, garbage collection and the distribution of electricity. Committees kept the phone working, the water flowing and the sewers operating.

After each round of war, the newest wave of Christian refugees was housed and fed by the party. Roads were repaired, bridges were rebuilt. When a car bomb exploded, Phalangist ambulance units rushed the wounded off to hospital, while other party workers cleaned up the mess. There may not have been any trains, but the buses ran on time. They were even subsidized by the party. So, too, was the food at the cut-rate supermarket cooperative run by the Phalange. "We are acting in the absence of the state," explained Dib Anastase, commander of the Phalange police.

The enclave was broken up into a network of wards directed by Popular Councils. They ran the neighborhood and even conducted quality-control checks at local stores. "What happens if a shopkeeper doesn't comply with party standards?" one council chief was asked by a reporter. "We twist his arm," was the succinct reply.

East Beirutis were supposed to be paying taxes to the Lebanese government, but, like their counterparts in the western part of the city, few did. Instead they paid the LF. Each dwelling was visited once a month by a party tax collector. This was no amateur operation; time and motion studies had determined the optimum area each collector had to cover.

Tax money from individuals was not the LF's only source of revenue. Far from it. Businesses and real estate were taxed, and there was a surcharge on every gallon of gasoline, every movie ticket, every meal served in East Beirut restaurants. Each truck that rolled through the LF checkpoint at Barbara, the northern border of the Marounistan enclave had to pay a toll based on the value of its cargo.

By far the biggest source of revenue was the illegal ports. The LF controlled the important Fifth Basin, the deep-water docks at the eastern end of the government-run Beirut Port, along with a string of smugglers' coves along the coast. The illegal ports robbed government coffers of an estimated $500 million a year, a quarter of the national budget. While ships stood at anchor waiting their turn at the pirate docks, Beirut Port – where importers had to pay government taxes – was virtually empty. At least 14 illegal ports dotted Lebanon's Mediterranean coast from Tripoli in the north to Tyre in the south. Most militias had at least one of their own. But by far the largest was the Fifth Basin, controlled by the LF. Shipping sources estimated it handled 50 percent of all Beirut commerce.

There was a sound economic reason for ships to use these illegal ports: They charged as little as 10 percent of the government's import fees. The fact that fighting more often than not closed the government-controlled port fueled the need for the illicit ports, a fact not lost on the militia leaders who decided where to point the guns.

Since insurers refused to cover ships going to the illegal ports, most of the cargo arrived in the leaky hulls of tramp steamers. Some of those same ships picked up a much more profitable cargo – Lebanese hashish destined for Egypt, Europe and the United States. The LF sternly denied that it was involved in the illicit hash trade, but foreign diplomats told a different story. They claimed the LF was in the business right alongside most of the country's other private armies. As one diplomat put it, "Drugs and weapons go together like peanut butter and jelly."

The private ports were illegal, but they were not secret. At one point during Amin Gemayel's reign, they operated only at night ("We don't want to embarrass the president," confided one LF official), but it was a farce. At Dbayeh port, located in what was generally regarded as Amin's personal fiefdom, the ships swung at anchor, cranes scratched the sky and containers piled up on the docks. When darkness fell, the port lit up like a football field, stevedores working in plain view of passing motorists on the main coastal highway.

At one time, Joseph Abboud was the chauffeur and bodyguard to Camille Chamoun, who served as Lebanon's president in the 1950s. Then Abboud set up the Dbayeh port with the blessings of his former boss. He soon had his own chauffeur and bodyguard – not to mention a string of houses, a yacht and an airplane. His fortune was made possible, Abboud told one reporter, by "the protection of a strong leader." He plowed some of his profits into an $80 million medical center named after President Amin Gemayel. Justified or not, that sort of thing won Gemayel the nickname, "Mr. Ten Percent."

One of the reasons the war had gone on for so long was that so many people were making so much money from it. The same families that controlled the guns owned the cement factories, the glass industry and the construction firms. After every round of destruction, they made a fortune putting back together again what their fighters had blown apart.

The click of the chips blends with the chink of ice in glasses as the croupier drags his stick down the length of the roulette table. The fat gentleman in the blue tux has just lost, by rough estimate, $2,000. He takes a swig of scotch, grabs a handful of chips from the mountain in front of him, and begins to cover the upper third of the table with little piles of red. Somewhere on the other side of the room, a champagne cork pops.

There isn't a seat to be had over at the blackjack tables. Even the high-stakes games are two deep. Beneath the crystal chandeliers, huge sums are being won and lost. Sometimes the dealers have trouble counting, and once in a while they drop the cards, but no one seems to mind. It isn't like the old days, with dazzling French maidens in the slot, but it's still the best action in town.

The Casino Du Liban was once a required stop for jet-setters, but since 1975 its patrons have been drawn primarily from the Christian elite. They come to see and be seen. War isn't going to stop them from having a good time.

When fighting engulfed East Beirut early in the conflict, the Christians began to develop the port of Jounieh to the north. Almost a decade later, the huge bay looked like a miniature Miami Beach. Hotels and exclusive beach clubs lined the seafront. Restaurants, movie theaters and video parlors crowded the hills above.

East Beirut, particularly the Ashrafieh neighborhood along the Green Line, took its share of battering. Many families had lost their homes. Others hung on, huddling in the basement whenever new fighting erupted. At night, the streets of Ashrafieh were as dark and deserted as those of West Beirut.

But a few miles up the coast, another world began. Jounieh and its environs were rarely troubled by inconveniences such as power cuts, and only occasionally was the area shelled. Neon lit the city. A typical night out might start with a fish dinner at Sultan Brahim's, followed by a little gambling at the Casino Du Liban or one of several other high-class gambling dens, all of which paid a cut to the LF. There was a huge electronic bingo parlor on the main road and cinema complexes offered the latest Hollywood movies. As in West Beirut, violence was the favorite theme. While Clint Eastwood blew away bad guys in Cinema One, young militiamen in Cinema Two laughed uproariously at Nick Nolte as he walked down the center of a sniper-infested street in *Under Fire*. They knew how long he would last in real life.

The evening usually ended under the pulsating lights of a disco, where the Christian young danced till dawn. The parties in East Beirut never seemed to end. Each week the front section of *Monday Morning* magazine chronicled some new national horror, while the back pages were full of photographs of nubile lasses in the latest Paris fashions and their tuxedo-clad escorts at yet another charity ball or nightclub opening. "Around the Clock" kept tabs on the primarily Christian social whirl as well as the doings of their role models in Monaco and Cannes.

"Why do you people always talk about our casinos and restaurants and never about our refugees and the damage Muslim shells inflict on this side?" Christian officials constantly asked reporters. "Why are you always showing pictures of the slums in West Beirut and the beaches here in the East?"

The comparison was a cliché after ten years, but not unfair. The vast majority of people in West Beirut survived under appalling conditions; the vast majority in East Beirut were far better off. On the Muslim side of the Green Line, tens of thousands lived without running water or toilets. Entire families existed in a single room, and the bombed-out shells of buildings were coveted for the shelter they provided. There was a handful of East Beirut-style beach clubs in the Muslim sector – places like the Druze-owned Summerland Hotel – but they were the exception to the rule. Not everyone in West Beirut was poor, but they all shared the same 8:00 p.m. curfew for months on end, the same frustrating power cuts, the same fear of armed men lurking in the shadows outside, the same sense of claustrophobia.

There *were* poor in East Beirut; there *were* refugees. During the September 1983 conflict alone, 150,000 Christians had been driven out of their homes in the Chouf Mountains. Plenty of Christians were living temporarily in schools and churches, but the key word was "temporarily." Most were quickly resettled in other parts of the Maronite enclave, and some moved into family homes up the coast. Those who did not have money were taken care of by the Phalangist party or the church. The LF provided the support lacking in West Beirut. The situation in East Beirut was far from ideal, the adjustment was difficult, people were forced to live in the dangerous sector along the Green Line, but visitors did not find the gutted buildings teeming with refugees so common in the West.

East Beirut *was* shelled. People *did* die there with grim regularity. But they had an escape valve. If East Beirutis needed a break from the tension of war, they could spend a weekend sipping arak at the mountain resort town of Broumanna or skiing at Karayah. Even people without much money could afford a day basking on the northern beaches out of range of the shells. In West Beirut, pinned against the sea, there was no escape.

The Maronite Christians had their mini-state in all but name. Making it official was their ultimate goal. They called their plan "political decentralization." A federal system would be established, dividing the country into political/religious entities based roughly on the Swiss model, which gives each state substantial autonomy. The federal government would have overall authority and would coordinate foreign policy, but each community would tend to its own affairs. The Lebanese Army was already made up of Christian, Sunni, Shi'ite and Druze brigades. The blueprint would have each army unit protect its own territory alongside the militias of that sect.

Critics called the concept partition. They were convinced it would result in a dismembered Lebanon carved up between Israel and Syria.

"Our plan is revolutionary," countered LF spokesman Naoum Farah, sucking deeply on a huge, rough-hewn pipe. "The country is already divided up against itself. This plan will overcome those suspicions, unifying the country while allowing each community to feel secure." It was also a convenient way for the Christians to hold onto their privileged status. The word "compromise" did not seem to exist in their vocabulary.

"We are willing to find solutions, not to make concessions," Karim Padradouni, a Christian political strategist, said in an interview with the *Daily Star*. "Let us be clear: if the price of ending the war is concessions on our part, then let the war go on."[3]

"We've still got time. Why should we compromise?" asked financier Cyril Bustros. "Why should we compromise and on what? Should we compromise on civilization? No, we can't. I don't think anybody can. What should we concede? Christianity? Civilization? Democracy? Can you concede these? I don't think we can.

"I know what's on the edge of your tongue," he said, leaning forward in his swivel chair. "What we call privileges. What are these privileges? Economically, the country's open to everybody. Now, some people worked more than others. If you put up more factories, that means you worked more. That's all. What's the privilege? Everybody speaks of prerogatives, privileges. What are they?"

"The Shi'ites would say those are the right to an equal amount of political say," his listener pointed out.

"This is what the federation could give. Instead of us abandoning what you say are privileges and them fighting to gain them, everybody would have the same privileges in his own community. Don't forget that we are in an ocean of non-Christians. The least we can do is try to find some guarantees to survive."

Survival. It preyed on the minds of the Christians. They had once been the majority but had watched helplessly as the high birthrate on the other side of the line expanded the Muslim ranks while their own numbers shrank with the Christian exodus.

"The question for us is to survive. We are ready to go on for another ten years. We are ready to fight." The words were those of a Christian housewife. It was the dominant sentiment on the streets of East Beirut.

"The best solution for Lebanon is to divide it," said a middle-aged businessman in a cafe. "You divide it and then we will do good, because now everybody hates each other and you can't live with them [the Muslims]. They think the same of us."

"It's very dirty politics in our country and I think the best solution is to divide it," concluded a teenager in a bright red Italian dress with a matching headband that held her teased hair in place.

"You know," added her sneering boyfriend, "there are too many fucking people here. We hope one day we can destroy them and make them run away."

4
Combatants

Lebanon is one of the most precarious places to visit, and yet ... one of the most pleasant. The visitor prepared to risk the hazards of civil strife, will be enriched by the experience.

—*Traveller's Guide to the Middle East*[1]

The main battlefield for the warring Muslim and Christian sects was a place called the Green Line. Its name conjured up images of lush parks, baseball games and picnickers nibbling sandwiches in the shade while little boys pulled model sailboats across a sparkling lake.

But on Beirut's Green Line, there were no rustling kites, no barking dogs, no laughing families. It was an ugly scar gouged across the face of the city. The half-mile-wide swath of destruction stretched from the heart of the port, past the crumbling facades of the once-majestic banks in the old downtown area, across the pitted expanse of Martyr's Square, beyond the shattered shell of the museum, and out to the ravaged hulks of factories in Shweifat, once Lebanon's industrial center.

The story of Beirut was the tale of two cities: Muslim West Beirut and Christian East. The Green Line divided them as effectively as any moat. The battlements of the Crusades had been replaced by sandbags, dirt berms, and empty shipping containers looted from the port. The rust-streaked boxes were piled on top of each other to block the narrow streets on each side of the no-man's-land, forming barricades to protect against snipers.

Walking along the Green Line during a lull was like striding across an abandoned movie set. A layer of broken concrete and glass crunched underfoot, the sound magnified by the deathly silence. This was once an area of proud old Ottoman structures. High windows once peered from under elegant arches. On the buildings that were still standing, the red tile roofs had collapsed. The facades resembled those of a cliff face molded by eons of rain and wind. They had been eaten away by billions of bullets. It was as if someone had built a structure of ice, then doused it with hot water, smoothing the contours. Inside, the buildings were honeycombed by holes broken in the interior walls to enable fighters to walk for a full city block without ever stepping outside, a handy trick in the heat of battle.

If the Green Line was the moat, the Murr and Rizk towers were the castles of the warring feudal lords. They stood on opposite sides of the no-man's-land, unfinished skyscrapers towering over the city, warring twins set a dozen blocks apart. On nights when the fighting was heavy, it was as if two behemoths were locked in battle, tossing fireballs back and forth high above the city. For a decade fighters in fortified positions in the two buildings had been trading rocket fire. Still, the structures stood, scarred but unbent. Beneath, mere mortals continued their fight. Rarely a night passed without at least a few shots being fired. Usually, hours of mortar exchanges were required before the fighters were allowed to sleep.

There wasn't a Beirut militia that didn't have at least a few of its own positions along the line. They each fought when it was convenient for them or suited the particular goals of their masters. The biggest challenge facing the "mainstream" militia leaders was controlling the splinter groups and the splinters of the splinters. Even when the key leaders agreed on a cease-fire, those small factions could easily sabotage things. A few rounds in the right place were all it took.

In the summer of 1984, a member of the French cease-fire contingent concluded that the Green Line was "a playground for crazies, weirdos and others with personality problems." The observer told the *Daily Star* about a troublemaker who arrived by motorcycle every evening at 5:00 p.m. He carried no weapon.

"The young man parks his motorcycle, then proceeds to comb his hair in the rearview mirror," the bemused Frenchman reported. Properly groomed, "he walks to a section of the Green Line that is controlled by his friends. Then, about ten minutes later, we invariably hear two rocket-propelled grenades fired from exactly [that] spot." After about 30 minutes, he "goes back to his motorcycle, still parked near our observation post. Again he looks at himself in the motorcycle mirror and combs his hair. Then he gets on his bike and rides away."

Sometimes, the paper quoted the observer as saying, the attack would provoke a battle that lasted for hours.

Even between clashes, the Green Line was a dangerous place to be. On most of the six main crossing points, snipers sat in wait. Some days, their orders were to allow normal traffic. Other days, they were given a chance to pick off passersby.

The Ring, the Fouad al-Awal Bridge, was the worst crossing point. A 300-yard-long overpass that cut through the heart of the Green Line, it was the fastest way from one side of Beirut to the other. It was also the deadliest. A four-lane highway flanked by tall buildings, it was completely exposed. There was no place to hide, no place to cut off. This was Sniper's Alley. Even when things were quiet, most motorists preferred to use one of the other traffic-clogged routes. But now and then some brave or crazy driver would challenge the men with the high-powered rifles. The snipers usually won.

This item was transmitted by Beirut's Suhufiya News Agency: "At exactly 1 p.m. a woman showing signs of insanity crossed [the bridge]. Not a single shot was fired at her. The snipers must have been too surprised to act."

To the snipers, killing was a game. For others on the Green Line, it was all they knew.

"The revolver was this far from his head," says the stocky young man, as he measures an inch or two between finger and thumb. "And yet I didn't, uh, the first shot, I was trembling." The words come haltingly.

"He kept looking in my eyes. That is stamped very deeply in my memory. He wasn't afraid. Maybe he was ignorant or something or he doesn't understand, but he was not afraid. He kept staring into my eyes, and to tell you something that I've never told anyone, the first shot didn't hit him. I was shaking too hard."

He looks down at his hands, the incident nine years before still bringing pain. "This is war," he says, shrugging. Somehow it doesn't sound like a cliché.

We'll call him Joe. That's enough. It's healthier for him that way. Lebanon is a place where enemies want retribution and "friends" don't hesitate to punish one of their own who has said too much.

When we spoke in the early 1980s, he was 26. He happened to be Christian – Greek Orthodox to be exact. His English may have been a bit sharper, but his experiences were those of many thousands of other young Lebanese men who had grown up with war.

Joe was a fighter, a member of the Lebanese Forces (LF), better known as the Phalange, the key Christian militia. He began his military training at the age of 14 and killed his first man at 17. He learned the art of war from the Palestinians whom he would later fight, one of those incongruities that made Lebanon so difficult to understand. That was in the years before the Christians and the Palestinians began to slaughter each other in the name of justice.

In those days, the PLO was a cause célèbre to many young Lebanese. While American college kids were marching against the war in Vietnam, young Beirutis – Muslim and Christian alike – were rebeling by hanging out with the PLO and the Lebanese leftist militias that gathered around it.

"I'd take a taxi across the line and when I'd get to the camps, I'd take off my jeans and put on camouflage fatigues," recalled Nadine Akhouri, a Greek Orthodox housewife. "I'd learn how to shoot a gun and throw a grenade. If my mother had found out, she would have killed me."

The PLO demanded establishment of a secular state in Palestine where Muslims, Christians and Jews would, theoretically, live side-by-side. Christians, such as George Habash of the Marxist Popular Front for the Liberation of Palestine (PFLP), were among the PLO's leaders. Lebanese and other Christians were welcomed by Arafat and Co. for two practical reasons: they could be pointed to as evidence that the PLO practiced the secularism it preached; and they provided more warm bodies. The PLO needed as many of them as it could get.

That many Lebanese found the PLO attractive should not be surprising. Before the country became a cauldron of Muslim–Christian strife, it was the birthplace of the region's secular political principles. In the cafes facing the tree-shaded campus of the American University of Beirut (AUB), young Arab intellectuals gathered to plot the political future of a region dominated by what they saw as "reactionary" monarchs who inherited power by birth or were installed by foreign "masters."

Numerous leftist, anti-sectarian parties grew up in Lebanon espousing the goals of Pan-Arabism: an Arab world united as one. Even though these groups counted many Christians – primarily from the non-Maronite sects – among their leaders, all played a role in Lebanon's 1958 "revolution" that challenged the existing Christian Maronite-dominated order and was put down with the help of 14,000 U.S. Marines.

And so when Joe arrived at the PLO training camp in the Tal Zaatar refugee camp in 1972, no eyebrows were raised. He said he wanted to join the struggle against the Zionist enemy. He even agreed to sign a pledge to undertake a mission inside Israel after his graduation. There was no reason for suspicion.

There should have been. Joe was there to learn from his enemies in order to use their knowledge against them some day. He was only 14, but he had already been indoctrinated by the Phalange.

"We had regular meetings every week," Joe recalled later. "The man that was in charge said we did not have enough experience in fighting, so we should take whatever chance we had to get it. We all knew the Palestinians had the best technique for war, so I decided I must have that.

"I had a good friend who was having his training in a Palestinian camp. His uncle was an officer and he used to take us to the beach. One day I said, 'Why are you training him and not me? What's the difference between him and me?' He said, 'No difference,' so he took me to Tal Zaatar."

Four years later, Tal Zaatar lay in ruins, a victim of Christian guns. A 53-day siege, coupled with saturation shelling, claimed the lives of at least 1,000 Palestinian and Shi'ite Muslim residents of the sprawling slum and left about 3,000 wounded.

Few fighting-age men came out alive. They were systematically rounded up and executed. Some of those captured during the siege ended up at the bottom of a ravine just north of the Christian port of Jounieh. A bridge there had become a favorite spot for getting rid of unwanted baggage. Cars would frequently pull up at night, and from the trunk would come one, two, sometimes a half dozen Palestinian bodies. Occasionally, they would arrive by the truckload. Often the bodies were doused with gasoline and lit before being pitched over the side. There was little water in the ravine and the rotting bodies just piled up. Beirut was not known for its sanitary standards. During the fighting in Tal Zaatar, Christians on their way to the beach would stop on the bridge to see if there were many recent additions, an indication of how the battle was going.

As a young militiaman, Joe had helped deliver bodies to that bridge. Now he was tired and disillusioned.

The setting was a fish restaurant just below the Casino Du Liban, overlooking Jounieh. The remains of the standard Lebanese seaside *mezza* – a meal consisting of an array of dishes – was spread out before us: piles of ravaged shrimp heads; clean-picked spines of deep-fried red mullet, known in Lebanon as *rouget*; and half-empty bowls of *moutabbal*, a dip made from mashed eggplant, and *hommos*, the chickpea paste that is the mainstay of the Lebanese diet. Empty arak bottles littered the table. The milky anisette liquor that went by so many different names throughout the Mediterranean – Pernod, ouzo, araki – had been flowing freely.

The ravine that had consumed so many Palestinian bodies was just a stone's throw away.

As always in Lebanon, the talk had turned to the war. Joe's thoughts had returned to those nights on the bridge and the bodies that crowded his past.

"I can't get to sleep at night. I spend more than four hours in bed every night before I sleep. I have to remember every face, every man. I must apologize to each one. I must tell each one that I am sorry. Then maybe I can get relieved and go to sleep. Every night is the same thing. You have something called a conscience."

It was a kind of confession, spoken clearly and without hesitation.

Lebanon's violence was often impersonal; machine guns spraying bullets into the darkness, mortar rounds launched from a half mile away, artillery fired blindly. It was hard to believe his memory could be so exact.

"Not to make this too tough on you," I prompted, "but how can you actually remember every face?"

"Every face ... every face." Joe paused, studying his folded hands, and resumed in a whisper, "every face. Maybe sometimes you can remember a group. It's very tough."

His voice rose. He was addressing the victims he was never able to look in the eye. "Sorry to all of you. I can't remember you."

He paused again, then looked up at me and said firmly, "But you *can* remember the faces you saw."

One face was carved indelibly in the memory of an inexperienced and frightened young man.

"The first three guys I had to shoot were Syrians. Syrian workers, not fighters. That's what hurts me most. They had nothing to do with the war, but a friend of mine was shot in the same hour. We heard that there were some Syrians fighting with the Palestinians and another friend of mine caught these three Syrians trying to go by the port to the other side."

He looked out across the black waters toward Beirut, eight miles away. Lights twinkled in both halves of the capital – city power was on this night. There was a dark patch in the center – the Port. Occasionally, a dull red flash pricked the darkness.

Joe stared for a long time at the place where he killed his first man, then turned back to me.

"He [his friend] told me, 'These three are Syrians. What do we do with them?' So we shot them." The words carried no emotion. He might just as easily have said, "So we offered them lunch."

"One of them kept looking directly at me." Joe's voice began to take on a hollow quality as he relived the horror of that day.

"When you shoot someone, you say, 'Kneel,' and he kneels; 'Look at the ground,' and he looks at the ground." His words began to come more quickly. "The first two did that. The third refused to look at the ground. He kept looking at me in the face. He was very courageous." There was admiration in Joe's voice.

The trembling teenager missed his first shot, but not his second.

"After this, I went to bed for 48 hours. I didn't eat. I couldn't sleep. I felt very sick. I remember them always."

If that first time was difficult, killing would soon become routine.

"If you want to talk about me, I've never shot a child, nor a woman. Never. Not even sniping. Never. I have never shot a man who, leave out those first three, was not wearing a uniform. Never."

He paused. Remembering the truth. "There were some exceptions," he admitted, dropping his eyes from mine. "Tal Zaatar."

The place where he learned the art of war. The place where he killed those who had taught him. Barely a Palestinian male of fighting age escaped.

"In Tal Zaatar, they took off their uniforms and put on civilian clothes. But except for Tal Zaatar and the first three guys, everyone I killed was in uniform."

"Armed?"

"No." The tone indicated the answer needed no elaboration. It was sufficient that the man was old enough to be a combatant. Kill the enemy when you have the chance, most fighters believe, or he might someday return with a gun and kill you.

One extremist Christian group, the Guardians of the Cedars, carried that concept a step further. Its philosophy: kill every Palestinian infant, since, after all, babies grew up to be "terrorists" who eventually had to be killed anyway. The group's leader, Abu Arz (Father of the Cedars) was also in favor of killing Palestinian women. Each female was, of course, the potential mother of a potential terrorist. Abu Arz, a Christian former policeman, had been born in Palestine.

Joe rejected such extremists, but the line between their actions and his sometimes blurred.

"When you have a good friend shot in front of you, you lose control. You do anything. When you have a good friend, not a guy you've known for a week, but a good friend who has saved your life three or four times and you've saved his life, and you begin to share even a girl when you find one, who you won't refuse no matter what he asks, when you see him shot in front of you, or shot ..."

Joe fell silent, staring at the reflection of the moon on the harbor.

"You must have someone to judge this guy," he concluded.

Those close relationships, forged under fire, had helped keep Lebanon's war aflame.

"Let me give you an example. Two friends. They grow up together, go to school together. The war began. The first says to the second, 'Yesterday I shot a man.' They are competing, which one to be the best. They are very young, so the second will look for an opportunity to be equal to his friend. That's the way it begins."

Killing was macho, all part of maintaining the right image. The young toughs swaggering down Hamra Street with pistols tucked into their belts knew that. So did the "water-skiers," punks hanging onto heavy machine guns mounted on the backs of open jeeps, who careened through the streets of the city sending pedestrians fleeing – pedestrians, the people they were supposed to be protecting.

"They kill because they're afraid of losing their image. That *heroic* image." Joe's voice dripped with sarcasm.

"They say, 'Kill him, go ahead. I don't care,' because they don't want to lose their image. Especially the older ones. They don't want to look like they're getting soft. They want to show the younger ones they are still the best.

"Those are the men who kill for pleasure, or to keep their pleasure. Maybe 60 percent of it is done for pleasure. Killing for me was never a pleasure. I killed from anger. There were times that I was so angry that you cannot imagine. I could do anything. Anything. A friend of mine gets shot and I got the most high level of anger. I could push anyone. If Amin Gemayel was near me, I could push him, step on him, to get the man I want."

"Most people have a handful of really close friends in their entire life," I observed. "But tens of thousands of Lebanese have been killed."

"It's the memory," he said flatly.

"You lash out once because your friend has been killed and ..." He interrupted before I could finish.

"And it becomes more or less like a habit. You have nothing to stop you from doing it. You've shot these three guys," Joe is talking of himself again, "so you've done it. Like they say in court, if you kill one man or a hundred, it's the same crime.

"So I did it. And did it. And did it." He gulped down the arak without looking at the glass. Silently, he prepared more for the two of us. It was a Lebanese ritual. First the clear arak was poured into a new glass for each drinker, then an equal measure of water was added, turning the liquor milky, and finally a few pieces of ice were added to each glass. The order must never be changed.

It gave him time. He concentrated on the drinks, avoiding eye contact. Only when he had made me a fresh drink did he look at my face. When he spoke, Joe answered the question that was on my mind. It was easy to see he had had this conversation with himself more than once, as he lay awake at night waiting for the ghosts to go away.

"If you want to say maybe I was drugged when I did this or this, no, I was 100 percent okay. No alcohol either. That means I have no excuse." It was as if the phrase "no excuse" was a whip with which he was beating himself.

"But the massacres – how can someone wipe out an entire village?" I asked, a question I had pondered since witnessing my first mass slaughter in Africa years before.

"When you massacre people, you are afraid someone will massacre you. When you have all your parents massacred in a village and they have nothing to do with the war, you will go to another village and massacre those who have nothing to do with the war.

"The fighters always kill those who have nothing to do with the war," Joe said, his face lined with disgust. "And the other side does the same thing. That's the problem. Always civilians, civilians. Because they have to go to work. They have to bring money to their families.

"It's the most dirty war in the world because the fighters are so safe. He has someone to pay a salary for him, his medicine, everything. He is very insured. But the civilian ..."

In fact, a study by Dr. Samir Khalaf of AUB found that 90 percent of the casualties in the first decade of the war had been civilians.

"I had no value for the civilians. I didn't think about them. What I was concerned about was the friend that was fighting with me. Only." Joe lit a cigarette and motioned to the waiter for another bottle of arak. He was in no hurry to end the conversation. Perhaps it was a kind of therapy for him.

"But aren't the civilians the people you are fighting for?" I asked.

"No." In light of the propaganda on all sides about defending the freedom of their respective communities, the answer was revealing. "When I was sitting on the front lines in '75 and '76, I didn't think about civilians. Perhaps I didn't know that a civilian existed in my everyday thinking.

"We were living in a fight. We barely see a civilian. We were always on the front line. We spent maybe three days without sleeping, then we slept for 24 hours without stopping. We didn't have time to think about civilians or even what we were fighting about. All we were concerned with was to kill this enemy, maybe protect this friend from dying, and not be killed ourselves."

The new bottle arrived, and he poured another round of arak.

"But didn't you have discussions about what you were fighting for?" I asked, finishing off the drink in my old glass.

"No." Joe stopped pouring and thought back for a moment. "No, we didn't have. Look, it was very tough. Every day you had a new experience. Every day you have a new weapon to learn on. Every day you have a new sight of a dead man getting a bullet in his head, his heart shot out. All that we thought about was our friend. Our friend always. If he gets shot, I have to carry him. If I get shot, he has to carry me.

"In a war, you can't think like you think now. You have a cloud in front of you. Danger doesn't mean nothing. Nothing at all. Tomorrow doesn't exist. Even today. The next hour doesn't exist. You have this hour. Whatever you want to do, do. The next hour you may not be here."

The arak bottle was in motion once more.

"Sometime you think you're invincible. When you have so much shelling on you, you think that it will pass. You're unhurtable. You are untouchable. You feel that after all this shelling, how could a bullet kill me?

"In 1975, I was passing a corner in a street. We were mixed between Palestinians [whom the Christians were fighting] and us. I passed this corner. I ran into a Palestinian who was crossing in the wrong direction."

Joe moved a few things on the table, illustrating the two men's relative positions with the empty arak glasses that had been piling up like the dead soldiers of his stories.

"We went to cross at the same time, so we hit. For three seconds, I didn't exist. For three seconds, I don't remember what I was doing. We stood there, this Palestinian and myself, in front of each other, without looking at each other's faces. My weapon in front of me and his weapon in front of him. We can't use them and didn't and wouldn't because, I don't know, for a few seconds we didn't exist. We forget everything. Our minds freeze. Everything stopped. Then he ran that way and I ran this way, automatically." The arak glasses slid off in different directions.

"After this, when I sat all alone, I began to cry. My tears went out and I went into a very cold sweat. I felt that I could be dead then. For the first time, I thought about death. Does it exist? At 16 years old, you don't believe something called danger, death. After this, I began to be very careful about crossing corners. We learn from our mistakes.

"But for the man when he goes to war at 16 or 17 years old, danger doesn't exist. When your officer runs, you run after him. If he dies, you will step on him and keep running.

"You know, the only thing I was thinking about when I sat there frightened was that I don't know how to drive a car. That was one thing I had not done. I was very worried that I must not be dead without driving a car." He smiled at how silly it seemed.

A member of the Phalange Special Forces, an elite fighting unit whose members joined for life, Joe had told his commanders he would not fight again unless the situation was desperate.

"I have run out of anger," he said, spilling some of his arak. He put a napkin over the damp spot and continued. "I'm tired.

"When the 1978 battles began, I swore before I got my gun that I would not shoot anybody. Whatever is happening, I'll take a prisoner. Let another kill him. I won't kill anyone."

"Kill" was Joe's euphemism for execute. In his mind, shooting someone in battle was natural and necessary.

"One day the Syrians came into a building and our commanders contacted us and said, 'The Syrians are in this building. Get them out of there.'

"During the fighting, I killed some Syrians and we caught three. One of them was tall, six feet, no hair, very black. All the guys wanted to kill him. I said, 'No, nobody will kill this guy. We'll give him as a prisoner to the responsibles and they will know what to do.'"

The Syrian had been in the area for some time. There were reports he had beat and killed local Christians. With his distinctive looks, there was little chance the Syrian was being confused with someone else.

"They said, 'We want to kill him. He did this and that.'"

A man at the next table glanced at us, clearly uncomfortable with what he had overheard.

"You know," Joe said, his voice taking on a confiding tone, "my mind began to change a little bit. I began to forget that I swore not to do this thing. I began to think, 'You know, the Syrians did a lot of things. Beat guys, killed them.'

"My guys were very angry. They really wanted to kill this guy. And I was going on their side. In one minute, I would have said, 'Okay.' It's the same mistake. I'm in charge. If I say, 'No,' nobody will kill him. But if I say, 'Yes,' I am killing him.

"There was just a hair between yes and no. All the guys were standing, no words. Just waiting for a yes or no. I said, 'No.'"

He exhaled, relieved that this had been his decision. "In 1978, I said, 'No,'" he continued proudly. "I was 20 years old and I said, 'No.' It was not an easy decision to take. They all said, 'You are a coward.' I didn't care.

"Maybe he was shot after, but I didn't do nothing. I said, 'No.'" Joe kept repeating that word. You could hear the pride in his voice; the feeling that maybe, just maybe, the incident had helped make up for all the times he had said yes.

Other military lines in Lebanon were difficult and dangerous, but the Green Line was the most permanent and consistently deadly. It had been there since 1975. Over the years, the demarcation had shifted a few blocks one way or the other according to the fortunes of war, but it had never disappeared. Occasionally, the Lebanese government exerted itself. The army moved in and the barricades came down. But, inevitably, they went back up again, usually in a matter of days. The perennial subject of discussion at Lebanese cabinet meetings was the "latest" plan to dismantle the mid-city dividing line.

The term "Green Line" had been borrowed from Cyprus, where a similar no-man's-land marked the division between the Turks and the Greeks. The name came from the green ink used to mark the line on official maps. Beirut maps did not show the division, green or otherwise, but it was indelibly inscribed on the souls of the Lebanese. Even in those rare moments when the bulldozers pushed aside the earthen mounds, the psychological barrier remained. Among the young, many had never glimpsed the world across the line.

A researcher at AUB once tested the geographical knowledge of Muslim students in West Beirut and Christian students in East Beirut. He showed them famous sights from around the world, such as the Statue of Liberty and the Eiffel Tower, along with popular landmarks on the two sides of Beirut. Most of the students correctly identified the American and French tourist spots, but when it came to their own country, few Christian students recognized West Beirut's seafront corniche and only a handful of Muslims knew that the underground caverns in the pictures were just up the coast in the Christian heartland.

Plenty of Christians and Muslims did cross the Green Line every day, but the fears of those who refused were well grounded. Thousands of Lebanese had been kidnapped or had disappeared since 1975. No one knew just how many. One estimate put the number of missing Muslims alone at 4,000. More Lebanese were kidnapped almost every day. Some abductions were political, others personal. Many people were kidnapped so they could be exchanged for someone kidnapped by the faction to which the individual belonged. Sometimes the kidnappers were looking for a specific person; usually, anyone from the other side would do. Muslim militiamen often waited at one of the Green Line crossings and just took the first (or first dozen) Christians who came along – or vice versa. Some of these victims were lucky enough to be traded back to their comrades; many were never heard from again.

"It's not very pleasant to say, but we have to face the truth. Most of these people were killed long ago," admitted Druze leader Walid Jumblatt, the one militia chieftain who rarely pulled verbal punches.

Thousands of women on both sides of the Green Line lived with nothing more than the memory of their men. One Muslim woman told the *Daily Star* of the morning Phalangist militiamen surrounded her home and kidnapped her three sons, shooting her husband.

"They [Christian Phalangists] came in the morning, surrounded the house and entered the bakery where my husband and sons were working. They were still wearing pajamas. The militiamen asked my three sons to follow them. My husband was afraid and tried to stop them from taking my sons, but he was unable to do anything. They fired at him, hitting him in the back.

"I went to get clothes for my sons, but when I got back they had already left. All of them – the militiamen and my three sons. Two days after my sons were taken I contacted [President] Amin Gemayel, who at that time was a high official in the Phalange Party. He told me categorically that my sons would not be released until a final solution was reached in Lebanon. I still remember his words.

"What are my feelings? You are asking me how I feel? I feel I can no longer feel. My sons are now 32, 31 and 23 years old. When they were kidnapped, they were 22, 21 and 13."[2]

Yet even in their quest for loved ones, the relatives of Muslim and Christian abductees could not bridge the great social divide and create a united movement to apply pressure across the political spectrum. For as they talked of unity, they sniped at each other, disparaging the claims of those across the line, demanding that *their* men must be released first. It was a pattern found in most other aspects of Lebanese life.

They warred on the streets and they warred on the playing fields. Sport was no equalizer for the Lebanese. It wasn't official, but the First Division of the Lebanese Soccer League broke down roughly this way: West Beirut had two Sunni Muslim teams, along with one each from the Shi'ite and Druze communities; East Beirut had three Maronite Christian teams and one made up of Greek Orthodox players; another Maronite team represented the pro-Syrian Franjieh clan in northern Lebanon; the Sunnis of Tripoli had a team; and the Armenians had two, one representing each end of the political spectrum.

Control of sport, like control of government, was in Maronite hands. The head of the Olympic Committee was a Gemayel, the directors of the athletics federation, the shooting team, and even the table tennis organization were Maronites. As in the war, the innocents – in this case, the athletes – were victims of the political divisions.

Mahar Abbas was a Muslim who held several Lebanese track records. As he tried out for the 1984 Lebanese Olympic team at the AUB track in West Beirut, Abbas spoke bitterly about factional politics. "I used to train in the east part of Beirut, in Baabda, and here [in West Beirut], the [Druze] PSP [militia] told me not to go back or they'll kill me."

Just staying on their own side of the line was no guarantee of safety for the athletes, however. Competition between Lebanese sports clubs was fierce. They all wanted the best athletes on their teams and the coaches were not particular about how they recruited. Abbas' friend Tarek Musawi, another record holder, discovered that. "They told him, 'If we see you training at AUB we will shoot you,'" Abbas said. "And they told him, 'A bullet won't cost us anything. One bullet for one [Lebanese] pound. You'll lose your legs for all of your life.'"

The racetrack was one of the few places where the Lebanese of all sects came together, if only rarely. Straddling the Green Line at the Museum crossing point, it was accessible to residents in both halves of the city. Gambling fever was non-denominational.

But even without politics, there was violence at the track. In the early 1980s, a winning horse was shot by an irate bettor just as the filly crossed the finish line. A few years later, a riot broke out when four favorites tripped and fell at the start of the race. The accident allowed a 91-to-1 long shot to win and the losers poured onto the track, tearing down the tote board.

To calm things down, track officials disqualified the race and announced they would refund all bets. That didn't please one bettor, who leaped from the stands waving a winning $12 ticket. As police hustled him away, he threatened to blow up the track unless officials paid up. As the next race was being run, a rocket-propelled grenade blasted through an outer wall, causing bettors to flee in panic.

Since adults acted like children, it was easy for Lebanon's children to act like adults. The grownups had their militias; the kids had the Scouts. Neckerchiefs, merit badges and the Scout sign were all part of it. But somehow, Robert Baden-Powell might have objected.

Amal scouts marched beneath portraits of the Ayatollah Khomeini chanting, "With blood, with spirit, we will sacrifice to you."

"We teach them Islam and the Qur'an and we prepare them to fight," explained one of their commanders at a rally in the Shi'ite slums. Druze Scouts, too, put a very Lebanese twist on the motto, "Be Prepared."

"In time of war, I am a fighter and in time of peace, I am a scout," one young Druze follower of Walid Jumblatt said, summing up his philosophy.

On the other side of the line, the Troop d'Jesuit wore the original Boy Scout uniforms and carried the official Boy Scout handbook, but the parts about tolerance and brotherhood seemed to have been lost in the translation.

"We have never shared any activity with any other [Scout] association, neither Christian nor Muslim," their leader, perched on a log in a mountain camp overlooking East Beirut, adamantly pronounced. "Not even with Christian Scouts."

Although the various Christian militias had joined together under the banner of the Lebanese Forces, these were Roman Catholic Boy Scouts. They wanted nothing to do with anyone else. They intended to remain pure.

Peace marches were bombed out of existence, young lovers from opposing factions were kept apart, television signals from one side of the city were jammed in the other.

These were the people the Reagan administration set out to unite.

Section II

Planting the Seeds

5

The Slippery Slope

And he, whose whole course of proceeding seemed like a deliberate crusade against Mohammedan susceptibilities, never appeared to reflect for one moment that he was thereby supplying the springs to an under-current of fierce and deadly fanaticism, which, however overborne and kept out of sight for the time, would be ready on the slightest occasion or opportunity to rise to the surface with an impetus almost resistless and overwhelming.

—Col. Charles Churchill[1]

When the men of the 32nd Marine Amphibious Unit (MAU) splashed ashore at the beach opposite Beirut International Airport on September 29, 1982, they were coming not to fight a war, but to administer first aid to a diplomatic black eye.

It had been just 19 days since they had climbed aboard ships at Beirut Port and bid Lebanon good-bye. The task of the 2,100-member Multinational Force (MNF), which also included French and Italian troops, was considered complete. The last PLO guerrillas, cornered in West Beirut by the Israeli invasion, had been evacuated. Despite nagging doubts about the wisdom of committing U.S. troops to as volatile a place as Lebanon, the mission had gone without a serious hitch. But the White House was not taking any chances. A full two weeks before the Marines were expected to leave, Washington ordered them back on the ships, and the Pentagon breathed a deep sigh of relief.

The fleet was barely over the horizon when the trouble began. In short order, President-elect Bechir Gemayel was blown up by an assassin's bomb, the Israelis entered West Beirut in direct violation of a solemn pledge to the United States, and squads of Phalangist militiamen bent on vengeance entered the refugee camps of Sabra and Chatilla in an operation closely coordinated with the Israeli army.

Yasser Arafat and a half dozen members of the PLO Executive Committee sat in stunned silence, gazing at the unedited images of slaughter that had just arrived from Beirut. Crowded around a tiny television monitor on a conference room table in a dingy Damascus office, the faces of these men who had survived three months of war and siege slowly turned gray.

Arafat, the consummate actor, was performing no more. Tears filled his eyes. He abruptly waved away a young aide who had entered the room, signaling for total silence so he could hear the anguished descriptions of what had happened from the survivors on the screen. The bravado was gone. The PLO chief was clearly shaken. He was responsible for the lives of those left behind – he and, in his view, the United States.

"When we left Beirut, we left Beirut under the protection of the Multinational Force," he shouted at me after the tape had ended, his voice cracking as it did whenever he was angry. "It had been agreed that they must stay for one month, and before they left they must consult with the Lebanese and with me!"

It was well after midnight. We had brought the tapes of the Sabra and Chatilla massacre to show Arafat after satelliting them to New York for that evening's broadcast in the U.S. Figures like Arafat normally gave us the news, not the other way around. This situation was unique. The massacre had taken place because Arafat had agreed to a peaceful evacuation of his fighters from Beirut. His reaction to what had happened was an important part of the story. But, in those days before satellite television, the reality was that, sitting in Damascus, he would not have been able to see the carnage until the footage shot by Western television reporters was eventually fed back to the Middle East and carried on Syrian television. That would take days. We were shortcutting the process.

"This shameful crime of genocide is an international responsibility, and first it is an American responsibility," he continued. Our camera was rolling now; he was beginning to perform. "It is not my responsibility. It is something touching the U.S. credibility, [and that of] the French and the Italians, and their honor, too."

Arafat felt that he had obtained a guarantee from U.S. negotiator Philip Habib that Palestinian civilians left behind in Beirut would be protected. The fourth clause of the evacuation agreement, the so-called Habib Document, specifically spoke of the need to protect "law-abiding and non-combatant" Palestinians. Arafat was convinced that he had been tricked.

Back in the United States, officials denied Habib had given an ironclad pledge, but they confirmed that the United State had, in effect, promised safety for the families the PLO fighters had left behind in Beirut. During negotiations over the PLO evacuation, "the question of retribution came up again and again," recalled one U.S. diplomat who was intimately involved in the discussions. "Habib was careful because he couldn't guarantee anything. He gave assurances based on assurances from the Israelis" that the civilians would be safe.

But the word "guarantee" *was* used in the final evacuation agreement: "The United States will provide its guarantees on the basis of assurances received from the government of Israel and from the leadership of certain groups with which it had been in touch."

Habib had been acting in good faith. His undertaking to Arafat to protect Palestinian non-combatants was based on two key factors: Israel's pledge that its forces would not enter West Beirut, and a promise from Bechir Gemayel, commander of the Lebanese Forces militia (the Phalangists), that he would prevent revenge killings.

Contrary to Arafat's claim, the Americans insisted there had never been a promise that the MNF would remain for a full month or that Arafat would be consulted before they left. The evacuation agreement called for the MNF mission to last for a "maximum" of one month. Once the PLO was safely out of Beirut, in the view of the Americans, there was no compelling reason for the Marines to stay. Israeli Defense Minister Ariel Sharon did not object; he didn't want the MNF there a moment longer than necessary for fear they would act as a shield for other "terrorists" who, he claimed, remained behind in Beirut.

When Bechir was killed, Sharon broke with alacrity his country's commitment not to enter West Beirut and helped undermine the word of the late Phalangist commander. Israeli troops rolled into the Muslim half of the city, ostensibly to "prevent chaos," while, according to an Israeli investigation, the Israeli chief of staff, Lt. Gen. Raphael Eitan, ordered "a general mobilization" of Phalangist units.[2]

"The Phalangist commanders were told by the Chief of Staff that the IDF [Israeli Defense Forces] would not enter the refugee camps in West Beirut but [that] the fighting this entails would be undertaken by the Phalangists," according to the final report of the Kahan Commission, which conducted the official Israeli investigation of the massacre. "The camps in question were Sabra and Chatilla." Eitan told the Phalangists they should use "their own methods" inside the camps.[3]

The Phalangists' job, Israeli officers later testified, was to "mop up" the "armed terrorists" allegedly hidden in the camps. The Israelis claimed that 2,000 fighters remained in West Beirut, but U.S. officials dismissed the figure as "highly inflated." No one disputed the notion that there were still thousands of fighters in the Muslim half of the city, but the vast majority were Lebanese members of local Muslim militias. It was the official

U.S. view that the presence of these militiamen was strictly an internal Lebanese affair of no concern to Israel, and that it was up to the Lebanese government to disarm them. Israeli officers, however, had nothing but contempt for the Lebanese government and its army.

The Phalangists were told not to harm civilians, but Eitan, Sharon and other top Israeli officials knew the militia's record of atrocities.[4] Even as Eli Hobeika, the Phalangist intelligence chief, and his 150 men entered Sabra and Chatilla on the evening of Thursday, September 16, at the request of Sharon and Eitan, the Israeli chief of staff was telling a cabinet meeting in Jerusalem that the Phalangists "now have just one thing left to do, and that is revenge; and it will be terrible."[5]

Israel's deputy prime minister, David Levy, expressed concern at the news that Christian militiamen had been sent into the camps. He feared that since they were acting under IDF supervision, Israel would be blamed for the inevitable outcome. "I know what the meaning of revenge is for them, what kind of slaughter," Levy noted. That did not deter the rest of the cabinet. According to the Kahan Commission, no one responded to Levy's comment, and the ministers proceeded to approve the text of a government statement justifying the Israeli invasion of West Beirut.[6]

The tanks had begun forming up before dawn. We found the long line of Merkavas and armored personnel carriers at the eastern edge of the port, just past the basin where PLO fighters had completed their evacuation a few days before. Huge blue and white Israeli flags billowed in the wind as the armor rolled through the devastation of the old downtown district. At each intersection, the drill was the same. A tank would crawl out into the crossroads, swivel its huge turret like the head of some evil carnivore looking for prey, then stand guard as the foot soldiers ran past, using its bulk as protection. The rumble of the armor and the Hebrew chatter on the military radios were the only sounds.

While cameraman Robert Moreno and soundman Hassan Harake recorded the scene, I kept expecting the blast of RPGs or a volley of gunfire at each corner. But by the time we emerged on the western side of the port, beneath the pockmarked sign that read "Crisis Tourism" (I never did figure out whether that was someone's idea of a joke or had once been a real office), the Israelis still had not encountered any opposition. The only figure there to challenge them was the bloated corpse of a dead fighter lying in the dirt beside the road.

Past the perforated tower of the Holiday Inn, along the seafront corniche, the Israelis jogged in single file. Occasionally, shots or explosions were heard, but they were from deeper inside the city where the invaders were encountering opposition.

The soldiers kept close to the buildings and walls, making themselves a more difficult target for snipers. We did the same. After covering the PLO for so long, there would have been a certain irony in being mistaken for an Israeli and killed. The situation was already bizarre enough. To stand in the street beside an Israeli tank looking up at my old apartment in an Arab capital was a situation I found difficult to fully absorb.

As we watched Israeli tanks rumble past the U.S. embassy a few hundred yards down the coast, one senior American diplomat commented dryly, "So much for 'free' West Beirut."

During dinner that night at the Alexandre Hotel, the press headquarters in East Beirut, we watched Israeli jets dropping flares over Sabra and Chatilla, blissfully unaware of what was happening inside, as Israeli Radio outlined the Jerusalem government's justification for invading West Beirut.

To U.S. officials, no justification was possible. Habib and his top assistant, Morris Draper, were furious. They felt betrayed.

When news of the massacre began leaking out the following day, the American anger turned to rage. The first call was to Amin Gemayel, presumed to be in charge of the Christian militia now that his brother was dead. Next, they got the Israelis on the phone. More than 12 hours passed between Draper's initial call to Bruce Kashdan, the Israeli Foreign Ministry representative in Beirut, and the withdrawal of the Phalangists.

The full extent of the slaughter left the Americans horrified. Arafat issued his denunciation, and Lebanese Muslims, whose trust Habib had won in the long negotiations, denounced Israeli–American duplicity.

U.S. officials would later point to Sabra and Chatilla as the place where the seeds of the American disaster in Lebanon were planted – a disaster that would spawn a global terrorist nightmare that few could even begin to imagine at the time.

"It's at that point that the slippery slope begins," said one diplomat, who was deeply involved in the formulation of U.S. policy, as he looked back over the years of bombings, assassinations and kidnappings.

After the slaughter in the camps, the word of the United States lay broken and soiled. U.S. policy was thrown into disarray. In addition to the immediate consequences of the massacre, Washington was worried about the impact it would have on the Reagan Middle East Peace Plan, which had been unveiled on September 1. All the diplomatic credits built up among Arab moderates during Habib's negotiations had been wiped out in one fell swoop.

The first priority was to prevent another massacre. The Sixth Fleet was turned around and Washington launched into urgent consultations with its European allies to cobble together a new Multinational Force to go back into Beirut. France and Italy quickly agreed to return. Britain would join later.

"This was not a deeply thought-out process," one diplomat recalled. "When we first organized the force to oversee the evacuation, a great deal of consideration was given to the implications. This time, we reacted from the gut. We simply had to do something and getting the Marines back seemed the most logical thing."

The Marine Corps had been picked for the original Beirut assignment over other branches of the armed forces because of its reputation for discipline and its ability to get in and out of places fast. If something went wrong during the PLO evacuation, Washington wanted to make damn sure logistical snafus did not leave American troops stranded in the middle of a war. Some people in the Reagan administration and the Pentagon had not been enthusiastic about sending in U.S. forces. They were worried about political fallout and military screwups, but Yasser Arafat had insisted that foreign soldiers must provide cover if his men were to evacuate and Ariel Sharon had refused to accept European troops without the Americans.

When American troops needed to be "reinserted" into Lebanon in the wake of the massacre, the considerations about which branch would be involved were more straightforward. The marines were on the ships just offshore and they had already seen duty in Beirut (though most had never set foot outside the confines of the port). The thought that Lebanon might turn into garrison duty more fitting for the U.S. Army was never seriously considered.

President Reagan certainly was not thinking in those terms. Asked at a news conference whether the Marines would remain in Lebanon until Israeli and Syrian troops withdrew, the president replied, "Yes, because I think that's going to come rapidly." Aides were caught off guard. What their boss really meant to say, they told reporters later, was that the U.S. "hoped" the foreign forces would leave before the Marines. It was not the last time that administration officials would reinterpret Reagan's comments on Lebanon.

Still, most administration officials were talking in terms of weeks when asked about the duration of the mission. Privately, a few were more cautious, estimating that the Marines might be there a minimum of four to six months.

Throughout their 17-month mission on Lebanese soil, the Marines liked to refer to themselves as "neutral peacekeepers." Neither term ever really applied. Their aim was certainly peaceful, but they were specifically told to stay out of the fighting; they should not actively intervene to "keep the peace." Theirs was a symbolic presence. Yet that presence was in support of one side in Lebanon's manifold war.

Their commander in Beirut, Col. James Mead, cheerfully told reporters that his men had come "to help our Lebanese friends." President Reagan defined just who those "friends" were in a letter to Congress on September 29:

> [The Marines'] mission is to provide an interposition force at agreed locations and thereby provide the multinational presence requested by the Lebanese Government *to assist it and the Lebanese Armed Forces ...* Our agreement with the government of Lebanon *expressly rules out any combat responsibilities for the U.S. forces.*[7]

For that one fleeting moment in Lebanese history, it all seemed so simple. U.S. and European troops were welcomed by virtually all of Lebanon's main armed factions. Each had given its assurance that the MNF would not be attacked. Amin Gemayel was Parliament's unanimous choice for president. His picture was plastered throughout West Beirut. Lebanon finally had a Christian president who was also the darling of the Muslims – a man who preached the need for a unified, pluralistic Lebanon and seemed to mean it. Whether he could control his own militia was still open to question, but U.S. officials believed that the Christian force would eventually fall into line. Later, as Gemayel's consensus crumbled, things would become far less clear-cut. The noble task of supporting a "legitimate" government would be transformed into a more questionable role of backing a besieged minority regime.

The only sour note in those early days was prompted by Israel's refusal to withdraw from Beirut International Airport – precisely the piece of turf the Marine contingent was supposed to secure. That caused a three-day delay in the Marine landing, further testing the already strained patience of U.S. officials.

The 1,300 marines who finally hit the beach that muggy September day had been assigned the airport largely because it was – relatively – the safest piece of real estate available. Located on the coastal plain just south of the city, the airport was an important symbol to the Lebanese. Whether it was open or closed was a barometer of the security situation. The airport was dominated by the Chouf and Aley Mountains. Deploying there violated the Marine doctrine to always take the high ground. But moving into the hills was not an option the marines had been given. The MNF was to guard Beirut and nothing more. Although U.S. officers would have preferred a more dominant position, they were confident that if trouble broke out, their men were in a far better position to defend themselves than the 1,500-member French and 1,200-member Italian contingents, which were assigned to the crowded residential and commercial areas of the city.

A man named Reagan was the first casualty of the Marine mission in Beirut. Twenty-one-year-old Corporal David L. Reagan of Chesapeake, Virginia, was killed and three other young marines were wounded, as they cleared away an unexploded shell left over from the Israeli invasion. A Marine spokesman said the device was a "cluster shell," a 155mm artillery round that contained 38 golf-ball-sized bomblets. Israeli use of these American-supplied devices, and the larger "cluster bombs," had sparked controversy during the war. Critics had charged that they were being employed in violation of U.S. restrictions. Congressional sources said Israel had agreed to use the lethal weapon only in defense against an attack by two or more sovereign nations. Neither condition existed in Lebanon.

White House spokesman Larry Speakes assured the nation that the regrettable incident would not undermine the Marines' mission. "It is our expectation that our people will not become involved in any combat that will result in loss of life."[8]

The same day, President Amin Gemayel, looking like the Good Humor Man in a blinding white colonial suit, stood on the Green Line and proclaimed: "There will be no more East Beirut and no more West Beirut. This is not a symbol of reunification. It is a reunification of the hearts."

For Lebanon and America, those were heady days.

If Amin Gemayel had any doubts about the firmly pro-American course on which he was launching Lebanon, he kept them to himself.

"The Americans were on a white horse. Everybody was talking about the American solution," a top Gemayel advisor later recalled as he sat in the battered Presidential Palace. Habib and the U.S. embassy in Beirut had thrown all of America's considerable influence into getting Amin elected. In return, the young Lebanese president "went hook, line and sinker" for the U.S. approach. "Nobody predicted the American plan would fail," the advisor lamented.

The U.S. approach was twofold. It consisted of a diplomatic drive to achieve the withdrawal of Israeli and Syrian forces from Lebanon, backed up by a show of support for the Beirut government, and a "fresh start" toward attaining a wider Middle East peace.

The Lebanese end of that policy would culminate in the ill-fated Lebanon–Israel Agreement, signed on May 17, 1983. The broad Middle East peace effort, which became known as the Reagan Initiative, had been outlined in a speech by the U.S. president in September.

The Israeli invasion of Lebanon had created "a new opportunity for Middle East peace," Reagan had told a nationwide television audience. The time had come for a negotiated settlement to help satisfy "the yearning of the Palestinian people for a just solution to their claims." To that end,

Reagan had proposed that Palestinians on the Israeli-occupied West Bank and Gaza Strip be granted "self-rule in association with Jordan." The status of Jerusalem would be negotiated, although it must remain "undivided." Reagan had also called for a freeze on Israeli West Bank settlements. Israeli Prime Minister Menachim Begin immediately rejected the plan out of hand, perceiving it as a direct challenge to his vision of the biblical "Eretz Israel" (Greater Israel).

Both aspects of the U.S. approach were based on the same set of assumptions. Radical Syria was defeated and isolated. It was in no position to cause trouble in Lebanon or challenge Arab moderates such as Jordan, Egypt and Saudi Arabia, which were more willing to make peace with Israel.

There was a sound basis for those assumptions. In the first weeks of the June 1982 Israeli invasion of Lebanon, Syria had lost more than 90 combat aircraft and hundreds of its tanks had been destroyed. In addition, its surface-to-air missile network in the Bekaa Valley had been wiped out. The diplomatic signals coming from Damascus reinforced the conviction among policymakers that Syria would, at worst, not interfere and might, at best, cooperate.

Experts outside the administration concurred. "There basically isn't a Steadfastness Front" left, Middle East analyst Judith Kipper of the conservative American Enterprise Institute told the *Wall Street Journal*, referring to the alliance of hard-line anti-Israel Arabs. She argued that in the wake of the Israeli invasion of Lebanon, Arab leaders "have clearly opted for the political option, a diplomatic solution, and they have looked to the U.S. for help."[9]

"Syria depends on being a central Arab actor," Adeed Dawisha of Britain's Royal Institute for International Affairs was also quoted as saying in the same story. "While not liking the U.S. initiative, the Syrians can't isolate themselves from it."

Syrian Foreign Minister Abdel Halim Khaddam himself added to the sense of optimism among U.S. negotiators. In an early October meeting with Secretary of State George Schultz at the United Nations, he reiterated his country's promise that the 30,000 Syrian troops in Lebanon would be withdrawn when Israel's 70,000-man army pulled out. That promise would form the basis of the May 17 Agreement, but between October 1982 and May 1983 circumstances would change.

Less than a month after the Marines arrived back in Beirut, President Amin Gemayel decided he liked the presence of U.S. and European troops so much that he wanted more. A lot more. Gemayel publicly proclaimed the need for a 30,000-man MNF and stunned U.S. officials during a visit to

Washington when he privately let it be known that he might need as many as 60,000 troops to stabilize his country. He envisioned the beefed-up MNF spread out across Lebanon to fill the void left when the Syrians, PLO and the Israelis departed. The Lebanese president was apparently having visions of a repeat of the Marines' 1958 performance, when 14,000 U.S. troops had landed to prop up President Camille Chamoun, who was being threatened by a Muslim revolt sponsored by Egyptian President Gamal Abdel Nasser. If the Eisenhower administration had not intervened in 1958 and had allowed events to take their natural course, a more equitable power-sharing arrangement is likely to have evolved and the debacle that would befall the U.S. two and a half decades later would probably never have occurred.

It's doubtful that Amin Gemayel spent much time pondering such twists of fate. He needed more U.S. muscle because he had virtually none of his own. The Lebanese Army had disintegrated early in the civil war and was in no position to challenge the militias. The Lebanese Forces, also known as the Phalangists, which had traditionally been the Gemayel family militia, were already turning on the president, whose palace was located on their East Beirut turf.

In West Beirut, the first signs of opposition were beginning to appear. Widespread roundups of suspected Muslim guerrillas and Palestinians by Christian units of the Lebanese Army, often using brutal tactics, set off anger and resentment. Two years later, when the government released a list of more than 700 people languishing in its jails without trial, many were found to be from that first wave of detentions in 1982. There were no similar sweeps of Christian militiamen in East Beirut.

When Gemayel ordered bulldozers into the sprawling slums beside the airport to level illegal dwellings – the only shelter for hundreds of thousands of Shi'ite Muslims and Palestinians – any hope he had of retaining a Muslim consensus cracked beneath the blades. Gemayel hadn't wasted any time making his intentions clear. The very day the new cabinet of Prime Minister Shafik al-Wazzan met for the first time was the day the bulldozers began rolling over squatters' homes in Haret Gharwani, 200 yards from the Marine bunkers. The Gemayel government's refusal to let other Muslims – Lebanese or Palestinian – rebuild their war-damaged homes only made things worse.

The three young men were sitting in the shade in front of a makeshift auto repair shop. It was really nothing more than two cement walls with a piece of corrugated metal laid on top as a roof. Rusty tools lay in the dust around the even rustier hulk of a Mercedes 200 that had seen better days. Oil covered everything, especially the coveralls of the men, who greeted us with suspicious silence.

They had reason to be suspicious. Few Palestinian men their age (mid-twenties) were left in the camp. The government had long since rounded up most of the others who had stayed behind when the PLO was driven out in 1982. These young men were lucky. They had valid Lebanese residence permits. Still, that was no guarantee of anything. In their minds, everyone was against them: the Lebanese Army, the Christians and the president.

They were probably right. Gemayel's government was on record as advocating the expulsion of all Palestinians who had come to Lebanon after 1948 (which constituted the vast majority), the Christian militias had long fought for just that, and the Army was now doing its best to make that goal a reality. The government had not yet begun the massive expulsions of women and children that many officials hoped for, but it was making life as difficult as possible for those who remained.

"Why don't you build a proper garage?" I asked the young men. I already knew the answer, but I needed them to say it on camera.

"We build, the government destroys," said the oldest of the three in Arabic. "Build during the night, and the next day the Army sends tractors to knock it down." He tossed the dregs of his tea into the dust. "We don't care about the garage; we can work here. But what about the children? They have no place to sleep."

The car repair shop was not the only makeshift structure in the ruins of Sabra and Chatilla. The Israeli bombs had stopped falling months before, but many homes were still open to the elements. From a rocking chair on the second floor of his home, an old Palestinian man looked out over the camp. His view was unobstructed: the walls of the house had been destroyed in the attacks.

Some of the buildings had roofs, others had walls, but few were completely intact. Plastic and bits of wood covered the gaps here and there, but the piecemeal repairs did not change the fact that these people were virtually living outdoors. Women cooked over open fires beside the winding paths and water came from a communal tap near the camp's entrance, just across from the mass grave where the victims of the massacre were buried.

Not all the camp's residents were Palestinian. Many were Lebanese Shi'ites driven from South Lebanon. The government didn't let them rebuild their homes either. Gemayel's men wanted the Palestinians out of Lebanon and they wanted the Shi'ites out of Beirut.

When Amin Gemayel's government had begun bulldozing neighborhoods flanking the airport runway, it had declared that the sprawling slums were a hazard to air traffic. No one ever suggested that the shantytowns might also be a hazard to those who had to live in them.

Gemayel's efforts to drive out the impoverished Muslims did nothing but increase the bitterness toward him and the Christians as a whole. In one breath, the American-backed president declared his commitment to a "new, united Lebanon." In the next, he ordered measures to erase – or at least remove from view – two of the country's largest, most underprivileged communities. And he offered their members no alternatives: no place to go, no reason for hope.

Some U.S. State Department officials might have been stunned by Gemayel's awesome request for a massive influx of troops, but President Reagan did not appear to be fazed by it. In a sweeping commitment, he declared that Gemayel "deserves all of our support" and assured his newfound ally that he could "rely on the help of the United States."

Washington planners began peppering their briefings with terms such as "vital interests," explaining that the United States had been presented with a "window of opportunity" during which it would be possible to mold a firmly pro-American nation out of the debris of chaos and war.

The Pentagon dispatched its first shipment of armored personnel carriers and artillery to the Lebanese Army and announced it would soon station a team of U.S. military officers to train and rebuild the government units. Marine officers were ordered to draw up contingency plans for placing another 5,000 to 8,000 men in Beirut. Officials at the Defense Department (including the Joint Chiefs of Staff) remained opposed to the idea of enlarging U.S. involvement in Lebanon. As an alternative, they began to explore the possibility of beefing up the MNF with soldiers from other countries.

Instead of sending in more marines, Defense Secretary Casper Weinberger and others preferred to use a team of U.S. trainers (the term "advisor" was avoided) to help teach the Lebanese Army to fight for itself. The ultimate aim was to double the size of the government force. The fact that two separate branches of the U.S. military – the Marines and the U.S. Army advisors – were based in Lebanon on what was essentially two different missions, would later add to the problems. While the Marines were proclaiming their neutrality, they and American soldiers were training and advising the Lebanese Army. Muslim militiamen who were locked in combat with the government troops were, understandably, a little confused.

On September 29, President Reagan had emphasized that the Marines would remain in Lebanon for "a limited period of time." By November 11, the schedule was already beginning to slip. "I can't give you a close-out date," he said at a news conference. "But I can tell you that we're trying to push as fast as we can on the two things that must happen. And that is the ability of the Lebanese government to heal the wounds and bring their people together and have control. But it also hinges on getting the three foreign factions – the PLO, the Syrians and the Israelis – out of Lebanon. We are pushing on that as fast as we can."

Unfortunately for the White House, the Lebanese and Israelis had not even agreed where to meet to discuss the issue. U.S. officials held Israel responsible for the impasse. The Begin government was demanding what Washington considered "unacceptable political concessions" from Lebanon. In return for a pullout, Israel wanted "normalization of relations" with Lebanon.[10] Jerusalem had originally expected to conclude a peace treaty with a government headed by Bechir Gemayel, but even Bechir had balked at that, and his brother Amin wanted no part of it either. Israel now accepted that there would be no diplomatic relations, but was demanding open borders, free trade and regular political and business contacts.

U.S. negotiators envisioned a simultaneous phased withdrawal of the Israeli, Syrian and PLO armies. Israel's position was that it would not pull out until Syria and the PLO had done so. Damascus was saying the exact opposite. Begin, meanwhile, was adamant that the talks take place alternately in Jerusalem and Beirut. If it agreed to that, Lebanon would be conferring de facto recognition on the disputed Israeli capital. Gemayel refused, saying that acceptance of those terms would antagonize Syria, something he could not afford.

The Lebanese were being forced into a corner and they didn't like it. They emphasized to U.S. diplomats that it was up to the United States to put the necessary pressure on Israel to back off its demands. Prime Minister Shafik al-Wazzan told reporters that Lebanon would "not be blackmailed into making political concessions." Security was the top of discussion, not politics. They were, the Lebanese told Habib and Draper, negotiating a withdrawal of forces, not a peace treaty or a structure for diplomatic relations.

Lebanon's objections were a harbinger of things to come. Those same complaints would be raised, in a much sharper tone, by Syria months later. It was no coincidence. During this period, the Lebanese were in close contact with Damascus. "We took care of the Syrians, while the U.S. dealt with Israel," one Gemayel aide would say later.

The Assad regime in Syria was becoming anxious at the direction the negotiations were taking. It had told both the Lebanese and the Americans that it was willing to pull its troops out of Lebanon if the Israelis did the same, but it had no intention of allowing the Begin government to make political and diplomatic gains from the invasion. Complicating matters was Syria's contention that it had an historic right to a special influence over Lebanese affairs.

While the Lebanese were calling on the United States to do something about Israeli intransigence, Washington was having trouble just talking to Jerusalem. U.S.–Israeli relations were bad and getting worse. Israel's refusal to withdraw from the airport had delayed the landing of the Marines. Begin had shot the Reagan Initiative dead in the water within 24 hours of its announcement. Israeli demands had stalled the withdrawal talks. The final blow was an announcement by Deputy Prime Minister David Levy that Israel would soon establish five new settlements on the West Bank in direct defiance of President Reagan's September 1 call for a freeze. Reagan had been slapped in the face.

Washington's response was unusually vehement. "We cannot understand why, at a time when we are actively seeking broader participation in the peace process, Israel persists in a pattern of activity which erodes the confidence of all ... in the possibilities for a just and fairly negotiated outcome to the peace process," State Department spokesman Alan Romberg told reporters.[11]

Weeks later, the two sides were locked in a bitter wrangle over aid. The Reagan Administration had requested $2.5 billion for Israel during fiscal year 1983. Congress wanted to increase the total. During intensive lobbying against the move, administration officials argued that giving Israel even more money would make it appear that the U.S. was rewarding it for the war and its intransigence.

Israel won. Over White House protests, Congress added another $200 million to the package. In Jerusalem, the Israeli cabinet innocently said it found the administration position "a bit astonishing," adding that it marked "an important shift" in U.S. policy toward Israel.[12]

Relations had slipped another notch.

Amin Gemayel's problems at home, meanwhile, were steadily getting worse. Christian–Druze clashes were intensifying in the Chouf mountains, the Shi'ites were growing restive, and the Phalangists – with Amin's father at their head – were ignoring him. Many Christians were saying he was a traitor. So tense were his relations with the Christian militia that the U.S. government did not press Gemayel to punish those responsible for the Sabra and Chatilla massacre. Phalangist influence over the officer corps of the Lebanese Army made the president's position even more tenuous. The situation meant that even if he had wanted to, Gemayel was in no position to begin imposing political reforms. Any effort to placate West Beirut's Muslims would only undermine what little authority he still wielded over the Christians in his own backyard. All this was a moot point, however. Amin Gemayel showed no more inclination to share power with the Muslims than had any of his predecessors. In some ways, he was worse than the others because he had built up expectations with his lofty talk of a "reunification of the hearts," then failed to deliver.

With pressure mounting from the left and right, Gemayel leaned a little harder on the Americans and Europeans, who were quickly becoming the pillars of his regime. In a November 30 speech, he asked them to double the size of the MNF "to help the Lebanese Army end the turmoil in the mountains." That turmoil was the first sign of what the Gemayel government, and the Americans, could expect as Syria's opinions were steadily ignored.

In December 1982, when Lebanese and Israeli negotiators finally sat down in a shell-battered beachfront hotel at Khalde, just south of Beirut, it was probably already too late to arrange a withdrawal deal that would work.

If there had been any chance at all, Ariel Sharon had taken a large step toward destroying it. During the drawn-out U.S. attempts to get the two sides to the bargaining table, Lebanon and Israel had been conducting secret negotiations of their own (of which Gemayel had kept the Americans informed). They culminated in a mid-December letter of agreement that outlined the broad scope of the talks and included a Lebanese commitment to eventually seek normal relations with Israel. Gemayel wanted the deal to remain a private understanding, while the U.S.-sponsored talks produced the public accord. But even before the secret deal was signed, Sharon brandished it publicly, announcing a breakthrough that – in his view – proved Israel didn't need the meddlesome Americans in order to reach an agreement with its neighbors.

Amin Gemayel was immediately thrown on the defensive. Muslim leaders denounced the private deal, which they said infringed on Lebanon's sovereignty. Syria voiced its anger in no uncertain terms. Therefore, when the Lebanese finally sat down to face Israel's chief negotiator, David Kimche, they were already feeling very boxed in.

Said one Lebanese official with the benefit of hindsight: "The act of conception [of the May 17 agreement] was part of the funeral process."

Time had doomed the accord. That was clear to the U.S. embassies in Beirut and Damascus. In early February, the embassy in Beirut sent a cable to Washington declaring emphatically that the negotiations would not succeed. What might have worked in November, the diplomats on the scene advised, stood no chance three months later. Syria had been given time to recoup, and the rulers in Damascus had begun to realize that they could call the shots.

Backing up this hardened position was a new feeling of confidence in Syria. Beginning in December, the Soviet Union had embarked on its largest foreign rearmament effort ever. Everything the Assad regime had lost during the Israeli invasion was replaced, in spades. In addition to modern T-72 tanks and new MIG and Sukhoi jets, Moscow deployed in Syria two batteries of SAM-5 missiles, among the most sophisticated antiaircraft weapons in the Soviet arsenal. This was the first time SAM-5s had been installed outside the Soviet Union. One battery of SAMs protected SCUD surface-to-surface missiles that could strike inside Israel. The 300-mile range of the SAMs also put U.S. aircraft carriers in the Mediterranean within their reach. With them came an estimated 5,000 Soviet technicians and combat pilots. Western military experts concluded that the Syrian armed forces emerged from the buildup far more powerful than ever before.

Moscow added icing to the cake. Receiving a secret message from the White House expressing concern at the deployment of the missiles, according to U.S. diplomats, the Kremlin curtly replied that any attack on Syria by the United States or its "protégés" would be considered an attack on the Soviet Union itself.

Syrian annoyance with the direction of the Lebanese–Israeli negotiations, meanwhile, was compounded by events elsewhere in the Middle East. Although Assad had played a spoiler role at the September Arab summit, the heads of state still adopted a plan that implicitly recognized Israel. The so-called Fez Plan, named after the Moroccan city in which the meeting had been held, fell short of the Reagan Initiative, but the two had many points in common. Then Assad watched helplessly as PLO chief Yasser Arafat gave Jordan's King Hussein the green light to begin exploring the possibility of talks with Washington, as called for in the Reagan plan. The White House proposal virtually ignored Syria. In its quest for a Jordanian–Palestinian confederation to administer the West Bank and Gaza Strip, the American initiative contained no provision for achieving an Israeli withdrawal from the Israeli-occupied Golan Heights of Syria.

Adding to the Syrian leader's discomfort was the fact that the other Arabs, slowly coalescing into a moderate bloc, were turning against him because of his support for Persian Iran against Arab Iraq in the Gulf War. Hafiz al-Assad was feeling isolated and he didn't like it.

Time and again the Syrians had privately indicated to diplomats and reporters that their ultimate goal was peace with Israel, but they refused to negotiate from a position of weakness. Not until the Arabs were as strong as Israel, the Syrians argued, could they win a fair and equitable peace. This had been a key reason for Assad's vehement opposition to the 1978 Camp David Accords, and it remained at the heart of his refusal to enter subsequent talks.

Assad's mind-set was succinctly outlined by Robert G. Neumann, former U.S. ambassador to Saudi Arabia, in *Foreign Affairs* magazine: "To the Arabs, the 'one peace at a time' formula constitutes a nightmare image of increasingly impotent Arab states having cut unfavorable deals with an overpowering Israel. Syria is particularly affected by this thought because, having long been isolated, it fears that under this scenario it would be the last, and therefore the weakest, to sign up."[13]

To Syria, the Reagan Initiative raised the possibility that after the West Bank, the Gaza Strip and the Sinai Peninsula were all returned to Arab hands, the Golan Heights would be the only piece of Arab real estate still under Israeli control, and no other Arab state would care.

By early 1983, the U.S. and Syria were on a collision course. U.S. policy in Lebanon and the Reagan Initiative combined to threaten the very foundation of the Syrian regime. Faced with the prospect of Lebanon, Jordan and the PLO each concluding peace with Israel, Assad had to act.

U.S. diplomats based in Beirut and Damascus perceived that, but theirs were voices crying in the wilderness. Policymakers in Washington accused the two embassies of being negative and dismissed the warnings. They seemed to have forgotten Henry Kissinger's Middle East maxim that there is "no war without Egypt, no peace without Syria." Secretary of State George Schultz and his special Middle East envoy, Philip Habib, believed that Syria's position was temporary. They were convinced, as one frustrated diplomat put it, "that Saudi Arabia can press the button and make things all right."

That reasoning was based on dollars and cents. The Saudis poured a billion dollars a year into Syria, and other Gulf states contributed several hundred million more. About half the money went to underwrite Syria for its role as a "confrontation state" against Israel. The rest went to subsidize the cost of Syria's army in Lebanon. The Syrians had entered the country in 1976 under an Arab League mandate to operate as the Arab Deterrent Force, much in the style of UN peacekeeping units, ostensibly to end the civil war. They initially fought to support the Christians, who were on the verge of defeat at the hands of the combined PLO and Muslim forces, then later switched sides. The subsidy was withdrawn when the Arab leaders decided at the Fez summit in September 1982 that they, too, wanted the Syrians out to enable the Gemayel government to reunify the country.

Since they were working for the same thing, Washington reasoned, the Saudis could use their economic muscle to strong-arm Damascus into going along with what would become the May 17 troop withdrawal agreement. The same applied to the Reagan Initiative. A 1981 statement by King Fahd, along with the 1982 Fez plan, had demonstrated that the policies of his country and the United States were on parallel courses. Thus, the administration believed, the Saudis could be counted on to bring Damascus into line.

U.S. diplomats in Riyadh, the Saudi capital, were not so sure. Beirut and Damascus weren't the only embassies saying things Washington did not want to hear. "The Saudis are cautious," one knowledgeable diplomat based in Saudi Arabia said at the time. "They don't like to arm wrestle. That's not how they work. They reason, they discuss, but they do not push."

"We don't deliver people," agreed a young American-educated Saudi prince who worked on the outer edges of the foreign policy establishment. "Our money gives us a certain entree, a certain amount of influence. But we do not pound on the table and say, 'You are not getting another riyal unless you do such and such.' We mediate; we try to achieve compromises. Of course, in the back of the minds of the people we are negotiating with is always the knowledge that we have plenty of money to reward them if things work out well."

The truth was, the Saudis were not about to push the Syrians around or try to intimidate them. Saudi aid to Syria and the PLO was as much protection money as an attempt to influence policy or support their Arab brothers. The House of Saud knew the potential threat the radicals could pose. Syrian-allied groups such as Dr. George Habash's Popular Front for the Liberation of Palestine openly called for the elimination of what they called "reactionary" regimes. The Saudis apparently believed that as long as they kept the money flowing, the sated radicals would not lash out and risk losing the cash.

The Saudis also had doubts of their own about the course of the Lebanese troops withdrawal talks, worrying that the accord could prompt a flow of Israeli goods into the Arab world.

Still, in late 1982 and early 1983, King Fahd did not refuse to help his American friends. Envoys shuttled back and forth between Damascus and Riyadh in search of compromise. The Saudis explained their position, and the Syrians did the same. In the end, the Saudi mediation upon which the Reagan administration had staked so much had no effect at all.

The Centurion tank loomed over Marine Capt. Charles Johnson as he stood directly in its path, blocking entry into the sector around Beirut airport that was controlled by the United States.

"You will not go through this position," the 30-year-old Wisconsin native informed the Israeli lieutenant colonel atop the turret.

"I am going through," the Israeli shot back, gunning the engine of the heavily armored tank as two others in the patrol did the same. "Over my dead body," Johnson coolly replied, drawing his pistol and chambering a round. After a brief conversation on his radio, the Israeli turned his tank off the road. With Johnson walking beside the lead tank, the two others suddenly took off at high speed, heading straight for Marine lines.

The American leaped aboard the commander's tank. "He was down in the turret," Johnson later told reporters back at the base. "I grabbed him with my left hand; I kept my pistol at the ready [pointing away] with my right hand."

"One thing we don't want to do is shoot each other," the Israeli told Johnson. The Marine's reply: "Yes, but if you keep doing things like this, the likelihood is going to increase."[14]

In Tel Aviv, the tank commander, Lt. Col. Rafi Landsberg, held a news conference of his own. He and his men had been on a routine patrol in an Israeli-controlled sector, he told reporters, when a Marine captain had come running toward them "waving his revolver like a cowboy." Landsberg said he had "invited" Johnson up onto his tank. Israeli officials implied that Johnson, a teetotaler, had been drunk. The Israeli tank commander himself laughed off the whole incident. "It was really all very amusing," he said.

Washington was not so amused. This was the sixth attempt by Israeli troops to probe U.S. lines. Throughout early January, marines along the perimeter had repeatedly been sent diving for cover by the Israeli practice of using reconnaissance by fire – blindly shooting in all directions during a patrol. The incidents were accompanied by Israeli claims that the Marines had failed to stop terrorists from passing through their positions. U.S. officials suspected that the Israelis were trying to discredit the MNF in order to strengthen Israel's bargaining position in the troop withdrawal talks. If Israel demonstrated that the peacekeepers couldn't stop the movement of Palestinian fighters in Beirut, U.S. assurances of security on Israel's northern border would ring hollow.

In a news conference, President Reagan said the effort to stabilize Lebanon was being impeded by Israel's "repeated efforts to go through the lines and do what was agreed that they would not do." Defense Secretary Weinberger charged that the latest Israeli action was "threatening," while other Pentagon officials flatly contradicted Israel's claim that its men had been on their own side of the line. They pointed out that Landsberg had been involved in two previous incidents and said it was unusual for an officer of his rank to lead a routine tank patrol. The Americans also reported that a group of Israeli officers with binoculars had taken up position on a ridge overlooking the site just before the confrontation with Johnson. Israeli officials called the U.S. response "shocking and ridiculous" and said Washington had blown the incident out of proportion.[15]

Marine officers in Beirut didn't think so. Their commander, Col. Tom Stokes, ended his tour in mid-February by telling the *Los Angeles Times* that by messing with his men, Israel had soured "probably the biggest cheerleader for the Israelis in the U.S. Marine Corps."[16] A month later, Col. James Mead, back for his second tour of duty, was angrily accusing the Israelis of endangering marines and civilians alike by their "gross lack of fire discipline ... and very poor tactics."[17] Israeli reconnaissance by fire still had Marines hitting the dirt, and the Israeli Defense Force, an army that received more U.S. military aid than any other in the world, was blocking U.S. Marine patrols and threatening and insulting U.S. troops.

In a letter to the secretary of defense, the outgoing commandant of the Marine Corps, Gen. Robert H. Barrow, demanded "firm and strong action" to stop the Israelis from putting marines in "life-threatening situations that are timed, orchestrated, and executed for obtuse Israeli political purposes."[18] Israeli commanders flatly denied that they were shooting anywhere near the Americans. Earlier U.S. protests and better lines of communications between the U.S. and Israeli forces (installed at Israel's request after the Johnson incident) had changed nothing.

Amin Gemayel felt the hot breath of Syria on his neck. Fighting in the Chouf mountains intensified as the Syrian-backed Druze forces stepped up their effort to drive out the Christian militia. Shelling spilled over into East Beirut, giving Gemayel a taste of things to come.

Fearful of antagonizing Damascus even further, he ordered his negotiators in the talks with Israel to dig in their heels. They must not compromise on the question of Lebanese sovereignty. They must not grant political concessions to Israel. The site of the withdrawal talks alternated between Khalde and the Israeli border town of Netanya, but the talks themselves barely moved an inch.

Gemayel appealed to his U.S. mentors to do something to ease the Syrian pressure. The Americans confidently assured him that once an agreement was in hand, Damascus would fall into line. Instead of negotiating directly with the Assad regime, Washington adopted a policy of isolating it.

The moribund talks dragged on. Israel demanded the right to operate in a security belt inside Lebanon. The Lebanese said no. Israel sought surveillance stations. Lebanon refused. Israel insisted on a "normalization of relations." Lebanon balked. Gemayel's chief negotiator, Gen. Antoine Fattal, tried time and again to confine the talks to the intended subject of security arrangements, but always failed.

The U.S. mediator, Morris Draper, and his bosses in Washington grew exasperated right along with the Lebanese. With U.S.–Israeli relations at what *Time* magazine called "one of their lowest points in a quarter-century," President Reagan lashed out.

"Israel is delaying unnecessarily," he said in an interview with a group of local television reporters from around the country. "For them not to leave now puts them technically in the position of an occupying force."[19]

Announcing that the United States recognized Israel's "just" concern that the fledgling Lebanese Army might not be up to the task of guaranteeing that Palestinian guerrillas would not flood back into South Lebanon once the IDF pulled out, Defense Secretary Weinberger suggested that the U.S. might be willing to expand the Marine mission to fill the void.

But Israel was not about to be pushed. "Just what the United States has in mind in guaranteeing the security of Israel's northern border I really don't know," Israeli ambassador Moshe Arens, who had just been named to replace Sharon as defense minister in the wake of the Kahan Commission report on the Sabra and Chatilla massacre, told the editors of the *Washington Post*. "We've had a long tradition, and I don't think we're about to go from it, that the only guarantee for Israel's security is the Israel Defense Force."[20]

More than just Lebanon was at stake. Administration officials suspected that Israel was dragging its feet in Lebanon to distract attention from a flurry of construction on the West Bank that threatened to sabotage the Reagan Middle East Initiative. While the United States was preoccupied in Lebanon, the Begin government was "creating facts" on the West Bank. The longer the Lebanon crisis continued, the more Jewish settlements could be built on the West Bank. The more West Bank settlements there were, the harder it would be for the United States to impose Palestinian self-rule on the territory.

If Israel's aim in Lebanon was to undermine the Reagan Initiative, it was working. U.S. credibility was being badly undermined. In a White House meeting in December, President Reagan had promised Jordan's King Hussein that he would deliver an Israeli withdrawal from Lebanon and a freeze on new West Bank settlements if the monarch would negotiate a wider Middle East peace. Hussein came away from the meeting with the understanding that Washington would achieve both goals by the time he actually sat down to talk with the Israelis.

Hussein was a worried man. He saw Israel's creeping annexation of the West Bank as a direct threat to his throne. In the king's view, Israel's aim was to drive the remaining 800,000 Palestinians on the West Bank across the river into Jordan, which had a population that was already at least 60 percent Palestinian. His fears were fueled by the comments of Israeli officials as they jousted with Washington over the future of the Occupied Territories. Moshe Arens summed up his country's attitude for the editors of the

Washington Post: "Israel's position is that a Palestinian homeland and state exists – Jordan."

Hussein genuinely wanted peace. He was realistic enough to know that the Arabs had no hope of defeating Israel in a war, but he faced a dangerous threat from the radicals led by Syria if he entered negotiations alone.

Former Jordanian Prime Minister Zaid Rifai (who would later return to that position) summed up the dilemma in a conversation at his home: "We are faced with a choice of committing military suicide, political suicide, or letting the patient die slowly of a terminal disease."

For six months, beginning in late 1982, King Hussein and Yasser Arafat danced a slow-motion ballet. Its aim was to find a formula that would enable the PLO chief to join in an effort to achieve a negotiated peace under the broad outlines of the Reagan Initiative. In the end, they never quite got into step.

One April night, Arafat went away and never came back. The two men had finally reached an agreement to explore talks with Israel. Arafat flew to Kuwait to obtain the blessing of the PLO Executive Committee, but opposition from Syria and the PLO hard-liners proved too great. Rather than risk dividing the PLO even more than it already was, Arafat bowed to the hard-liners and scrapped the accord.

Syria was booming its opposition daily on Damascus Radio. "President Assad and PFLP leader George Habash discussed the anti-Palestinian conspiracies and the need to confront the Zionist, imperialist conspiracies aimed at liquidating the Palestinian cause and imposing a capitulatory settlement at the expense of the Palestinian peoples' inalienable rights," the station reported on April 4.

"America has to make its promises more tangible if it expects us to take such a risk," PLO Executive Committee member Dr. Hanna Nasser argued in Amman during the Hussein–Arafat talks. "What are they offering us? They say they will give us the West Bank, but they can't even get Israel out of Lebanon."

"The credibility of the United States is being put to the test," Arafat's spokesman, Mahmoud Labadi, declared late one evening in the living room of a guest palace where his boss was housed in Amman.

Some PLO officials believed that if a Lebanon withdrawal accord had been initialed in February, Arafat might have been able to convince his recalcitrant lieutenants to give him the go-ahead to talk to Israel.

Arafat was no statesman. He inspired his men in combat, yet he had no broad vision in times of peace. Give Arafat a decision to make, went the old Middle East saw, and he will put it off every time. It can be argued that Arafat should have been able to see that the split between the PLO moderates and hard-liners was inevitable, but he still hoped to hold his organization together. If he was going to wager the long-term viability of the PLO against the possibility of winning a homeland, the United States was going to have to make the odds more attractive by demonstrating that it could make good on its promises.

Hussein might have understood Arafat's decision, but the PLO chairman did not even have the decency to tell him to his face. For five days, Hussein waited for his guest to return from Kuwait. Finally, an envoy arrived carrying a whole new set of proposals.

Hussein had had enough. He issued a statement declaring that Arafat's about-face had set their talks "back to where we were in October 1982." Worse yet, the new proposals contained what was, to the king, a mortal sin: They "did not give priority to saving the land."

Hussein's initial anger was directed toward Arafat, but a set of interrelated factors involving U.S. Middle East policy had combined to torpedo the peace effort:

- The collapse of U.S. credibility caused by Washington's inability to get Israeli troops out of Lebanon or achieve a freeze on settlements in the West Bank.
- America's failure to exert (in Arab eyes) any serious pressure on Jerusalem to comply. While Congress was vetoing new arms sales to Jordan, which had indicated a willingness to consider peace talks, it was increasing aid to Israel, which had emphatically rejected them.
- Pressure and threats emanating from a newly confident and increasingly angry Damascus regime. The assassination of PLO moderate Dr. Issam Sartawi hours before King Hussein pronounced the death of the talks with the PLO was a powerful signal to Arafat of what might happen if he did decide to negotiate.
- Washington's refusal to deal directly with the PLO until it explicitly recognized Israel and accepted UN Resolution 242, which called for an exchange of territory for peace (the U.S. position was based on a promise made to Israel by Henry Kissinger when he was secretary of state). Arafat had implicitly recognized Israel's right to exist, but he argued that to do so publicly would leave him nothing more to bargain away at the negotiating table. He wanted U.S. recognition of the PLO in return for making that final step.

Looking tired and defeated, the Hashemite King of Jordan sat at the head of a long table flanked by American reporters. Framed between portraits of his assassinated grandfather, King Abdullah, and his great-grandfather

Hussein, the leader of the Arab Revolt, the Jordanian monarch methodically recounted the steps that led to the collapse of his talks with Arafat and the PLO. Twice the previous day he had spoken by telephone with President Reagan, each time outlining the reasons for the statement he had just read.

"Lebanon," Hussein said he had told Reagan, "caused us enormous damage and damaged American credibility as well."

The Israeli presence in Lebanon, the Begin government's position on the Reagan Initiative, the "troubles of the people suffering in the occupied areas," the construction of new settlements on the West Bank, all these, Hussein sadly explained, "represent obstacles in the path to progress on a just and lasting peace." Together, he said, these factors had undermined U.S. credibility.

Hussein was also bitter about the Reagan administration's refusal to deal directly with the PLO. He could not and would not speak for the Palestinians. The Arab League and most nations of the world recognized the PLO as the "sole legitimate representative of the Palestinian people." But the issue went beyond that. Palestine, Hussein told the reporters, was not his to bargain away. If he did reach an agreement with Israel on his own, he might be accused of "losing" Palestine, and the accord would be worthless. If the PLO and other Arab states were directly involved, the chances of a widely accepted peace were better. That was why he was arguing that ultimately an international conference of all parties to the conflict, including the Soviet Union, should be convened to put its imprimatur on any final settlement.

But Hussein also wanted the PLO at his side in the preliminary talks. He was convinced that for the PLO to cede its right to speak for the Palestinian people would be to strip it of all stature. The United States had been willing to negotiate with the Vietcong – why not the PLO?

As the noise of children playing in the hall filled the room, Hussein mused about the future of his country and his throne. The Jordanian monarch was a survivor. One story popular around his kingdom told of how the life of young Prince Hussein had been saved when a bullet struck a medal over his heart during the assassination of his grandfather. Many other attempts on his life had followed after he reached the throne. Israel had warned him of several plots, but Jordanian sources said their own intelligence service had also detected several Israeli-inspired attempts to unseat him.

The king himself feared the worst from across the Jordan River. "We see ourselves as the next target from Israel in the future," he told the reporters, "whether it is in the long or short term."

Hussein did not close the door to negotiations completely. He and Arafat would continue trying to find the right formula despite their mutual dislike and distrust. Each time, the king would repeat his warning that it was "the last chance" for peace. It began to sound like he was crying wolf, but there was a limit to how long Hussein could act as point man, drawing fire from the radicals. If the United States did not eventually come through with something concrete in return for Hussein's efforts, high-level Jordanian sources privately warned, the king might be forced one day to turn his back on negotiations and adopt a hard line in order to survive.

Two years later, Hussein was in Damascus embracing Assad.

"Is anybody down there?" the Marine officer bellows into the bullhorn as he points it toward crevices under the jutting concrete. "If anybody can hear me, please shout." No matter how many times he calls, the answer is always silence.

Arc lights illuminate the haunting scene like a movie set. Hundreds of marines and Lebanese rescue workers swarm around the wreckage. Ambulances wait to receive the dead and wounded.

At the heart of it all stands the U.S. embassy in Beirut, its central section collapsed like a house of cards. The date: April 18, 1983. The first blow against the United States has been struck.

Hours earlier, a young man wearing a black leather jacket and driving a pickup truck containing an estimated 2,000 pounds of TNT had slowly approached the embassy's curving driveway on the Beirut seafront, then gunned his engine and raced past the Lebanese guards, crashing into the building's entrance. The massive explosion had devastated the heavily armored lobby and brought down all seven stories above. In his penthouse office, U.S. ambassador Robert Dillon was temporarily pinned under a wall.

In all, at least 63 people were killed, including 17 Americans, 33 Lebanese employees of the embassy, and more than a dozen other people in the building or passing by. Worst hit was the CIA. Members of the Beirut CIA station had been meeting with the agency's top Middle East expert when the suicide bomber struck. In addition to the visitor, Robert C. Ames, the Beirut station chief and seven other agency employees were killed. U.S. intelligence in Lebanon had suffered a body blow. So had U.S. policy.

President Reagan pledged that America's commitment to Lebanon and the Middle East would not waver. "This criminal attack will not deter us. We will do what we know to be right," he said in a statement delivered at Andrews Air Force Base.

Visiting the smoking embassy ruins, President Gemayel confirmed his faith in the United States. "Those responsible for this crime had united in death innocent Lebanese and Americans and strengthened the determination of our two countries to continue to work together," he said, with as much hope as conviction.

Ordinary Lebanese were skeptical. The embassy, like the Marine contingent (which would be hit six months later), was a symbol of U.S. strength. If it could be destroyed, they wondered, what hope was there for Lebanon? If the United States could not protect *itself,* how could it protect their country?

Voices in Washington were also asking why the embassy had been so vulnerable. Since the 1979 takeover of the U.S. embassy in Tehran, security at the Beirut embassy had emphasized defense against mobs. The walls of the lobby had been reinforced and the main doors had been sealed up. Gun ports had been installed, a huge supply of tear gas for the Marine guards had been laid in,[21] and interior doors had been built so the embassy could be compartmentalized to seal off invaders in one section of the building. Outside, however, there were no gates blocking the driveway and although the diplomats had discussed constructing a wall around the building, that had never been done.

Appearing before a congressional investigating committee, Under-secretary of State Lawrence Eagleburger testified that such an attack was "virtually impossible to defend against if the driver is prepared to commit suicide."

It was not the last time that excuse would be heard.

Islamic Jihad (Islamic Holy War) had come of age. "Shadowy" was the adjective most often attached to the name. When anonymous callers to the French news agency AFP and a Beirut newspaper claimed responsibility for the embassy bombing on behalf of Islamic Jihad, little was known about the group. It had claimed to be behind a 1982 car bombing at the French embassy that had taken twelve lives, a grenade attack that had wounded five marines in March, and a series of other minor actions against French and Italian peacekeepers; but otherwise, it was largely a mystery.

Attacks on the French had started after it became known that France was providing arms to Iraq for its war against Iran. The bombing of the U.S. embassy bore the hallmarks of a blast 16 months before that had leveled the Iraqi embassy in Beirut.

Circumstantial evidence pointed to Iran and the mysterious men who spoke for Islamic Jihad seemed to encourage that speculation. The bombing of the U.S. embassy was "part of the Iranian revolution's campaign against imperialist targets throughout the world," an anonymous caller told the leftist Lebanese newspaper *al-Liwa.* And there was a special warning for the foreign peacekeepers: "We shall keep striking at any imperialist presence in Lebanon, including the Multinational Force."

The CIA would later trace the trail back through Syria to Iran. Intelligence sources said the agency intercepted a series of cables from Tehran to its embassy in Damascus that appeared to link the Khomeini regime with the embassy bombing. One cable authorized payment of $25,000 for a terrorist attack in Lebanon. Others asked that twelve Iranians be assisted in moving through Damascus to Lebanon. U.S. intelligence officials would eventually conclude that the operation had been a combined effort by elements of the Iranian and Syrian intelligence agencies, working with the assistance of a former PLO security official in Beirut and a team of others. But at the time, Washington was reluctant to emphasize the Damascus connection for fear of further antagonizing the Syrian leadership and thereby making it even more difficult to convince them to go along with a pullout from Lebanon.

Congress, meanwhile, supported the White House decision to stand firm. It required only that the administration seek congressional approval if it sent any more troops to Lebanon. Ironically, an old Vietnam hawk was one of the few who demanded that the Marine contingent, the size of which had crept up to 1,500, be pulled out. "I think we're headed for trouble," growled Republican Senator Barry Goldwater, reading the handwriting on the wall.[22]

Secretary of State Schultz launched himself into the effort to win a troop withdrawal agreement with new vigor. Schultz had avoided getting directly involved in the talks, working instead through his Middle East envoys as they toiled to drag the two sides to the bargaining table. Arriving in Beirut in the wake of the bombing to underline America's determination to hang tough, Schultz was intent on wrapping up an agreement at almost any cost. The talks did not skip a beat, reconvening in the presence of the secretary of state the day after the blast in a conscious signal to whoever was behind the bombing.

After another two weeks of shuttling between Beirut and Jerusalem, Schultz, with the help of Habib and Draper, had his deal. The Lebanese had given, literally, miles of ground. Israel had won most of what it sought. The agreement was not the peace treaty the Israelis had hoped for, but it was not far short. The preamble might easily have come from the Camp David Accords.

Israel had its recognition: "Recognizing their right and obligation to live in peace with each other as with all states, within secure and recognized boundaries. ..."

And its peace: "[T]he state of war between Israel and Lebanon has been terminated and no longer exists."

As well as the right to guarantee its own security from within Lebanese territory. A 25-mile "security zone" was established that would be jointly patrolled by eight teams of Israeli and Lebanese troops; Israeli officers would be stationed at two "liaison centers" in South Lebanon; and Israeli intelligence agents would be allowed to operate in the area.

The agreement detailed exactly how many men the Lebanese Army was allowed to station south of the Awali River (8,682), who would make up the units, where they would be allowed to move, and the type and number of weapons they could carry.[23] The Lebanese Air Force was not allowed to fly over South Lebanon without giving Israel prior notice.

The brigade stationed between the Zahrani River and the border was to consist of recruits from that area. The requirement essentially guaranteed that the bulk of the troops would come from the Israeli-sponsored South Lebanon Army (SLA), the militia that had established a buffer zone along the border years before. One of several side memoranda to the formal agreement stipulated that its commander, Maj. Saad Haddad, a cashiered Lebanese Army officer, would be in charge of "anti-terrorist operations" in the newly formed government brigades. The Lebanese government had wanted to put Haddad on trial for treason.

The accord did not grant Israel its original goal of diplomatic relations between the two countries, but it did set out the next best thing. It set up "liaison offices" in the two capitals, viewed by most observers as embryonic embassies, and included an agreement to begin negotiations on "normalization" of trade and other ties within six months. Since rules concerning the interim period were not mentioned, Israeli officials assumed that the de facto open border would continue to operate.

There was one very large catch: the accord was contingent on the withdrawal of Syrian and PLO forces from Lebanon. Secretary of State Schultz called the agreement a milestone. Syria roared that it meant "Arab surrender."

"Lebanon will become an Israeli protectorate and a base for spying on the Arab world," state-run Damascus Radio charged in an angry commentary, referring to Israel's sophisticated listening post on Lebanon's Mount Baruk, which allowed the Israelis to monitor activities deep inside Syria. "This agreement means Arab surrender, and Syria will not allow either Arab or Lebanese interests to suffer. Syria will not abandon its position in defending every inch of occupied Arab land." The rhetoric was underlined by a new round of shelling of the Lebanese capital.

U.S. diplomats saw a faint ray of hope between the gathering clouds. In some of its commentaries, Syria had used phrases such as "in its present form" when talking about its rejection of the accord. Although Damascus had increased the size of its Lebanon garrison by 10,000 men over the previous two months, Schultz and his negotiators believed Assad might be staking out a bargaining position and waiting for the right deal.

"I don't think Syria wants to wind up responsible for Israeli occupation of Lebanon," Schultz said hopefully as he prepared to visit Assad.[24] In Damascus, he heard nothing but the same hard line. After his talks with the Syrian president, Schultz suggested that it would be better for the Lebanese to handle the negotiations with Syria, while the United States concentrated on Israel.

Things move slowly in the Arab world. Whether it is negotiating over a carpet or a country, interminable rhetoric and gallons of sweet tea must be absorbed before the slightest progress can be detected. It can be excruciating for restless American tourists – or secretaries of state.

Hafiz al-Assad wanted attention. Schultz's predecessor, Alexander Haig, had never even bothered to visit Damascus. Now that Schultz had finally shown up, the Syrian strongman intended to savor the moment. Let the Americans bow and scrape a little to remind them that Syria cannot be ignored, his actions seemed to say. Schultz apparently didn't have the patience for it.

Henry Kissinger spent 130 hours drinking tea with Assad on 26 separate trips during his shuttle diplomacy. Schultz pulled out after two visits and just nine hours of talks with the Syrian leader.[25]

The United States could negotiate with Assad from a position of relative strength (eroding by the minute). Left on its own, Lebanon could do little more than plead. Behind closed doors, Beirut and Damascus were talking, but it was not what Schultz wanted to hear.

Lebanese Foreign Minister Elie Salem met with a reception in Syria that chilled him to the bone. According to the Beirut newspaper *l'Orient le Jour*, his Syrian counterpart, Abdel Halim Khaddam, said coldly, "You were a university professor. Return there. Isn't that better for you?" Khaddam then mentioned a prominent Lebanese journalist and critic of Syria who had been murdered after having his writing hand soaked in acid. As if the hints were not already overt enough, Khaddam pointedly added, "[former Egyptian President Anwar] Sadat imagined that he benefited from a consensus. Today, he doesn't know what hell he is burning in."

Syria had the United States and its client government in Beirut on the defensive. In a rare coinciding of interests, Damascus and Jerusalem together had destroyed Reagan's Middle East Initiative (for quite different reasons). Now it was in Syria's power to strike down his Lebanon policy as well.

Syrian surrogates in Lebanon were mobilized and, as the Beirut cabinet gave its stamp of approval to the agreement with Israel, Druze leader Walid Jumblatt, former prime minister Rashid Karami, and the leaders of two other leftist militias met at the home of former president Suleiman Franjieh to coordinate strategy. Their opposition would eventually coalesce into the National Salvation Front, dedicated to the overthrow of Amin Gemayel.

In Gemayel's palace at Ba'abda, the president and his advisors still believed Assad could be brought around or isolated. Their confidence was bolstered by private expressions of support from around the Arab world. Egypt, feeling lonely in its peace with Israel, openly welcomed the May 17 agreement. Kuwait, Saudi Arabia and the Gulf states cautiously recognized the accord as an expression of "the free will of the Lebanese people."

But on May 17, as the troop withdrawal agreement was being signed in consecutive ceremonies in Lebanon and Israel, it was the Lebanese who were feeling isolated. Syria severed the main roads between the two countries and cut all telephone and telex links. Beirut lost contact not only with Damascus, but also with the portions of its own territory occupied by Syrian troops. The border between the two countries remained open, but the roads were blocked at the checkpoints guarding Syrian-controlled areas. Travelers from Beirut were denied access to both the Bekaa Valley and the northern port of Tripoli.

The message was clear: if the Gemayel government persisted in its "act of submission" to Israel, Syria would effectively claim half of Lebanon as its own. The widespread suspicion that Syria had long coveted the fertile Bekaa, from which it reportedly derived $1 billion a year in hashish exports alone, lent credence to the threat.

The following day, Damascus announced that America's chief Middle East envoy, Philip Habib, was no longer welcome. Arab hospitality had come to an end. "It has been decided not to receive Habib in Syria because we have nothing to discuss with him and because he is one of the most hostile American diplomats to the Arabs and their causes," the Syrian News Agency announced. That was "not the spirit we had hoped for," the State Department lamely retorted.

Privately, Syrian officials charged that Habib had lied to them back in the autumn about the terms of the withdrawal accord. They had agreed then to go along with it, they told reporters, because they, too, wanted Israel out of Lebanon. The presence of Israeli artillery within reach of Damascus was no small factor. But, the officials said, they had insisted all along that

Israel must not make political gains from its invasion. Habib, they claimed, had promised that it would not.

Habib's usefulness was at an end. Syria held him responsible for Lebanon's capitulation and the Israelis had lost confidence in him. They believed the outspoken diplomat had been against them since their invasion in June 1982.

By late May 1983, confidence at the Lebanese presidential palace had evaporated. Lebanon's leadership was suffering from a bad case of nerves. Efforts to negotiate with Damascus on terms even more favorable than the Israelis had received were rebuffed. Arab states that had supported Beirut's move only weeks before were buckling under Syrian pressure. Kuwait publicly switched horses. "Any agreement concluded with the Zionist enemy must be discussed by the Arab states collectively so they may take the final decision at the proper time," Kuwait's government announced after the visit of a Syrian envoy.

The Syrian blockade had been quickly lifted, but the veiled threats of a permanent cutoff persisted. To Lebanon, the trading middleman of the Arab world, such barriers would be disastrous. Damascus was not in the mood for pity. Syria, Khaddam reiterated, would "spare no effort to foil" the agreement. Syria's Lebanese proxies stepped up the pressure. Rumblings of civil war filled the air.

"I cannot conceive that Syria will remain adamant in its present position and expose Lebanon to the infinite dangers that we face," Lebanese Foreign Minister Salem said, almost by way of prayer. "The choice is between withdrawal [of foreign forces] with this agreement, or the extinction of Lebanon."

U.S. officials remained convinced that without the agreement, Israel would stay in Lebanon indefinitely. From the sidelines, they quietly reminded Gemayel that he needed them and they wanted the accord.

A key figure in the palace at the time later remembered the mood: "The president realized the atmosphere had cracked, but he also feared that if the pact were jettisoned, the Americans and the Israelis would be even more angry. We were trapped. Imagine there are five swords drawn at you, and each one says, 'If you take this step, I'll kill you.'"

Soon after, Hafiz al-Assad threw away his sword and rolled out the artillery.

6
Under Fire

Ludicrous! Nay, rather humiliating and degrading; that
the representatives of the five great Christian powers of
Europe should have been authorized and commissioned by
their sovereigns to interpose between the [combatants] ...
then forced to stand by helpless spectators. ...

—Col. Charles Churchill[1]

It didn't look like much. A battered metal tube resembling a drainpipe
protruded from the street near the airport parking lot. Marine officers in full
battle dress stood around nodding knowingly as three Lebanese Army
soldiers tried unsuccessfully to dislodge it from the asphalt.

The 122mm Grad rocket was the first salvo in a barrage of rockets and
mortars that fell on the airport and nearby Shi'ite neighborhoods on August
10, 1983. First Lt. Neal Morris, a 26-year-old executive officer with the
Headquarters Company, was making a dawn visit to the latrine behind the
building housing the Battalion Landing Team (BLT) headquarters when
the Druze–Christian clashes in the mountains spilled down into the Marine
compound.

"I heard the round coming in, and after I realized what it was, I was
making myself a low profile," he told reporters later. "I crouched down
[and] I felt the pain." Morris got a dozen stitches in his right leg and the
Marines got a taste of what was to come.

This wasn't the first time the Marines had taken fire. In late July, Ken
Densmore, a Navy air traffic controller, had been in the airport control
tower when it had been hit during an artillery barrage. He and two marines
had received scratches and minor injuries, but none of the shells had
landed inside the Marine compound. That attack had been over almost as
soon as it had begun. On August 10, the shelling continued sporadically
throughout the day. As Druze militiamen besieged a Lebanese Army
position in the mountains, rockets crashed into the airport, a Lebanese
Army training camp, and the area around the presidential palace and the

defense ministry. Several that missed their targets also fell on the Shi'ite slums that lined the runway.

Hysterical women and angry men crowd the alley where a car is in flames. Behind it, three men carry the broken body of an elderly woman from a collapsed cinder block building. She was in bed when the house took a direct hit.

"This from Gemayel," shouts one man, pointing at the body. "He made this."

"The Kataeb, they kill us," a woman screams, using the Arabic word for Phalange. She clutches her bathrobe closed with both hands.

Twelve people died in the August 10 shelling and more than 40 others were wounded. In the eyes of the Shi'ites in the slums, the Christians were responsible. In fact, their allies, the Druzes, were killing them. Druze leader Walid Jumblatt wanted to make a point to the government, so he was shelling the area around the airport. Just because innocent people who were his allies were being slaughtered in the process was no reason to hold back. Lebanon's warlords had never allowed such minor details to get in the way.

Before long, Lebanese Army artillery positions that lay just a few hundred yards north of the Marine bunkers were ordered into action. Orange flames licked from the barrels of the 155mm howitzers as rounds hurled over the heads of the Americans toward Druze-held areas in the mountains. The Marines watched the escalating battle with growing consternation, logged the position of the militia guns (they would not be referred to as "enemy emplacements" for another few weeks), and finally fired four illumination mortar rounds over the Druze positions to register their displeasure at having 122mm rockets raining down around them. The guns fell silent, but not for long.

"The army has orders to be an army," proclaimed Prime Minister Shafik al-Wazzan in a radio broadcast. "The government wishes to inform the public that it is going ahead with its national reconciliation and security policies." The Lebanese route to compromise would once again be through the barrel of a gun.

The Marines went on Condition One, their highest state of alert, for the first time since the 24th MAU had arrived in May. The bunkers that had seemed snug enough for the past three months suddenly looked awfully shallow. The shovels came back out and new sandbags were filled, as officers using loudspeakers to compete with the boom of the Lebanese Army's artillery shouted orders: "Keep your helmets in hand. Keep your flak jackets handy. Work on those bunkers." The marines didn't need any encouragement.

Jumblatt took things a step further by kidnapping three government ministers who went to the mountains to try to reason with Druze religious elders. In return for the ministers' freedom and an end to his shelling of the airport, Jumblatt demanded the resignation of the Wazzan cabinet, the withdrawal of the army from the mountains, a guarantee of equal rights for all religious communities, and a halt to the use of the airport for military purposes.

To Walid Jumblatt, the Lebanese Army and the Phalange were one and the same. The Phalangists had moved into his mountain fiefdom under Israeli sponsorship. He had no choice but to acquiesce. Now that the Israelis were planning to redeploy to a new front line on the Awali River south of his enclave, Jumblatt planned to push the Phalangists back out. He had no intention of voluntarily allowing Gemayel's army in to support the Gemayel family militia and extend what he saw as the Christian occupation of Druze lands.

Robert McFarlane, who had replaced Philip Habib as President Reagan's Middle East envoy a few weeks earlier, drove down to the Marine compound to boost morale. A former Marine himself, McFarlane consulted briefly with Col. Timothy Geraghty, the 24th MAU commander, in the operations hooch. When the shells started coming a little too close, McFarlane emerged from the sandbagged building ramrod stiff, calmly walked to his armored limousine and disappeared in a squeal of tires and whirl of bodyguards. No one in Beirut had much doubt that the shells were Walid Jumblatt's version of a calling card. The Druze leader just wanted to remind McFarlane that other people in Lebanon besides Gemayel also wanted to be heard.

McFarlane had come to the Middle East to pick up where Habib and Schultz had left off in trying to convince Syria to withdraw from Lebanon and thus save the May 17 agreement. But he had quickly become bogged down in trying to shore up Gemayel and save him from his internal opponents. As one diplomat associated with the McFarlane mission put it, "You come to Lebanon to deal with the big issues and spend all your time trying to turn the water on."

Gemayel had snubbed the new envoy when he first arrived in late July. The Lebanese president was apparently miffed that President Reagan had welcomed Israel's plan for a partial withdrawal from the Beirut area to positions farther south. He was worried that the Israelis would dig in even deeper on their new front line and stay there. He wanted them out completely and he wanted the Americans to turn the screws on Jerusalem to make it happen. He was also rebeling at sudden pressure from Washington to compromise with his enemies, something U.S. diplomats had refrained from insisting on during the wrangling over the May 17 agreement, out of a belief that Gemayel could be pushed only so far at one time.

"During the period of negotiation, in a word, nobody was willing to address the question of power sharing until after the negotiation was completed," U.S. ambassador Robert Dillon told a congressional committee in December 1983. "So it was not until the summer of 1983 that we were able to get people to address that question."[2]

But once they did address it, Gemayel dug in his heels. There could be no negotiations on power sharing, the Lebanese president insisted, until the country was free of the Israelis and Syrians. Gemayel, diplomats who dealt with him reported, had a bit of a problem maintaining a firm grip on reality: "One minute he was on the verge of resigning, then, after some minor tactical success, he would say no to compromise."

When McFarlane arrived on July 31, Gemayel was in one of those "no to compromise" moods. He wanted Israel out of Lebanon completely, he wanted the army to take over the mountains, and he wanted Walid Jumblatt's head on a platter. The fact that nobody outside the palace grounds much cared what Gemayel wanted did not deter him. His view of the world around him was slightly different from that of most other people. As he put it in a speech, "Ninety-nine point nine percent of the Lebanese people" supported his government. In fact, in the year Gemayel had been in office, he had done nothing for the Muslims, while succeeding in alienating the Christians. A barometer of his true position had come in late July. To avoid getting shot out of the sky on his return from Washington, the president of Lebanon had made a secret midnight landing, reminiscent of an illegal arms shipment, at his own airport.

In Robert McFarlane, Gemayel found someone willing to treat him like a real president. When the U.S. envoy finally saw him on August 2, Gemayel quickly knew this was a man who was on the same wavelength. McFarlane arrived flanked only by his private staff. Ambassador Dillon was not invited, nor was anyone from his embassy. The Lebanese president had grown bored with Dillon's incessant calls for compromise and his repeated demands that Gemayel negotiate with annoying rivals like Walid Jumblatt. McFarlane and others in the Reagan administration were equally bored with what they saw as the embassy's negative attitude. As McFarlane and Gemayel talked in the unfinished palace the young president was building for himself in his ancient family seat at Bikfaya, Amin Gemayel knew things were about to change.

McFarlane emerged from his tête-à-tête with the Lebanese president and announced to a horrified embassy staff that he was ordering a halt to all contacts with Druze leader Walid Jumblatt. Dillon tried reason, then anger.

Both failed. McFarlane stood firm, so the U.S. ambassador fired off a cable to Secretary of State Schultz arguing that such a prohibition was diplomatic insanity. Schultz passed the dispute to Reagan (since McFarlane was part of the White House staff), who eventually rescinded the order. By that time, however, the president's action would be a moot point. The shelling would have started in earnest and the Middle East envoy would be scrambling to arrange a meeting with the one man who could stop it – Walid Jumblatt.

McFarlane was not the first to ignore Jumblatt. Habib, too, had pretty much given up on the Druze warlord (who had gone into self-imposed exile in Syria and Jordan after an assassination attempt in Beirut). In May, around the time the Lebanese–Israeli Agreement was being signed, the Beirut embassy proposed that one of its political officers fly to Amman, Jordan, to see Jumblatt and make one last effort to bring him around. Habib rejected the idea, convinced that Syria was pulling Jumblatt's strings. Until the United States could win over Damascus, Habib believed it was useless to reason with Jumblatt.

McFarlane's move took Habib's thinking on that occasion several steps further. His immediate priority was to prevent a civil war in the mountains that threatened to pit Jumblatt's militia against the Lebanese Army. While few disputed his analysis that Syria was providing Jumblatt with the wherewithal to fight and was egging him on, McFarlane seemed to overlook the fact that the confrontation in the Chouf was first and foremost an ancient, localized dispute with historic fears, hatred and grudges at its heart.

McFarlane's conviction that his decision to boycott Jumblatt was the correct one was strengthened when the Druze leader kidnapped the three Lebanese ministers. The U.S. envoy was outraged at what he saw as uncivilized behavior bordering on terrorism. It was the instinctive reaction of a man who didn't understand that this was the way Lebanon worked. If he had bothered to ask, the experts in his Beirut embassy would have been happy to explain that such tactics were not unusual among any of the Lebanese factions, including the one headed by President Gemayel.

McFarlane did not appear to be much interested in what the resident diplomats had to say. His job was to pull America's chestnuts out of the fire of Lebanon and the embassy was telling him that doing so would be harder than he had thought. So the new envoy chose his own route, embarking the United States on a policy of trying to prevent civil war and achieve unity in Lebanon by isolating the very man most openly at odds with the government.

After the meeting at the palace, morale in the U.S. embassy in Beirut plummeted. The diplomats had been ignored when they had warned that the May 17 agreement was doomed. Now they were being ignored again.

It was clear to everyone that Ambassador Dillon was finished. Three weeks later, Dillon announced he was temporarily taking leave of Ronald Reagan's foreign service to become deputy commissioner general of UNRWA, the UN agency dealing with Palestinian refugees.[3] There, at least, his understanding of Lebanese politics would be valued. By deliberately omitting Dillon from the talks with Gemayel, McFarlane had sent the Lebanese leader a message that the ambassador's unpleasant counsel could – and consequently would – be ignored. He, McFarlane, would be Gemayel's conduit to Washington.

As he shuttled around the Middle East, McFarlane's reception in Damascus was scarcely better than that accorded Habib, whom the Syrians had ultimately refused to see. The new envoy's message was much the same as Habib's: Syria must withdraw from Lebanon.

Syria "does not attach any importance to any new envoy," the government newspaper *Tishrin* said before the McFarlane visit. "By virtue of its bitter experience with the United States, Syria will not expect anything good from Washington other than fresh pressure." Syria was saying that it would leave Lebanon once the Israelis withdrew. The argument was based on the fact that Syrian forces had been invited to Beirut by the Lebanese government (to save the Christians from the Palestinians in 1976); Israel had invaded. Washington wanted the two armies to withdraw simultaneously.

And still the guns kept up their refrain. Battles continued in the mountains between Druze fighters and Christian and Lebanese Army troops. Jumblatt freed the Lebanese ministers, but he kept up the military pressure. With the full backing of Syria, he was adamant that the army must not enter his fiefdom and that Christian militiamen who had taken up positions there with the help of the Israelis must leave.

"Just as we have ensured the security of Beirut, we shall ensure the security of the Chouf," President Gemayel told the Druzes. That was exactly what they were worried about. Christian officers imposed the government's will in Muslim West Beirut. Scores of Muslims had been summarily rounded up and imprisoned, while their slum dwellings were destroyed. Demonstrators who tried to stop the destruction of their homes had been shot by the army. Jumblatt was not going to let the same thing happen on his turf.

Even Muslim supporters of the government were despairing about the direction the Gemayel regime had taken. "I find myself constantly alerting the administration to the many mistakes that have been committed by the various agencies," former Prime Minister Saeb Salam, a respected Muslim elder statesman who had firmly backed Gemayel, said forlornly in mid-August. "Solidarity behind the regime is eroding."

Jumblatt saw no difference between Christian Phalangist troops and the Christian-dominated units of the Lebanese Army, which took orders from a Christian president who had shown no inclination to share power with the Muslims. He was also having trouble seeing the difference between the Lebanese Army and the U.S. Marines who were backing it up.

"If somebody starts shooting at them, tell them to shoot back, don't just keep running," a Marine sergeant explains to a translator who passes the sage advice on to a line of Lebanese Army recruits.

"Okay, let's go. *Yallah, yallah*," the sergeant screams at the raw soldiers as they start slowly across an open field toward the yawning rear door of an American chopper that sits with its huge blades whirling.

As soon as the last recruit stumbles on board, the machine lifts into the air, rears its tail, then races toward the mountains. Minutes later, the helicopter is back. As it hovers a few feet off the ground, Lebanese soldiers spill from the door, crashing to the earth with bone-wrenching impacts, tripping over each other, and dropping their weapons. Eventually, some lift themselves up and meander back across the field toward a dirt berm that is the nearest cover. The marines watch, shaking their heads.

"Run, you idiots. *Yallah*," screams the exasperated sergeant. "Oh, forget it. You were all dead ten minutes ago anyway." He motions to a lieutenant. A line of trees walks forward — at least that's what they look like. They are actually marines in full battle camouflage. Small, leafy branches are entwined in the netting of their helmets. Their faces are smeared with green and black camouflage paint that blends with the dapple of their camouflage fatigues. At a signal, they sprint across the field, clamber aboard the chopper and are airborne in seconds.

When the helicopter returns, the marines leap out, instantly flopping belly-down in combat positions on the ground, providing 360-degree cover, then hustle back across the field, screaming at the top of their lungs to intimidate the enemy as they charge.

These marines were teaching the Lebanese what soldiering was all about. The task primarily belonged to a unit of U.S. Army trainers based at the Lebanese defense ministry. They were assigned the job of rebuilding the Lebanese Army, which had largely disintegrated during the civil war. The American soldiers rotated through Beirut, with about 100 on the ground at any given time. When the Lebanese were buying artillery, U.S. artillery experts came to show them how to use it; when they bought tanks, specialists came to train tank units. Since the previous November, the Lebanese Army had blossomed from a 17,000-man Christian-dominated militia (with only about 2,000 combat troops) to a 34,000-man force that was taking on a more multiconfessional character.

Sixty percent of the officers were still Christians (Muslims made up 60 percent of the enlisted ranks). The army commander, Gen. Ibrahim Tannous – widely respected by the foreign officers as a dedicated, professional soldier – retained close ties with the Phalangists. Christian army units were responsible for many of the abuses in Muslim West Beirut. And there was still a great deal of suspicion between the sects. But the army was inching in the right direction. Men and boys who had fought each other across the civil war lines were actually volunteering to join the national army to fight for their country. It was a big step. Given time, the army could become the country's salvation.

Senior Americans in Beirut were impressed. "I think the progress that the Lebanese Armed Forces have made in the past year is nothing short of remarkable. They've come a long way. Certain units have the capability of carrying out the mission right now, and I'm optimistic they can do that," Col. Timothy Geraghty, the 24th MAU commander, said in late August.

The problem was that the army was working for a man who apparently cared only about one community. Amin Gemayel had already ensnarled himself in a confrontation with the Druzes and other Muslims were growing restive. There was a danger that he would provoke a divisive conflict before the army was unified enough to survive it intact.

The Marines were helping the U.S. Army to train the Lebanese Army because they were bored. You could only fill so many sandbags. Marine officers decided that by helping to pound the raw recruits into soldiers, they would keep their own men sharp and speed the day when they could all go home.

Walid Jumblatt certainly wanted the Americans to go home. He was having a hard time figuring out where his Lebanese enemies ended and the Americans began. The Americans trained and equipped the Lebanese Army. U.S. diplomats were advising Gemayel on how to survive and were pressing forward with a troop withdrawal scheme that, in the eyes of Jumblatt's Syrian patrons, would reward Israel for its invasion. They were also backing Gemayel's demand that the Lebanese Army enter the mountains when the Israelis withdrew.

Once again, it all evoked echoes of Col. Charles Churchill's observations a century before:

[A]s if in open mockery of his professions of neutrality, the general excuse for his criminal collusion, the [Turkish ruler] actually sent five camel-loads of ammunition to the headquarters of the Maronite forces; and having thus supplied them with the means of carrying on the war, the next day, to save appearances, sent them an order to make peace with their adversaries, on pain of suffering the severest penalties.[4]

At the airport, the problem of telling the Lebanese Army from the Marines was not just metaphorical. American and Lebanese positions were interspersed throughout the compound. In some places, the two forces actually shared checkpoints. On one corner of the tarmac, just yards from Marine bunkers, were the Lebanese Army helicopters Jumblatt said were being used against his troops. Aging Hawker Hunter jets that he claimed were being readied for action over the Chouf stood nearby. Across the street from the Marine headquarters was the main Lebanese Army training camp. Just north of the Marine artillery was the Lebanese Army artillery. Even the Marines accepted the fact that the Druze gunners in the mountains a few miles away might not always hit what they aimed at.

With the Lebanese artillery surrounding the Marines hard at work against the Druzes, Jumblatt had a message he wanted reporters to pass along: "I'm just giving this small advice to the U.S. Marines to stay away from Lebanese Army positions. It's better for them and better for me. If they don't, they could get caught in the crossfire [and would] unfortunately suffer the consequences."

Jumblatt wanted a dialogue on power sharing. Gemayel, echoing the stances of the Christian Maronite militia, said that could only come when all foreign forces withdrew. As the standoff continued, Lebanon slid inexorably toward open civil war.

Once more, Lebanon's bloody history was repeating itself.

"At length, the Maronite patriarch, mad with vexation and disappointment, again fulminated the thunders of his wrath," Col. Churchill had written of the confrontation a century before. "'Maronite or Druze supremacy,' he declared, 'the blow must be struck, and he who strikes first will have two chances to one in his favor.'"[5]

"The situation is no longer bearable," Maronite patriarch Pierre Gemayel, father of the president, now proclaimed with great melodrama. "The people are no longer able to endure. Let the war take place and let the stronger win. Let the world assume responsibility as it watches the death of a people and a civilization."

Yet again, outsiders were to be blamed for the bloodlust of the Lebanese.

Like father, like son. Amin, too, tossed the mess squarely into the foreigners' laps. But he differed from his father in one respect: instead of just blaming it on the foreigners, he also wanted them to clean it up.

"It is time for the Multinational Force to adopt the method that will prevent the loss of hope among the Lebanese," he told Western diplomats. Translation: "Save me." And the Americans almost bought it. U.S. military sources said consideration was being given to sending a reinforced unit of marines and European troops into the Chouf to form a buffer when the Israelis withdrew from the area. The proposal was strongly backed by McFarlane. The chairman of the Joint Chiefs of Staff, Gen. John Vessey, flew to Lebanon to discuss the proposal with Gemayel. The Pentagon had not been keen on the idea of sending the Marines to Beirut in the first place and it was even less enthralled with the suggestion that it send Americans into the mountains.

The proposal was vetoed when, in a rare show of agreement, Schultz and Weinberger both ruled that it would be too risky. Even without a U.S. presence in the mountains, many in Washington and Beirut remained convinced that America's adopted Lebanese waif would grow up to be big and strong.

"Romeo Yankee. Romeo Yankee. This is Foxtrot, over." The voice of the young, acne-scarred corporal can barely be heard over the thump of the helicopter as it lifts off. Constant radio contact with base is standard procedure for any patrol in Hay-es Sellum, the sprawling Shi'ite slum known to the Marines as Hooterville or Khomeiniville.

As the marines stride along the unused railroad track that once linked Syria and Egypt, a gray-whiskered Arab in a white *keffiah* falls into step behind them, smiling at the last man in line, who does slow 360-degree turns to cover the rear.

At the edge of the slum, small children run out to greet the marines. A little boy walks hand in hand with one American, while an older child runs out to shake hands with another marine, the first black person he has ever seen.

"Ain't this wild?" a lance corporal asks with a wide grin. The narrow street echoes with shouts of hello, as children and adults approach the marines, selling everything from cigarettes to kebabs. The marines aren't allowed to buy any of it or eat the food they are given as presents, for fear it might be poisoned. The Khomeini posters plastering the walls of the neighborhood are a reminder that not everyone out here is friendly.

On the other side of town, three jeeps flying American flags from their antennae cruise the winding streets of the old downtown district along the Green Line. In Martyrs Square, the marines stop to take in the awesome destruction, then head up toward Sabra and Chatilla, pulling into the cratered infield of what was once the Cité Sportif, the city's main sports stadium before the PLO took it over as an arms dump and training camp. It was the first target of Israel's fighter-bombers when they hit Beirut at the start of the 1982 invasion.

Dirt-caked Palestinian children clamber through holes made in the stadium walls by the Israeli bombs and run toward the marines as they gaze into a deep crater. The Americans take turns having their pictures taken in front of a portion of the stands that has collapsed, then remount their jeeps, drive past the makeshift homes and shops set up under the parts of the stadium that are still standing, and head back to base.

There wasn't much to do on patrol, on foot or in a jeep, except "show a presence," like the mission said. Things didn't always go smoothly. Some Lebanese would motion threateningly as Marine patrols walked by. Others would run out of doorways, hit an American, then run off. Extremists in the camps wanted to provoke the Marines into lashing out and turning the people against them.

Mostly, though, the reception the Americans received was friendly. The Lebanese genuinely liked having them around. The Marines provided a buffer between the people in the camps and the Israelis. For that alone the slum-dwellers were grateful. Things wouldn't stay quite that friendly for long.

"The colonel doesn't buy that Chicken Little crap," Maj. Bob Jordan confided as the camera crew packed up their gear. It was August 24 and Col. Geraghty had just been interviewed about the recent shelling of the compound and the gathering storm clouds over the Chouf. Jordan, the Marine spokesman in Beirut, was putting things in slightly more explicit terms than Geraghty had been prepared to do.

"All these people are running around saying the sky is going to fall down. He doesn't see it that way," Jordan explained. "Once the Israelis pull out, we feel confident the Lebanese Army can deploy in the Chouf."

The comment reflected the guidance coming from Washington. The day after 1st Lt. Neal Morris had been wounded in that salvo of Grad rockets on August 10, White House spokesman Larry Speakes told reporters, "I don't think you are going to see these people [the Marines] step into the line of fire." The White House thought the Marines had been effective so far because "we have seen a country rise out of chaos to some reasonable restoration of peace."

Geraghty himself expressed the belief that the Marines could stay out of any fighting that did occur. "A lot of the shelling and the activity around not only here but a number of other places in Lebanon are part of people sort of guarding turf and sending messages to one another," he said, lifting his helmet and rubbing the blonde stubble on his head. "Specifically, the rounds that have landed within the perimeter here have not, we feel [been] directly targeted at the Marines. It's been spillover and indiscriminate firing that has occurred [and] has not been specifically identified for the Marines.

"They have the capability of laying a whole lot on us at any time," the colonel acknowledged. "We're prepared to handle that."

Geraghty dismissed Jumblatt's warning that the Marines should move. "Our mission is to support the Lebanese government and the Lebanese Armed Forces in reestablishing sovereignty and control within their own country. We plan to continue that mission."

Five days later, the sky began falling down.

The Cobra helicopter gunship hangs suspended for a brief moment as the Zuni air-to-ground rocket streaks toward its target. A Druze armored personnel carrier erupts in a cloud of smoke and debris, relieving a Marine unit pinned down at a small post outside the main airport perimeter. The gunship pivots and joins a second Cobra. Together they race back and forth across the smoking battlefield like a pair of angry bees as a Huey transport chopper swoops in to a "hot" landing to pick up American casualties. All three choppers have taken fire from Muslim positions on the ground, as the Marines have been doing since before daybreak.

Already one American is dead. Staff Sgt. Alexander Ortega, a 25-year-old from Rochester, NY, died instantly when his tent took a direct hit. Donald Losey, a 28-year-old 2nd lieutenant who was with him, won't survive the flight to the USS *Iwo Jima*. They are the first American servicemen to be killed in action since the attack on the USS *Mayaguez* in Southeast Asia in 1975.

Before Monday, August 29 was over, 14 other marines would be wounded. Most of the mortar rounds and rockets were pounding the Lebanese Army base at the airport, but the Marines were getting their share, too.

Their defenses had not been built to withstand an artillery onslaught. The mission was one of "presence," Washington kept telling the Marines. They were only supposed to "show the flag," and their positions were built with that in mind. Sandbagged guard posts were silhouetted against the skyline, the American flag flying proudly overhead. The marines inside operated in full view of passersby, demonstrating America's commitment to Lebanon. That was fine as long as all the Lebanese wanted them there, but as the summer of 1983 drew to a close and the sniping and shelling increased, "presence" meant "target." Geraghty ordered his men to start digging in.

The metamorphosis of the defenses outside Geraghty's own office summed up the change. In late July, when the first shells fell on the airport, the headquarters staff was ordered to dig foxholes outside the low, one-story building. When rounds started coming in fast and furious in late August, they began burrowing deeper and laying boards across the top of the holes. By early September, reinforced bunkers would be in place with heavy beams supporting several layers of sandbags, protecting the dugouts. In December, after the bombing of the barracks, the entire headquarters operation would be moved permanently underground.

The Marines, trained to take the offensive, were getting a lot of practice imitating groundhogs. "We're trying to dig it up as much as we can. No matter how deep you dig, it's never deep enough," said a bare-chested corporal as he filled sandbags in a new bunker. "You dig real fast when one hits pretty close. Today one hit pretty close and we were digging with our hands, trying to do down deeper, though it's never deep enough."

"We just keep digging in until you hit water or rock," added his buddy, chopping away at the side of the ditch with a spade. "Seems like that's all basically we came here to do."

"It's not something you do a whole lot of training for," Capt. Paul Roy, the Alpha Company commander, conceded. "You don't sit back there in the U.S. and practice this sort of thing. Or practice to dig holes so deep that you can't get hit. And that's basically what we're doing right now."

The day Ortega and Losey were killed, Geraghty maintained a tight rein on his men. The Marines were allowed to return fire with their personal weapons only when they had a confirmed target that was actually firing at them. Unless their lives were in jeopardy, approval to fire had to come from Geraghty himself. The Marine commander held back the heavy guns for fear of escalating the violence and spilling innocent blood. Finally, shortly before noon, he ordered the 155mm howitzers at Charlie Battery, the artillery company perched on a small hill adjacent to the Shi'ite slums, to be armed with illumination rounds. The six shells burst in the air over a Druze rocket emplacement in the foothills to the south. The idea was not to inflict harm but to tell the gunners that the Marines knew exactly where they were and could take them out at leisure.

The Druzes didn't get the message. In Lebanon, strength was respected. Mercy equaled weakness. The rockets and mortar rounds kept raining down on the airport. When another salvo of illumination rounds from the guided missile cruiser USS *Belknap* still failed to get the message across, Geraghty ordered Charlie Battery to try again, this time with high explosives. Those the Druzes understood. The gun emplacement was obliterated, setting off a forest fire on the hillside that burned for the rest of the afternoon.

The Marines had fired their artillery in anger for the first time. In his logbook, Geraghty recorded "3 Druze KIAs and another 15 wounded," observing wryly: "The howitzer battery certainly reached out and touched someone."[6]

U.S. troops had been under attack and were defending themselves, but in the eyes of the Druzes and the Shi'ites on the other side of the line, they were defending the Lebanese Army. Jumblatt had already said he had nothing against the Marines. Their positions were interspersed with those of his enemy and he had warned that if they didn't move, they would become embroiled in the conflict. That was just what was happening. In the eyes of the Muslims, the Marines were taking sides. They had watched Lebanese Army airborne units stage an early morning helicopter landing on the airport runway directly behind the bunkers of the Marines' Alpha Company, using the Americans as a protective shield. As the Lebanese troops had formed up on the runway between Alpha Company and the headquarters area, their officers had joined Alpha Company's commanding officer, Capt. Roy, in one of the Marine bunkers. The American officer pointed out known militia hiding places in the buildings facing them. Satisfied about the location of their targets, the Lebanese officers had then ordered their men to move out and marched directly through the Marine lines as they stormed the slums.

To Muslim gunmen on the other side of that field, the sight of the enemy advancing from the Marine bunkers left little doubt that Gemayel's army and the Americans were working together. It was at about that time that the mortar rounds and rockets began pouring into Marine positions. One of those rounds wounded four marines in the Alpha Company command post where Capt. Roy had stood giving directions to his Lebanese counterparts. Alpha Company's Second Platoon, where Ortega and Losey were killed, was just down the line.

The trouble had actually begun the morning before. A group of Shi'ites were putting up posters of Imam Musa Sadr, their missing spiritual leader, when a carload of gunmen drove by and took a few potshots at them. The Lebanese Army rushed into the area to prevent problems and ended up doing just the opposite. The troops fired on a vehicle that refused to stop at a checkpoint, the fighters inside shot back and all hell broke loose. Shi'ite Amal militiamen poured into the streets. One group attacked an army position, kidnapped five soldiers and stole their armored vehicle. That got army headquarters mad. It ordered units into the slums, provoking fierce battles that closed the airport and left a pall of smoke hanging over the city.

The shelling of an army post on the West Beirut seafront Saturday night was a hint that the incident that had provoked the mess might not have been quite as spontaneous as it seemed. The Muslim leadership had been waiting for an opportunity to move against Gemayel. Impatient with his failure to institute political reforms, angry at the May 17 agreement with Israel, and egged on by Syria, the Muslims had been poised to strike. Now they had their excuse.

Weapons were no problem. For centuries, Lebanese boys had been taught by their fathers to wrap their weapons – first swords, later assault rifles – in oilcloth and bury them in the garden, out of reach of the latest conqueror. The spot would be marked by a flower or plant distinctive enough to jog the memory months or years later, but not so distinctive that it would draw the attention of the invader. In more recent years, a vast honeycomb of tunnels, some big enough for a fleet of trucks, had been dug beneath the city. Despite repeated sweeps through West Beirut by the Israelis and the Lebanese Army searching for arms caches, huge stockpiles remained, most of them turned over to the Muslim militias by the PLO during its evacuation the year before. What Amal and its allies had not secreted away, Syria supplied.

Sunday was supposed to be a day off for the marines. The compound was sealed off to the press to give the officers some relief from the incessant badgering. Hot dogs and hamburgers were usually thrown on the grill. The idea was to relax and have fun. It never seemed to work out that way. For some reason, the Lebanese always chose Sunday to make trouble. As the conflict intensified, barely a Sunday went by without an attack on the Marines, a car bomb in the city or some shelling at the beach. By Wednesday or Thursday, a cease-fire would be back in place. On Friday, Muslim militiamen would take the day off to pray, they would spend Saturday shopping and on Sunday they would start stirring things up again.

This particular Sunday, some French legionnaires, fellow members of the Multinational Force, had been invited to the Marine compound for hot dogs and beer. The party broke up early when stray small arms rounds started zinging by. Within hours, marines were engaged in combat with Muslim militiamen for the first time. The units involved were caught up in fighting at isolated posts manned jointly with Lebanese government troops. In the general scramble to confront the Lebanese Army, these positions were obvious targets for Amal and were soon being pounded by machine gun fire and rocket-propelled grenades (RPGs). Later, officers privately admitted that the Marines probably wouldn't have become directly involved if they had not been standing alongside the Lebanese Army. At one point, they said, Amal militiamen went so far as to approach the Marines and tell them to go back to their own bunkers. The gunmen said they had no quarrel with the Americans. The same message would be repeated several times over the next few months.

To an American boy sitting in a bunker 5,000 miles from home, that was the closest thing to a dare. The U.S. Marines were not going to cut and run just because some "ragheads" pointed a few AKs at them.

Geraghty and his officers had a more sophisticated view, but it boiled down to the same thing. The mission statement they had received clearly stated that it was the Marines' job to "deny passage to hostile armed elements in order to provide an environment which will permit the LAF [Lebanese Armed Forces] to carry out their responsibilities in [the] city of Beirut."[7]

From the other end of the AK, things looked a little different. The opportunity had finally come to drive Gemayel's Christian army back to its own side of the city and the Americans were protecting them. The Muslims had told the Marines that they didn't want to pick a fight. They had even given them time to ask their headquarters for permission to leave. Yet the Americans insisted on standing there with the Lebanese Army. When the Americans had arrived in Lebanon, hadn't they said they were going to be neutral and work for the good of *all* Lebanese? Well, if they wanted to choose sides, so be it.

Regardless of their intention, the Marines' stance played right into the hands of the men who had been sent to Beirut with the express purpose of stirring up trouble between the Marines and the people of the slums. More than 300 of these Lebanese Shi'ite militants had been trained in Iran, according to Western intelligence sources, at a camp just north of the holy city of Qom. The vanguard of this group had begun slipping into Beirut in February and March, about the same time the first isolated grenade and sniper attacks on the foreign peacekeepers had begun and about a month before the suicide attack on the U.S. embassy. Their supply lines stretched back to the Iranian Revolutionary Guards' barracks outside Baalbek.

The Marines had first spotted these infiltrators in late August when the bulk of them had moved into the slums around the airport. That was when the sniping had begun in earnest. Many of the Shi'ites wore rust-mottled camouflage similar to the uniforms of the Syrian army. Others could be identified by their red armbands. These new arrivals were mainly from a group called Islamic Amal, headquartered in Baalbek. As the name implied, it was a breakaway faction of Nabih Berri's Amal. The staunchly pro-Khomeini leader of this group, Hussein Musawi, had once served as Amal's military commander. He had split with Berri over the Amal leader's failure to order his men to confront the Israelis during the 1982 invasion.

With these new arrivals had come Iranian advisors, sophisticated Soviet Dragonoff sniper rifles, and a plan to provoke the Marines. Watching the gunmen move openly among the gutted buildings facing their perimeter, U.S. officers knew that their mission had entered a dangerous new phase.

The call came in late afternoon. The informer told our Lebanese office manager that gunmen were about to take over the building our office was in. It overlooked the Prime Ministry, which they were planning to attack. Grabbing tapes, equipment and typewriters, we staggered to the elevators, stopping long enough to tell friends in the Reuters news agency office that they had better clear out. With telexes, news wires and a staff of several dozen, they felt they couldn't leave. Bad call. They spent the next few hours hiding under desks as hooded gunmen ducked in and out of the windows, trading fire with government soldiers.

The streets of West Beirut were crawling with militiamen. We had just come back from the neighborhood near the state-run television station, which had been taken over by Amal. Hidden snipers in apartment buildings dominating the station prevented anyone from approaching. Viewers who turned on their television sets saw a picture of Imam Musa Sadr filling the screen while a voice announced that the group "warns for the last time against this dangerous course of the army." It also declared its unswerving rejection of this course and is prepared to resist to the end, until the army becomes an army for the whole nation. Amal had taken over the TV station because government troops had occupied its headquarters in Borg al-Barajne.

As Lebanese Army units swept through the southern slums near the Marine compound, the militiamen doubled back behind them and overran West Beirut itself. Government installations, army barracks, police stations and key buildings were besieged.

Making our way to the presumed sanctuary of the Commodore Hotel, we passed dozens of gunmen at checkpoints along the streets. It was as if someone had set the clock back to 1982. Explosions and gunfire echoed through the city.

Dumping the elements of our makeshift office in a hastily rented suite, three of us headed back to record the battle. As we approached the crossroads between our office and the prime minister's compound, we could hear gunfire close by. Experience had taught us that when you're near fighting, you don't pull out from behind cover until you know what's waiting for you. The driver, not one of our regulars, seemed to have forgotten that, wantonly racing toward the inter-section at breakneck speed. I shouted in Arabic for him to stop. He hesitated, and, at the last second, jammed on the brakes as 50-caliber machine gun bullets chewed up the street a few feet ahead.

The hooded gunmen occupying the building overlooking the prime minister's office were from the Mourabitoun, the Sunni Muslim militia.

Down the street, Shi'ite Amal militiamen had a Lebanese Army unit surrounded at the Murr Tower. The government troops were firing from the upper stories, but Amal already occupied the lower floors. East Beirut was also being hit. Druze gun emplacements dropped shells around the Presidential Palace, the Defense Ministry and several Christian neighborhoods. By nightfall, more than 30 people were dead, about half civilians, another 130 were wounded and West Beirut was firmly in the hands of the Muslim militias.

They were bitter in the bunkers on Tuesday. Marines out at Alpha Company had heard on the radio that Washington was saying they had taken "spillover" fire aimed at the Lebanese Army. Marines sitting in the sandbagged foxholes at Alpha Company's Second Platoon, where Ortega and Losey had died, said they had actually seen some of the Muslim gunmen aiming rifles and RPGs directly at them.

"When you saw the guys that were shooting at you," Cpl. John Ruffner was asked, "were you pretty convinced they were shooting *at* you?"

"Certainly, certainly were, sir," he said, without hesitation. "I was looking right down the barrel of their guns. It felt good to finally start hitting back."

At another position up the line, the sign in front of the platoon canteen used to read, "The Can't Shoot Back Saloon." A while back, that had been changed to, "The Can Shoot Back Saloon." The newest version: "The Did Shoot Back Saloon."

"What's with those assholes in Washington?" asked one marine as he shaved over a sawed-off oil drum that doubled as a sink. "We're gettin' our butts shot at and they say this isn't combat. How many of us are supposed to get killed before it qualifies?"

Their boss, Capt. Paul Roy, was more cautious, but he also found it hard to believe that someone out there didn't have it in for the Marines. "There were so many rounds that came in, some of which landed on us, some of which landed across the airstrip. I don't know if we were the target. I don't know if they were meant for us." He hesitated, obviously thinking about his men who had died, balancing that against the guidance he had received from above. "We were taking direct fire from the ville [slums]. We don't know who we were taking direct fire from or why. We had a very difficult time."

U.S. Green Berets on the other side of town were also having a tough time. The soldiers, part of the training mission attached to the Lebanese Army, were trapped in the seafront Cadmos Hotel, not far from the wreckage of the old U.S. embassy. Lebanese government troops shared the hotel with them and the Druzes had decided they wanted to storm the place.

Since the April bombing of the embassy, the diplomats had been working out of apartments in the Durraford Building, where many had been living before the attack, as well as in a few extra offices set aside for them in the British embassy down the street. A section of the seafront corniche between the two buildings, about three blocks long, had been barricaded with barbed wire, concrete blocks and sandbags. The two lanes closest to the beach were still functioning, but the rest of the area was off-limits. Ninety marines were there to make sure it stayed that way.

Saleh, the boss of the Druze militiamen in the neighborhood around the embassy compound, was on good terms with the Americans. His men had helped evacuate the wounded the day the embassy was bombed and had sealed off the area to make sure that there was no looting. Now the Americans relied on his help to prevent further attacks. Saleh frequently had dinner with the embassy's security officer, Al Bigler, at the Spaghetteria, a favorite seafront haunt of diplomats and reporters at one end of Druze turf. This was a situation the Marines, who were at war with the Druzes on the other side of town, had a hard time understanding.

On Tuesday, Saleh showed up at the embassy with a group of about 20 Druzes from the neighborhood to tell the Americans he was about to storm the Cadmos. They might, he suggested, want to pull the Green Berets out before he ordered his men to attack. Like some of the Shi'ites around the airport the previous day, he emphasized that his quarrel was not with the United States, and went off to give the Americans time to think about it. Some of the people with Saleh said they were happy to have the Marines defending the neighborhood, but they wanted the Lebanese government troops out.

Not long after, boats and helicopters carrying Lebanese Army reinforcements landed on the beach beside the Cadmos. Saleh was convinced he had been tricked and flew into a rage. He had been trying to do the Americans a favor and now they had tipped off the army. The streets around the embassy compound were soon swarming with heavily armed, hooded Druze gunmen, while a loudspeaker on a mosque across from the hotel began broadcasting a taped message: "To our beloved Lebanese Army, we do not want to hurt you. The regime has thrown you as prey of the Phalangist conspiracy, so do not obey orders and do not shoot."

As Bigler and Bob Pugh, the embassy's deputy chief of mission and ranking American on the scene, tried to calm Saleh and convince him that the arrival of the government troops had nothing to do with them, a pair of U.S. Cobra helicopter gunships appeared overhead and several American naval vessels came into view offshore, a reminder to Saleh of what he faced if he attacked. Finally, after several hours, an evacuation of the Green Berets was arranged.

Saved from their "enemies," the Americans were almost killed by their "allies." As the convoy carrying the first batch of U.S. soldiers drove from the hotel toward the embassy compound, artillery rounds began exploding overhead. The shells were airbursts, timed to detonate before they hit the ground, thus inflicting maximum casualties. They were being fired by Lebanese Army batteries on the other side of the Green Line. Gemayel's officers had laid in the rounds to stop the Americans from pulling out of the Cadmos. The government wanted the Green Berets there as a buffer between its men and the Druzes. They were going to keep the Americans in the hotel even if they had to kill them to do it.

Saleh, his men, Bigler, Pugh and the marines all ducked for cover and the Druze officers' suspicions about U.S. collusion with the army quickly disappeared. The remainder of the Green Berets stayed in the hotel and Saleh put off his attack.

The tank rumbled slowly along Hamra Street, its 50-caliber machine gun firing blindly straight down the long thoroughfare. As we cautiously peered around the corner of the An Nahar newspaper building, the gunner let loose with a burst that chewed like a buzz saw through the trees lining the sidewalk, sending branches crashing down to the street. The gunner swiveled and sprayed the front of a clothing shop on the corner opposite us, shattering the plate-glass windows.

Ten thousand government troops were systematically working their way forward on three axes, dividing and retaking West Beirut. Muslim militiamen were falling back toward the sea in the face of the armored advance. At the other end of Hamra, gunmen had been taking up positions on rooftops and in windows, readying their RPGs to try to cripple the tanks and armored vehicles. We had circled around from behind the militia lines to find the Lebanese Army, using alleys and climbing over walls to avoid the open areas between the two sides.

As cameraman Sean Bobbitt and soundman Nick Follows recorded the scene, the tank rolled steadily past us, then stopped beneath, of all things, a bullet-marked cinema marquee announcing the current feature: Apocalypse Now. The turret swung right, and the barrel lifted and fired. We were enveloped in the deafening concussion as a corner of a building a block away exploded.

Troops moved up behind the tank. Unlike most members of the Lebanese Army, these men looked like soldiers. They moved with military bearing. The sleeves of their U.S. Marine-issue camouflage uniforms were rolled up over bulging biceps, and many wore olive-green sweatbands tied around their heads. This was the Eighth Brigade, the first unit fully trained by the Americans. Over the next six months, this tough group of 3,000 men would bear the brunt of the task of propping up Amin Gemayel.

While this column worked its way down Hamra, another unit moved along Corniche Mazraa from the Museum crossing on the Green Line. In most parts of the city, the militiamen were harassing the advancing troops, then melting away. Near the Soviet embassy, just off Mazraa, one group was putting up a determined stand. Explosions rocked the area as tanks fired into apartment buildings and the irregulars responded with rockets. Much of the shooting was coming from hidden snipers, making it extremely dangerous for anyone or anything to move.

It was an axiom of Beirut coverage that New York television producers weren't much interested unless you had pictures of people with guns shooting at each other. Diplomatic intrigue and erudite analysis usually bit the dust if there was no "bang bang" involved. Given the choice between crucial political developments and mindless violence, mindless violence won out every time.

Once we had enough mayhem on tape to satisfy even the most bloodthirsty armchair warrior, Sean and Nick decided it was time for me to do my stand-upper, the correspondent's brief appearance on camera to establish that he was actually at the scene of the story. For protection, we squatted beside a wall, on the other side of which there was a lot of smoke and nastiness. Nick clipped a neck microphone under my flak jacket and I said something vaguely intelligent about the implications of the day's fighting. I could barely hear myself over the fighting going on behind me. With all the ambient noise, Nick was unable to monitor the sound quality in his earphones. After two or three takes, we figured we had to have one that was usable, and since none of us wanted to stick around any longer than was absolutely necessary, we headed for the car.

The problem with doing stand-uppers in combat is that you can't repeat them if you find out later that something didn't work, which was exactly what happened when we looked at the tape back at the Commodore Hotel. There I was, squatting in front of a wall wearing a flak jacket, breathlessly saying something dramatic about war, amid absolute silence. Not a sound could be heard except my voice. The few wisps of smoke in the background could have been from a neighbor grilling steak.

The flak jacket, it seemed, had shielded the mike from all the background noise. The only thing to do was hit the hotel roof and try it again. There was plenty of smoke hanging over the city, and continued sniping in the neighborhood would provide the sound effects. It should look fine, we told ourselves.

It did until the shell slammed into the roof directly across from us. Actually, that would have looked quite dramatic if I hadn't dived right out of view of the camera. Shrapnel rained down around us as Sean steadied himself and shouted for me to try it again. I did, and so did the guy with the artillery. I had just finished (the delivery was a little shakier than usual) when anther shell crashed into the building on the opposite corner. These boys weren't kidding around.

We ran down to our temporary office and announced it was time to move again. A top-floor suite with one wall that was almost all glass somehow didn't seem to be quite the right place at that moment. The three of us, along with producer Lucy Spiegel and videotape editor Jan Sandle, grabbed everything we could and headed down to Nick's fourth floor room. We had just set up when another round hit the building across the street. We were beginning to think someone didn't like us. We pulled a table out into the hallway and, just as we finished setting up the editing gear, an explosion threw us to the floor. The doors of the neighboring rooms were torn from their hinges and we were engulfed in a cloud of dust, glass and bits of plaster and wood. The room below us had taken a direct hit. Choking on the dust, we took stock. Miraculously, everyone was okay. We grabbed the gear, videocassettes and typewriter (I was never going to get this story written at this rate) and headed for the stairs, which were littered with broken glass.

The Commodore lobby was chaos. Some people were running for the basement shelter, some were running for the telexes, and some were just running around. Nobody had been hurt, but there were a lot of angry reporters. If these people wanted to kill each other, fine, but shelling the Commodore was against the rules (our rules, anyway). And to do it right when we were on deadline.

The basement was a cross between the newsroom of a big city paper ten minutes before the first edition closed and a hurricane disaster relief shelter. Beleaguered Lebanese families sprawled on the floor while television camera crews climbed over them. Reporters, some in flak jackets, pounded away on portable typewriters. Shouts of "Who's got some paper?" and "Anybody know what the Marine casualty count is?" mixed with the wail of crying babies.

The rumble of shells regularly shook the building. In order to drive the militiamen off the streets, Christian President Amin Gemayel's Christian-commanded army was shelling the Muslim half of its own capital. From the front door of the hotel, we could see smoke rising over the city. By nightfall, Beirut Radio was reporting that the "operation" had been "successful." The army was again in control of West Beirut. Hundreds of cars had been destroyed, along with scores of apartments and shops.

The operation had been successful, but the patient was dying.

7

A Village in Revolt

> That Maronites in the mixed districts exclaimed, "We
> cannot exist with the Druzes, either they or we must be
> destroyed or leave this country," while their hostile prepa-
> rations, their military organization with military names,
> together with the incessant purchase of arms and
> ammunition, embittered still more the feelings of the
> Druzes, already exasperated by the former attempts made
> on their independence.
>
> —Col. Charles Churchill[1]

The scene looked a bit like one of those old Frankenstein movies where
the villagers armed with pitchforks and scythes marched to the castle
demanding that the monster be put to death. Old women dressed in
widows' black with white headscarves waved rusty swords over their heads.
Little boys hoisted ancient bolt-action rifles with both arms. One old lady
kept stabbing the air with a kitchen knife, looking like a mad woman who
has just dispatched her family and is in search of more victims; all that
was missing was the blood dripping from the blade. The crowd chanted and
shouted. Occasionally, the wail of an excited woman rose above the din like
the scream of a charging Indian.

Even the setting was right: a medieval town square with narrow lanes
leading off between stone buildings with red tile roofs. Only the gas station
was out of place. In the movie, they would have marched toward a castle
perched on a hill. Instead, the self-appointed spokeswoman frantically
explained what the commotion was all about. She waved her hands wildly,
adjusting and readjusting the scarf.

"We are here to defend ourselves," she shouted, an hysterical edge to
her voice. "We fight against the Phalangists, then we fight against the
Lebanese Army, and then if we feel that the Israeli army will be against us,
we are going to fight against her." A big job for such a little group of people.

"You take this message to President Reagan," someone else chimed in. "You tell him we know that America is playing tricks on us, so we advise America, we advise Mr. Reagan himself not to play tricks on the Druzes. He can play tricks on anybody else, but never on the Druzes."

One of our camera crews happened to stumble on the scene while on a routine drive through the Chouf Mountains. I was watching the videotape back at the office, trying to decide whether it would fit in that day's story.

The villagers had been surprised, but pleased to see the camera. It had given focus to their chanting. If they felt silly standing out there like a bunch of high school kids at a pep rally, they hadn't shown it.

A half dozen fellows wearing cowboy hats and crossed bandoleers of ammunition had watched the excitement. One guy, the nonconformist in the bunch, wore a red headband with a huge peacock feather stuck in it. The young thugs looked as if they had just stepped onto the wrong sound stage. They were good at standing around posing, but as I watched the tape, I wondered whether they would be any more effective in battle than the little old ladies with swords.

The fierce Druze warriors of legend were there, too. If they had sent out to central casting, they couldn't have done better. These were proud, strikingly photogenic old men with weather-beaten faces and huge, snow-white handlebar mustaches. Their uniform of white knitted skullcaps and baggy pants with a flapping foot-long crotch hanging down like a skirt made them look as if they had stepped out of a sepia photograph from another century.

This was Aabey, an otherwise pleasant little Druze village perched high in the mountains overlooking Beirut. Hidden in the woods nearby was some of the artillery that had been shelling the Marines at the airport for weeks. Like most of the mountain people – Druze, Christian and Sunni – the people of Aabey were friendly, open folk. On the surface, there was nothing particularly warlike or violent about them. But this day, the people of Aabey seemed to have taken leave of their senses.

"We are going to fight everybody who comes here who is trying to put our heads down. We will not put our heads down. Always we have to put our heads up, up, up!" Imat Hamse was a frumpy, middle-aged woman, but there was a certain dignity, a certain defiance in the way she thrust her chin forward. There was also a certain absurdity. At issue was not an invasion of enemy troops, not an occupation by foreign soldiers, but the deployment of the Lebanese Army, the government force, in the Druze sectors of the mountains.

Lebanon's Druzes and Christians had valid reasons for being suspicious of each other. A century and a half of mutual destruction accounted for that. But this seemed to be taking paranoia a step too far.

In the confusing array of obscure Muslim sects, the Druzes were among the most obscure. They were a schism of a schism of a schism. Their roots led back to Shi'ite Islam, but the tie was tenuous. So secretive was the Druze religion that even most Druzes didn't know the details of its teachings. Women and children were told almost nothing. Of the men, only about 10 percent , *al-uqal* (the initiate), were allowed to study the ancient manuscripts. The rest, *al-juhhal* (the ignorant), were not even expected to pray.

To say that the religion was obscure was no slight. The Druzes themselves admitted as much. *The Druze Faith* by Dr. Sami Makarem, a Druze professor at the American University of Beirut (AUB), was one of the only books ever produced with the blessing of the religious authorities that provided a ray of enlightenment for the ignorant ones. It summed up the religion this way: "Druzism is an esoteric faith. To understand it one needs to be acquainted with Arabic esoteric terminology and with the way esoteric beliefs were written. The latter include deliberate disarrangement of arguments, brevity, and the introduction of trivial subjects while discussing issues of utmost importance."[2] A real incentive to delve further.

You couldn't *become* a Druze. They hadn't accepted converts since the year 1043. They believed in reincarnation and also that the soul moved closer to God in each new life. Since all Druzes, according to their teachings, were incarnated from the original band of converts, there was no room for new arrivals.

Essentially, the Druzes incorporated the teachings of all the main Eastern and Western religions. Their founder, Hamza ibn 'ali, had argued that before the arrival of the Druze faith, man was not yet far enough developed to absorb the true nature of God. Therefore, the divine message had been unveiled in stages through history by Buddha, Abraham, Moses, Christ, Muhammed and the other prophets of the world's religions. According to Makarem, by the time the Druze religion was proclaimed in 1017, the converts "had been prepared by all those religions and philosophies that enriched their minds and cultivated their souls."[3]

Fleeing religious persecution back in those misty times seems to have been a full-time occupation for most sects that refused to toe the official line. A few years after they raised their heads, the Druzes began to feel the lash. The religious bosses in Egypt didn't like being told their faith was outmoded. Drowning, immolation, impalement on spears, crucifixions – the Druze believers suffered them all. Their legends even tell of men having their heads cut off and hung around the necks of their wives or daughters. Massacre, back then, was an art form.

The Druzes headed for the hills, ending up in the mountains of what are now Lebanon, Syria, Jordan and Israel. There they spent centuries waging intermittent war against their Maronite Christian neighbors. At times, the two persecuted sects cooperated under Turkish, and later French, tutelage in jointly governing their mountain redoubt. But over the space of 20 years beginning in 1841, they fought a series of bloody wars that upset the balance of power in the mountains, built a wall of hatred between the two sects, and began the endless round of retribution that continues today.

It has become a cliché in the Middle East that the word Druze was sandwiched between the adjectives "fierce" and "warrior." The reputation was built back then. Massacre begot massacre. The Druzes usually came out on top. Legend has it that the bloodshed between the two religions began in earnest in 1841 when a Maronite shot a partridge on the property of a Druze. The story has the ring of truth. Plenty of other battles have been sparked by just such trivial incidents.

In 1983, the people of Aabey and their fellow Druzes were still holding a grudge. The Lebanese Army wanted to enter the mountains to replace the Israelis, who were preparing to pull back to a new front line on the Awali River a few miles south. The Israelis had grown tired of being caught in the crossfire of Druze–Christian clashes. They were an army of occupation and had contributed to the tension in the Chouf by playing one faction off against the other for their own purposes, but they also served as a buffer between the two groups. The Lebanese government feared that if its army didn't fill the void left by the Israelis, full-scale war would erupt between the two sects. It was also worried that the Druzes would fortify their fiefdom and the government would never get it back.

To many outsiders, Druze leader Walid Jumblatt's refusal to allow the Lebanese Army into the mountains appeared little more than an attempt by a petty warlord to protect his turf. All rhetoric aside, he was in charge up there and wanted to keep it that way. And therein lay Lebanon's problem: too many chiefs and no Indians. Everybody wanted to be in charge. If they couldn't run the country, they would be boss of whatever section of it they could take and keep.

There was no doubt that the army was run by a Christian-dominated officer corps with strong Phalangist leanings, and no one could dispute the fact that Gemayel had failed to address the deep and legitimate grievances of the Muslims. But in the view of the U.S. diplomats who had come to sort things out (and that of a lot of other people), Lebanon's only chance as a nation seemed to lie in the government's imposing some semblance of order. As long as Gemayel controlled nothing more than his palace and the Ministry of Defense, his presidency was a joke. He was not going to achieve unity or control overnight, but he had to make some move toward sovereignty over the fiefdoms. He had to show that his army was more than just another militia.

Jumblatt didn't see it that way. The artillery shells he lobbed onto the airport and Christian East Beirut eloquently announced his position. In case anyone misinterpreted the message, he laid it out in words. "We have to make them [the Phalangists] understand by the language they know best that we will not tolerate their presence, nor that of their army, in our areas," he said in late July.

Shi'ite leader Nabih Berri, whose militia controlled the vast slums south of the capital, backed Jumblatt's stand. He had his own turf to worry about. If Gemayel successfully exerted his authority in the mountains, he might start getting ideas. The Christian president's next step would probably be to try to put the screws to the Shi'ites. "Sending the army into the mountains," Berri predicted with usual bombast, "will herald the beginning of the end for the Lebanese Army and for Lebanon as an entity."

The people of Aabey feared that it would also mean the beginning of the end for them. Not three miles away lay the army lines. While President Gemayel made speeches about how the army represented all Lebanese and not just one sect, Aabey's residents could look down from their village and see Phalangist militiamen manning bunkers side by side with the government troops. They were under no illusions.

The Phalangists owed their presence to the Israelis. The Christian militiamen had moved into the area under Israeli protection in the summer of 1982 during the siege of Beirut. It was Israel's present to its local ally. The Druzes didn't like it, but there was nothing they could do. Most of the Christians were natives of other areas of Lebanon, and, like gunmen all over, they quickly started acting like bullies.

"They started setting up roadblocks, making incidents against the Druzes," Afif Talhouk, an Aabey villager, later recalled. "Over loudspeakers they would shout very obscene words to the Druzes and say they're going to be thrown out of this country, this country is not theirs. This was followed by acts of sniping, abductions, murders."

Finally, fighting broke out and the Phalangists were pushed out of Aabey. But they weren't pushed far. Druze militiamen controlled the neighboring village, but the Christians and the Lebanese Army were perched at its edge. The people of Aabey were convinced that if the army was allowed to come back, the Phalangists would, too, and this time they would come with a vengeance.

President Gemayel insisted that if only the Druzes would put down their weapons and let in the army, everything would be all right. The Druzes didn't believe a word of it. The fact that the Phalange was the Gemayel family militia didn't do a lot for the president's credibility.

Seen from a bunker at the airport with Druze shells falling all around, the confrontation appeared deadly serious. Sipping fresh-squeezed lemonade in the cool shade of Kamal Hamse's broad front porch in the center of Aabey, we found talk of imminent death and destruction harder to accept. The setting was blissful, the air crisp and clean. The silvery green leaves of acres and acres of olive trees shimmered on the slopes of the rolling hills. Far below, the airport runways slashed a white X through the slums on the southern edge of the city. Beyond, Beirut lay shrouded in a polluted haze. From that vantage point, the Lebanese capital gave the illusion of a thriving metropolis. Hidden from view was the society trying hard to die.

Kamal's house was the village meeting place. If you sat rocking on the porch swing for an hour or two, you could chat with just about anybody who counted. They would stop by for a quick coffee or just to say hello. These weren't grim warriors preparing for battle. Everybody seemed to be smiling, enjoying themselves. It all had the air of a church group getting ready for a raffle, or maybe the headquarters of a small town political campaign.

Kamal was a rosy-cheeked, cherubic man with a perpetual smile. His wife was everybody's mother. They gave Lebanese hospitality a whole new meaning. No matter how many times we visited Aabey, we were never allowed to leave the house without a *mezza*, a massive spread of meats, salads and several desserts.

A few years before, the Hamses had decided they had had enough of Lebanon's violence, so they had packed up and moved to Virginia. They invested their savings in a cheese store in a suburban shopping mall just across the Potomac from Washington and worked hard to make a new life.

"We had any kind of cheese you could think of – French, Italian, Swiss, everything," Kamal recalled proudly, handing me another iced lemonade.

"It smelled like heaven," his wife added, taking a deep breath as she remembered the aromas.

But heaven collapsed. In June 1982, they took time off to come back to Lebanon for their son's wedding. A few days later, the Israelis invaded and the Hamses found themselves trapped. "We couldn't leave. There was fighting all around. We were afraid to leave our house here in the mountains where it was safe," Kamal said sadly, looking across the mountains toward the sea.

The war kept them away too long. The shop went out of business. With no money to start again, they had no choice but to stay in Lebanon. "At least we still have the house," Kamal added with unfailing optimism.

The first time we stopped by, a day after the rally, we drank our ritual coffee then started to make our excuses to go in search of the local militia commander. "Relax," Kamal insisted. "I've already called for him. He's on his way." Sure enough, a little while later a serious-looking young man with a walkie-talkie arrived to fill us in on who was where and doing what to whom. What a way to cover a war.

Kamal arranged for a steady stream of visitors at the house each time we visited over the next few weeks. Everybody who stopped by had to have his or her say, whether articulate or not, whether he or she knew what they were talking about or not. They droned on as we drank our lemonade and nodded politely, enjoying the crisp, cool air that was so refreshing after the humidity of Beirut.

Their fears were summed up by one pleasant gentleman who worried that his two-day growth of beard might make him look shabby to American television viewers. "We are afraid that if the army is allowed to come here, they will bring the Phalangists, who will create a new Sabra and Chatilla in the mountains." A massacre like the one in which Christian militiamen slaughtered in cold blood hundreds of Palestinian civilians.

The local religious leader spoke of the same thing. He sat proud and erect on the carpet-covered floor of his simple house. A tall, thin man of about 40, Sheikh Aby Affid Muhammed Farash was an imposing figure in his flowing robe, round flat-topped hat designating his rank as a religious elder, and long, black beard. Yet there was gentleness about him, a friendliness, reflected in his concern that his Western guests might be more comfortable on chairs than on the thin mats spread on the floor.

The simple, rustic chamber where he received us was built of logs. It was a room designed for teaching. A single log pillar stood in its center. This was where the Druze men gathered to discuss their religion and its meaning. Sheikh Muhammed sat there with his back to the pillar like some modern-day Socrates addressing his students. The analogy was no coincidence. Weekly lectures formed the core of the Druze religion; philosophical discussion took the place of the formal rituals of most other faiths.

We, and an entourage of translators, military men and villagers who had joined us along the way, were arranged on mats lining the walls. I shifted uncomfortably, trying to find someplace to put my long legs. Shoes had been left outside; sheets covered our stockinged feet and legs. To show an Arab the bottom of your foot was to insult him. Somehow though, I felt that if that happened, the sheikh would understand. Despite the deference shown him by even the most grizzled fighter, this did not seem a man bound by ancient rules.

Sheikh Muhammed was the senior religious figure in the area, but the Druze sheikhs were as much a political force as a religious one, and his message this day was secular.

"The sheikh wants you to understand why the Druzes are fighting," the translator told us after Sheikh Muhammed had spoken for some minutes in Arabic. "The Druzes are not against the Christians. We have always lived side by side. There was no conflict between the Druzes and the Christians in our area until the foreign Christians came." This was a reference to the Phalangist fighters from other regions who had been brought in by the Israelis. "Now we must defend ourselves. President Gemayel says he wants unity, but he has done nothing for us. He is a Phalangist, no different than his brother. His army is the same as the Phalangists. We will not bow to him. We will not give up our dignity."

The sheikh's voice was gentle, hypnotic. The exotic setting, his impressive presence, and the obvious esteem in which the other Druzes held him, combined to create a unique atmosphere. It was only when his words were translated into the same stale phrases that the spell was broken.

"The Phalangists want to kill us, to wipe up out," intoned the translator. "If the army is allowed to come here, there will be a massacre."

Wherever you turned in Aabey, there was that word – massacre. Still, it was hard to accept that these people really expected such a thing to happen. It was a good word, lots of shock value. People can justify a great deal by saying that they're trying to protect themselves against a massacre. Like shelling the airport or rocketing Christian residential areas. As much as we grew to like these people on our frequent visits, we couldn't forget that they were killing people – including U.S. Marines – in Beirut.

Yet it was hard to believe. Here they were, old men, young girls and everybody in between, running around in green fatigues playing war. At the open-air kitchen across from Kamal's house, plump, middle-aged women in flowered dresses and motherly smiles prepared home-cooked meals for their sons and grandsons at "the front." It looked more like a Pillsbury Bake-Off than a military kitchen. Three giggling teenage girls were loading trays of food into a Land Rover to take down to their boyfriends near the edge of town. Gold earrings and bracelets set off tight-fitting military-style uniforms that set off tight little unsoldierly rear ends.

Down at the front, the atmosphere was like that of a Boy Scout camp. Teenage fighters, some in hand-me-down uniforms, others in jeans, horsed around in the shallow ditches that passed for the village defenses while the food was spread out on the ground.

Once we had scooped up handfuls of flyblown meat and cold mashed potatoes with them, we were initiated into the gang. Now they wanted to share their secrets – the hidden cave that wound deep into the mountain, the artillery and stockpiles of weapons secreted there. "For Marines," one of the militiamen said, pointing to a 120mm mortar hidden under a tarpaulin.

We had just received a new shipment of bulletproof vests from New York. The label claimed they would stop anything short of an armor-piercing bullet, an impossible boast. Normally, we wore flak jackets, which covered a greater portion of the body than the new vests. The flak jackets had saved numerous lives – my own included – but if the vests really did what they claimed, it would be worth switching. There was only one way to find out.

Our newfound friends were in favor of anything that let them fire their guns. We went inside the cave so the shooting didn't start a battle and set up a vest on a shovel, which we stuck in the dirt. If anyone had been wearing the vest when the first round hit it, they wouldn't have lived to tell the tale. By the time our Druze friends were finished with it, there wasn't enough left to bury. We decided to stick with the flak jackets.

All the excitement left our Druze comrades with a hefty thirst, so it was back to camp for scalding-hot sweet tea in sticky glasses with an inch of sugar lying on the bottom. Nothing quite so refreshing on a hot summer day. As we chatted, the inevitable question arose: "Why don't the Americans go home?" Always a tough one. You could dodge and weave, or perhaps provide a briefing on domestic U.S. politics, but this didn't seem quite the right place for those tactics. So I reverted to an old standby, answering a question with a question: "Why do the Druzes shell the Americans?"

"Because they are with the Christians. They protect Gemayel," Rashid, the apparent commander of the group, replied, disgust evident in his voice. Rashid was a wiry young man in his late twenties. His command of the English language indicated an education at odds with the dirty fatigues, wild curly hair and unkempt beard. Someone translated what he said into Arabic and the rest of the fighters nodded vigorously.

"We like Americans. We don't want to fight them. We have nothing against them," Rashid continued. This was something that never failed to amaze me. Even when the United States was shooting at the Lebanese, they would tell you how much they liked Americans. "But it is best the Marines go home."

"Do you really think you can beat the Marines?" I asked him.

"If we fight them, they will learn what the Druzes can do," a younger boy answered. With long brown hair and a soft face, he might have been mistaken for a girl if not for the shadow of hair on his upper lip.

"But the fleet is sitting out there," I retorted, gesturing toward the sea. "They've got jet fighters and helicopter gunships." I wasn't trying to scare them or wave the flag, but it was obvious that if the Marines kept getting shelled, the heavy firepower would eventually be called in. These were nice kids; I wanted them to understand what they were up against. Their ancestors had earned the Druzes a reputation as fierce fighters, but this wasn't 1862.

"They've got enough naval artillery out there to take the top of this mountain off without even coming within sight of the shore," I told them. "How can you fight that?"

"We will fight them," Rashid replied confidently. "They will learn."

8
Choosing Sides

All who knew the temper of the rival sects, and the
passions by which they were animated, saw that civil war
between them, not withstanding its temporary suspension,
was from henceforward merely a question of time.

—Col. Charles Churchill[1]

"Direct hit on first platoon!" a lance corporal shouts from his vantage point on
a corner of the Battalion Landing Team (BLT) barracks roof.

"There's one in the water!" someone else on the other side of the building
immediately adds.

"Impact on the hanger!" yells a third marine, as a trio of mortar rounds walks
across the runway.

From a small bunker on the southeast corner of the roof, a handsome young
captain, unlit cigar clenched firmly between his teeth, relays the reports to the
operations center at the other end of a military telephone.

All around the roof, marines using binoculars, the sights of TOW wire-guided
anti-tank missiles, and a sophisticated electronic targeting apparatus concentrate
on locating the sources of the fire, but the rounds are coming so fast and furious
that the men can barely keep up.

"Incoming!" screams a marine, as the whine of a shell pierces the thunderous
explosions in the distance. Some of the two dozen marines and reporters hit the
deck behind the sandbags encircling the roof. "Nah, it's going the other way," says
one corporal, spitting out a stream of black juice from the chaw of tobacco
bulging in his cheek. The round hits well out of range.

Out over the Marine lines, a Cobra gunship dances like a spider on a web to
avoid ground fire, while a monstrous Sea Stallion helicopter, the Marines'
workhorse, lowers a howitzer into position, the chopper's seven huge blades
straining against the weight of the artillery piece.

In the midst of the chaos, marines with nothing particular to do at the moment
lean back against the sandbags on the roof and open cans of C rations or sit
scribbling graffiti on their helmets. Down below, a column of Lebanese troops run

behind one of the hangars, while Marine jeeps race along the runways carrying officers or supplies to the line companies.

Four days after the government put down the late August revolt in West Beirut, war has erupted again, this time centering on the mountains.

"Willie Peter at four o'clock," reports one of the men on the TOW sights. A cloud of white phosphorus rises like a huge evil genie over a Lebanese Army position near the Khalde junction. Flames shoot up among the buildings just above the crossroads.

The Marines had heard on the radio that Washington was still saying they were not involved in hostilities (even though the Pentagon had authorized $65 a month "hostile fire" pay on August 31). The Americans were just taking "spillover" fire, according to a White House spokesman. The men in Beirut didn't buy that for a minute.

"If this isn't combat, I don't know what is," one young captain said as he emerged from the operations room. "Even [the Druzes] aren't that bad at aiming. This is way behind the demonstration stage. They fire small arms at us; we fire small arms back. They fire artillery at us, we fire artillery back. I call that combat."

Marines in the line companies were bitter about what was being said in Washington and strained at the leash held by their commander, Col. Geraghty. He understood their frustration. He was feeling it, too. But the colonel saw the broader picture and he didn't want his unit to get involved in a war. The MAU officers were walking a fine and treacherous line between defending their marines and provoking the other side. The men in the ranks only saw the shells and bullets falling around their foxholes.

"Most of the time we just sit around and wait to get hit," Pvt. First Class Mark Hutchison complained one day outside his tent. "It's not much fun at all. The bad part is you can hear them fired and, you know, hear the little whistle from the rocket as it comes for you."

The predominant sentiment on the lines was, "Let's go take out the bastards."

"Either we go in or move out," said a marine in a bunker facing the mountains in early September. "We're serving no purpose just sitting here."

"You know, we're supposed to keep the peace, yet the airport is closed. We're sitting all around the airport. That ain't done no good," Lance Cpl. Dave Chapman reasoned.

Geraghty's policy of holding off return fire as long as possible prompted a lot of grumbling. "We're taking rounds from RPGs and all sorts of rockets," Alpha Company's radio operator reported. "And it took us four hours to get fire from our arty [artillery]. What [do] they do? They shoot illum, illumination. It just don't make sense. Here we are – we had mortar rounds hit here in front of the bunker. If it was not for this berm, hell, half of us would have been dead."

The tanks were dug in on the southeast side of the runway facing the Druzes at Sweifat. They were having the same problem. "Antitank weapons were shooting directly at us, and it was going right over us and we had to get clearance to shoot back," one of the men manning an M-60 tank recalled a few days after the battle. "They were shooting right over us, sir. It was five minutes before we could shoot back. It was a hot five minutes. We could have got killed if they had been fatal." He paused and smiled. "And then we took them out."

Some of the men wondered who was shooting at them and why. Staff Sgt. Richard Smith didn't bother to speculate on who his enemy was anymore. "I take direct fire from someone, they're trying to kill me. They're the enemy."

Motivated. That's the word Marine officers liked to use to describe their men. "They're all motivated and ready to do their job," they would tell reporters. And they were. Despite the grumbling, most of the marines felt that they were helping "give the Lebanese time to sort themselves out," as one man put it, or "hold the place together," in the words of another. Deep down inside, they realized Geraghty had good reasons for holding them back. The marines knew *he* was on their side, but they weren't so sure about Washington.

"From a lot of stuff we've been hearing on the news, it seems like nobody back in the States really cares about what's going on," one depressed sergeant said. "'Marines take stray rounds in Beirut,' 'Marines caught in the crossfire.' You know, one day when they were shooting at us the whole day, we got one line, 'Marines caught in the cross fire.' It's like they forgot about you. We're over here and not getting support from back there, so why should we be here?"

Lebanon's latest round of war had exploded in the early hours of Sunday, September 4, 1983, when Israel began its long anticipated redeployment to the Awali River, midway between Beirut and the border. The Israelis were not leaving Lebanon; they were just moving a few miles south, where their occupation force could better protect itself. Columns of trucks and armor rumbled down from the mountains while jets and helicopters kept a vigil overhead. As the Israelis withdrew from their mountain positions, Christian and Druze fighters scrambled to claim them for their own. Fighting between the two militias broke out immediately. From then on, observers in Beirut could plot the progress of the Israeli withdrawal by watching the

Christian–Druze battles slowly creep down the mountain ridges from the towns of Aley and Bahmdoun and across the Chouf.

The United States had tried to stop the move. McFarlane prevailed upon the Israelis to delay their withdrawal for a week while he and his aides tried to patch together a last-minute agreement with Druze leader Jumblatt that would allow the Lebanese Army to move into the mountains. To the Marines' executive officer, Lt. Col. Harold Slacum, the precipitate Israeli withdrawal meant "open warfare was a foregone conclusion."[2]

A few days before, President Gemayel, under heavy but belated U.S. pressure to begin implementing reforms, issued a statement inviting his opponents to a national reconciliation conference "to chart Lebanon's future within the framework of territorial integrity and total sovereignty." The fact that he made the call only after coming close to losing West Beirut in the August revolt and now faced a battle for control of the mountains was not lost on his enemies. Trying to demonstrate evenhandedness, Gemayel ordered the army to deploy in East Beirut, the first time he had issued such an order since taking office. But he did so only after getting permission from his father and the other Christian leaders. It was a cosmetic gesture. The Christian militiamen kept their weapons and there was no roundup of "troublemakers" as there had been in West Beirut. Gemayel would have to do a lot more if he was going to prevent war.

The Lebanese president's true attitude had been displayed in a nationwide speech a week earlier in which he had made only a halting gesture in the vague direction of reform: "The political, economic and social shape that the Lebanon of the future must take is a subject [that] ... must be looked into quickly." But the heir to the Gemayel Christian Phalangist dynasty couldn't quite bring himself to go all the way. "The prerequisite," he had told his disappointed Muslim viewers, was that such discussions must take place "in a purely Lebanese atmosphere," that is after the foreign forces were gone. In other words, no reform now.

His invitation on the eve of a new civil war was a clear case of too little, too late. Jumblatt, Shi'ite leader Berri and the Syrians knew they had Gemayel on the run. The Muslims had spent all of August demanding a national dialogue on reform, but now that it was finally being offered, they weren't interested. The Muslim militia leaders sensed the possibility of achieving their aims through the barrel of a gun, and the blanket shelling employed by the army to retake West Beirut was a convenient excuse for rejecting negotiations.

"We now consider ourselves in a state of war with Gemayel. There is no room for dialogue," Jumblatt told reporters the day after the offer was made. The next move, he said, was "fighting, only fighting, with all we've got."

Given the choice between talking and fighting, the Lebanese had, true to form, chosen the latter. It had always been thus. That was one of the lessons Israel had learned since its invasion. When McFarlane approached Jerusalem with a request that the redeployment to the Awali be put off, he was not met with much enthusiasm. After all, Washington had spent the last year trying to get the Israelis and the Syrians to withdraw.

In one sense, Israel's presence in the mountains had been a stabilizing factor because Israeli troops kept the Muslims and Christians apart. But Jerusalem bore almost as much responsibility for the fighting that erupted after its troops left as the Lebanese themselves.

The Phalangist militiamen would not have been in the Druze-claimed areas of the mountains in the first place if Israel had not brought them in under its wing. The Israelis were also arming both sides. Jerusalem had been supplying and training the Phalangists since 1976. Its relationship with the Druzes was more recent.

Walid Jumblatt was probably the only man in history to have both the Israelis and the Syrians as allies. During the invasion, he had reached an accommodation with the Israelis. His men were told not to oppose the advancing Israeli troops. Later, he demonstrated that he could act as a buffer between the Israelis and their enemies. His men could make sure the Palestinians (also his sometime allies) did not slip through to Israeli lines after the pullback. In return, Jumblatt was allowed to continue running his fiefdom, and he obtained a de facto political counter to Syria. If Damascus pressed him too hard, there was always the subtle threat that he would go over to the other side. It was a dangerous game that had to be played carefully.

Jumblatt was cultivated by Druze officers of the Israeli Defense Forces. The 60,000 Israeli Druzes were the only non-Jews drafted into the country's military. Their ties with their Lebanese cousins were strong, so strong that once the Chouf war erupted, the Israeli daily *Haaretz* reported, some 1,333 Druze members of the Israeli Defense Forces petitioned the chief of staff to be allowed to fight alongside the Lebanese Druzes (they were turned down). These officers and others whom one U.S. diplomat scornfully called "the Lawrences of Lebanon" – a reference to their penchant for using local forces for their own ends in the style of T.E. Lawrence (Lawrence of Arabia) – developed a working relationship with Jumblatt and began funneling weapons to him. According to Western military sources, the arms consisted mainly of AKs, ammunition and light mortars captured from the PLO. Jumblatt's ammunition dump was further fortified, according to these sources, just before the Israeli withdrawal.

Meanwhile, other Israeli officers kept the Christians happy. The two-pronged policy meant that, in theory, Israel would win no matter which faction triumphed in the inevitable conflict. As one diplomat put it, "Israel was eyebrow deep in both camps."

The worse the fighting after the pullout, the more Israel stood to gain. Jerusalem had been telling the world that it was helping to keep order in Lebanon. When the Chouf went up in flames, the Begin government could sit back and say, "I told you so." The bloodshed would strengthen Israel's argument that chaos would return to South Lebanon as well if it withdrew from that area.

Israel, it seemed, was employing a tactic the Turks had found so effective a century before, as Colonel Churchill had observed:

> Not being allowed to rule it in their own manner, they took spiteful sat-isfaction in seeing it laid waste by anarchy and disorder. They hoped, indeed they felt assured, that the inevitable crisis must come, when the two sects would again stand opposed to each other in hostile array, when they might once more play their own desperate game.[3]

The Americans justifiably feared that if there were no agreement between Gemayel and Jumblatt for the deployment of the Lebanese Army in the mountains as the Israelis withdrew, a bloodbath would result. This sudden fear said a lot about Reagan administration policy in Lebanon. A month before, President Reagan had told interviewers that the Israeli redeploy-ment was "welcome" and "gives us some needed leverage" with the Syrians. The statement had angered Gemayel, who worried that a partial Israeli pullback to a more readily defensible position would make it even easier for them to remain in his country indefinitely. At about the same time, U.S. envoy McFarlane had severed communications with Jumblatt.

Now, after a lot of bloodshed, the White House and its envoy realized the true implications of the redeployment, Jumblatt's crucial role in the general scheme of things, and the need to put the screws to Gemayel to produce a power-sharing arrangement that would be acceptable to Syria and the Muslims.

Begin agreed to delay for a week. When Washington again began demanding more time on Saturday, August 27, the Israeli prime minister told the Americans to forget it. He knew the two sides were no closer to an agreement. Another few days were not going to make any difference. Israel had lost two dozen men in the mountains since September 1982. More than 100 others had been injured. Domestic opposition to the prolonged occupation was mounting. Enough was enough.

The order was sent.

Thunder rolled down from the mountains in endless waves. The ridge between Aley, Bhamdoun and Soul al-Gharb was trembling under the punishing exchanges. Each angry flash in the hills was followed by the sound of the impact a few seconds later. In the time it took for the noise to reach us, there would be several more explosions.

Aley itself was taking the most brutal battering. Smoke poured from burning buildings, leaving a gray pall over the Druze-held village. Watching the battle from the next ridge, it was difficult for us to believe that anything could still be alive under that barrage. We had expected fighting when the Israelis withdrew, but the scale of this battle shocked us. One building in particular was taking tremendous punishment. An unfinished structure silhouetted against the sky on the crest of a hill, made distinctive by a large Eiffel Tower-shaped antenna on the roof, it was being pounded incessantly from Christian positions. Each time the building was hit, its tenacious defenders fired back.

The Phalangist militiamen with whom we were sharing our vantage point in a row of shops decided to lend a hand. They had been using this position, tucked into a curve on the Beirut–Damascus highway, as an observation post, radioing target coordinates to the artillery batteries, telling them when to adjust. Now a tank rolled up behind us to join the fray. Hidden by the row of shops, the tank backed into the center of the highway, raised its barrel and fired over our heads. For ten minutes, the tank continued to pound the Druze positions, before grinding up the hill and out of sight, leaving deep tread marks in the road.

Tanks fire, then leave — standard military practice. Return fire is inevitable. We knew that. We did not leave. The view was too perfect. The pictures cameraman Erik Durshmeid and soundman Pierre Denaud were getting were fantastic. Every time we thought about packing it in, the tempo on the ridge would pick up. Besides, we told ourselves, the tank had been hidden when it fired. The Druzes probably didn't have the slightest idea where the shells had come from. Deep down inside, I knew staying was the wrong decision.

I realized how wrong as I was getting into the car. The first mortar landed about 25 feet to my left. Shrapnel rained down on the roof as I dived under the dashboard, fully expecting the windshield — or worse — to come crashing in on me. A split second later, the second round hit the highway divider about 15 feet to my right. Bits of metal and concrete showered through the open door. I lay still for a moment, waiting for the third round that never came.

Erik, Pierre and driver Ayad Harake were still standing outside their car, parked next to mine, when the mortars hit. By all rights, the second round should have killed them all. They were just across the street from it. The only thing that saved them was the fact that the mortar clipped the far side of the highway divider. The three-foot high concrete barricade had shielded them from most of the debris. Still, Ayad later found a piece of the shrapnel lodged in the flap of his flak jacket.

A mile down the hill, we found Lebanese Army troops camped at an abandoned villa that had housed their Syrian counterparts years before. A column of tanks, armored personnel carriers, jeeps and trucks was parked along the road. We asked an officer whether the vehicles were on their way to join the battle. "Our orders are to remain here," he said firmly.

After months of threatening to send the army into the mountains, Gemayel had ordered his forces not to move. He had no choice. His top commanders told him he could have West Beirut or he could have the mountains. He could not have both. The army high command and its U.S. trainers had been proud of the performance of the troops when they had retaken West Beirut the week before. Aside from a handful of defections to militia ranks, the army had held together. It had not split along religious lines. The men had fought well. Dead soldiers had been shot in the face and chest, not in the back. Still, only a small portion of the government troops had completed their training. The army, Gemayel was told, was not strong enough to take on the task of holding West Beirut and fighting its way into Druze-held areas. Privately, the officers were afraid their men would be chewed up if they tried.

The government issued a statement charging that Israel had withdrawn without coordinating the move with the Lebanese Army. Newspapers accused Jerusalem of double-crossing Gemayel. A military spokesman in Tel Aviv, in effect, said Gemayel was a bald-faced liar. "Advance notice of the pullback was given to representatives of the Lebanese Army, the Druze and Christians in all sectors," the spokesman claimed. "Throughout the night efforts at arbitration were continued ... however, all attempts failed ... The Lebanese Army ... made absolutely clear that it has no intention of entering the area being vacated by the IDF."

The Christian militia, which had been so full of bluster when it thought the army would be there to back it up, suddenly sounded very subdued. "We don't know what happened," complained Phalangist commander Fadi Frem. "Yesterday, we were tactically ready to move out and the Lebanese Army would move in. Now we are facing a war." Perhaps Amin Gemayel, who had taken so much flak from the Christian militia since assuming office, allowed himself a private smirk.

Yet the government troops were providing some support to the Phalangists. A Christian president could not allow fellow Christians to be wiped out without putting up a fight. More to the point, Gemayel's own regime was in danger. An army artillery battery hidden in a pine grove near the Defense Ministry kept up a steady barrage in the direction of Aley, drawing Druze return fire that was pummeling Christian East Beirut, including the area around the Defense Ministry and the palace. From the ambassador's residence in the mountaintop palace compound, Robert McFarlane had a ringside seat to the show his policy had helped produce. Beirut lay spread like a map at his feet. Smoke from scores of fires across the city rose toward the heights he occupied. Shells crashed into both sides of the capital with monotonous regularity, as they would for most of the week. Christian residential areas as far north as Jounieh were being battered by guns in Syrian territory on the other side of the mountains. Muslim neighborhoods from the airport slums to the seafront corniche were being pounded by Christian artillery in return.

Christians were being driven out of dozens of mountain villages as the Druzes pushed forward and the Christian militia was in deep trouble in the crucial battle for Bhamdoun. Government shelling alone would not be enough to save the Phalangists. Nor would Israeli warnings to Syria to stay out of the fighting, or a proclamation in Jerusalem that Bhamdoun had suddenly become a "red line" that the Druzes should not cross. Israel even sent jets to strafe a column of Druze-manned Syrian tanks that was heading for Bhamdoun, a message to Syria not to let its armor get involved. Despite all that, Bhamdoun fell to the Druzes early Tuesday and Israel didn't do a thing. Reporters visiting the town found the bodies of executed Phalangist militiamen, their hands bound behind their backs, lying in the streets of the shattered resort town.

In a reprise of the autumn of 1841, "the whole of Said Bey's [Jumblatt's] districts were thus given over to fire and sword; and for a month the work of destruction, rapine and murder was unintermitting ... [T]he Muslims hourly vowed death to the Christians."[4]

The army was more effective south of the city. Within hours of the Israeli pullout, Druze militiamen had seized the strategic Khalde junction just south of the airport. The crossroads were crucial because from there the Druzes could link up with the Shi'ites, creating an unbroken supply line from Damascus to West Beirut. Supported by artillery firing over the heads of the Americans, government troops fought their way past Marine positions along the beach and drove the Druzes back into the foothills. Other units regrouped in the airport compound, again using Marine forward lines as a buffer and drawing Druze fire on the Americans, then moved out of the airport's rear gate in an attempt to surround the Druze force. At one point, the Marines opened fire with small arms on a building housing a concentration of Druze fighters that threatened the government troops.

The following morning, as the Lebanese Army pushed into the foothills above Khalde, the Marines mortared artillery positions from which the Druzes had shelled the American bunkers, injuring four marines in what was still officially being described as spillover fire. This served only to reinforce the Muslims' growing conviction that the Marines had taken sides against them. From the safety of Damascus, Walid Jumblatt, never one to pass up an opportunity to win a few propaganda points, charged that the Lebanese Army had retaken Khalde only after "heavy artillery support" from the Marines.

Gemayel, meanwhile, was beginning to panic. The West Beirut revolt had created in him a sudden interest in negotiations. The mountain war prompted an immediate announcement that the May 17 agreement with the Israelis was being "frozen." Exactly what that meant, no one outside the palace was quite sure. Whatever, it was not enough to satisfy Syria, which smelled blood. Damascus called on fellow Arab states to seal Lebanon's borders and cut off all diplomatic, economic and military ties with the "traitors" who occupied the Lebanese Presidential Palace.

Washington, too, stepped up its rhetoric. The deaths of two more marines in shelling Tuesday, September 6 prompted the Reagan administration to dig in its heels even deeper. With the aircraft carrier *Eisenhower* and the guns of the Sixth Fleet sitting off the coast, another 2,000 heavily armed marines en route from East Africa, and Marine artillery batteries hitting the Druze-controlled hills, a White House spokesman reminded the Syrians "that we do have considerable firepower offshore, and they should be circumspect in their own active involvement in instigating violence in the area."

This muscle flexing got Syria's back up even more. "Syria does not fear American threats, nor will it retreat before the American fleet or give in under pressure," Damascus Radio proclaimed. The antagonists had entered the classic spiral of escalation.

The latest marines to be killed, 19-year-old Lance Cpl. Randy Clark and 25-year-old Cpl. Pedro Valle, had died in a barrage of rockets and mortar rounds from the Shi'ite slums. Two other marines had been wounded. For the first time, Col. Geraghty admitted that the Americans had been the target. "The fires are specifically directed and are being adjusted at and over Marine positions," he told reporters.

This comment came as no surprise to the marines in the bunkers or the reporters who had been watching their steady slide into the conflict, but it marked an important turning point. The United States was finally admitting that it was no longer viewed as neutral by all sides, the assumption upon which the entire mission had been based. Up to that point, Marine officers later said, they had had to go along with the official "illusion" that they were not a target, because to admit that someone was firing at them would have required retaliation, and that would have shattered the image of neutrality. The short-term satisfaction of hitting back would have jeopardized the long-term goal of uniting Lebanon.

The following day, September 7, American F-14s from the *Eisenhower* and French Super Etendard jets from the aircraft carrier *Foch*, which had arrived off Beirut earlier in the week, streaked over the city. The French were angry over the shelling of the French MNF headquarters, located in the elegant old French ambassadorial mansion on the Green Line, that had left a French officer and his driver dead. The deaths brought to 16 the number of soldiers France had lost in Lebanon. Neither the French nor the American jets attacked, but their presence alone was designed to intimidate. The multinational fleet moved closer to shore for the same reason. U.S. guided missile cruisers, Italian frigates and French destroyers patrolled the waters a few hundred yards from the beach.

Twenty-four hours later, in the first use of U.S. naval firepower in Lebanon, the five-inch guns of the frigate USS *Bowen* silenced a Druze missile battery that had been harassing the Marines.[5] President Reagan phoned Geraghty and vowed "whatever support it takes" to stop attacks on the Marines, and Marine spokesman Maj. Robert Jordan told reporters at the airport that, "If the threat continues to increase, we will continue to increase our response."

By Friday, September 10, the USS *New Jersey* was on its way to Beirut (the battleship's 16-inch guns were the largest in the U.S. Navy), and London announced that Buccaneer long-range bombers were being dispatched to British bases in Cyprus.

Meanwhile, McFarlane and Saudi mediators scurried between Damascus and Beirut, alternately threatening, cajoling, warning and pleading. According to one diplomat, Gemayel was told the honeymoon was over; it was time to start making some serious concessions fast. Syrian President Assad was given a proposal for a peace conference and was warned that he had better tell his Druze and Shi'ite clients to keep their hands off the Western troops. None of the players took much heed.

After meeting with McFarlane, Jumblatt promised to tell his men not to fire at targets near the MNF troops, but the shelling and rocketing did not stop. The Assad regime dismissed the warnings as "cheap threats." Gemayel vacillated between resigning and ordering everything short of an invasion of Syria. His grip on reality was slipping once again. With the four nations of the MNF under mounting domestic pressure to withdraw, an aide to the president called reporters to the palace and, with explosions reverberating through the building, put out the word that Lebanon wanted the Americans and Europeans to beef up their contingents and send them into the mountains to make Syria "think ten times" before advancing.

The demand for more troops was immediately followed by a request from the commander of the Lebanese Army, Brig. Gen. Ibrahim Tannous, that the Americans provide direct support for army units at Souk al-Gharb, a mountain town Christian militiamen had handed over to the government a few days before. Tannous painted a grim picture of the situation there. The American-trained Eighth Brigade had taken heavy losses, ammunition was running low and units trying to reinforce the trapped men had been driven back by Druze artillery. Souk al-Gharb was in danger of falling. The village was the last line of defense before the Presidential Palace. If Soul al-Gharb was overrun, Tannous warned, the government would collapse.

With this plea, Tannous raised the specter of Palestinian and Iranian involvement. Military briefers began talking of a force of some 2,000 commandos from Syrian-backed PLO factions (dissidents who opposed Arafat) fighting alongside the Druzes. Stories were circulated of teams of infiltrators, speaking Palestinian-accented Arabic and Farsi (the language of Iran), slipping into army positions under cover of darkness and axing to death the occupants in their sleep. A few bodies, which the Defense Ministry claimed were those of Syrians and Palestinians, were dragged out for reporters, who also spotted small groups of PLO fighters in the Druze-held mountain town of Bahmdoun. Jumblatt denied that Palestinians were fighting beside his men, and various Damascus-based PLO leaders said the same.

Then Yasser Arafat, anxious not to appear left out, announced that some of his men were indeed involved in the battle as "volunteers." Jumblatt was livid and the Lebanese government had its evidence. Robert McFarlane and the White House seized on the issue as proof that Gemayel was up against foreign invaders. There was no doubt that some Palestinians were in the mountains helping the Druzes, but sources deeply involved in the discussions at the palace later said there had never been any conclusive evidence of direct large-scale Palestinian involvement in the fighting. In the fog of battle, it was difficult to come up with hard facts. There were many different versions of the level of Palestinian involvement. Gemayel's version was the most extreme and that was the one the Reagan administration supported.[6]

Gemayel had the Western powers over a barrel and he knew it. The United States, France, Italy and Britain had staked their prestige on the creation of a strong Lebanese government. By failing to distance themselves from Gemayel as it became clear that he was not pursuing a path that would unite Christians and Muslims, the four Western governments were being tarred with the same brush as he. Now Gemayel was in danger of falling and he was drawing them into a war that should not have been theirs. As the noted historian Barbara Tuchman succinctly put it in her classic *The March of Folly*, "In a dependent relationship the protégé can always control the protector by threatening to collapse."[7] Tuchman demonstrated how that rule had helped suck the United States into Vietnam. In Lebanon, it was happening again.

Listening to Tannous' presentation, McFarlane became an instant convert. The request for help in the mountains fit right in with his efforts to broaden the U.S. role in Lebanon. The special envoy had been a supporter of the proposal to send the Marines into the Chouf before the Israeli withdrawal. He had also favored allowing small groups of marines to go into the mountains as cease-fire observers. McFarlane had one goal: preserve Amin Gemayel. In the envoy's eyes, and in those of his bosses at the White House, America's future in Lebanon rested on the survival of Gemayel's presidency. As the McFarlane team plotted strategy to support the beleaguered brigade at Souk al-Gharb, the Cassandras of the U.S. embassy in Beirut were again cut out.

The embassy was skeptical of Tannous' tale of gloom and doom. The resident diplomats knew that every Lebanese faction would do everything possible to draw in outside support. They had seen the Christians cry wolf in 1981 over the plight of their forces at Zahle, dragging Israel into a confrontation with Syria in the Bekaa Valley "missile crisis." They were not convinced that Souk al-Gharb would fall without U.S. intervention.

Embassy political officers laid out their objections in a memo to Ambassador Dillon:

- Intelligence showed that the Lebanese Army defenders of the village were in far better shape than Tannous claimed. One company had been badly mauled, but the balance of the force was in good shape.
- The United States had no quarrel with the Druzes. Jumblatt was the Lebanese Army's enemy, not America's. The mission of the Marines was to act as a neutral presence, not as a tactical ally of the Lebanese Army.
- Shelling Souk al-Gharb would not work. The U.S. could not put enough in to make a real difference in the war. The action would be a political gesture that would tear off once and for all the already tattered cloak of neutrality.

The Chouf war had been preordained. This was a self-inflicted disaster. In spite of the objections of the embassy staff, McFarlane sent a telegram to the White House requesting that the fleet be ordered to shell Druze positions above Souk al-Gharb to protect American lives. Tannous' ax-murder stories had clearly made a big impression on the special envoy. According to those familiar with Tannous' arguments, the envoy believed that if Souk al-Gharb fell, the Presidential Palace (and the U.S. ambassador's residence where McFarlane was staying) on the next ridge would be overrun soon after. In short order, the government would collapse, the Druzes and their allies would pour into Beirut, American diplomats and civilians would be endangered, and the Marines would be besieged.

Dillon strongly objected. If McFarlane wanted to shell the Druzes to support Gemayel, then he should say so. The claim that screaming hordes of bloodthirsty Druzes led by ax-wielding Iranians were going to descend on the city to slaughter Americans was simply not true.

Americans who knew Beirut may have dismissed McFarlane's scenario, but it all sounded quite plausible to Ronald Reagan. Besides, accepting the pretense that Americans were about to be killed was the only way the White House could order the naval guns to open up in support of the Lebanese Army without seeking congressional approval. The administration was already engaged in a tug-of-war with Capitol Hill over the War Powers Act, which required the president to obtain the endorsement of Congress before involving U.S. forces in a foreign war. Plenty of people on the Hill said he had already gone too far without consulting them.

At a weekend meeting with Secretary of State Schultz, Secretary of Defense Weinberger, Joint Chiefs of Staff Chairman Gen. John Vessey and National Security Advisor William Clark, Reagan – over the strong objections of his secretary of defense – agreed to allow U.S. forces to fire in support of the Lebanese Army on three conditions: (1) The U.S. commander in Beirut concluded that Souk al-Gharb was in imminent danger of falling; (2) the attacking force was non-Lebanese; and (3) the Lebanese government requested support. A spokesman in Washington called the policy "aggressive self-defense."

The order was sent down through the chain of command to Beirut. As it arrived, so did the USS *Tarawa* carrying another 2,000 marines and four Harrier Jump Jets rigged for ground-attack missions. What followed was a week-long battle of wills between Geraghty and McFarlane. The envoy wanted Geraghty to give the order to fire immediately, but the Marine commander balked. There were an estimated 600 artillery tubes in Druze- and Syrian-controlled territory. Geraghty already had his own artillery in action almost every day, as well as carrier-based jets flying regular recon-naissance flights to defend his marines. If he openly took sides with the

Lebanese Army, the colonel was convinced all those guns in the mountains would be turned toward his men in retribution.

The Marines were sitting ducks. They owned the lowest piece of real estate around. The airport was located on the coastal plan, dominated by mountains on two sides. Those mountains were controlled by their would-be enemies. It was not a situation into which the Marines would have put themselves voluntarily. They had been trained to take the high ground, but this mission was not supposed to have involved combat. The territory they occupied had been chosen according to political, not military, criteria. So there they sat, looking up at the people who were trying to kill them. To the old Vietnam hands, the whole thing dredged up uncomfortable memories of the North Vietnamese rout of the French at Dien Bien Phu in 1954.

Despite the firepower of the fleet and the Marines' own artillery and heavy mortars, the Druzes and their Syrian backers had the distinct advantage. Their guns were scattered throughout what the military men called sawtooth mountains, hidden among a series of ridges. Naval gunfire has a flat trajectory, limiting its effectiveness in reaching targets on the far side of peaks. The Druze and Syrian guns had no such problems. They could, as one Marine officer put it, "fire right down our throats." The U.S. tubes at Charlie Battery did not suffer from the disadvantage of the fleet's guns, but they were far too few to make a difference. Geraghty feared that support for the Lebanese Army would mean massive casualties among his own men. Like the resident diplomats at the embassy, he also suspected Tannous was trying to drag the Marines into Gemayel's war. The Marine commander had bluntly laid out his objections when Washington had asked for his opinion. When the White House imposed the new Rules of Engagement, he balked at ordering the naval fire on the grounds that all three conditions had not yet been met.

McFarlane wanted to send a message to Damascus with the Souk al-Gharb shelling. Although the diplomat had no direct authority over the Marine commander, he sent word back to the White House to put pressure on the Pentagon to have it order Geraghty to open up.

McFarlane's military aide, Army Brig. Gen. Carl Stiner, who reported directly to the chairman of the Joint Chiefs of Staff, John Vessey, was enlisted in the fight. The telephone lines between the ambassador's residence and the airport burned up with the heated exchanges between Geraghty and Stiner. A Marine officer who walked into the operations center during one such call heard Geraghty shouting, "General, do you realize we'll pay the price down here? We'll get slaughtered. We're totally vulnerable."

The head of the U.S. training mission, Col. Tom Fintel, and the commodore of the fleet, Capt. Morgan France, both supported Geraghty's stance. So did his superiors at the Pentagon, much to McFarlane's chagrin. In addition to their suspicions about the Gemayel government's political motives, the military men also worried that the Lebanese Army line officers at Souk al-Gharb, accustomed to years of street fighting, were not experienced enough at conventional battles to provide a cogent evaluation of their situation.

Meanwhile, the Defense Department launched a massive operation to resupply the Lebanese Army. Code-named Rubberwall, it was the largest air and sea lift since the 1967 Arab–Israeli War. The United States would end up supplying the Lebanese Army with some 40,000 155mm artillery rounds alone in the month-long Chouf war. The idea was to take the pressure off the government troops without directly involving Americans in the fighting.

Back in Washington, the political dance between McFarlane and Geraghty was reflected in conflicting messages from various branches of the administration. While the White House was setting the stage for direct U.S. involvement in the war on the basis that Americans were under threat, Marine Corps Commandant Gen. P.X. Kelley was telling a congressional committee that there was no "significant danger" to the Marines, adding in a television interview, "I believe whoever is shooting at us is shooting at where we are, not who we are, because of our strategic and visible positions."

If he was right, there was no need to shell Souk al-Gharb. If he was wrong, according to the original mandate, the Marines should leave Lebanon.

On the night of September 16, Geraghty compromised and employed his new authority to order the destroyer USS *John Rogers* and the frigate USS *Bowen* to use their five-inch guns to counter artillery batteries located, in the words of a Marine spokesman, "deep inside Syrian-controlled areas of Lebanon." Warrant Officer Charles Rowe said the U.S. ambassador's residence and the Defense Ministry had both been shelled, thereby "endangering American lives." The actual threat to the Americans, however, was questionable. The ambassador's residence was just a few hundred yards from Gemayel's palace, which many suspected was the real target. And while Fintel and his military training staff had offices in the Defense Ministry, that building also happened to be the headquarters of the army the Druzes were fighting.

The action marked the first time the ships had struck behind Syrian lines. The temperature immediately rose. "In reference to the U.S. military spokesman's statement in which he announced that the Sixth Fleet off the shore of Lebanon shelled areas in which Syrian forces are present," said a warning broadcast on Damascus radio, "we emphasize that if any shell from land, sea or air falls in areas where our forces exist, we will shell the source of the fire."

The Christians, meanwhile, had been doing more than sitting back with their fingers crossed hoping the Americans would take sides. They were trying to provoke U.S. involvement. When he justified the naval firing, Rowe spoke of the shelling of the ambassador's residence and the Defense Ministry. He didn't mention that the embassy compound in West Beirut had also been mortared. There was good reason for omitting that. U.S. military sources said that the shells came from Phalangist batteries in East Beirut. America's Christian "allies" apparently thought they could trick the U.S. into retaliating against the Muslims. It was a pattern that would continue until the Marines finally pulled out six months later.

The hours that led up to the naval shelling had been busy for the Lebanese government. With the latest Saudi-sponsored attempt to reach a cease-fire collapsing, Gemayel ordered his air force into action to counter what was described as an assault by several hundred Palestinian guerrillas who were attempting to break through the Souk al-Gharb front and link up with other Palestinians who had infiltrated Beirut. (By constantly talking about the Palestinians, Gemayel was doing his best to distract the world from the fact that he was fighting a civil war and to make his Muslim troops forget that they were killing fellow Muslims.) Five 1950s-vintage Hawker Hunter jets that hadn't seen action for almost ten years limped into the air from a makeshift runway on the highway near Byblos in the north. Two of them didn't stay in the air long. One was shot down over Souk al-Gharb, its pilot taking a dip in the Mediterranean before the USS *Eisenhower* picked him up. Another was hit by antiaircraft fire and barely made it to the British base on Cyprus. Syrian jets were soon overhead, asking Beirut tower for a weather report just to make sure the Lebanese pilots knew they had company, and the Israelis took to the air to keep an eye on the Syrians.

Saturday night, the Lebanese Army's position took a turn for the worse. Shi'ite militiamen attacked government positions in several West Beirut neighborhoods for the first time since the army had put down the revolt two weeks before, raising the threat that the Muslims would open a second front in the war.

The crunch came 24 hours later. Shortly before dawn on Monday, September 19, the Druzes and their allies unleashed a fearsome artillery barrage against Lebanese Army positions at Souk al-Gharb. U.S. officers who watched the assault from the Defense Ministry for several hours estimated that shells rained down on the village at the rate of one a second. Even at bargain basement prices, that was millions of dollars worth of ordnance. Shouting to make himself heard over the earsplitting explosions, the ranking Lebanese officer at Souk al-Gharb radioed the Defense Ministry with a chilling message: his own ammunition was running out. He could hold out for only another 30 minutes. Tannous, the Lebanese Army commander, contacted Fintel, then got Geraghty on the horn and formally requested help. This time the Marine colonel was ready to comply. By radio, he contacted Capt. Morgan France, commodore of the fleet offshore.

Up until this point, neither Geraghty, Fintel nor France had been convinced that all three of Washington's conditions for intervention had been met: that Lebanese Army defenses at Souk al-Gharb were about to collapse; that large numbers of Palestinians were reportedly among the attacking force; and that Tannous had formally requested help. Now, as he watched the tremendous punishment the Lebanese Army was taking under the Druze artillery barrage, Geraghty decided that this time the danger of Souk al-Gharb falling appeared real. The intense pressure from McFarlane had helped Geraghty reach that conclusion. He was a military man answerable to a chain of command that stretched to the Pentagon – and ultimately the White House. That chain had helped shield him from some of the political heat, but not all of it. He knew that the president had approved the decision to shell Souk al-Gharb a week before. McFarlane had no power to give orders to the Marine commander, but he did represent the White House. Tim Geraghty could only buck the system so long.

If Geraghty had not ordered the U.S. Navy into action and Souk al-Gharb had fallen, the Marine commander might technically have been guilty of disobeying orders. But once he was satisfied that the Lebanese Army was "hanging on by its fingernails," Geraghty did not hesitate to step in. "I think, my personal opinion, that it would have been unconscionable for us to stand by and not provide support for them in that moment in time where they required it," the Marine colonel later told an administration fact-finding commission, "because I am convinced that if the Lebanese Army had been defeated, probably it would have brought down the government, which was our support."[8]

So the United States took the final step over the line. A-6 Intruder fighter bombers catapulted from the deck of the *Eisenhower* and the five-inch guns of the frigate *Bowen*, the destroyers *John Rogers* and *Radford*, and the nuclear-powered cruiser *Virginia* opened up. The jets were equipped with 1,000-pound bombs, but as they made their identification runs over their targets, the decision was made that an air strike would signal too great an escalation of the conflict. Using the Navy was enough. The planes ditched their bombs in the sea and returned to the carrier.

The first time the ships had fired, on September 8, just four shells had been directed at Druze targets. When the *John Rogers* and the *Bowen* fired at artillery "endangering American lives" eight days later, they had launched a total of 72 rounds. When the four ships unleashed their firepower to save the Lebanese Army at Souk al-Gharb, they pulverized Druze positions with 360 five-inch shells.

Geraghty was painfully aware of the implications. "That clearly changed our roles," he told Marine Corps historian Benis M. Frank. "It's a milestone. ... It moved us from a previous, very careful, razor edge of neutrality that we were walking."[9]

As the guns cooled down, the commander of the Sixth Fleet, Vice Admiral Edward Martin, issued a statement containing the official U.S. justification for the barrage: "Successful [Lebanese Armed Forces] defense of the area is vital to the safety of U.S. personnel, including U.S. multinational forces, other U.S. military and the U.S. diplomatic corps presence."

In keeping with the conflicting signals, Maj. Robert Jordan, the Marine spokesman at the airport, added quietly that "there was no direct threat" to Americans. In the smoke that hung over Souk al-Gharb that Monday afternoon, it was just possible to detect the last vestiges of U.S. neutrality.

America's allies in the MNF were livid. None had been notified in advance of the U.S. plan to act in support of the Lebanese Army. They feared that their own troops would suffer the consequences.

"One has to be very wary of deeper involvement," warned British Prime Minister Margaret Thatcher. The Italians, too, muttered angrily.

"French policy is not in gear with American policy," complained French Foreign Minister Claude Cheysson. "If the Americans want to take the place of the Israelis, that's their responsibility, not ours." Despite the grumbling, France late in the week ordered its Super Etendard fighter bombers to launch their first air strike against targets behind Syrian lines in retaliation for shelling of the French MNF headquarters that wounded four more soldiers. President Francois Mitterand personally approved the air raid.

The Italians, meanwhile, watched helplessly as their entire ammunition dump went up in a huge fireball after a direct hit from a rocket. Since they didn't own an aircraft carrier, they asked Britain for permission to move a squadron of F-104 Starfighter jets to the British base on Cyprus to be on standby the next time they were hit. Consciously or not, all four nations were slipping off the fence of neutrality.

The damage to America's shattered image as a peacekeeper was compounded when reporters ran across a group of Marine Corps and U.S. Army trainers in Souk al-Gharb the day after the shelling. They were there on Geraghty's orders to assess the plight of the Lebanese garrison, but to

Gemayel's enemies it was further evidence that the Americans were fighting alongside the government troops. For exactly that reason, Geraghty had resisted a classified message from Washington two weeks before ordering him to send observers into Souk al-Gharb.

"When a reporter walked in Tuesday and asked, 'What's your bartender doing in Souk al-Gharb?' recalled Bob Jordan, "I knew we'd been caught."

The news the inspection team brought back confirmed the fears of U.S. officers and the embassy: the Lebanese Army brigade at Souk al-Gharb had exaggerated its position. The Americans came away convinced that the army could have held on without the support of the Sixth Fleet. The United States had been suckered once again. Years later, long after the Americans were gone, the Lebanese Army was still holding off the Druzes at Souk al-Gharb.

The observers returned to the mountain village the following day and the ships continued firing for much of the week in response to shelling against the ambassador's residence, the embassy and the Marines, but the massive conventional retaliation Geraghty and others had feared never came. The presence of F-14 Tomcat fighters from the *Eisenhower* and Super Etendard fighter bombers from the *Foch* crisscrossing the skies over the capital might have helped discourage attempts to get even. The USS *New Jersey*, carrying more firepower than the dozen other U.S. ships in the flotilla combined, arrived on the weekend, underscoring the jets' message.

That message was not meant for the Druzes or the Syrians alone. After months of blaming Damascus for the trouble in Lebanon, Reagan decided the strings were being pulled from even farther away. "There is no question that there is influence by the Soviet Union, which has put people in there, and weapons systems and is urging [Syria] to support – and they have supported and they are supporting – some of the internal Lebanese factions ... with supplies and, we believe, sometimes with manpower," he told a group of broadcasters at the White House a few days before McFarlane finally managed to cobble together a cease-fire with help from Saudi Arabia. By then, the casualty toll for the three weeks of fighting stood at four marines killed in action and at least 30 wounded. More than 800 Lebanese combatants and civilians were dead.

Reagan's talk of "Soviet sponsored aggression" was like music to Amin Gemayel's ears. He wasted no time jumping on the bandwagon. "We are fighting against the Warsaw Pact," he said in an interview with the *Los Angeles Times*. "You have many Soviet experts in the Lebanese mountains with the Syrian Army."[10]

A century and a half of Byzantine struggle with scores of factions, sects and families backed by dozens of foreign sponsors battling for a baffling array of conflicting economic, religious and political goals all boiled down to East against West in the mind of Amin Gemayel. "You have two clans – the Syrians and the Soviet Union on one side, and Lebanon and the Free World on the other side," he told his interviewer. It was the kind of face-off Ronald Reagan could understand.

Once again, the U.S. embassies in Beirut and Damascus sent cables arguing "not so." Moscow didn't have those kinds of levers over Assad. The Soviets had provided Syria with $2 billion worth of weapons and equipment, but they couldn't call the shots in Damascus. Assad was his own man. Besides, Moscow didn't need to get directly involved in the conflict; things were already going its way. This was not an East–West confrontation, the cables repeatedly emphasized, Syria was not a Soviet surrogate. Damascus had historic interests in Lebanon that stretched back long before the Soviet Union even existed. The embassies might as well have saved their energy. McFarlane saw the war in Lebanon as a Soviet-inspired attempt by Syria to destroy U.S. interests in the Middle East. The White House just saw red.

Two weeks after the shaky cease-fire went into effect, Reagan was warming to his theme. "Can the United States or the Free World stand by and see the Middle East incorporated into the Soviet bloc?" he asked rhetorically during his weekly radio address on October 8. "What of Western Europe's and Japan's dependence on Middle East oil for the energy to fuel their industry?" That was the first anyone in Lebanon had heard about having oil under the country's rubble.

"We don't know, if we continue, we may have at Souk al-Gharb [American] Pershing missiles and in Aley [Soviet] SS-20s," Walid Jumblatt wryly observed after hearing about Reagan's comments.

While the Reagan administration was reiterating its commitment to Lebanese democracy, Gemayel announced the introduction of censorship. The latest bulwark of the Free World didn't like some of the things Muslim newspapers were saying about him.

Two days after the United States fired on Arab soldiers for the first time in support of its Christian-controlled client government, Secretary of State George Schultz told the House Foreign Affairs Committee that the MNF's "task is a peacekeeping mission, not a war-fighting mission. Its job is not to take sides in a war but, on the contrary, to help provide a sense of security for the legitimate government of Lebanon."[11]

What the Reagan administration didn't seem to be able to grasp was that by propping up Amin Gemayel's regime, it *was* taking sides. In Ronald Reagan's world, the good guys wore white hats and the bad guys wore black. In Lebanon, all the hats were gray.

9
Victims of War

The Christians were allowed to keep their arms, but not to stir out of [Deir al-Kamar]. Convoys of mules carrying flour were sent up to them from Beirut. They were frequently, however, intercepted by the Druzes. Sufficient [food] only reached its destination to enable the Christians to keep body and soul together. ... The Druzes had cut off the supplies of water. ... Whenever a Christian showed his face beyond the town, he was instantly cut down. Many asked permission to leave, but were sternly refused.
—Col. Charles Churchill[1]

There was something strange about the heap of broken concrete. Rubble was certainly nothing unusual in Lebanon, but instead of the usual jagged edges protruding in all direction, this hill of wreckage was smooth. It looked as if a whale had thrust its back up through a cement ice pack and dived again to the depths without breaking through completely.

This was all that was left of Kamal Hamse's house. If you looked closely, you could just see one edge of the swing peeking from between the broken concrete that buried the porch where we had once sat sipping lemonade. The Phalangist demolition teams had done their job well: a few satchels of explosives in the right places and the building had collapsed onto itself. The cement roof had settled at eye level, the huge slabs giving it the appearance of a broken ice pack.

The tidy stone wall that surrounded the property was untouched. From the street, we walked through the open gates, up the slate path and past the rhododendrons, coming face-to-face with a ruin surrounded by other ruins. The Phalangists had worked their way through Aabey systematically dynamiting the homes. Artillery tears great jagged chunks out of buildings; bombs scatter the wreckage for hundreds of yards. Each of these buildings had collapsed on itself. Aabey looked as if it had been ravaged by an earthquake, not a war.

The houses that had not been dynamited had been burned. Black scorch marks stained the walls of those houses still standing. Furniture had been consumed, roofs had collapsed, but the structures themselves had survived. Many were ancient stone buildings made of heavy blocks. To wreck them would have taken more dynamite than it was worth. They stood, violated but intact.

Sheikh Muhammed's home had been easy to destroy. A heap of charred logs and blackened stones was all that remained of the holy shelter. The sheikh was dead. He and his acolytes had been executed when the Phalangists overran the town in the first days of the September war. Several other villagers had died, too. Druze officials would later claim that 47 people had been slaughtered in Aabey. Most villagers had escaped to Beirut as the fighting began. They were lucky. Just down the hill was Kfar Matte, where the bodies of at least 40 Druze men, women and children were discovered months later. They had been gunned down in cold blood.

Aabey had fallen in the first days of the September Chouf war. As the Israelis withdrew and the mountains erupted, Lebanese government forces and Phalangist militiamen had rolled into Kfar Matte, then turned toward the Druze militiamen defending Aabey.

"They were raining bombs on us," Kamal said later in Beirut. "On Tuesday, the commander came to me and said I must get my wife out. He said their defenses were about to collapse and I did not have much time." Kamal and his wife grabbed a few valuables and jumped in their car. On the edge of town, Christian snipers opened up, shooting out one of Kamal's tires. He kept going and made it safely to Beirut. Two days later, Aabey fell.

Overall, the war was a defeat for the Christians. Jumblatt's Druzes overran scores of Christian-controlled villages. Christians were driven out of 52 towns and villages and the Phalangists claimed hundreds of Christians had been massacred. Outsiders were never able to confirm the accuracy of those figures, but it's difficult to overestimate the level of horror in Lebanese wars. The term "ethnic cleansing" may have been coined in Yugoslavia years later, but the concept was an old one in Lebanon.

Months after the September war, a spine of destruction scarred the lush green mountain ridges where the Christians had lived for centuries. Driving down the rutted roads, it looked as if a mad giant had stomped through the mountains, crushing everything in his way.

Kfar Matte and Aabey were among the few places where the Christians had advanced. There they vented their rage for the losses elsewhere. There they got even for the campaign of massacre and destruction they claimed had been unleashed against Christian villages by the Druzes.

Back in August, the people of Aabey had struck us as melodramatic in their warnings of an impending Phalangist massacre, but they had been right. They knew their history and what their countrymen were capable of far better than we. That was obvious as we walked the streets of Aabey several weeks after the cease-fire was arranged in late September.

As in any town that has been occupied by an invading army, the streets of Aabey were littered with the broken remnants of people's lives: the books, papers and pictures of no interest to the looters, who always seem to draw some vicarious pleasure from ruining what they don't take – like a rapist spitting on his victim after the act to strip away any vestige of self-respect.

Walking through the familiar streets, I found a diary lying in the dirt in front of a house that slumped drunkenly to one side. Its pages had been torn out. A few yards away, a muddy photo album. The plastic cover had been stepped on, but the pictures inside had survived – snapshots of children playing, a school graduation and a smiling family at a lawn party. It took me a few seconds to realize that under the wreckage in front of us was the ivy-covered porch on which the smiling group had posed. I put the album in my shoulder bag to give to Kamal to pass on to the family that had lived in the house.

Some armies might have tried to deny responsibility for the kind of thing that happened in Aabey. Not the Phalangists. Their green cedar tree symbol was stenciled on walls, doors and the hulks of automobiles. And the Phalangist fighters were still there, too, racing around in beat-up Range Rovers.

When we first pulled into town, Aabey seemed completely deserted: No checkpoint on the outskirts of town, no one in the streets, no sounds. Only the total silence of a dead village. Not even the chirp of a bird. Sometimes you can't help wondering if the birds don't sense the evil in a place like Aabey and move on. A more logical explanation is that they've been driven off by the noise of battle. But when you are walking an empty street in a wrecked town expecting to see a body, or worse, in each doorway, it is easier to believe in evil than logic.

Eventually, the Phalangists found us and ordered us out, but not before a session at their local headquarters, the village school.

Kiddie chairs, the kind with the chair connected to the desk, were heaped outside the door. Phalangist fighters lolled in the shade of the courtyard inside, leaning back against the cool stone. "Phalange" was spray-painted in bold letters on one wall. A row of hangman's nooses was drawn on another. Underneath, someone had sprayed "Rock & Roll."

As we waited for the inevitable argument over the fate of our videotapes, we noticed a fighter emerge from one of the doors wearing a T-shirt emblazoned with the motto, "Kill 'em all and let God sort it out." He looked as if he was already working on it.

Kamal Hamse knew his village had fallen to the Christians. He knew there had been destruction. He had no idea it had been so bad. He sat staring at the television monitor, stunned. A barely audible whistle escaped from his lips as he watched the camera pan over the remains of what had once been his home. The rosy cheeks were gone; the usually smiling countenance was grim.

When the screen went blank, Kamal turned slowly toward me, shaking his head. The fight had gone out of him; the perpetual optimism had been used up like the videotape. "Myself, I have lost the work of 22 years. I don't know if I can rebuild this building or the things inside," he said as he rose, shoulders sagging, to return to the apartment where he was staying with friends and tell his wife they had lost everything. Again.

Months later, after the Druzes had retaken Aabey, Kamal Hamse braved the mines planted in the road leading into his village to survey the damage. Walking through the gates of his property, he took one glance at what remained of his home, and his head slumped, eyes closed. His cherubic face took on a new look, a kind of resigned acceptance.

"*Ma'alesh*" ("It doesn't matter"), he said in a whisper. "Ma'alesh." He lifted a small automatic camera. His wife would want to see.

In the old days, Kamal had been proud of his "cave." The heavy stone cellar, part of the basement of an ancient building, was a perfect shelter during shelling. The cellar had survived the explosions that had destroyed the house. Fire had consumed the furniture, the mementos and the bar, but the arched stone ceiling was still there.

"We can build the new house on top," Kamal said, some of the old optimism beginning to return. Rummaging through the ashes, he found a glass bottle, the kind antique stores sell, still in one piece. He held it toward us. "It remains." There were tears in his eyes. A single, useless bottle salvaged from a lifetime of work. He held it as if cradling the family jewels.

"The important thing," Kamal continued, composing himself, recapturing a little more of the old optimism, "the important thing is that I return to my village. The place where my family grew. We say when we have children, everything can be returned."

As he spoke, you could see the old Kamal returning. The slumped shoulders straightened just a little, a hint of confidence returned to the voice. It was as if by trying to convince us that it would all be okay, he was convincing himself.

"Maybe in a few weeks you will return to this place and you will see all of this rebuilt," he said. "We are going to return back to it and rebuilt it better than it was, no matter what." All that was needed was peace, money and workers – none of which Kamal had.

"We say [we are] sorry for what happened here," Kamal explained as we walked toward the cars. "What happened here is a great atrocity they have done with poor people, with civilians, people who were not military. Those who were living in these houses, they were killed some of them, and now we feel great that we returned back."

Yet he would remember always the Christians who wrecked his home and his life. "I don't hate the person who did it. But of course," he paused, realizing the truth, "of course, we have to hate them a little. Not much, but a little."

Down a winding lane, we came across an old man standing in the street studying what was left of the village where he had been born and hoped to be buried. He ran sooty fingers through his short gray hair and nodded sadly. His shoes were scuffed and his pants dirty from climbing through the charred rubble. When he saw us, he smiled. He did not bemoan his fate; he did not curse those responsible. Instead, he apologized. "You are welcome in our country here," he said, thrusting his arm forward to shake hands. "But we cannot invite you to our house because it is ruined."

The whoosh of an incoming artillery round sent us diving for cover. For a second, the shell sounded as if it was going to land right on us. Shrieking as it passed directly overhead, it left behind a roar like that of a speeding freight train. It was at least ten seconds before we heard the impact, a deep rumbling sound from the next ridge. We were between whoever was firing and whomever they were firing at.

With the first explosion, the old man picked up the conversation as if nothing had happened. "We want peace only." A second deep-throated roar rolled across the valley. "We want peace." Again the screech of incoming shells. We instinctively ducked. The shells sounded like they were barely clearing the treetops. We could feel the pressure swell against our eardrums as the projectiles parted the atmosphere above our heads.

The old man calmly looked up at the sky as if expecting to see the shells as they passed by. "I think the *New Jersey* is shelling us," he said, matter-of-factly. "The Americans think that we are their enemy. We are not. We want peace. We have no reason to hate them."

At the shrine of Emir Abdullah, there *was* reason to hate. The dome-shaped vault, burial place of the Lebanese Druzes' only saint, had been wrecked. Huge stones from the collapsed walls blocked the entrance. It looked as if there had been a cave-in.

"They've blown the shrine, they burned it. They dug [up] the grave and we don't know why." The voice of Dr. Shawki Ghraizi, a member of the board that ran the Druze community, shook with rage. "Because of hate maybe. They hate us."

An antique candelabrum still hung from the arched ceiling, but beside it the sky was visible through a hole ripped by the blasts. Dappled light merged with shadows thrown by candles flickering in the dark burial chamber. Three women knelt in front of a makeshift altar built from a few stones and a slab that had once covered the grave. The two older women wailed softly, as if afraid to disturb the holy spirit that dwelt there. The youngest, a striking raven-haired beauty in her early twenties, was lost in silent prayer, face buried in her hands. A black-and-white checked Palestinian keffiah shrouded her head like a veil.

A perfectly round, metal-gray stone the size of a basketball stood on the altar. In the darkness, it bore a frightening resemblance to a human head. There were no facial features. Instead, a carved pattern made the orb appear to be wrapped in cloth. It was the focus of the women's worship.

Beginning with the youngest, each touched her forehead, then her lips, to the stone, repeating the movement three times. When the women were finished, Kamal and the other men stepped forward to do the same. No one would tell us the significance of the stone; no one would say why it was being kissed. The ritual, the cavelike shrine and the mysterious round stone hidden in the shadows, left us feeling that we had witnessed something not meant for Western eyes.

As others filed toward the altar, two soldiers began tearing strips from a red cloth that had once been part of the shrine. A tiny piece was handed to each person present. The girl in the keffiah held out her arm as a strip was tied around her wrist. The holy relics would be treasured for generations, a reminder of the Christian sacrilege.

Watching the cloth being distributed, I asked Dr. Ghraizi if he felt hatred for those who had destroyed the shrine. "At the moment, yes, but later on, we are the people who forgive," he replied. He was adamant that there would be no retribution. "We don't treat them the same way they treat us."

The Christians just over the mountain had a different story to tell.

The old peasant woman in faded widow's black leaned over the sooty iron cooking pot, stirring the thickly bubbling porridge with a big wooden ladle. Her face was deeply lined, a road map of misery. Around her, other women stirred their own pots. A few families sitting on the cold stone were already eating, but they took no more pleasure in their food than the old woman. Shouting children ran among the cooking fires, while their fathers sat in the shade of the stone walls of a church, talking grimly or staring off across the valley.

The once flourishing Christian community of Deir al-Kamar was now nothing more than a running sore on the body of the mountain, one of many created by a plague of destruction. A middle-aged father in a dirty undershirt and torn pants held his hand up to shield his eyes from the sun as he looked toward the palace at Beiteddine directly across the valley and muttered an Arabic curse. The ancient seat of the Turkish governor was now controlled by Walid Jumblatt's Druzes, who had systematically destroyed the Christian villages in this section of the Chouf and cornered their fleeing inhabitants here in Deir al-Kamar, where they had been trapped for a month. With the refugees were about 2,500 Christian militiamen, remnants of the routed Phalangist forces.

Flour and other essentials were brought in by Red Cross convoys – when the Druzes allowed them to pass – but there were no fresh vegetables or red meat; the only water came from the fountain in the village square. Anyone who tried to leave was shot by the Druze snipers who guarded all approaches.

There was a hiss as the old widow accidentally dripped porridge from her ladle onto the flames, sending smoke curling up the height of the tall monument behind her. The stone memorial had been built in memory of the more than 1,000 Christians who had been massacred by the Druzes after the month-long siege of Deir al-Kamar in 1860. Their descendants were trapped here again. They only hoped history was not about to repeat itself.

Inside the church, dozens of families had set up home. Some slept on the pews, others on the cold stone floors. A few had brought cots. Ropes were hung from the rafters and draped with blankets to create a modicum of privacy. A handful of lucky families had moved into the choir loft, away from prying eyes.

"They no let us go. They no give us food," said one father, grabbing me by the arm and shoving a flat loaf of pita bread in my face. "This all I can give my family."

The refugees brought with them tales of massacre and carnage. They spoke of Druzes entering their villages and slitting the throats of women and children, of young men lined up against walls and gunned down. There was no way to corroborate the stories, but they mirrored others we had heard from refugees in Beirut. History, and the monument outside the church, gave them a ring of truth.

We had been allowed into the town on Jumblatt's orders. He was under intense international pressure to permit the Christians to leave. U.S. jets had repeatedly flown over the town in symbolic support. Jumblatt was pressured into promising he would not attack the town, although his men couldn't resist lobbing in the occasional shell. Now the Druze leader wanted to prove through the news media that the Christians' situation was not as desperate as they claimed. To make sure reporters didn't smuggle anyone out in their cars, we had to walk the last few hundred yards of the exposed road leading into the town. When we left, Druze snipers bounced rounds off the blacktop behind us to discourage anyone from following.

Earlier, addressing a gathering of Druze elders and officers in a vaulted stone chamber of the Beiteddine Palace, Jumblatt had railed against the "foreign fleets that stopped us from kicking the Phalangists out of Souk al-Gharb." He warned that if Gemayel did not scrap the agreement with Israel and share power with the Muslims, he would soon learn that "the cease-fire is not the end of the battle." Many of the Druze warriors in the gathering wore the traditional baggy black pants and white wool skullcaps. Outside, fighters holding Druze banners had flanked the arched doorways as Jumblatt and his retainers had arrived from Mukhtara, the ancient family palace.

A feudal warlord, an ancient palace, a besieged Christian fortress. If not for the cameras, we might well have stepped back into another century.

In a sparsely furnished house behind Deir al-Kamar's central square, Emile Rahme, an East Beirut lawyer who was doubling as the local Phalangist commander, painted a bleak picture of the situation he faced: "We have 40,000 people here. We are surviving, but that is all. We have eaten all the apples from the trees, killed all the chickens. Now we exist on one piece of bread a day." He, too, held up the obligatory disk of pita bread. "The Western world must save us. We appeal to you to ensure the people of Deir al-Kamar do not die. You have your ships out there," he pointed toward the sea, "your *Eisenhower*, your planes. Syria wants to destroy the Christians of Lebanon. It is your duty to help us." It was the old story – blame one set of foreigners for the trouble and demand that another set bail them out.

When Jumblatt finally agreed to an evacuation in mid-December, it became clear there had never been more than about 12,000 people in Deir al-Kamar, half of them residents of the village. Conversely, the 2,500 militiamen totaled just over half the number Jumblatt had claimed were there. Even when the floodgates were opened, the Phalangists tried to convince the refugees not to leave. Christian leaders wanted to use the international pressure resulting from the plight of those besieged at Deir al-Kamar to force Jumblatt to allow them back into their villages, thus giving up some of the ground he had gained.

Lebanon's population ebbed and flowed with the tides of war. Government officials estimated that 400,000 people fled their homes between August and December 1983. Since the war had begun in 1975, somewhere between one-half and two-thirds of the population had been forced to move at least once.

From the beginning in the mid 1970s, the civil war drove thousands out of homes along the Green Line. Whole neighborhoods of Christians and Muslims were uprooted and shifted to the appropriate side of the military rift. In places such as Karantina and Damour, populations were driven out to make room for refugees who belonged to the same religion as the men with the guns. Some Beirutis moved to the mountains to get away from the fighting; others returned to the south.

A few years later, many of the latter, along with tens of thousands of poor Shi'ite peasants, abandoned their farms and orchards in South Lebanon to escape the heavy hand of the PLO. Driven out of their own country and, more recently, Jordan, the Palestinians behaved like most other armies of occupation as they entrenched themselves in what would become known as Fatahland, ruling with forced labor, extortion, robbery and fear. When the area became a battlefield, with the PLO and Israel trading rockets attacks and air raids, many more Shi'ite made their way to Beirut, settling in the Belt of Misery, the burgeoning shantytown that grew up around the airport.

In the 1982 Israeli invasion, the Lebanese milled around like ants whose nest had been disturbed. The first instinct for those in the south was to head north, but the front line quickly overtook most of them. Those who stayed in South Lebanon soon discovered they had made the right choice. Peace was restored (although it would not last), and soon many from Beirut were streaming south again to escape the Israeli bombs and siege of the capital. Muslims with money fled to East Beirut and then on to Cyprus, Europe or the United States.

The evacuation of the PLO brought Beirut's population back for a time, and things settled down under the warming rays of hope. Gemayel's roundups of Palestinians and Shi'ites caused many families to start thinking again about heading south, which was precisely the government's intention. The Lebanese Army sweep into West Beirut in the first days of September 1983 confirmed the fears and sent a cavalcade of beat-up Mercedes, with mattresses, pots and pans lashed to the roof, streaming toward Sidon and Tyre. Those refugees were joined by tens of thousands of Christians and Muslims from the mountains when the Chouf war broke out there a few days later.

Close to 150,000 mountain villagers ended up behind the "safety" of the new Israeli front line: thousands of Christians, allies of the Israelis, went on to Tel Aviv itself. In fact, so many Christians were crossing the border to fly out of Ben Gurion Airport that the Israeli airline El Al set up a ticket office on the border. Other fleeing Christians congregated in the Lebanese mountain town of Jezzine, while Sunni Muslims gathered in Sidon and the majority of the Shi'ites settled around Nabatiyeh. All lived with relatives, in schools, churches or mosques, or wherever they could find a roof. It would be only months before Israel's Iron Fist policy to counter the increasing attacks would drive many north yet again.

Mahmoud Abu Ali was sitting on a cinder block scraping mud from an old boot the first time I met him. It was a pointless exercise. A sea of mud surrounded him and the leaden sky held a promise that the swampy bog would stay that way for some time.

Mahmoud's damp, leaking building was in a prime location in the slums on the southern edge of West Beirut. Just across the street was the swanky Summerland

Hotel, where in the summer bikini-clad beauties in high heels basked beside the Olympic-size pool sipping champagne during the day, then dancing the night away at the disco after lobster or filet mignon in the Four Seasons dining room. Mahmoud's family also had a great view of the sea – through the holes in their walls. The four-story apartment house had been bombed by the Israelis, shelled by the Christians and rocketed by the Lebanese Army.

There wasn't much between the Abu Alis and the elements. Some rooms had no walls, while in others the walls were like Swiss cheese. Not a single window had glass. No one slept on the top floor because there was no roof. The rain formed wide puddles there and leaked down to the floors below. Plywood, plastic bags and cardboard had been nailed over some of the holes to block the damp winter wind.

While his daughters continued collecting water in empty plastic bottles from the tap outside (the only source for the Abu Alis' building and the army garrison next door), Mahmoud invited us into his "living room," where several other middle-aged men were sitting playing cards. I settled into a torn pink chair with the stuffing spilling out. My companions chose the "couch," the back seat from an abandoned car. The women were dispatched to make tea over the open fire out back, while Mahmoud talked about his life.

The Abu Alis were Shi'ites. This was not their real home. They owned a house in Hay-es Sellum, a neighborhood on the Muslim side of the Green Line, but the fighting there had driven them away two months before. Mahmoud had been afraid for his wife, their eight children and his mother-in-law. Since then, they had been sharing this decaying structure with eight other families, sleeping nine to a room. "It is too difficult," he lamented. "But better to live like this than die at home."

Mahmoud had no idea whether his own home was still standing. His wife had pleaded with him not to go back to check. "She afraid I killed," he said with a sad smile.

I asked whether he blamed the Marines for his plight. "People die before the Marines come, but many die when they shoot," he replied. "Why Marines shoot? We like Americans. Why they make trouble for us?"

Mahmoud was the only one of the men in the building who had a job. He was a policeman. He had been for 19 years. Each day, he reported for work, enforced what passed for Lebanese law and order, then returned to his decaying hovel. The other families survived on their meager savings, odd jobs the men were able to pick up, the charity of Muslim organizations, and begging. Theft probably also played a role, but no one mentioned that.

"I want to work, but no one give me job," explained Abdel Latif Abda, a man of about 50 with a weather-beaten face, rough hands and a shock of graying hair.

His two wives had 20 children between them. His sick mother also lived with them, the damp winds adding to her misery.

The economy had thrived for much of the war, one of the reasons the conflict was able to drag on, but now business, too, was collapsing. Before, people suffered with money in their pockets. Now they just suffered.

Leading the way up the broken stairway, pointing out the hole in the floor on the second landing, Abdel Latif gave us a tour of his "apartment": three rooms on the third floor. In the first, a girl of perhaps three years old was curled up in a blanket on a door that had been laid on the floor to insulate her from the cold, damp concrete. A biting wind whipped through the uncovered window. Blankets and a few mattresses were scattered along the walls. This was the children's room. The next chamber was a combination kitchen, living room and bedroom for the adults. A beat-up kitchen table with a few rickety chairs was the showpiece of the house. It had recently been salvaged from the Italian troops when they had pulled out of the building next door. A poster of the Imam Musa Sadr decorated one peeling wall. More mattresses were piled in the corner beside three empty ammunition crates where the food was stored. There was another car seat under the window.

One daughter, a skinny girl of about 15, was sweeping the floor when we came in. Two others were on the balcony hanging wet clothes on a line. (The first sign that a building had been taken over by refugees was always the wash hanging from the front balconies.) They all giggled at the sight of us and fled into the third room, where they slept. Like most Shi'ite women, the mother and all her daughters wore scarves over their hair.

Abdel Latif stood in the middle of the room and spread his arms. "This is how we live. We survive, not more. It is all we can ask."

Squatting was a way of life for tens of thousands of Lebanese. By the autumn of 1983, property owners – primarily Sunnis – had stopped constructing new apartment blocks, not because of the war but because of the squatters. As soon as a new complex was complete – and often well before – it was overrun by poor Shi'ite or Palestinian families. Each time fighting flared up around the airport or Christian artillery pounded the slums, masses of refugees poured out of the Belt of Misery into downtown West Beirut, breaking down the doors of empty apartments, setting up house on construction sites, or taking over movie theaters to get away from the fighting around their homes.

Landlords who owned partly empty buildings took to dumping concrete into toilets, chopping holes in the roofs and smashing all the windows in an attempt to make their apartments unlivable, often to no avail. People whose own homes often had no plumbing and were battered by shelling were usually not put off by such inconveniences.

The Abdas had been in their present home for four months. It was the most recent of a series of buildings they had stayed in since arriving in Beirut from South Lebanon during the 1978 Israeli incursion. In especially bad times, the Abdas camped under the trees in the Sanaia Garden, a public park in West Beirut across from the prime minister's office. It was a choice between danger and despair. When fighting flared up, hundreds of families crowded onto this patch of grass, commuting between the park and their embattled neighborhoods, depending on whether the rain or shellfire was heavier.

The Abdas, Abu Alis and others had moved to this refuge by the sea both for shelter and safety. The building next door had been a neighborhood barracks for Italian peacekeeping troops. But recently the Italians had been replaced by a breakaway Lebanese Army unit loyal to Shi'ite leader Nabih Berri and Abdel Latif and his friends feared that soon there would be more fighting and they would have to flee again.

"I wait myself like a little child in front of his father," Berri said of the president after one particularly heavy round of army shelling on the Muslim slums. "I wait to see at least one word that he is sorry [that] more than 100,000 people are out of their houses. Children without fathers, fathers without children." Yet Christians were left wondering when Berri was going to take his own advice and apologize for those in East Beirut whom his guns had left homeless.

The basement was dark, depressing. A few hurricane lanterns threw yellow light on the four old men in pajamas playing cards on an empty crate. Children played with plastic trucks and dolls on the floor. Many people dozed on cots in the darkness toward the back. Notably absent were young men of fighting age. The voice of a female disk jockey introducing the next tune blared from several radios scattered around the room. The Voice of Lebanon, the main Christian radio station, was kept on constantly for news of the fighting. The urgent beat of the bulletin theme song broke in whenever the direction of the shelling shifted. In the corner, half a dozen women sat in a circle knitting. A black-haired woman of about 40 with a cardigan sweater draped over her shoulders held up a half-completed blue wool blanket for us to see.

"This much since we came," she said, raising her eyebrows in a look that said, "What can you do?" "I'll probably finish before we leave here."

The 45 Christian residents of the building had been in that basement for five days while Druze and Shi'ite guns shelled their East Beirut neighborhood. There were couches, chairs, even a refrigerator. We commented to one of the men about how well furnished the place was.

"It is our second home. We spend much time here," he said with resignation. Plastic bags of flat pita bread were piled on a table beside empty *hommos* bowls. A long-handled pot for making Arabic coffee stood on a small gas burner. Stores of food and water were kept in the basement for the long sieges. Whenever there was a lull in the shelling, the women ran upstairs to prepare proper meals.

Ashrafieh, East Beirut's answer to Hamra, was one of the Christian neighborhoods that abutted the Green Line. It was a favorite target of the Muslim gunners. The area had been badly battered in the civil war before the Syrians stepped in to save the Christians, had become a battlefield after the Syrians switched sides, had been besieged and shelled by the Syrians when the Phalangists got too cocky in 1981, and had been intermittently shelled by the Muslims ever since.

This autumn day, the Lebanese Army and the Druzes were locked in one of their daily squabbles over Souk al-Gharb. Jumblatt's men weren't making any headway, so they were shelling the airport and East Beirut, partly because there were Lebanese Army and Phalangist guns in both places, partly out of frustration.

"Always the shells, always the killing," said an unshaven, balding man in pajamas. Many of the men never even bothered to change into street clothes, since they certainly weren't going out into the street. He shrugged and raised his hands palm up. "What can we do?"

"All we want is peace. We do not want to fight," his wife insisted.

Others on the Muslim side were suffering just like them, we reminded her. Couldn't the Lebanese compromise for once to silence the guns?

"We are a peaceful people. We do not hate the Muslims. We are all equal. We are all Lebanese. But the Christians built this country. They [the Muslims] will not take it away [from us]. We will fight to defend what is ours. We are ready to fight."

Strange how such a peaceful people were always poised to pull out a gun.

I instinctively ducked at the crack of the rifle. The people around me paid it no mind. Their attention was riveted on the back of the truck, heaped with sacks of flour and tins of oil. This Shi'ite neighborhood hard up against the Green Line was a warren of poverty, a breeding ground of despair. In this neighborhood of hastily built shelters now a decade old, relief workers reported, 80 percent of the men had no jobs. The $50 or $100 a month offered to those who joined the Shi'ite militias was a lifeboat for their families. Although the Gemayel regime should have viewed government programs to distribute food and provide jobs as a matter of self-preservation, these things did not exist. The food on the back of the truck was being handed out by Berri's Amal movement. For the Shi'ites crowded around waiting for their share, Amal's name literally did mean "Hope."

No matter where you went in Lebanon, no matter how bad the situation, you never saw starvation. This was partly because of the close-knit family structure. A man lucky enough to have a job often supported his own wife and children as well as the families of his brothers and sisters. And if the family unit failed, the militias and the warlords who ran them usually took care of their people. Lebanon was still a feudal society.

The convoy of trucks piled with food had left the well-stocked warehouse an hour late. The shelling from across the line that usually tapered off by morning had continued this day until almost noon. Even as we had watched workers load the trucks, several shells had crashed into an apartment building a block away.

"*Ma'alesh* (It doesn't matter)," one of the drivers told us as we hid among sacks of grain inside the warehouse. "It is just a little shelling. They want to make sure we are awake."

Crowds of people waited for the trucks at each stop along their regular route. At each distribution point, a supervisor stood with a clipboard to make sure no one got more than his or her fair share. Young girls, middle-aged men and old women all jostled for position as the rations were handed out.

Bent under the weight of a sack of beans, a women in a full-length black *chador* (body veil) waddled into the open between two buildings where the sniper on the other side of the line could see her. Several shots rang out, but the woman made it to the cover of the next house.

"It is like this every day," said the Amal official supervising the distribution, an extremely unmilitary-looking man of about 30, who was cross-eyed behind thick glasses. "It is dangerous. But the people, they need food."

Most of the food was bought locally, but some was donated by other countries. I pointed to the cans of cooking oil embossed with a pair of hands clasped on a red, white and blue shield, the symbol of U.S. aid. "You take aid from the Americans and fight the Marines?" I asked, only mildly surprised. He just shrugged and smiled.

The rhythmic clang of metal against metal echoed through the room. The weights tapped out a mournful dirge as they slid up and down on the steel cable. Silhouetted against the Beirut skyline, the lonely figure stared out the large plate-glass windows while the crippled legs strained against foot braces to lift the weights with painfully slow regularity. If he had not motioned us to his side, we would never have recognized this gaunt-faced man with his wasted frame and spindly, scarred legs.

"Do you remember me?" The voice was almost pleading. He wanted assurance that he was still the man he had once been. He knew he was not. "From Aabey. The day we shot the jacket."

Rashid no longer looked like a commander. A sickly pallor had replaced the healthy flush of a fighter. A vicious scarlet incision crawled across his right knee and down his calf. There were no scars on his left leg, but it, too, had withered from disuse. It had taken months of therapy before he could move the leg, bend the shattered knee, slide one foot in front of the other. Like the other cripples who surrounded him in the West Beirut rehabilitation center, Rashid faced a long, exhausting struggle if he was ever to walk normally again.

He motioned down at the maimed leg. "A tank shell, when they overran us." A vivid picture sprang to mind of Phalangist troops overwhelming the sparse Druze defenses at Aabey, of Rashid and his friends lying in the pitifully shallow trenches as tank shells crashed around them. He was reluctant to talk much about that day.

"They came," Rashid said with an involuntary shudder. "Many died."

"But at least you survived. And you didn't lose your leg," I said, trying to lift the gloom.

"*Ilhamdulillah*" ("Thanks be to God"), he replied automatically. "But there is no strength." The words were filled with resignation, the sense of shame at his weakness palpable. A nurse came over and told Rashid his exercise period was over. It was time for the whirlpool treatment. As Rashid hobbled painfully toward the door, fighting to keep his balance, one foot sliding hesitantly in front of the other, a boy of about 16 rolled up beside us in a wheelchair. He made a short, harsh speech in Arabic.

"He say it because of the Americans the man and all the others wounded," the Lebanese nurse translated. She picked up a beach ball and began throwing it to a ten-year old girl sitting on a bed. The exercise helped restore balance and strength to the crippled body. "He says the Americans make all the trouble."

The boy had been crippled in the 1982 Israeli invasion. The girl had been paralyzed the following summer during a clash between the Marines and Shi'ite militiamen near the airport. A bullet had hit her in the back while she was inside her house.

"He says if the Americans no come here to help Gemayel, the man and the girl would not be hurt, and if the Americans no give Israel bombs, he would be okay," the nurse explained without emotion. It was obvious that she agreed with his analysis.

The argument oversimplified things enormously. It ignored the fact that the Lebanese had been killing each other long before the Americans came along. But this was not an idea a 16-year-old had come up with by himself. Right or wrong, oversimplified or not, it was a belief most Lebanese Muslims shared.

10
The Seeds Sprout

If one permits the infidel to continue in his role as corrupter of the earth, his moral suffering will be all the worse. If one kills the infidel, and thus stops him from perpetrating his misdeeds, his death will be a blessing for him. For if he remains alive, he will become more and more corrupt. This is a surgical operation commanded by God the All-Powerful.

—Ayatollah Khomeini[1]

"Two men with Mediterranean skin tones have been overheard in a Paris cafe saying that a major complex will be hit in Beirut." That, according to officials who saw it, was the gist of a warning that passed across Col. Geraghty's desk three days before a hate-filled Muslim warrior achieved martyrdom for himself and the annihilation of 241 U.S. servicemen by driving a truck loaded with explosives equivalent to 12,000 pounds of TNT into the lobby of the Battalion Landing Team (BLT) headquarters.

The CIA advisory, part of the National Intelligence Estimate of October 20, 1983, was buried in the avalanche of raw intelligence dumped on the Marines every day. It indicated that Hussein Musawi's Baalbek-based Islamic Amal organization was the group most likely to carry out the attack, but that appeared to be no more than educated guesswork. The report did not say what kind of complex had been targeted, what it would be hit with, or when.

In retrospect, the advisory seems like a critical piece of intelligence. At the time, it was nothing more than yet another vague and nearly useless bit of hearsay, lost in a barrage of equally oblique hearsay. Rarely were there specifics; rarely were the Marines told "this group is going to do this thing at this place on this day."

"The problem was the intelligence was basically the sky-is-falling type of information," Capt. Morgan France, the task force commodore, told congressional investigators after the bombing. "I think that that is intelligence, but on the ragged edge of intelligence. ... Every imaginable threat, terrorism, was coming across our desks. We were working up plans of action. But it was like chasing your tail. Who were these people, what were they about? – that type of information specifically, a little more specific, we could have used."[2]

The spooks were good at finding out the location of the conventional threats – the artillery and tanks – but they were of little use when it came to countering terrorism. Part of the reason was that the United States was relying largely on the Lebanese. Before 1982, agents inside the PLO had helped the agency keep track of the world of the Muslim militias. That resource was lost with the PLO evacuation. America's intelligence-gathering ability in Lebanon was further crippled when the CIA Beirut station was virtually wiped out in the April embassy blast. Those in a position to know said it was never properly rebuilt.

As the commander of the Marine battalion that preceded Geraghty's in Beirut put it: "My [intelligence officer] can tell me what's going on in the Bekaa Valley and he can tell me what's going on in Tripoli. ... We have no foggy idea what's going on right outside our gates. We have no capability of tapping that and understanding how those people out there are feeling about us, if there's anything going on."[3]

For the Americans, the close-knit Shi'ite terror cells, whose members were often related or had known each other from birth, were almost impossible to penetrate. That left the United States largely dependent on the Lebanese government's Deuxieme Bureau, which was run by Christians, and the Phalangists' intelligence operation. While those groups might have had agents inside or with access to some of the Shi'ite groups, they also had an ax to grind. Just as the Lebanese Army wasn't above shelling the Americans to keep them involved in the fight against the Muslims, the intelligence services were not above feeding the United States false information that served their own purposes.

One example was the alleged role played by Shi'ite cleric Muhammed Hussein Fadlallah in the Marine bombing. Lebanese intelligence put out the word that Fadlallah blessed the suicide drivers the night before the attack. That story quickly gained credence in Washington, which was anxious for a name, aside from the nebulous Islamic Jihad, on which to hang blame. The cleric consistently denied involvement in the bombing and, despite the best efforts of reporters and diplomats, no independent evidence surfaced to directly implicate him. Considering Fadlallah's links to Hizbullah and other Iranian-backed groups, however, the story remained very plausible. To anyone familiar with the workings of the Lebanese intelligence services, it was equally plausible that the Christians had made up the story to smear a Muslim leader they regarded as a threat. Ironically, the publicity resulting from Fadlallah's alleged role in the bombing helped transform a relatively unknown cleric regarded by many extremists as a member of the establishment, into one of the more influential figures in the Shia religion.

From the Lebanese and colleagues in other contingents of the MNF, the Americans received plenty of vague warnings (between May and November, the Marines were told of more than 100 car bomb plots) but little hard data. The Marines were given lists of the models and license numbers of cars said to be carrying explosives (they were looking for a white Mercedes and an Opel pickup truck the day of the bombing), but nothing as to where the bombs were assembled or when and where they were supposed to hit. As the Long Commission, the panel appointed by the Department of Defense to investigate the bombing, concluded: "Seldom did the U.S. have a mechanism at its disposal which would allow a follow-up on these leads and a further refinement of the information into intelligence which served for other than warning."[4]

Most of the raw intelligence ended up on Geraghty's desk as precisely that, *raw* intelligence. It was up to the Marines to evaluate the threats and put them in context. Marine intelligence officers in Beirut were ill equipped to properly evaluate the reams of unprocessed information. The Long Commission found that Marine counterintelligence personnel earned their trench coats after nothing more than a five day U.S. Air Force seminar. "This course provides an excellent overview of terrorism," the commission reported, "but does not qualify an individual to instruct others regarding terrorism, nor does it provide sufficient insight into the situation in Lebanon to prepare an individual for that environment."[5] As Shi'ite resentment toward the Marines had risen in pace with American involvement in the fighting, that lack of intelligence expertise had become crucial and, finally, fatal.

In their testimony before Pentagon and congressional investigators, Geraghty and a wide variety of other Marine Corps officers from the commandant on down repeatedly maintained that they never expected a *truck* bomb. All their preparations were aimed at stopping a *car* bomb because that was what the intelligence was predicting. The Marines were working on this assumption despite the fact that a pickup *truck* was used in the attack on the U.S. embassy. Antiterrorism experts from the European Command who investigated the embassy blast had even predicted that a more spectacular attack was still to come. U.S. military forces in Beirut, those investigators warned, constituted the "most defined and logical target." They told the Marines of their concerns, but the visitors had no mandate to recommend changes in the Marines' security, even though they answered to the same boss, Gen. Bernard Rogers, commander in chief of U.S. forces in Europe.[6]

While it can be argued that Geraghty and his aides should have been able to make the leap of imagination from a pickup truck bomb to a truck bomb, the MAU commander was denied one piece of valuable information that might have helped him reach the conclusion that cars were not the only threat he faced.

The bomb that leveled the BLT consisted of thousands of pounds of standard explosives packed around cylinders of propane gas and hexogen, a sophisticated explosive compound that multiples the force of a blast many times over. The gas-enhancement process had been employed in the April embassy bombing and in several other explosions in Beirut before that. The FBI report on the embassy blast outlined the technique and warned that it was relatively easy to employ. Oxygen, propane or various other gases could be used. In a city that was one big arms dump, where bottled gas was used extensively for cooking and heating, making a gas-enhancement bomb was a cinch. But Geraghty never saw the FBI report, nor was he briefed on the agency's finding. The CIA and the Department of State received copies, but the Pentagon, with 1,500 men in Beirut, did not.

According to the Long Commission, "If DOD elements had been provided the relevant data pertaining to the characteristics of the explosive device employed against the U.S. embassy in Beirut, the USMC Commander may have acquired a better appreciation of the catastrophic potentialities arrayed against him."[7]

The unseen terrorist threat was not uppermost in Geraghty's mind. Much more real were the shells falling out of the sky almost every day. Geraghty had been a marine for 24 years, including a 22-month tour in Vietnam. All his training had prepared him to fight a conventional war, and he was doing that now. He knew how to protect his men against artillery. That was why he billeted so many marines in the BLT, with its reinforced steel and concrete shell. Here they would be safe from just about any conventional weapon. As for the terrorist threat, Marine officers were relatively confident that the coils of barbed wire and the fence that separated the BLT from a nearby airport parking lot would stop a car or slow down a small truck long enough for the guards to load their weapons and shoot its driver.

Geraghty was never specifically told he could not dig tank ditches (simple trenches into which vehicles would fall), install tank traps (crossed sections of metal railway ties that looked like three-foot high versions of a child's jacks), or build dirt embankments. In his view, however, such fortifications would create "Fortress America" in direct conflict with his mission to "show the flag."

"The vulnerability was there and recognized by all of us," he told congressional investigators aboard the *Iwo Jima* just days after the bombing. "What I want[ed] [in terms of security] was not what I could get because of the mission, the presence mission, and by virtue of my location."[8]

Geraghty wanted the high ground, as any marine would, and he wanted to be someplace other than a busy international airport with workers, caterers and passengers wandering among his positions. But he recognized that this was a political mission that carried with it a whole new set of rules. According to his interpretation, he told congressional investigators, "It was a mission where we were not to build up any permanent-type structures ashore."[9]

"What I would have had to virtually [do], to preclude this kind of attack, is to have major concrete bunkers completely surrounding the perimeter with zigzag entrances and that is put[ting] up a barricade," he added, testifying before the full committee two months later in Washington. "You couldn't do it ... at the airport."

Concern that his men would look like an army of occupation also prevented Geraghty from setting up his own checkpoints on the roads approaching their positions (though cars *were* searched by Americans at the gates of the Marine compound itself), leaving the Marines dependent on the Lebanese Army to screen out potential vehicle bombs. But searching cars required work, and the Lebanese troops rarely did much more than wave as the cars went by. "They just don't check. That is part of the problem," Geraghty explained to the members of Congress, who didn't understand how a five-ton truck filled with explosives had managed to elude a Lebanese roadblock. "The Lebanese, they just do things differently."[10]

Even so, Geraghty ordered the sentries at the gate where the bomber entered to keep the ammunition clips out of their weapons. He worried that an overanxious marine might accidentally shoot a civilian in the parking lot since "the fields of fire were Beirut International Airport, and it was, again, not an ideal situation, but one we had to live with."[11]

Critics would later claim, with the benefit of hindsight, that Geraghty could have established tougher defenses without turning the Marine compound into Fortress America. But at the time, the colonel didn't see it that way and none of his superiors suggested that perhaps he was erring on the side of visibility. When the Marine Corps commandant, Gen. P.X. Kelly, visited Beirut, he did not, according to Geraghty, question the deployment of so many marines in the BLT or the security around the base. Nor did Secretary of the Navy John Lehman, Robert McFarlane (a former marine) or any of a host of diplomatic VIPs, Reagan administration representatives and military brass who passed through Beirut airport in the summer and autumn of 1983. The lack of criticism or guidance led Geraghty and his officers to the fatal conclusion that their "high-visibility" interpretation of the "presence" mission was the correct one.

When the Marines arrived in Lebanon, their orders said they were to have a non-combat role. The Lebanese Army was supposed to protect them. The rival militias had all, supposedly, given their blessing to the deployment of the Americans. But the September war saw the Marines locked in battle, fighting the Druze and Shi'ite militias. Instead of the Lebanese Army protecting the Marines, the battle for Souk al-Gharb saw the Americans protecting the Lebanese Army.

"By the end of September 1983, the situation in Lebanon had changed to the extent that not one of the initial conditions upon which the mission statement was premised was still valid," the Long Commission concluded. "The image of the USMNF [U.S. Multinational Force], in the eyes of the factional militias, had become pro-Israel, pro-Phalange and anti-Muslim."[12] Some of the government's enemies were determined to do everything they could to sever the U.S. pillar propping up Amin Gemayel. The suicide drivers took the most direct route.

Administration figures from the president on down repeatedly used the term "cowardly" to describe terrorists who blew themselves up with their victims. To the Shi'ites, it was just another act of war.

"Is it cowardly for me to set out on a mission to attack my enemies knowing that I will die?" asked Akram, an Amal militiaman, as we sat drinking sweet tea in a building facing the Marine positions. Sandbags blocked windows without glass. The Amal symbol was scratched in charcoal over the peeling paint on the dirty wall. "Are the Marines more brave fighting and trying not to die? Is it more brave to shoot bombs from the sea? We have no *New Jersey*," he said, referring to the U.S. battleship standing off the coast. "We do not have jet planes. We have many trucks, so we use them. What is the difference between dropping a bomb on a building from the sky and driving it from the street?"

Americans who knowingly sacrificed themselves in places like Pork Chop Hill and Iwo Jima were given medals. Shi'ites who accepted suicide missions were denounced as fanatics.

It had taken Sgt. Shefly Walkman five minutes to go from his barracks, 15 yards from the BLT, to the latrine, take an early-morning leak, and return. He knew that because as he walked back into the long, one-story building that housed some of the administrative offices, he glanced up at the clock. It read 6:20. He took a few more steps "and then BOOM, everything started crashing in on me."

The force of the explosion threw the marine to the floor. He was momentarily stunned. "My first thought was that we got hit by an artillery round because everything in front of me was blowing and the building was behind me." It didn't take him long to realize something far worse had struck.

"After the black, the building started crumbling in and everything. I got up and all I could hear was somebody yell 'help me.' So I went outside and started looking around and I saw a bunch of people running toward the BLT building, so I got in and started running with them and got down there and looked at the building, and said, 'Wow, a minute ago it was here and now it's gone.'" He shook his head, remembering back. "Oh man, after that I stood there a minute and looked around and said, 'Man, this is totally messed up.'"

There was an eerie stillness around the ruins of the building in those first moments after the blast, like a scene from a science fiction movie set in the aftermath of a nuclear war. Trees that were not uprooted had been shorn of their leaves and most of their bark. Pieces of uniforms were draped in the branches. Cement dust blanketed the ground like snow. "I walked almost up to the building. I didn't see nobody. I mean nobody was nowhere near me. I just stopped for a minute, then I turned around and I looked, I looked back there and all of a sudden bodies just, like, popped up. They were just there. I just had to look real good 'cause they blended in with the rubbish," the black sergeant said, shuddering at the memory.

"I walked over to one and grabbed it by the hand and turned it over, and I knew he was gone 'cause both of his eyes were gouged out." No artillery round could have caused all this, he told himself.

"At first, the only thing I thought about was, 'Let's get the wounded out,' because all the time all I was hearing was, 'Help, help, help, I'm hurt.' There was a couple under there, I could hear 'em hollerin' but I couldn't get to them. I just stood there, listening to them. I was saying, 'Are you all right?' and they just kept saying, 'Help, help, help.' Wow. I had to take that and wait for the bulldozers to come."

After several hours spent dragging the twisted and crushed remains of marines out of the rubble, Walkman was assigned to the team on the airport tarmac bagging bodies for shipment home. That's when he found some of the guys he used to play basketball with on other, more peaceful, Sunday afternoons outside the building that no longer existed.

"A couple of them, the bodies that they brung in, was the same people I was playing ball with." The big marine from Miami slumped over a little and looked away. "It was a real shock to me, 'cause when they opened one of the bags I looked at the dude and I was gonna ask him, I was gonna say, 'Yo, watchyou doin'?'

Then I thought, he be dead. The same dude that I played ball with, then I saw him laying there. I was gonna ask him what he was doing." Walkman looked down at the dirt he was sifting through his fingers. "Times sure changed real quick on us."

There was a bitter irony in the historical fact that it was a Christian holy war against Islam which had given birth to the violent jihad that would come to plague the West. That conflict had been waged on the very soil now soaked with the blood of U.S. marines.

To Americans struggling to comprehend this seemingly alien concept of martyrdom that now plagued them, St. Bernard of Clairvaux's exhortations to the Christian knights of the Second Crusade carried a chillingly familiar message:

> Rejoice, brave warrior, if you live and conquer in the Lord, but rejoice still more and give thanks if you die and go to join the Lord. This life can be fruitful and victory is glorious. Yet a holy death for righteousness is worth more. Blessed are they who die in the Lord. But how much more so are those who die for Him.[13]

For centuries after the Prophet Muhammed's conquest of Mecca, Muslims had interpreted the Qur'anic injunction to jihad (holy war) as a call for an internal spiritual struggle and an external struggle to create a true Islamic community.

It was not until Christendom's brutal and unprovoked war of conquest in the First Crusade (1096–1146) that jihad once more came to be viewed in a military context. In the first of what would be five major Crusades that dragged on for almost 100 years, Frankish knights carved a bloody path from Antioch down the coastline of the Levant, through what is now Syria, Lebanon and Israel, leaving a legacy of hatred and fear in their wake.

"These ironclad giants from the West looked like monsters to the Turks and Arabs, who had heard stories of their cannibalism," wrote historian Karen Armstrong in her study of the impact of the Crusades on modern politics. "The amirs and rulers of the cities granted them free passage and supplies, begging only that they might be spared."[14]

But not all would be spared. In 1099, the European Soldiers of Christ breached the walls of Jerusalem and slaughtered some 40,000 Muslims, as recounted by the jubilant Crusader Raymund of Aguiles:

> Wonderful sights were to be seen. Some of our men (and this was more merciful) cut off the heads of their enemies; others shot them with arrows, so that they fell from the towers; others tortured them longer by casting

them into the flames. Piles of heads, hands and feet were to be seen in the streets of the city ... in the Temple and porch of Solomon, men rode with blood up to their knees and bridle reins. Indeed it was a just and splendid judgment of God that this place should be filled with the blood of unbelievers since it had suffered for so long under their blasphemies.[15]

In fact, Christians and Jews had long lived under the protection of the Muslim rulers of Jerusalem, who accepted them as fellow People of the Book, a situation the Crusaders ignored.

The Jerusalem massacre and subsequent bloody campaigns by the Christian Crusaders ultimately led to the rise of a devout and learned young Muslim military leader who would become known as Nur ad-Din, Light of the Faith. This reluctant soldier called for a return to the fundamental principles of Islam, largely abandoned by the corrupt and feuding rulers of the Caliphate, and claimed that a defensive jihad against the invaders was the duty of all Muslims.

"It was, therefore, the Crusaders' brutal behavior in the Near East, not an atavistic love for violence inherent in Islam, which revived the practice of the jihad in the Middle Ages," Armstrong notes.[16]

Nur ad-Din was not waging war against Christianity per se, but rather against an army of invaders that happened to be Christian. This distinction was enshrined in the Qur'anic passage which had granted divine support for the Prophet Muhammed's jihad against the non-believers of Mecca: "If Allah did not repel aggression by means of those who fight against it, there would surely have been demolished cloisters and churches and synagogues and mosques, wherein the name of Allah is oft commemorated."[17]

These foreign armies had invaded and occupied numerous Turkish and Arab states. By 1109, along with Jerusalem, Haifa, Jaffa and Acre had all fallen under their swords. Tripoli, Beirut, Tyre and Sidon were also in Crusader hands, and the invaders had marched on Baghdad itself, home to the Caliph, but were driven back. Four separate Crusader states had been established in the heart of the Islamic lands. Nur ad-Din's campaign was a jihad of self-defense. The Qur'an, Nur ad-Din told his troops, made clear they had no choice but to fight: "Permission to fight is granted to those against whom war is made, because they have been wronged, Allah indeed has power to help them, to those who have been driven out of their homes unjustly only because they said, 'Our Lord is Allah.'"[18] Those words, which provided Nur ad-Din with religious sanction for his jihad against the Crusaders, would resonate through the centuries. They would be taken up by Nur ad-Din's successor, the famous Muslim general Saladin, who would ultimately crush the Crusader armies and drive them into the sea, forever enshrining himself in Islamic history.

Almost a thousand years later, as the Marines battled their unseen enemy in a city Saladin once wrested from Crusader control, his heroic specter remained enshrined in the Arab consciousness. It could be seen in Baghdad, where Iraqi leader Saddam Hussein, who, like the famous general, was born in the Kurdish town of Tikreet, styled himself as a modern-day Saladin. It could be seen on the West Bank, where a fundamentalist group calling itself the Saladin Brigades carried out attacks on Israeli troops and settlers. And, most ominously for the Marines, it could be seen in Damascus, where a huge mural of Saladin's decisive victory over the Crusaders hung on Hafiz al-Assad's office wall.

Saladin was gone, but his legacy remained. So, too, the memory of his glorious victory over the foreign invaders who had occupied Muslim lands. To many Muslims, the thousand-year-old battle continued.

The U.S. was resented in many parts of the world for what was termed Western imperialism. Modern Arab fundamentalists had another name for American Middle East policy: *"al-hurub al-salibiyya,"* the "Wars of the Cross," more simply translated as "the Crusade."

The Marines were numb in the immediate aftermath of the blast. Their emotions had been cauterized. The rush to rescue the wounded and dig out the dead left little time to contemplate the disaster. But in the following days, as the reality sunk in and the men realized that the buddy they had filled a thousand sandbags with was gone or the unit they used to belong to didn't exist anymore, in Col. Geraghty's words, "quiet fury" set in.

We heard a lot of talk of "strengthening resolve" from the officers and, indeed, the bombing had increased the determination of some marines to stick it out. "It's my job, sir," they'd tell us. But once you got beyond the stock phrases they had been brainwashed with since boot camp, the marines were individual human beings who reacted to the trauma of the bombing in a lot of different ways.

Some, like a young private from Kentucky named Irwin, felt he owed it to the dead marines to keep going. "You gotta learn that, hey, if your buddy falls, you just gotta keep going so the mission can get accomplished. If we just quit, or forget our discipline, forget who we are, marines, and just go crazy, the mission won't get accomplished and then they're dead without no purpose. So that's what we gotta do, we gotta keep our mission, keep our discipline, so then they had a reason for dying."

That discipline had been drilled into them from the day they had shed their civvies. Now it was paying off. "That's what Marine Corps discipline is all about," said Pvt. 1st Class Martin Julio. "You just have to bite your teeth, like biting on a bullet, just keep moving."

After months of being shot at while civilians in Washington said they weren't in combat, a lot of marines had a bitter taste in their mouths. "Maybe now they realize how serious it really is," Cpl. Randy Barefoot said.

Hit back. That was the gut instinct of every marine. To a man, they wanted to kick ass. The question was, kick whose ass? "We can't hit back 'cause we really don't know who done it," reasoned Cpl. Thomas O'Hara.

As the days after the bombing turned into weeks, the anger and hatred melted into frustration. They couldn't lash out, but they couldn't leave, either. The marines of the 24th MAU were getting fed up. Discipline wasn't the only quality the Marine Corps valued. The drill instructors at Parris Island and Quantico had also hammered in aggression until it was an instinct.

"Marines are supposed to go in and take land, and the army is supposed to come in and take [over]. But we're just sitting here being peacekeepers. From higher echelon, they won't let us do nothing else, so we just gotta sit around and take the punishment," complained Cpl. Thomas Fenning one day in early November when a few marines sat down to bitch out of earshot of their officers. "We were hurt real bad when the BLT blew up. What we're supposed to think about that? You know, they come in and blow up our BLT, over 200 some people are dead. All my really good friends, they're dead." He took off his helmet and wiped perspiration from the red indentation on his forehead left by the sweatband. "It's just like high school. One day you may skip school and somebody goes in there and they blow up the school. Now all of your friends are dead. How would you feel then? That's the way I look at it."

"You want to kick some ass?" I asked, already knowing the answer.

"If they let us, we would," he replied with a determined nod.

"I think we should either do something, get the job done, straighten the place out, if not leave," Pvt. 1st Class Robert Lockland agreed. "It would be better for us to go on the offensive than just sit around, 'cause they know exactly where we're at. Right now we're sitting ducks and they can do anything at any time."

"We've always been told, 'take the offensive.' Go on the offensive, do our job, fight for our country. Here we're just sitting here and dying. Lance Cpl. Robert Brady was talking now. Dappled light from the camouflage netting overhead shaded his face. "That's the way I feel. We're not doing nothing over here really, except for dying. Most of my friends are gone in the BLT. I think it's a bunch of nonsense here really. If we're gonna come over here and make peace, the only way you're gonna make peace over here is to go in there and knock out all these people. Either that or just pull us out if we're not gonna do anything."

Brady was committed to his role as peacekeeper; he just wanted to go about it a little differently. "I'd like to see peace. And the only way we're gonna achieve peace is going in there and taking some names, kicking some ass. That's it."

"Revenge, just revenge" was what New Yorker John Chipor longed for. "Walking through the foothills, just getting even. What they do is murder. Nowheres in the world is murder accepted. Why should it be accepted here?"

Outside of Geraghty's command hooch, a bunch of guys on a jeep were wishing for just about the same thing. Cpl. Ethel Goodwin thought it was time to "take a side here, because if they keep saying we don't have an enemy, I'd like to go home. 'Til I find the enemy, take me home, but if you ever find one, let me know, I'd be more than happy to come back 'cause I had a lot of friends down there [in the BLT], a lot of friends."

Like plenty of other marines, Goodwin wanted to get his hands on the man responsible for the bombing. "I'd take five minutes with him. It'd make me feel real good and if all my friends [were] looking down on me, I'm sure it would make them feel good."

Cpl. Mike Wildemouth was also champing at the bit to stomp on somebody. "We're sitting here, we've been sniped at, we've been shelled, the nastiest destruction we had down at the BLT, and all we do is sit here. I mean our hands are tied by higher authority. Everyone here has lost a friend, a lot of good friends, and our colonel is doing as best as he can, but his hands are tied. The fact is we can do nothing. We can sit here and hold onto our guns and hope someday we'll find an enemy, since we ain't got one now."

If some of the Marines weren't sure what they were doing in Lebanon, Ronald Reagan had no doubts. With the scroll of a TelePrompTer, the United States suddenly had "vital interests" in Lebanon.

"Lebanon is central to our credibility on a global scale," he said at a news conference the day after the bombing. "We cannot pick and choose where we will support freedom, we can only determine how. ... If Lebanon ends up under the tyranny of forces hostile to the West, not only will our strategic position in the eastern Mediterranean be threatened, but also the stability of the entire Middle East, including the vast resource areas of the Arabian Peninsula." The dominoes were on the march.

Experts pointed out that foreign armies had been marching across Lebanon for centuries and it had not made a bit of difference to the United States. "We have a history of presidential declarations that we have 'vital interests' here and there, and the phrase is used much too loosely," argued Richard Parker, who had served as U.S. ambassador to Lebanon in 1977–78. "Lebanon doesn't have any intrinsic strategic importance to us."[19]

Dean Brown, president of the Middle East Institute, agreed. "Strategically, you have to ask yourself, is it of importance? The answer is, 'Only by way of denying it to someone else,' because it does sit there on the eastern Mediterranean. The Americans have never had any military facilities of any kind there, nor has anyone else," said Brown, who had formerly filled a number of diplomatic posts in the area, including a stint as President Gerald Ford's special envoy to Lebanon in 1976.

Middle East expert William Quandt, a National Security Council staff member under Jimmy Carter, shared that view: "Your main interest was to keep it from becoming a flashpoint."

The Reagan administration seemed to be doing exactly the opposite. The United States would not be intimidated by terrorists, Reagan vowed. America would strike back once "the perpetrators are identified." Two days later, the United States invaded Grenada. That night in Beirut, cynics in the press corps sat around the Commodore bar wondering how many Shi'ite truck bombers U.S. troops would find on the Caribbean island.

While he flexed his muscles, Reagan also held firm to his perpetual optimism. According to the *Washington Post*, in a private meeting on the eve of the Grenada invasion, he attempted to reassure congressional leaders worried about the disintegrating situation in Beirut. The president reminded them of the warm send-off Filipinos had given U.S. troops at the end of World War II. "People were lining the streets, waving American flags, and thanking the Americans for liberating them," one participant in the meeting quoted Reagan as saying. "Sooner than you think, in a few weeks perhaps, this situation can be repeated in Lebanon, with our troops leaving and the people rejoicing."[20]

With the Grenada operation (using marines who had been on their way to Beirut), Reagan released the safety value on the frustration that had been building up in Middle America. Patriots waved the flag and hoisted beer in barroom celebrations across the country. We had finally shown "them" that they can't mess with the U.S. But amid the euphoria of Grenada, some voices still asked why Americans were dying 5,000 miles from home in Lebanon to back one faction against another in a centuries-old cycle of mindless violence. President Reagan had an answer: "We're not somewhere else in the world protecting someone else's interests. We're there protecting our own. The area is key to the economic and political life of the West," he advised his countrymen in a national television broadcast on October 27. "If that key should fall into the hands of a power or powers hostile to the Free World, there would be a direct threat to the United States and to our allies."

The fate of the Free World, then, was resting on the stooped shoulders of a bunch of petty warlords who sat down behind green baize-covered tables at the Intercontinental Hotel in Geneva at the end of October and shouted at each other for a few days. They had caused the Lebanese mess in the first place. On their hands was the blood of the better part of 100,000 dead, and they kept on battling with other people's lives well past the time they would have had to retire in any other profession. Now they were supposed to try to sort it all out at a National Reconciliation Conference. Leaving out President Gemayel, newcomer Nabih Berri and Walid Jumblatt – whose father would have been there if he had not been assassinated years before – the average age of the participants was 78. Jumblatt called them "ossified relics."

Suleiman Franjieh, a wiry little men who as president had presided over the beginning of the civil war, glared across at Phalangist patriarch Pierre Gemayel, whom he blamed for murdering his son. Next to him was Rashid Karami. As prime minister under Franjieh, he had refused to order the army into action to stop the Christian–Muslim confrontation at the beginning of the conflict in 1975. Another former president, Camille Chamoun, who had laid the groundwork for civil war in the late 1950s by blocking Muslim political gains with the help of 14,000 U.S. marines, blinked myopically through Coke-bottle glasses, while former Parliament Speaker Adel Osseiran, a member of one of the old establishment Shi'ite families regarded as sellouts by most of the people in the slums, tried to control the trembling of an advanced case of Parkinson's Disease.

At the opposite table sat the man who represented the new wave of Shi'ite political power, Nabih Berri. President Gemayel, ever anxious to avoid concessions, had tried to exclude him from the conference. Yet another former prime minister, Saeb Salam, was the only one smiling. His influence had been on the decline of late and he was happy just to be back in the thick of things.

On the third side of the square, President Gemayel was alone at a table. That was fitting. Nobody in the room much liked Amin, except maybe his father, and even he seemed to be having doubts. Amin faced the Saudi and Syrian observers, living reminders of where the real power in Lebanon lay, who sat at a table that completed the fourth side of the square.

The participants had been dragged kicking and screaming to the negotiations because Saudi Arabia had so ordained and because Syria smelled concessions in the wind. Even Lebanese warlords had to take orders sometimes. ("Are you threatening us?" Chamoun challenged Syrian Foreign Minister Abdel Halim Khaddam at one point during the meeting. "I am threatening Israel and anyone who collaborates with it," Khaddam had replied icily.)

So they handed in their guns downstairs (Franjieh moodily refused to submit to a search after he set off the metal detector), left their bodyguards outside, and spent five days talking instead of shooting. In the end, they agreed that Lebanon was an "Arab" country, that Israel should withdraw and that political reforms should be explored. Then they adjourned to go back to Lebanon to continue killing one another. They were supposed to meet again in two weeks. It took four months and another war before the talks reconvened.

The fighting might have slowed a little during the conference, but the actors wasted no time resuming their roles once it was over. Even before the participants in Geneva signed the final document, one group that wasn't invited to the talks, Islamic Jihad, was at work once again. Another suicide bomber in another van packed with explosives rammed the gates of the Israeli security headquarters in the southern Lebanese town of Tyre, leveling the building and killing some 40 people, including at least ten Lebanese and Palestinian prisoners being held in the basement. Israeli jets were soon pounding Palestinian positions in the mountains. The Jerusalem government was determined to strike back against "terrorists." It apparently didn't care which terrorists it hit.

Twelve days later, the Israelis bombed bases bear Baalbek, where Shi'ite militiamen were being trained by Iranian Revolutionary Guards. The following day, as dozens of fighters who had died in the Israeli raid were being buried, more than a dozen French Super Etendard jets from the aircraft carrier *Clemenceau* swooped in to attack another training base, the Sheikh Abdullah barracks, in retaliation for the October 23 bomb. The United States praised the raid and warned that it, too, might soon have to strike. Defense Secretary Casper Weinberger charged that "circumstantial evidence" pointed to Iranian involvement, with the "sponsorship, knowledge, and authority of the Syrian government." Western intelligence officials were convinced that the October bombings, and the April attack on the U.S. embassy, had been organized in Baalbek.

The raids brought temporary gratification at the price of long-term pain. At the funerals of those killed in the air raids, Shi'ite clerics made fiery speeches demanding jihad against the West. "They have waged open war on us, and war they will get," promised Sheikh Subhi Tofeili, the leader of the pro-Iranian Hizbullah party in the Bekaa. Other militiamen who were still living, he said, had already undergone their funeral rites and were prepared to meet Allah. "America, France, and Israel started this war. Our fighters, who wear their death shrouds, shall go after them in Lebanon and elsewhere."

The seeds of hate Iran had planted the previous summer had grown tall on a diet of Western mistakes. Increasing numbers of Lebanese Shi'ites were clamoring to give their lives to punish the West, confident that Allah would reward their sacrifice.

The concept of martyrdom, giving one's life for Allah, was common to all Muslim sects. The Qur'an taught that the paradise awaiting fighters slain in jihad was far more glorious than the present: "And those who are slain in the way of Allah, He rendereth not their actions vain. He will guide them and improve their state, And bring them into the Garden which He hath made known to them."[21]

While acknowledged by Sunni Muslims, the themes of martyrdom and suffering dominated the Shi'ite religion. The deep-rooted quest for martyrdom could be traced back to AD 680, when Husain, grandson of the Prophet Muhammed (and, according to Shia belief, his religious inheritor), was massacred along with his family and followers at Kerbala in present-day Iraq. The battle against the vastly larger forces of the Umayyad Caliph (the inheritor recognized by what is now the more numerous Sunni branch of Islam) was essentially a suicide mission "intended to show up the brutal and sinful character of Umayyad rule and thus inspire a spiritual and moral revival."[22] Shi'ites each year commemorate Husain's martyrdom with the feast of Ashura, to Western eyes a bloody and brutal event during which some participants ritually beat themselves with whips and chains.

In Lebanon, the beginning of the end for Israel would come during Ashura in 1984, when hundreds of Shi'ites marched through the South Lebanese market town of Nabatiyeh literally whipping themselves into a frenzy, then attacked an Israeli patrol and set a jeep on fire.

Among the crowd was a father, whose back was covered with bloody self-inflicted welts, carrying a young son of perhaps five years old. Caught up in the throes of devotion, the father used a razor to cut small incisions in the son's scalp, then slashed his own head, smiling madly as the blood ran down over his face. Other men ran through the streets waving bloody T-shirts and frantically rubbing their wounds to make the blood flow more quickly.

To devout Shi'ites, self-inflicted mutilation was a badge of honor, a symbol of belief. The more blood they shed, the more they loved Allah. Most Westerners view death as the loss of something precious. To Shi'ites brought up in poverty and misery, dying opened the door to a better world.

Picture yourself as a 20-year-old man living in a squalid refugee camp, sharing a flimsy cinder block shelter with a dozen brothers and sisters, your father and your grandfather. Your mother and baby sister were killed in an Israeli bombing raid several years back and another brother was shot by the Christians. Your family has existed on handouts and odd jobs since it left South Lebanon, fleeing Israeli attacks and PLO thugs who bothered the girls and made you dig bunkers without pay. Now the Americans, who give the Israelis their bombs, have come to Beirut and are killing Muslims and helping the Christians. There are men who say you must obey the Qur'an and destroy the unbelievers. They offer you much money to fight and, if you are martyred, they will support your family. To die for Allah is to escape from the misery, strike a blow against those who created that misery and ensure a better life for the family you leave behind.

It was the same mentality that stirred Iranians to volunteer in droves for the privilege of inviting certain death by running across Iraqi mine fields. So he could be sure of his ultimate destination, each *basiiji* (volunteer) was given an inscribed metal disk that the mullahs told him was his "key to Paradise." During a visit to a POW camp outside Basra during the Iran–Iraq War, I had once asked a young Iranian *basiiji*, who was perhaps eleven years old, if he still had his key to Paradise. With a glance toward the Iraqi guards a few yards away, he reluctantly nodded.

"Could I see it?" I asked, through a translator. The boy reached into the waist of his POW uniform and brought out a metal disk. The inscription contained a set of numbers. The key to Paradise was nothing more than what Americans knew as a dog tag.

Husain's spiritual and moral revival had succeeded in spades, but it had also spawned a cult of martyrdom. Graves in the main Tehran cemetery in the late 1970s were decorated with pictures of the young men and women who had sacrificed themselves before the Shah's guns. Beirut in the 1980s was plastered with posters showing photographs of fighters who had died in battle or suicide missions. (This was not unique to the Shia. The PLO had done the same thing.) Later, when car bomb attacks on the Israelis in South Lebanon became almost a daily event, the suicide drivers began videotaping farewell messages that were broadcast on Lebanese television. (The Shi'ite successes inspired Sunni Muslims and members of other Lebanese nationalist groups to adopt the tactic.)

One such message came from "The Bride of the South," 19-year-old Sana'a al-Muhaidli. Her gentle face was seen on television screens across the Arab world after she rammed an explosives-packed car into an Israeli military convoy on the road to Jezzine, killing herself and at least two Israeli soldiers.

"Oh, Mother! How happy I will be when my flesh leaves my bones, and when my blood surges into the soil of the South while I am exterminating those Zionist enemies," Sana'a proclaimed joyfully in the message televised after her death. "Do not be angry with me because I left home without telling you. ... I have not left to get married or to live with anyone. I have gone to meet the courageous, honorable and happy martyrdom. My last will is to be called The Bride of the South." To celebrate her "wedding," Sana'a's family dutifully wore white to the funeral and distributed candy in celebration.

There was an historic role model for the young men and women who drove the car bombs. We know these raiders as the Assassins.[23] Formally known as the Nizaris, members of this eleventh-century Shia breakaway sect operated from mountain strongholds in Persia and Syria, sending suicide raiders who had been promised a place in Paradise to murder their enemies. Bernard Lewis, author of a book about the sect, described its members this way:

> For their victims, the assassins were criminal fanatics, engaged in a murderous conspiracy against religion and society. For the Ismailis, they were a corps d'elite in the war against the enemies of the Imams; by striking down oppressors and usurpers, they gave the ultimate proof of their faith and loyalty, and earned immediate and eternal bliss.[24]

Headed by the "Old Man of the Mountain," Hasan-i Sabah, members of the sect saw themselves as priests carrying out a holy mission. At Hasan's fortress of Alamut in northern Persia, according to a legend first related in the West by Marco Polo, there was a huge, lush garden "running with conduits of wine and milk and honey and water, and full of lovely women for the delectation of all its inmates." Potential Assassins, according to this tale, were drugged and placed in the garden, where they awoke thinking they were in Paradise. When their services were needed, they were drugged again and brought before Hasan, who told them they would return to Paradise only when their mission was accomplished, whether they lived or died.

Lewis describes Hasan's methods like this: "Others before him had vented their frustration in unplanned violence, hopeless insurrection, or in sullen passivity. Hasan found a new way, by which a small force, disciplined and devoted, could strike effectively against an overwhelmingly superior enemy. ... This was the method that Hasan chose – the method, it may well be, that he invented."[25]

The word used to describe the organization of the sect was *al-Da'wa* (the Call). Eight centuries later, al-Da'wa resurfaced as one of the organizations behind Islamic Jihad.

Manzariyeh Garden was the twentieth-century equivalent of Alamut. In this sprawling park in the hilly northern suburbs of Tehran, militants from across the Islamic world were being trained to form a permanent unit of *shaheen* (martyrs) ready to die on command. Many were Lebanese; others came from Saudi Arabia, Kuwait, Bahrain and even as far away as Morocco.[26]

In daily religious classes, leading clergymen sought to inspire the recruits through a carefully crafted appeal to Islamic duty and the close familial ties of Arab and Persian culture. Not only was a place in Paradise awaiting each martyr, the mullah said, but by leaving this unimportant world now, the young men could reserve a room in Paradise for the parents they loved.

The clerics used verses by Persian poet philosophers to describe the futility of the West's attempt to resist the spread of Islam:

The bird is flying over the earth,
The foolish man is trying to hunt the bird's shadow
And he runs and runs
Without knowing that the bird is flying over his head,
And without knowing where the bird is going.[27]

Once the world was cleansed of the corrupters of the earth, the young militants at Manzariyeh and other camps scattered around Iran were told, the Shi'ite Messiah, the missing Twelfth Imam, could return and Paradise would exist on earth as well as in heaven. Each martyr would then be appointed "commander of the earth," the title inscribed on the red headbands many of them wore.

Practical lessons were also taught at Manzariyeh Garden, such as how to rig a car bomb and how to blow up a building. In the days of the Shah, when Manzariyeh was the site of national and international Boy Scout jamborees, scouts earned their merit badges swimming in the park's large pool. Now, would-be suicide bombers trained there for waterborne assaults.

No longer would a cleric in Beirut or Tyre have to waste days or weeks inspiring one of his followers to give his life in an amateur attack. A trained corps of martyrs was now ready to strike. Martyrdom had become part of the establishment. As one Iranian exile who monitored events in his country put it, "You get a job, you join the army, or you become a martyr."

Iran readily accepted volunteers from around the world, but Lebanon held a special place in Tehran's plans. With nearly a million Shi'ites, Iranian-trained clergy already in place and almost permanent turmoil, Lebanon was fertile soil for the first Islamic revolution inspired by the ayatollah's success against the American-backed Shah. There, too, was a readily accessible battleground with willing recruits for the war against the ultimate enemy of the revolution.

The Prophet's grandson Husain had set the religious precedent for martyrdom, the Qur'an contained Allah's sanction, the Assassins had provided the tactics and the Iranian Revolution supplied the modern inspiration and support. An Islamic Republic had been created and the "Great Satan" had been brought to its knees. What had been achieved in Iran could be achieved again.

It was never easy to reconcile the chants of "Death to America" with the friendly reception that usually greeted me when I told militiamen that I was an American. The Imam al-Mahdi mosque in the slums near the airport was a stronghold of the most extreme Shi'ite faction, Hizbullah (The Party of God). That's where the gunmen brought Iranian Chargé d'Affairs Mohammed Nourani the day the Lebanese government had summoned him to announce that Lebanon was breaking diplomatic relations with Iran due to the presence of Revolutionary Guards in Baalbek. (Left unsaid was U.S. pressure on Gemayel to take the step because of Iran's apparent role in the bombings.) But Iran's Hizbullah supporters in Beirut refused to let Nourani go. To show their support for Iran, they had sent gunmen to escort the Iranian diplomat to the mosque and began a sit-in protesting the government's move.

When I arrived with our Lebanese camera crew, Nourani sat stoically on the floor at the front of the room, flanked by bearded mullahs. Bareheaded and wearing a Western-style business suit without a tie, the diplomat looked incongruous tucked between the gray-bearded mullahs clad in flowing robes.

The crowd, mostly fighting-age men, was enraptured by the rantings of an elderly sheikh who sat cross-legged at a microphone near Nourani, fulminating about U.S. imperialism and Washington's puppet Amin Gemayel. Occasionally, the tirade would be interrupted by a chant of "Allah Akhbar (God is Great)" from the crowd assembled on the dirty carpets. Militiamen with AKs flanked the clerics up front and stood guard at the back of the room. One of them handed me a statement, translated into grammar-school English and photocopied on a cheap machine, denouncing the cutoff of relations with Iran and complaining that, among other things, "the Lebanese regime has given all his [sic] political cards to the big devil and the enemy of all Muslims, the U.S.A."

Pictures of Ayatollah Khomeini and the Imam Musa Sadr hung behind the speaker. Posters depicting exploding car bombs and fighters with AK-47s treading on blood-covered American flags decorated the gray cement walls. There was a pile of shoes outside the door and an overwhelming odor of sweaty feet inside.

I tagged along behind the crew, trying to make myself small and inconspicuous, as they wound their way toward the front of the mosque, stepping over and between the young men seated on the floor. Muslim worshippers were usually tolerant of camera crews taking pictures in their mosques, but this was the stronghold of the extremists. The theme this day seemed to be "death to the imperialist unbelievers," and I, quite obviously, was an imperialist unbeliever.

About halfway to the front, I felt a tap on my shoulder. It was one of the gunmen who had been eyeing us since we came in. He and Hassan, our sound technician, had a short conversation in Arabic.

"He is asking if you would mind staying in the back of the room," Hassan translated. "Since you are not Muslim, you are not supposed to go near the front. But he says it is all right for you to stay in the back. He hopes you don't mind."

The gunman said something else and looked toward me expectantly. "He says he hopes you are not offended. It is the custom. He says he is sorry," Hassan explained.

Here I was, an American among the craziest of the crazies, the people who were running around driving car bombs into buildings, who had just essentially kidnapped the top diplomat of the country that gave them their guns to show him how much they liked him, and they were worried that they might have offended me by asking me not to wander around their mosque. I assured him that I understood and slipped quietly to the back. As I stood there near the shoe racks, the same gunman joined me and started to apologize again in broken English.

"*Ahlan wahsalan* (Welcome)", he said, taking my hand. "No problem Americans. You good man. Americans good." Funny, that wasn't what the mullah up front was saying. "Reagan bad. Marines bad. You good."

Another fighter walked over cradling an AK. He was about 15. "You America?" he asked. I reluctantly let on that I was. "Brother my father America. Take-sas. Ka-boo-wee." He jumped up and down, giving a bad imitation of his cowboy uncle in Texas riding a horse.

No matter where you went in Lebanon, everybody seemed to have ties to the U.S. Amal leader Nabih Berri had a Green Card (U.S. permanent residency). His former wife lived in Detroit. (He had divorced her largely to placate the radicals.) His security chief carried a U.S. passport. One of Amal's military commanders had gone to college in Chicago. Despite those links, Berri and his men were being drawn into battle with the Marines largely through the successful efforts of Iranian-backed extremists, like these fighters of Hizbullah, who set out to provoke clashes. The clashes created bitterness and the bitterness prompted more clashes.

"Me go America someday, maybe," the fighter with the relative in Texas told me. (I could see him filling out the visa form. Occupation: Islamic militant.) But that wouldn't stop him from slaughtering imperialist Americans in the meantime.

"Why is he here?" I asked, motioning to the Iranian diplomat.

"Iran good. We like. No want him go," the candidate for U.S. citizenship explained.

"What happens if he tries to leave?"

His face lit up with a big smile: "We kill."

That was how they dealt with their friends. We were the enemy.

11
Spillover

Kill a man, one is a murderer;
Kill a million, a conqueror;
Kill them all, a God.
—Jean Rostand[1]

"Ultimate protection from a determined suicide attack is impossible." The words had a familiar ring, but U.S. Chargé d'Affaires Philip Griffin was not talking about the Marine bombing, the attack on the French barracks, or even the April blast at the U.S. embassy in Beirut. He was referring to the destruction of his own U.S. embassy in Kuwait. The date: December 12, 1983.

One side of the three-story administration building had crumbled. It looked like the face of a cliff after a rock slide. The suicide bomber had raced 50 yards down the residential street in front of the embassy past the Kuwaiti guards manning a machine gun, smashed through the sheet-metal gates (one headlight was still embedded there), and veered left toward the imposing administration building without a single shot having been fired.

Four people (plus the driver) were dead and 20 were wounded, but a streak of good fortune prevented the disaster from being far worse. As in Beirut, the explosives were packed around gas cylinders, but most of them failed to blow up. The bomber drove right past the long, low building that housed the ambassador's office, political section and consular department, where dozens of people were lined up waiting for visas; and the administration building stood for about 90 minutes after the blast, allowing those inside to evacuate before it collapsed. None of the dead was American.

Luck had saved the United States; security expertise had had nothing to do with it. There had been plans to move and reinforce the gate, but eight months after the Beirut embassy bombing and seven weeks after the Marine blast, the plans still had not been implemented. Embassy officials blamed their inaction on budget cuts by Washington and delays by the Kuwaitis.

It may indeed be impossible to achieve "ultimate protection from a determined suicide attack," but you can try. A year later, the compound

188

would be ringed by cement "dragon's teeth" barricades, the walls would be raised and reinforced and the gate would be moved and strengthened. It might still have been possible for a suicide bomber to inflict serious damage, but he would have had to work a lot harder.

Within 90 minutes of the attack on the U.S. embassy, five other bombs exploded across Kuwait that December day and a sixth was discovered and defused. The targets included the French embassy, a housing compound for American employees of the U.S. defense contractor Raytheon, the airport, a natural gas refinery and a power station. Those blasts also could have been worse, but they were all booby-trapped cars and trucks not manned by suicide drivers, so none of them exploded closer to their targets than the parking lot or outer wall. In Beirut, an anonymous voice claimed responsibility for the attacks in the name of Islamic Jihad.

When investigators sifted the debris around the U.S. embassy, about all they found of the suicide driver was a charred skull and a finger, but it was enough for the forensics experts to trace the fingerprints and identify him as Raad Aqueel al-Badran, an Iraqi wanted by his government for a series of bomb blasts against police stations. Badran, who was traveling on an Iranian passport, was a member of al-Da'wa, an Iranian-backed Iraqi underground Islamic group fighting to overthrow Iraq's secular president, Saddam Hussein. But al-Da'wa's tentacles reached beyond Iraq and Kuwait. One name mentioned in connection with al-Da'wa's Lebanon branch was that of Muhammed Hussein Fadlallah, the Iraqi-born Lebanese Shi'ite cleric regarded as the spiritual guide of Hizbullah. Eight hundred years after al-Da'wa of the Assassins, the same name and same tactics were still being used.

As the Kuwaitis tightened the noose on Badran's collaborators, they uncovered more evidence linking the conspirators to Iran and Lebanon. In a string of raids, the Kuwaitis uncovered explosives, detonators and weapons that suspects allegedly confessed had been hidden in empty gas canisters and smuggled into Kuwait from Iran on fishing boats. Scores of Shi'ites were rounded up and questioned; hundreds were deported. Of the 17 people eventually tried and convicted for the bombings (four others were sentenced in absentia), 14 were Iraqis and three were from Lebanon. The fate of this group would become inexorably intertwined with the fate of the Americans in Beirut.

Their leader carried papers identifying him as a Lebanese Christian, Elias Fouad Saab. His real name was Mustafa Yousef. He and one of the other terrorists sentenced to death were cousins of Hussein Musawi, the Baalbek-based Islamic Amal leader suspected of involvement in the Beirut bombings. Musawi was also believe to have been involved in the 1982 kidnapping of

David Dodge, then acting president of the American University of Beirut. Dodge, who had been held for a year, had eventually ended up in Iran before being flown to Damascus and released after the intervention of Rifaat Assad, the Syrian president's brother.

America's troubles in Lebanon were beginning to boil over and it looked like Iran had turned up the heat.

"This is the last warning for the American and French forces," the caller to the French news agency AFP snapped in Arabic. "We shall give them ten days to leave Lebanon; otherwise we shall make the earth shake underneath their feet."

The announcement followed an attack on December 21, in which another truck loaded with explosives had been driven into yet another French position in West Beirut. Dirt barricades had deflected the blast, which collapsed two apartment buildings across the street. Eight Lebanese civilians were crushed to death and a French sentry was killed. Christian snipers across the Green Line accounted for a tenth casualty, a Lebanese rescue worker who had come to help dig out survivors.

At the same time, a time bomb went off at Mr. Pickwick's, an imitation British pub where U.S. Marine guards from the embassy liked to hang out. The Americans who had been drinking at the bar escaped unhurt, but four more Lebanese died, bringing the night's tally to 14 dead and more than 40 injured.

In the previous few weeks, two U.S. planes had been shot down during raids against Syrian antiaircraft batteries that had been firing on U.S. reconnaissance flights. One pilot, Lt. Mark Lange, was killed and another, Lt. Robert Goodman, Jr., ended up a captive of the Syrians. (He would be freed on January 3, 1984, when Rev. Jesse Jackson visited Damascus.) The Israelis, who had just concluded a new "strategic partnership" with the U.S. (even as the Reagan administration was trying to convince Muslims it was being even-handed), had continued their raids on Iranian and Shi'ite camps in the Bekaa; the battleship *New Jersey* had been hurtling Volkswagen-size shells at Druze concentrations in the mountains; other U.S. ships were regularly pounding positions behind Syrian lines; and the new Marine unit, which had replaced Geraghty's 24th MAU in mid-November, had quickly become bogged down in the same violence as its predecessor. Two weeks after the 22nd MAU landed, eight marines had been killed and two more wounded by a single shell that crashed into their bunker. Despite plenty of talk about cease-fires, an awful lot of guns were blazing.

In Washington, dirt-filled dump trucks and cement barricades appeared around the White House and other government buildings as President

Reagan warned that "up to 1,000" more suicide bombers were being trained in Lebanon. Nervous members of Congress talked of the terrorist war spreading "to our shores." The director of the FBI did nothing to dispel those fears. "This suicide-mission concept, which has now been expanded in a key way, presumably could just as easily take place in the U.S.," William Webster said.

And as if things weren't rumbling enough already, Islamic Jihad was now promising to "make the earth shake." It was not shaping up to be a very merry Christmas.

Somewhere in one of the textbooks I read at journalism school it said that reporters were supposed to stand back and observe stories as disinterested third parties. Around Christmas, it dawned on some of us that we might, in fact, have a vested interest in this particular story. The embassy compound had been turned into a fortified armed camp, the Marines had burrowed underground, and guess who now constituted the next largest – and oh, so accessible – group of Americans in Beirut?

The press corps had thinned out a little for Christmas, but the Commodore Hotel was still turning them away at the door. Every American newspaper that could afford the price of a plane ticket had at least one reporter in town. In the old days, we took pride in the fact that the Commodore was the Anglo-American hangout (most of the French and German reporters stayed in another hotel down the street). Now we would have happily chipped in to pay for the honor of housing a few scribes from Iran's Islamic Republic News Agency.

Talk at the bar began to center on the subtleties of the latest message from Islamic Jihad. Two or three translations were circulating. Of particular interest to us was the first line. Had the caller warned "the American and French forces" or "the Americans and French"? We opted to believe the former. It wouldn't make sense for the terrorists to drive us out. They needed us to report on their exploits. Didn't they?

The Commodore's silky manager, Fouad Saleh, laughed off all the concern. Whenever a worried reporter at the bar raised the possibility that his hotel might get blown to kingdom come, Fouad bought another round of drinks and tried to change the subject. Besides, he'd say with a sweeping gesture, with all the Shi'ites working in the Commodore, Islamic Jihad would never blow the place up – a rather weak argument when referring to people who took one-way trips in explosives-packed vehicles. When I took him aside to see what he really thought, Fouad said he had quietly laid on extra guards who were letting only people they knew park cars next to the building.

Some of us thought seriously of switching hotels, but each had its own disadvantages. Like reporters for the last nine years, we decided the Commodore remained the least of all evils. Our concern was probably exaggerated anyway, we told each other.

My Lebanese friends thought I was crazy. They refused to set foot in the place and didn't even like to drive past it. Lying in bed at night, I could feel the fatalism of the Lebanese taking hold. Logic told me Islamic Jihad needed us around to tell the world about their actions, my gut said the hotel was an awfully tempting target. But there was nothing I could do about it short of leaving, and I couldn't very well do that. As long as the Marines were in Lebanon, CBS had to be there. And since I was the Middle East correspondent, that meant I had to be there. I knew that other reporters who were veterans of Beirut shared my concerns, but we were prisoners of the story.

Christmas 1983 was a grim time in West Beirut. An 8:00 p.m. curfew was in force. Electricity was rationed. When we ventured out to dinner, it was just the gunmen and us on the streets. You could still get an excellent meal on white linen at places such as Quo Vadis or sip hot sake at the Tokyo while Mama-san, the jovial Japanese woman who ran the place, dished out fresh sushi and sashimi, but your dining companions were likely to be other reporters with maybe the odd Norwegian diplomat thrown in. The Lebanese stayed safely at home. The arrangement had its advantages: you never had to wait for a table, service was great and you certainly got to know the management. But Beirut was a little short on Christmas cheer. With Muslim fundamentalists running around blowing up bars and breaking into apartments where there was loud music, most get-togethers were canceled. Few residents were willing to risk having more than one or two couples over for a quiet dinner.

The Commodore decided to hold a huge party on New Year's Eve, the night Islamic Jihad's deadline for the Americans and French to leave expired. Lights were strung, a band was hired and a feast was prepared. A couple of hundred drunken Americans, with a handful of other foreigners sprinkled in, were going to dance the night away to blaring Western music. Everybody in town was talking about it, most of them wondering how big the explosion would be. I opted for a quiet evening at a friend's house. I was getting fatalistic, but I wasn't yet suicidal.

Americans were worried that there was danger when too many of them gathered in one place. They soon learned that individual Americans were also at risk.

Malcolm Kerr had dedicated his life to the Middle East. Throughout the region, the 52-year-old educator was known as a friend of the Arabs, an American who cared. Friends say that when he was offered the presidency of AUB in the spring of 1982, Kerr jumped at the chance. Even after Acting AUB President David Dodge was kidnapped that summer, Kerr didn't hesitate to leave the safety of his post at the American University in Cairo (AUC) for the uncertainty of Beirut.

In the middle of January 1984, Kerr was assassinated with a silencer-equipped pistol in the hallway outside his office. The anonymous voice of Islamic Jihad again claimed credit. It didn't matter that Kerr was a friend of the Arabs. He was "the victim of the American presence in Lebanon," the called said. The voice also ended our Christmas time debate about whether U.S. and French servicemen were the only targets.

"We promise you that not one American or Frenchman will remain in this country. We will take no different course and shall not waver," the caller vowed. Islamic Jihad was beginning to develop a certain degree of credibility.

We held the day ...
They ruled the night,
And the night seemed to last as long as
Six weeks on Parris Island. ...

The words of the Billy Joel song about U.S. Marines in Vietnam ran through my head as we crouched in the darkness watching the light show. Exploding shells and smoke lit the battlefield like special effects at a rock concert. The airport was one huge stage as the Marines fought their unseen enemies. Strobe-like flashes illuminated the scene in cameos that lasted milliseconds. Swarms of tracers raced back and forth, resembling meteor showers unable to decide where to land. On the far side of the airport, flames licked toward the black sky. Every few minutes, whole sections of the tableau were illuminated by starbursts, shells that parachuted to earth like lazy falling stars, stripping the cover of darkness from would-be infiltrators trying to probe the Marine lines.

Domingo Rex, a Mexican cameraman, and Azziz Akyvakas, his Turkish partner, were busy trying to record some of the battle when we found ourselves at the center of attention. An illumination round had burst right above us and was slowly settling to earth. Since the unfinished building on which we were perched between the airport and the sea had no roof or walls, we were standing out there like the main attractions at a turkey shoot. The marines had obviously seen us with their night vision scopes and wanted to take a better look. I just hoped they could tell a camera from a rocket launcher. I told Domingo to turn the camera sideways on the tripod to show its profile, then I shouted as loud as I could, "CBS! TV! Americans!"

We had done a lot of dumb things in Lebanon, but this ranked right up there with the best of them. It was another example of being trapped by the story. The Marines were under what appeared to be a massive attack on this evening in mid-January, 1984. We were there because the other networks had their crews hidden in similar buildings all around the airport. They were there because we were there. As we had left the hotel together, we all knew the danger of being mistaken for a militiaman by the Marines, but we also knew we couldn't ignore such a battle.

The starburst settled into the sea behind us. We stood still, giving the Marines time to send up another. We didn't want to look as if we were trying to slip away in the darkness. With the second shell, a voice called out something from the Marine positions. They were about 300 yards away, across the road, and we couldn't make out what they were saying. Didn't they have a bullhorn? Working on the assumption that they wanted us out of there, we picked up the gear and walked slowly down the stairs in full view of the Marines, while I kept shouting "CBS" and "Americans" until I was hoarse.

As we loaded the car under the glare of yet another illumination round, an NBC crew drove up. We suggested that they might not find it healthy to hang around. They took off and so did a second car that came racing out from behind the building. Our presence had drawn a little too much attention for the comfort of the militiamen – probably artillery spotters or snipers – who had been sharing our hiding place.

When cameraman Sean Bobbitt and soundman Nick Follows went out the next morning to Sweifat, the Druze industrial town on the southeastern edge of the airport, they found a lot of angry people. They were led to a doctor's office that had been gutted. The dentist's clinic next door was a total wreck. A plastics factory was the source of the huge fire we had seen the night before. Tank rounds had ignited its contents and they had burned for hours.

"Why are the Americans shooting against us?" asked one man who stopped his car in front of the crew. "We are a few people; we are a small sect here in Lebanon. Why are you shooting against us? We called them here to make peace. Now look what happened."

None of them wanted to talk about the fact that the buildings had a clear line of sight on the Marine positions and that the area was regularly used by snipers. None of them would deny that the militiamen had staged an attack from there the night before. Nevertheless, it was the Marines whom people blamed, not the militiamen.

"I get all my money and open these shops and look what happened," complained a middle-aged businessman as he gestured toward the row of wrecked stores.

"We're sorry about that. We can't control where we take fire from," replied Maj. Dennis Brooks, the Marine spokesman, when told what the residents on the other side of the line had been saying. "If people are gonna fire on us, are gonna move into civilian areas and fire on our positions, we will return fire to those areas."

The peacekeepers, whose mission Ronald Reagan had told Congress "expressly rules out any combat responsibilities," were dropping the pretense. They were sick and tired of being picked away at by gunmen hiding behind civilians. In the beginning, they had clenched their teeth and taken it, then they had fired warning shots, then they had hit targets away from built-up areas, and finally they had retaliated in kind.

The new policy, according to Brooks: "If you hit me, I'll hit you back a lot harder."

12
Taking the Hint

At last, the long deferred but inevitable day arrived. The
sun ... rose resplendent on the French tricolour, but only
to shed glorious rays on its humiliation ... a general feeling
of commiseration was excited in all breasts at this pitiful
exit of the advance guard of a great nation.
—Col. Charles Churchill[1]

The Commodore Hotel vibrated as if its foundations had been shaken by an
earth tremor. We were in the heart of the business district, a dozen city blocks
from the sea. Tall buildings surrounded us on all sides. And still, every time the 16-
inch guns of the battleship *New Jersey* fired, windows rattled in their frames and
curtains rustled as the wall of pressure slammed into the city. So fearsome was
the power of those guns that with each volley, the 59,000-ton battleship was
shoved several feet sideways in the sea.

Sitting at a typewriter trying to pound out a script about the latest outbreak
of shelling on the airport, I could feel the force of the air press in on my eardrums
a few seconds after every deep-throated rumble.

"*New Jersey* diplomacy." That was what the local press had dubbed America's
latest endeavor to sort things out. Watching from the States, Middle East scholar
Fouad Ajami had another phrase for it: "The fireworks of a frustrated power."[2]

For a while there had been a lot of talk about a new security plan that
was going to end the war. It was supposed to create buffer zones between
the militias and, most important to Washington, declare the airport neutral
territory. Ronald Reagan was hopeful, as usual; Amin Gemayel was enthusiastic. Syria shot it down.

At first, word was, all the warlords had agreed, except for one or two
minor "technical details." Well, maybe they weren't all that minor. After
a couple of euphoric weeks in which the Lebanese convinced themselves
(again) that they could see the light at the end of the tunnel, the power was
cut off. By mid-January 1984, the airport was closed and it was painfully

196

clear that the security plan was nothing more than another cease-fire that was going nowhere.

Clear to everyone, that is, except Reginald Bartholomew, the new U.S. ambassador to Lebanon. In late January, he gathered together his top advisors to review the situation. Between them, according to participants in the meeting, the Lebanon veterans painted a picture of gloom. The political officers predicted that the Muslims would soon resign from the government, while the military experts said they expected a major new outbreak of fighting. So bleak was the prognosis that several of those present recommended the evacuation of embassy wives and children. After listening to the sobering assessment, Ambassador Bartholomew vetoed an evacuation and, according to witnesses, announced cheerily, "Well, *I'm* optimistic."

Meanwhile, the new Middle East envoy, Donald Rumsfeld, made the rounds, but he was doing no more than running in place. Rumsfeld had replaced Robert McFarlane, whom President Reagan had promoted to National Security Advisor, presumably so he could employ on a global scale the skills that had proved so effective in Lebanon. It took Rumsfeld three trips to Damascus before Assad finally condescended to receive him. Even then, the Syrian president set the tone by announcing before the meeting, "Peace cannot be established under the American gun barrel."

The chairman of the Joint Chiefs of Staff, Gen. John Vessey, was apparently thinking the same thing when he visited Beirut in January. After a round of talks with Gemayel and his army commander, and a tour of the Marine compound, Vessey took a senior U.S. official aside and told him to do whatever he could to convince the Lebanese to ask the Americans to leave.

The Joint Chiefs of Staff had long ago decided that the Marines' position was untenable. The Pentagon was examining a variety of options, including a pullback to the fleet. Vessey and his colleagues realized that the Reagan administration was not prepared to withdraw unilaterally and leave the impression that the United States had been driven out by terrorists. But if the host government said, "Thank you, you can go home now," the U.S. would have a good excuse to do exactly that.

Brig. Ibrahim Tannous, the highly respected commander of the Lebanese Army, agreed to go along with the plan for a price: $600 million and six months. That was the value of the hardware American experts calculated the army needed to bring it up to strength and the amount of time it would take to train the new recruits.

It was a small price to pay to buy a way out. As one senior U.S. military official put it, "The U.S. has left bags of money behind when we abandoned other places. This is cheap."

The groundwork had been laid.

An insistent pounding beckoned to me from the other side of a layer of fog. Gradually, the haze lifted and I focused on the source. I emphatically did not want to get out of bed. When I had finally lain down sometime around 2:00 a.m., I hadn't slept for 36 hours. I had spent the previous night on the filthy floor of the hotel's basement while shells crashed outside and half a dozen taxi drivers entertained the assembled neighborhood with bongos and tambourines. Then I went out and got shot at some more. Now that the fighting had subsided, I had hoped to get at least six hours in the sack.

Cursing, I pulled on a pair of pants and opened the door. Lucy Spiegel, my producer, was standing there wearing a robe and a look of panic, waving a telex in my face. "The Marines are leaving!" she shouted, storming into the room. "Reagan has ordered them out! I just found this telex from the foreign desk downstairs."

"When are they going?" I asked, throwing on a shirt and a pair of shoes.

"I don't know. It doesn't say," she said, looking incredulously at the telex. "They could be gone already for all I know. I can't believe they didn't call me to tell me this."

New York regularly woke us up with inane queries, minor housekeeping, or to ask why we hadn't done our expenses. They had let us sleep through the announcement that U.S. military involvement in the country we were covering was about to end. Questioned about it later, the people on the foreign desk said they hadn't wanted to disturb us.

Much to my relief, the Marines were still there when our car came skidding up to the compound a little while later, but they were already packing. About 250 "nonessential" personnel were being moved out to the ships that day. The officers said it had nothing to do with Reagan's announcement, which had not "officially" reached them yet. According to Gen. James Joy, the 22nd MAU's commanding officer, the "redeployment" was part of a previously existing plan "to test a sea-basing concept that would provide amphibious support as opposed to the more traditional means of support." Joy and his spokesmen would stick to that story until they and a couple of bodyguards were about the only men left on the beach.

The British didn't try to disguise their withdrawal as anything other than what it was. By 8:00 a.m., their entire 110-man contingent had packed up, lock, stock and teapot, and cleared out for Jounieh, where helicopters were waiting to ferry them to the safety of HMS *Reliant* offshore.

No matter what you said about Ronald Reagan, he was a convincing communicator:

January 16: "There are terrorist elements who know they cannot succeed in their cause while the Multinational Force is there."

February 2: "He [House Speaker Thomas 'Tip' O'Neill, Jr.] may be ready to surrender, but I'm not. ... If we get out, that means the end of Lebanon."

February 4: "Yes, the situation in Lebanon is difficult, frustrating and dangerous. But that is no reason to turn our backs on friends and to cut and run. If we do, we'll be sending one signal to terrorists everywhere – They can gain by waging war against innocent people."

February 6: "The commitment of the United States to the unity, independence and sovereignty of Lebanon remains firm and unwavering."

February 7: "I have asked Secretary of Defense Weinberger to present to me a plan for redeployment of the Marines from Beirut Airport to their ships offshore. This redeployment will begin shortly and proceed in stages. ... These measures, I believe, will strengthen our ability to do the job we set out to do."

February 22: "We are redeploying because, once the terrorist attacks started, there was no way that we could really contribute to the original mission by staying there as a target just hunkered down and waiting for further attacks."

The fact that Beirut was falling apart had a lot to do with Reagan's sudden change of heart. So did the rising chorus of congressional dissent and the plunging election year polls. Reagan had once told reporters that he would consider pulling the Marines out "if there was a complete collapse and there was no possibility of restoring order." That was happening now, with a vengeance.

The Lebanese prime minister and other Muslims in the cabinet quit, Muslim militiamen retook control of West Beirut, the army split along religious lines, with Muslim troops laying down their weapons or joining the rebels, and the entire city was being shelled into dust.

On Sunday, February 3, after Prime Minister Wazzan submitted his resignation, Gemayel went on television. The Lebanese president sounded like a schoolboy pleading for the other kids to like him. He still didn't want to share his candy, though. "Everything is open to discussion," he said, referring obliquely to the May 17 agreement, but even with his government collapsing around him, Gemayel refused to give in to Muslim demands to scrap the accord. Nor did he actually offer to share power. Even the Americans, who insisted that he stand by the May 17 pact with Israel, were flabbergasted at Gemayel's continued failure to form a genuine coalition cabinet. The Reagan administration still wanted it both ways.

The United States didn't give up, though. Carrier-based warplanes bombed artillery positions in the mountains while naval guns opened up in a U.S. bid to prop up its tottering ally. But the situation was far beyond American help. On Monday, half of West Beirut was engulfed in fighting as Shi'ite and Druze militiamen battled it out in the streets with army units that remained loyal to Gemayel. By 1:30 in the afternoon, the government had clamped a total curfew on the Muslim sector of the city. Anyone outdoors would be shot. With so many Muslim soldiers joining their co-religionists or standing aside, however, government loyalists were outgunned. By nightfall, Gemayel's army had resorted to blanket shelling.

Lying in the hotel basement, we listened to artillery rounds scream in at the rate of one every few seconds. We knew Druze guns up in the hills were pounding Christian areas just as mercilessly. I had once asked Walid Jumblatt what he thought about at times like that, when he ordered his men to point their guns toward neighborhoods full of women and children.

"You don't think on such occasions, you just react. It's purely reaction," he said, stretching out his long, scrawny legs.

"But you know it's going to prompt shelling on Muslim civilian areas," I reminded the Druze warlord.

"I know that." He raised his bushy eyebrows and shrugged his bony shoulders in a gesture that suggested it was out of his hands. "It's terrible, but it's part of the Lebanese political game."

"How do you justify—" He broke in before I could finish.

"There are no justifications. And we haven't been able to reach a gentlemen's agreement not to shoot our civilian areas." Jumblatt's answers were always abrupt and matter-of-fact. No embellishments. He didn't care what anybody thought. Interviewing him was like talking to an unrepentant juvenile delinquent.

"Does your conscience bother you?" I asked.

Big sigh. "Of course," he said, his voice rising in pitch as if to say the answer was obvious. "And there's no way to avoid that. But I told you, it's purely an automatic reaction."

A series of "automatic reactions" between February 3 and February 7 left somewhere in the neighborhood of 250 people dead and many times that number wounded.

In his statement announcing the "redeployment" (read by a spokesman), President Reagan said he had authorized naval gunfire and air strikes to support the Gemayel government and promised to "vigorously accelerate" the training program for what was left of the Lebanese Army. On Wednesday, February 8, just hours after the announcement, the *New Jersey* let loose with the most sustained attack on antigovernment positions since the Marines had arrived. For nine hours the battleship dropped more than 250 16-inch shells on the Syrian and Druze gun batteries that had been bombarding East Beirut, while the destroyer *Caron* lobbed in another 300 5-inch rounds.

It was all window dressing. Ronald Reagan's Lebanon policy, starring George Schultz and Robert McFarlane, was as dead as the corpses stacked in the refrigerators at the AUB hospital morgue.

John Stewart, the U.S. embassy spokesman, was having a hard time explaining why the families of diplomats and nonessential embassy personnel were climbing onto helicopters just behind him when the U.S. government felt that the evacuation of the other 1,500 American civilians in West Beirut was "not justified at this time." Although Stewart couldn't say it, the White House was gambling with the lives of its citizens in an attempt to keep Gemayel in power. A full-scale evacuation, Washington feared, would send the wrong signal and might be a blow from which Amin Gemayel could not recover. So, if you didn't work for the government, you were on your own.

"If somebody calls or comes down and asks what we think of the situation and what [they] should do, we at least would recommend them reconsidering the necessity for being here," the usually elusive Stewart said, making his first appearance before reporters since the February crisis had begun.

"Yes, but how do they get out if they do reconsider?" he was asked.

"Well," Stewart stammered, "in the last couple of days, they would find it very difficult to do so."

Difficult indeed. The airport was closed and fighting blocked all roads out. Just getting Stewart's unreassuring message was a challenge, since the embassy's phones weren't working and most U.S. citizens who came to the embassy gates were unceremoniously told to go away.

The sound of the *New Jersey*'s big guns was what most shook the confidence of many American residents of the Lebanese capital, even some of those who had stayed through many other rounds of war. Washington said the ship was firing to protect Americans in Beirut, but many of those same citizens wanted to call the White House and tell the president not to do them any favors. Schultz and McFarlane had pushed hard for the naval action to demonstrate U.S. resolve and to counteract the loss of face brought by the withdrawal announcement. But the American residents feared that it would only make things worse for them, compounding the damage already inflicted by what they saw as a naive and misguided policy based on ignorance.

Walid Jumblatt underscored their concerns when he charged that Druze villagers were being slaughtered under the brutal barrage (a claim never backed up with evidence) and warned darkly of "serious consequences" for American civilians in West Beirut.

The next day, as the Marines helped British officials airlift their nationals out of the seafront compound shared by the two embassies, Washington finally bowed to pressure and announced helicopters would start evacuating holders of U.S. passports and residence cards in the morning. Bring one suitcase and leave your guns and pets at home.

Once word spread among the militiamen that the Marines were leaving, the Americans at the airport were pretty much left alone. An odd round fell here and there, but this *really was* spillover fire. The gunmen had lost interest. Even when the Lebanese Army's Fourth Brigade south of the airport disintegrated (the Christian officers jumped on helicopters and boats and took off, leaving their Muslim troops to join the militias), while Druzes from the mountains and Shi'ite militiamen from the slums linked up at Khalde thus encircling the Marines, it was all very low-key. Gunmen who raced up and down the coastal road between the main Marine compound and U.S. positions on the beach sometimes waved, sometimes sneered, but never interfered with the Americans as they packed up and shipped out their gear.

Some marines were bitter when they heard the news that they were pulling out. The president's words left them feeling kind of hollow inside when they thought of the friends they had lost. "He said they did die for a reason, to keep peace," said a corporal sitting on the ground outside his tent. "But then when you pull out like this, you know their lives didn't amount to nothin'."

"Alan Soifert, he got shot up there on the road." Staff Sgt. Claude Sabo talked slow and sad. "I took his place here. I think we're letting him down real bad."

But most of the men were happy to be getting out alive. "We all feel pretty good," said Lance Cpl. Nick Mattola.

"Last days of Beirut," shouted Sgt. Troy Matthews with a big grin. "I think it's great. Perfect. Fantastic."

Where U.S. military and diplomatic expertise had failed, American PR know-how was called in to save the day. With the same vigor with which it had sought to save Lebanon from itself, the Reagan administration set out to put the best possible face on an election year failure.

A salty Army colonel by the name of Ed McDonald was sent in from European Command in Germany to ride herd on the media. On the rare occasions when he unbuttoned his lip, the answers that came out were opaque. McDonald's vague style was in sharp contrast to the informal openness of the Marine spokesmen, whose noses were put out of joint by the arrival of McDonald and three other Army officers. The Army team had been brought in on the orders of Gen. Bernard Rogers, commander in chief of U.S. forces in Europe (directly above the MAU in the chain of command), who told them what to say.

Reporters never heard the word "withdrawal" or "pullout" escape McDonald's lips. Instead, he used the term "redeployment." The Marines weren't leaving; they were "redeploying to the ships," or so McDonald and his bosses wanted the world to believe. After a McDonald briefing, you were never quite sure exactly how many marines were still ashore or when they would leave. For weeks, we watched men and equipment pile onto landing craft and helicopters, but according to McDonald, the operation still hadn't started. Finally, on February 21, McDonald fessed up: the "redeployment" had officially begun. But he stayed vague on when it would end, right up to the final weekend, when the last amphibious vehicles crawled off the beach and bobbed toward the fleet like a family of seaborne hippopotami.

The idea was to make the pullout so drawn out, so routine, so boring, that viewers and readers back home would have grown fed up with it by the time that final, humiliating day rolled around. McDonald and his staff also set out to ensure that no single image would forever symbolize the U.S. failure in Lebanon. And the media managers succeeded. Although marines splashing onto beached troop transports and the sight of militiamen raising the Amal flag over abandoned Marine bunkers were telling pictures, neither began to approach the classic photograph captured seconds before the last chopper lifted off the roof of the U.S. embassy in Saigon.

The only ceremony took place in the monochrome shadows of the hour just before dawn. As a squad of marines stood at attention, the last American flag was lowered over the last bunker, while *The Star Spangled Banner* blared from a cheap tape recorder. There was barely enough light to take a picture.

The most enduring memory of that final day in Beirut came after the last marines were aboard ship. It was the sight of angry fireballs licking from the barrels of the *New Jersey* as it aimed a few parting shots into the descending dusk, like a spoiled little boy throwing one more rock before ducking behind his mother's apron.

In the early days of the Marine mission, the Reagan administration had set for itself several goals: the creation of a strong Lebanese government, the reconciliation of the warring factions, the withdrawal of foreign forces (Syria, Israel and the PLO), and a secure northern border for Israel. As far as the administration was concerned, the May 17 agreement was the key to it all and Syria was the main roadblock to peace.

On February 26, 1984, as the final Marine platoon loaded back on board ship, Amin Gemayel's government was teetering on the verge of collapse; the Lebanese Army had disintegrated; Muslim militias were in control of West Beirut; Syria, Israel and the PLO still occupied 90 percent of the country; and rockets were again falling on settlements in northern Israel. Three days later, Amin Gemayel flew to Damascus and threw himself into Hafez al-Assad's warm embrace. Not long after, the May 17 agreement was formally scrapped.

"I don't think ... that you can say that we have lost as yet," President Reagan declared a couple of days before the redeployment was complete. Maybe not, but as the last marines walked down the beach, the only witnesses were a gaggle of reporters and a small knot of grim-faced young fighters waiting to radio Muslim militia units to move in.

There were no waving flags, no cheering crowds and no victory parades.

Section III

Whirlwind

13
Jihad

For they have sown the wind, and they shall reap the whirlwind.

—Hosea 8:1–14
Old Testament

The two unshaven men in red-striped pajamas looked drawn and haggard. They sat on a couch wedged between U.S. ambassador Reginald Bartholomew and a French diplomat, casting furtive glances at the pack of pushing and shoving reporters and camera teams on the other side of the coffee table.

It had been just a few hours since their chains and blindfolds had been removed and they had been brought to Nabih Berri's apartment and told they were free. Both men were still dazed, uncertain who had held them or why.

"They said very little to me and they asked very little of me," explained Prof. Frank Regier, who had been taken from his home on the AUB campus two months before, in January 1984. "I don't think they wanted information from me. I think they just wanted me."

Chained to the bars of a window, his hands and feet bound, his eyes blindfolded most of the time, Regier assumed from the "bang, bang of the cannons" that all three of the places where he had been held were in Beirut. The blindfold meant that the only face he saw the entire time was that of his fellow captive, French construction engineer Christian Joubert, who worked for an Islamic relief agency.

That left Regier with a lot of time to think. "I believed I would get out eventually," he told the gathered reporters. "I sometimes questioned whether my sanity would be intact by that time."

As Nabih Berri told it, Regier and Joubert were rescued by Amal. Three local boys who were out shooting birds happened to climb over the wall of the house the pair had been moved to a few days before. Peering in a window,

207

they saw the two foreigners sitting on mattresses on the floor, chained, blindfolded and gagged. They told an older brother, who informed neighborhood Amal officials. Berri then ordered the rescue.

Amal officials were vague about who was behind the kidnapping and whether they had been caught. Berri said the captors had been out when his men stormed the building. The *Daily Star* quoted a member of the rescue team as claiming that one kidnapper was captured. Regier himself was visibly reluctant to talk about the subject, leaving the strong impression that he was under orders to keep quiet.[1]

The secrecy had a lot to do with the fact that Nabih Berri was walking a tightrope. The Amal leader was against attacks on foreigners. He knew the value of the Western community in Beirut and – now that the Marines were gone – he wanted the foreigners to stay. The rescue was evidence of that. He also had a vested interest in neutralizing or crushing extremists who were challenging his leadership of the Shia community. But to admit that Shi'ites had been arrested by his militia for kidnapping foreigners would be to play into the hands of those in other sects who wanted to brand Shi'ites as terrorists, as well as those within the Shi'ite community who would use it as evidence that Berri was siding with the Americans against his own people.

Regier was free, but two other Americans were still missing. Jeremy Levin, Beirut bureau chief for the Cable News Network (CNN), had been grabbed as he walked to work on March 7; CIA station chief William Buckley had been captured as he started his car in the same neighborhood a week later. Also in early March, another American who worked at the embassy, Marine Col. Dale Dorman, had been shot and wounded just around the corner from where Buckley was kidnapped.

Who was responsible and why? Publicly, there was only silence. Privately, contact had been made. It came in the form of an envelope slipped under the door of an AUB professor. A message scrawled on the outside ordered that the envelope be delivered unopened to the U.S. ambassador. Inside, according to sources familiar with the contents, were pictures of Regier, Levin, Buckley, Joubert and Hussein Farrash, a Saudi diplomat kidnapped in mid-January. There was also a note demanding a trade: the five captives in return for the 17 Shi'ites convicted of the bombings in Kuwait.

The Americans and French had been chosen as hostages because the 17 had been convicted of blowing up the U.S. and French embassies. The kidnappers figured Washington and Paris could get their comrades off. The Saudi was targeted because of the enormous influence his country wielded over Kuwait.

The men behind the bombings used the name Islamic Jihad, but U.S. intelligence would later identify them as members of the Musawi clan; their leader was a Shi'ite by the name of Imad Mugniyeh.

With his small band of followers, Mugniyeh would become, in the words of one U.S. security official, "the number-one kidnapper." But he would also become much more than that. This was the "former PLO security official" behind the first U.S. embassy bombing in Beirut and his name would be linked to much of the mayhem that followed.

A father of five born in 1962 to a respected Islamic jurist, Mugniyeh had a personal reason for launching the wave of kidnappings against Americans: the boss of the Kuwait operation, Mustafa Yousef, was his brother-in-law. One of Yousef's accomplices was a Mugniyeh cousin. They had been sentenced to death and in the best tradition of Lebanon, Mugniyeh was abducting others to get them back.

So from an early date, the fate of the hostages was linked directly to the fate of the 17 in Kuwait. The rest of us wouldn't know that for at least several months, when word began leaking out through sources in Europe and the Middle East. Administration officials privately told the families about the Kuwait connection in mid-May 1984, while publicly denying the link for more than a year. At the same time, it quietly sent word through Algerian and Gulf mediators that it would not give in to blackmail.

The first official confirmation followed a July 5, 1985 videotape from the hostages in which they outlined Islamic Jihad's demands. Not until they were handed a script of that statement did the kidnapped Americans know why they were being held.

There had been a collective sigh of relief among Americans in Beirut when the Marines had left. Now we were all holding our breath. We had assumed the threat against Americans had ended with the Marines' withdrawal. Driving out the Multinational Force had been the terrorists' goal, hadn't it? But by the time Buckley was taken, we knew something was very wrong.

We tried to rationalize what was happening. Regier was kidnapped while the Marines were still ashore; Levin had upset several Lebanese with militia connections, so he might have fallen victim to a personal vendetta; Buckley was generally understood to be a CIA agent and was thus automatically at risk; as a soldier, Col. Dorman was a likely target for any number of groups. When three men wrestled Rev. Benjamin Weir into a white Peugot 504, shoved his wife aside and drove off, no amount of rationalization could explain it away.

Some hopeful Americans in Beirut speculated that Weir's kidnapping on May 8, 1984 might be connected with a Muslim campaign against Christians – he was, after all, a missionary spreading the gospel – rather than an anti-American act.

However, it also looked very much as if Regier's luck had been Weir's misfortune. The kidnappers seemed to be replacing the hostage they had lost.

The speculation ended the next day. "The Islamic Jihad Organization is determined that not one American will be left in Beirut, as we made clear with the attack on the Marine base in October 1983," said a caller to the French news agency AFP.[2] In addition to claiming credit for Weir's abduction, the anonymous voice confirmed that Buckley and Levin were also in his group's hands.

Jerry Levin first knew he wasn't alone when he angrily banged his food dish on the floor one day because dinner was late and "much to my shock, someone banged back." That someone was Ben Weir, but neither man knew the identity of the other until much later, when they were both free and safely back in the U.S.

From what he heard during the morning visit to the bathroom, Levin suspected that there was more than one other prisoner. The daily routine called for the captives to knock on the bathroom door when they were ready to return to their cells. By the time he escaped in February 1985, Levin was regularly hearing three other sets of knocks. But he never saw his fellow captives or his captors. For more than eleven months, Jerry Levin never saw the face of another human being.

The first six months were the toughest. A scarf was wrapped around his head like a turban and he was ordered to keep it pulled down over his eyes at all times, even when the guards were outside the room. "Sometimes they would rush in and try to catch me with it off," Levin later recalled. He kept it knotted so it didn't accidentally slip off, "always a frightening possibility and an even more frightening event, because I was always afraid I might still be getting it back together just as one of them came bursting in to check up on me." Either way, like Regier before him, Levin would be beaten, often without warning, without reason. He gave his tormentors silent names: "Mad Mean Mike," "Sadistic Sam," "Angry Al." Later he would come to know one youth by the name he gave himself, Imad.

Shackled to a radiator with a chain too short to even allow him to stand, blindfolded, alone 24 hours a day, Levin tried to maintain his grip on sanity by making lists in his head: the operas he had seen, the books he had read. "I would spend a whole day making a list, then lose count and start over again," he said later, back in the States. "It sounded crazy, but it kept me going."

Every once in a while, he would stretch out on his mattress and try to catch a glimpse of daylight by peering under the turban, just to make sure the world was still out there. Even with the mask, he was ordered to sit or lie facing the wall whenever he heard his jailers unlocking the cell door. "They told me that if I saw their faces, that was it."

Levin consciously tried to prevent himself from talking out loud and became worried that his control was slipping when he realized that he was thinking about himself in the third person, watching himself as if from a distance. "I caught myself thinking, 'and then Jerry did this, and then he did that.' I knew I had to do something, so I began talking to God."

Levin, a Jew whose wife was a devout Christian, emerged from the experience "born again." "I felt His hand on me," he said six months after reaching freedom. "He pulled me through."

A few hours after his kidnapping in Beirut, the CNN reporter was wrapped head to toe in packing tape (an experience other hostages would also endure) and loaded into the false bottom of a truck, a compartment normally used for smuggling weapons and explosives. From the movement of the truck and the length of the trip, Levin knew he was being taken to the Bekaa. He later confirmed that when he surreptitiously scratched out a tiny hole in the pane that covered the window of his room and saw the Baalbek ruins and Mt. Lebanon to the west. Levin didn't know it at the time, but he was being held in a building just outside the walls of the Sheikh Abdullah barracks, headquarters of the Iranian Revolutionary Guards. This was the region the Musawis and Hizbullah ruled.

There was at least one attempt to rescue him. On May 16, one week after Weir was abducted, Amal militiamen stormed a house in Beirut's southern suburbs where they believed Levin and another American were being held. They found evidence that the building had been a hideout, but the Americans were gone.

Nine months – and several moves – later, Levin got himself out. His captors had been getting sloppy. Several times they had left his chains loose enough for him to slip off. He thought about escape but hesitated each time, imagining what might go wrong. "I guess I was just chicken," Levin said later, laughing softly when he recalled those moments. "Finally I told myself that if I got the chance again and didn't go, I was a coward and deserved to stay where I was." Perhaps more than anything else, the fact that his first anniversary in captivity was coming up made Levin determined to escape. "That was one anniversary I knew I couldn't celebrate."

When he next found his bonds loose enough to slip, Levin tied his blankets together and climbed out onto a balcony where he lashed the blankets to a railing and lowered himself down to the ground, just like in the movies. After a terrifying run down the mountain, his feet clad only in two pairs of socks, with dogs barking in the distance, Levin reached the startled soldiers manning a Syrian Army checkpoint.

He was taken to the Syrian headquarters in Baalbek and questioned about where he had been held. The Syrian officers told him that they wanted to try to rescue the others. With the Bekaa a virtual province of Syria, parceled up amongst two dozen Syrian intelligence officers and thousands of regular troops, skeptics in Washington had long claimed that Damascus knew where the Americans were being held and could rescue them at any time if it wanted.

Levin described the empty apartment building in a complex of largely unoccupied buildings just outside a very high wall. Directions were double-checked, details noted, in what was either a genuine Syrian effort to find and free the other Americans or an elaborate ruse. Although Levin had lost his glasses the day of the kidnapping and was nearsighted, he later said his recollection of the building's location was "quite precise." On the afternoon of February 14, he and the Syrians returned to Baalbek. From various locations in and around the town, he pointed out where on the nearby mountain his prison was located. And while the Syrians chose not to drive near where the Americans were being held, Levin recalled, "I described so many extremely recognizable and unique landmarks close to the building, there was no way they could not pinpoint its location."

After Levin emerged from captivity, there was widespread speculation that he had actually been set free. The story of his escape, according to this argument, was part of a deal with the kidnappers. U.S. officials publicly credited Syrian President Assad with helping to win Levin's freedom. The reporter himself stood by his account, but even he admitted he may have been allowed to escape for reasons best known to others.

One incident, however, seems to indicate that wasn't the case. When Rev. Weir was released in September 1985, the clergyman held a news conference in Washington to reiterate the kidnappers' demand that the 17 prisoners in Kuwait be freed. Afterward, he met privately with the families of the remaining captives to tell them what he could about their loved ones. Jerry Levin, who had been working with the families to publicize the case, was with them.

"So you're Jerry Levin," Weir said, taking the lanky reporter's hand. "Boy was there a commotion after you escaped. They were really upset."

A quick week off among the pine forests of northern Sweden had revitalized me. The crisp, clean air had cleared my head. Just strolling the streets window-shopping had helped untie that knot I had been carrying around in my gut since Weir's abduction.

Settling back into the leather first-class seat of the Swissair jet streaking toward Beirut, I took a sip of champagne, unfolded the *International Herald Tribune* and was punched in the gut. The story, written by my Beirut colleague J. Michael Kennedy of the *Los Angeles Times*, quoted U.S. intelligence reports as warning that one hundred Shi'ite terrorists were preparing to storm AUB and the embassy to kidnap as many Americans as they could get their hands on. As an added touch, the attackers would have dynamite strapped to their bodies so that if they were shot, they and their captives would go up in a ball of flames. That knot I thought I had left in Sweden suddenly crawled back out of its hiding place.

The American warning was based on an advisory from the Christian-run intelligence branch of the Lebanese Army. The detailed breakdown of how the assault was going to be launched claimed that the terrorists were members of Hizbullah. "The plan is prepared and its execution is soon," according to an English translation of the report, which the embassy had given to AUB officials. "Purpose of the operation is to put pressure on the U.S. and reduce pressure on Iran which is surrounded by enemies and unable to export its oil."

The AUB campus was immediately placed off-limits to embassy staffers, Marines began to patrol the area around faculty apartments housing American professors, and new barricades were erected around the fortified embassy compound where the diplomats had been sharing cramped living space since abandoning their own apartments after Buckley's kidnapping.

But in the uproar, some people began to wonder whether the embassy had been taken in by Christian intelligence operatives playing on the Americans' well-founded fears in order to discredit the Muslims. Hizbullah itself charged that somebody was out to give it a bad name (God forbid) and the group issued a statement denouncing "these attempts against our reputation." Genuine or not, the threat sent a shudder through the dwindling community of Americans who had been holding on in Beirut.

"Academic, missionary or press?" a young American woman with fiery red hair asked as I arrived at a dinner party in the home of an AUB professor. "You have to be one of the three. We're all that's left."

It was no exaggeration. Throw in the handful of U.S. citizens married to Lebanese nationals and that was the extent of the American community in West Beirut by the summer of 1984.[3] After the scare over the mass kidnapping, the embassy announced that the 50 or so remaining diplomats were being moved to apartments in East Beirut.

The professors and relief workers who had remained through the February evacuation (or returned after it) were committed to helping the Lebanese. The vast majority of the country's people wanted and needed their skills, the teachers and relief workers believed. Many remained determined that a small band of fanatics would not drive them away. But others were beginning to have second thoughts.

"They depend on us. We can't just leave. What kind of education would they get?" ecologist David Evans had said back in February when asked why he had not departed in the evacuation. "We tried it in September [the previous evacuation]. We felt terrible being away. We didn't know what was happening with our students." A few days after the helicopters had brought Evans and his wife, Henriette, also a teacher, to Cyprus, they boarded a boat back to Beirut. "We were willing to come back any way we could."

Three months later, David Evans had experienced a change of heart. "Back then, we had hope," he explained at his farewell dinner party. "We thought things would get better. We were determined to stay. Ask us how we feel now and you'll get a different answer. It's time to go." His wife, a Lebanese Maronite Christian, nodded firmly. "It's all changed. There's no point in taking the risk." With the end of the semester coming up, David was planning to leave soon, but he wouldn't say exactly when. "I'm too short," he explained with an embarrassed laugh.

The Rices, who had come to say goodbye, were digging in their heels. He was an agriculture professor; she taught in the English department. Both were Americans and committed to staying, even though they were living in a self-imposed prison.

"Bob never leaves campus," said Laura, a very collegiate-looking woman in her late twenties whose severe good looks were accentuated by red hair pulled back in a tight bun. The low-cut T-shirt with thin straps she was wearing on this warm evening left her shoulders bare and a generous portion of cleavage on display. This might have been standard uniform on a California campus, but it was a political statement in a city where Muslim fundamentalism was on the march. "I go out once or twice a week for shopping, but usually with someone else. I don't go off like I used to, so we don't have as much fresh fruits or vegetables. Is it worth getting kidnapped for a couple of oranges?"

"I don't see any point in going out anymore," added Bob. "Why take the chance?"

"We're staying though, unless it gets worse," Laura said with calculated bravado. You could tell she had used the words before. "But I don't know what we're waiting for. What more can they do to us? They've killed us, they've kidnapped us, they threatened to blow us up." The words were eerily similar to those of the Lebanese restaurant owner who had been bombed months before.

A week later, David Evans left. He asked a friend to administer his final exams, then had the papers sent by driver to him in Jounieh, where he graded them before getting on the boat that afternoon.

"It's crazy, impossible," one of his colleagues exclaimed, "but it's symptomatic of what's going on. People here are terrified." Whole departments were leaving, the teacher said. Some of the 40 remaining American professors were taking sabbaticals; others said they were going just for the summer, but few were expected back. Almost everyone would be looking for another job.

Joseph Curtin was a frightened man. The four abductions of Americans had been bad enough, but the mass kidnapping story had really spooked him. Unlike the AUB staff, who could stay within the relative safety of the campus walls, Curtin had to walk the streets. His job as Beirut director of Catholic Relief Services (CRS), a leading conduit for U.S. aid money, gave him a high profile. His visits to inspect projects being funded in the Shi'ite slums made him an easy target. Worse still, Curtin was the last American relief worker left in West Beirut. The odds were not good.

Joe Curtin had spent a lot of time in nasty places, but Beirut made his other posts look like vacation resorts. "I like hot spots. I've spent most of my career in them, but this is different. With all the [U.S.] aid money I handle, if there's a list, I just know I've got to be on it," he said over lunch one day.

"I'm becoming paranoid. Whenever anyone speaks to me in English, I ignore them," he said. "The other day, I was standing in front of the office waiting for my driver and this guy walked up the street and started staring at me. Of course, the more he stared, the more nervous I got, which made him stare even more. I looked at him, he looked at me, and I was convinced that was it, they'd come for me. I turned and ran into the office and locked the door. It turned out he was the neighborhood nut." Curtin, a short man in his late thirties, laughed nervously.

Curtin felt he had pressed his luck in Beirut long enough. CRS had agreed. He was being transferred back to the relative tranquillity of Southeast Asia.

"This isn't like shelling or fighting or bombing. I've been here for three years through all of it; civil war, the PLO, the Israeli invasion. This is by far the worst. I don't need this anymore."

Curtin's replacement in Beirut was a 53-year-old Roman Catholic priest, Father Lawrence Martin Jenco. On January 8, 1985, as he drove to work, Father Jenco was kidnapped.

"You are Joseph Curtin, are you not?" the frightened priest was asked when he and his kidnappers had reached the terrorists' safehouse in the Beirut slums.

"No, I'm Father Martin Jenco."

"You are not Joseph Curtin?" the startled gunman demanded again.

"No, I'm not."

What followed was a frantic few minutes as the kidnappers rummaged through Jenco's bag, searching his documents, matching the photographs against his face. There was no doubt; they had taken the wrong man.

Over the course of the next few hours, dozens of important-looking men in suits and ties streamed through the small apartment. Hushed conferences were held. There were loud debates in Arabic. Still without a blindfold, Jenco watched and waited while these strangers argued over his fate.

Finally, a decision was made. The captive was not Joe Curtin, but he *was* an American. The situation could be salvaged. A well-dressed man approached the bound priest and looked him directly in the eye. "Father," he said softly, "I am so sorry." With that, Jenco was blindfolded, wrapped in packing tape, hidden in the wheel well of a truck and driven to the Bekaa.

Like trout fishermen on a crystal clear stream, the kidnappers sometimes went after specific quarry; the rest of the time they cast blindly. There was no doubt that most, if not all, of the men kidnapped by June 1984 had been personally targeted. Regier was abducted from his home at AUB. Jerry Levin was grabbed as he walked to the office, following the route he took at roughly the same time each day. The gunmen who dragged Buckley away cut off the CIA agent's car in front of his apartment building when he was leaving for the embassy at the usual time on March 16. Weir's abductors were waiting in a car in front of his house when he and his wife walked out to go to work.

There was another pattern, too. All of the men kidnapped were in their fifties or sixties. Perhaps it was coincidental; perhaps the kidnappers had concluded that older men would put up less of a struggle. Either way, the pattern continued until Terry Anderson, chief Middle East correspondent of the Associated Press, was dragged from his car after an early morning tennis game in March 1985. Anderson was 37 when he was taken, but by that point, there were few other Americans left in West Beirut to choose from.

Getting nailed by accident also remained a possibility. In May 1984, a West German was picked up and held overnight while he convinced his kidnappers he was not American. The same would happen to other Europeans in the months to come. One Irish UN official found himself in real trouble when the gunmen holding him said they had never heard of a country called Eire, which is what it said on his passport. Finally, they found it on a map and let him go.

Samir Khalaf, a Lebanese sociology professor at AUB, was jogging one evening at about dusk when a car started pacing him. "I slowed down and they slowed down. Finally, I stopped and they stopped. One of them leaned out of the window and asked me in English what time it was. I suspected something, so I replied in Arabic and pulled down the hood of my sweat suit. They said, 'Oh, we thought you were a foreigner,' and drove away. I'm sure if I had been an American, I wouldn't be here right now."

Somebody tried the same trick on George Mall, a very American-looking videotape editor for ABC News, and a female friend from CNN outside the building that housed the Australian embassy. "We were standing in front of the apartment waiting for a taxi when a car pulled up and the driver stuck his head out the window like he wanted to ask us something," Mall recounted later over a stiff drink. "Like dummies, we said in English, 'Can we help you?' He just pulled over to the curb and sat there." It didn't take much of the silent treatment to make the couple nervous enough to go back inside. The driver left. When they figured the coast was clear, the pair came back out with two other friends, a *Time* magazine photographer who was as blonde as Mall and another obviously Western female from CNN.

No sooner were they on the sidewalk than two cars screeched up, disgorging gunmen. "We bolted into the lobby, slammed the front door, rushed into the apartment and locked the door. The gunmen hung around outside a good half-hour before they left.

"These guys were real serious," Mall added, in a tone of respect.

Within days, two other reporters had an equally unsettling conversation just down the block. Ray Wilkenson of *Newsweek* and ABC's Charles Glass were walking back to the Commodore Hotel when gunmen in a beat-up Chevy stopped to ask who they were. The reporters handed over Wilkenson's British passport and said Glass, an American, was British, too, but had left his passport at home. After much arguing, the gunmen gave the passport back and drove off. "I don't know what they wanted," Glass said later. "Whether we were who they were looking for or not. We tried to ignore the others and deal with the one guy who seemed to be somewhat reasonable."

A few minutes later, the gunmen were back to repeat the exercise. "I thought we were in trouble then," Wilkenson recounted in understated British tones. Again the "reasonable" member of the team apparently overruled the other, and again they drove off, this time for good.

"I told everybody I could about it," Glass said. "Berri, Fadlallah, Jumblatt. I'll probably get these guys in trouble for being so inefficient."

It would not be Glass's last brush with kidnappers. He would be abducted during a visit back to Lebanon in 1987 and held captive for two months before managing to escape.

Todd Robertson, an American reporter for the Reuters news agency, was just climbing onto his motorcycle outside the office late one night when a carload of thugs brandishing guns pulled up and ordered him into the back seat. They had apparently been waiting for him, or any other foreigner emerging from the building.

Then began a wild ride through the maze of streets and alleys along the Green Line, with Robertson sandwiched in the back seat between two gunmen, while a third tagged along behind on the reporter's motorcycle. The kidnappers made no attempt to avoid checkpoints. They readily identified themselves as Hizbullah and were waved through.

After a seemingly aimless drive, the gunmen stopped and ordered Robertson into a shed on the side of the road. "I looked in the door and was convinced they were going to shoot me in there," he told colleagues later. "I was shaking uncontrollably, but I refused to go in. 'Shoot me if you want to,' I shouted at the guy, 'but do it in the open. I'm not going in.'" Suddenly, the driver yelled to the gunmen threatening Robertson. The would-be killers jumped back in the car and roared off, leaving the trembling and bewildered reporter standing alone, wondering why he was alive and free.

Were these abortive kidnappings? If so, were the gunmen part of the same group that abducted the others? It was something we all wondered about and debated. We had a strong suspicion that these chance encounters were more likely to involve freelance gangs who figured they could jump on the bandwagon or maybe even sell their prizes to the "real" kidnappers. The experience of three other reporters months later provided evidence that not all the kidnappers believed they were carrying out the will of God.

Steve Hagey, a slow-talking Tennessean who was UPI's Beirut bureau chief, picked a hell of a night to have dinner with a couple of friends at the Relais de Normandie restaurant.

"I got about five steps into the place and saw the guys with guns who had about 15 or 20 patrons lined up against the wall," he said later.[4] At first, he thought it was a joke. "There's this guy standing there with a tablecloth around his face. I looked at him and laughed." Mistake number one. It certainly took the heat off the other guests.

"He jammed a gun in my gut and asked, 'You Amerikani?'" In short order, the gunman relieved Hagey of about $300 in Lebanese money he had in his pocket and found his tape recorder. "You CIA!" he announced. What started as an ordinary heist had struck gold.

Hagey and his companions, Reuters reporter Bill Maclean, a 29-year-old Canadian, and Maggie Fox, a 25-year-old freelance radio correspondent, were bundled into a car. The four gunmen ordered Hagey to direct them to his apartment.

"We were scared stiff. We hardly looked at each other. We had walked into a robbery and now our worst fears had come true: we were being kidnapped."

At Hagey's apartment, his glasses were pulled off and the three reporters were blindfolded with shirts and socks. The apartment was ransacked. A stereo, cameras and clothes were packed up. Hagey was asked if he had any money hidden there. When he said no, a gun barrel was pressed behind his ear. He told them to try the filing cabinet. "The whole time I smelled them eating tangerines."

The three reporters were forced to help carry the loot down to the car, then they went to Maclean's apartment and repeated the process. That's where things turned ugly.

Maclean and Fox were taken into the bedroom and Hagey heard the gunmen arguing. One of them emerged looking crazed and blindfolded Hagey with a tie. The reporter was convinced they were all going to die.

"It was strange. I kept expecting to hear a knife or gurgling or something. The whole time I was really calm. I figured I was dead anyway." The next thing he knew, Hagey was lifted up, carried outside and put in the trunk of a car. When he asked where he was being taken, the gunmen told him to shut up. "At that point, I figured *halas*," Hagey recalled, using the Arabic word for "finished." "I was glad for Bill and Maggie, but I figured this was it for me."

Hagey was taken into the Shi'ite slums south of the city where his captors made several stops. He was shifted to a small pickup truck and later to a Volvo sedan while the apparent leader of the group disappeared into a succession of nondescript houses. The gunmen seemed to be looking for someone or someplace. Later, one of his guards, who had been tormenting the reporter by slapping him and waving a gun in his direction, told Hagey they were calling Hizbullah to sell him. If the boast was true, they apparently couldn't find a buyer.

In the alley outside one house, his guards ranted about Reagan and the CIA, promising that they would force all Americans to leave Beirut. "I said, 'Let me go and I'm outta here.'" Instead, the guard put a gun to Hagey's head and told him, "We send you home tomorrow. In a box. We like to see your American blood in Beirut."

"He pressed the gun tighter against my head and said, 'Steve, this is your last night. What do you think of that?' Then he laughed and dry-fired several times. I slumped against him, it just went out of me," Hagey admitted. "A fist flew out and one of the other guards hit me in the face with the flat of his hand while they shouted about Reagan and the Kataeb [Phalangists]. I tried to tell them that *suhifi* [reporters] were okay, that not all Americans were bad, but they wouldn't listen."

Apparently unable to auction off a fit, young news agency reporter, the gunmen wrapped a jacket around Hagey's head to cover his eyes and took him to a house somewhere nearby. There he was blindfolded again and made to sit in the corner of a long corridor. Hagey was hoping he would be allowed to get some sleep. The gunmen had other ideas. Since they couldn't sell him, they decided to shake him down.

"One guy came up and patted me on the shoulder and asked if I was okay. I whispered that I was fine. Then he told me they wanted $100,000. I told him I didn't have that much money." That was all right, the gunman assured Hagey, they would take a check.

The reporter tried to convince them that no one would cash his check for $100,000, but they wouldn't listen. One of Hagey's checkbooks was produced and a gunman announced in broken English, "We want sex."

"You can image what went through my mind. Panic. Then I realized he didn't say 'sex,' he said 'six.' They wanted six checks totaling $100,000. Half of me wanted to cry and the other half wanted to laugh. I thought, 'God, deliver me from this so I can tell the story.'"

As he wrote the checks, Hagey told the gunmen six didn't divide evenly into 100 and asked if $96,000 would do. After he had written two $16,000 checks, he again tried to explain to the gunmen that the checks would bounce. "I figured that they were going to hold onto me and would get even madder when they went to the bank and couldn't cash the checks." This time he succeeded. The apparent leader nodded and left the room, only to return a moment later with a Czech-made Skorpion machine pistol and a silencer that he slowly screwed onto the barrel.

"It was about a foot long. I figured, here it is. They've swatted the mouse around, had their fun. I'm gonna die and there won't even be any noise."

Hagey braced himself for death as the weapon was pressed against his chest, waited a long moment, then watched incredulously as the gunman silently mouthed the words, "Boom, boom."

The easygoing Tennessean bristled in anger at the memory. "You know, working in Lebanon, you can't help but have some sympathy for these people and all they're going through. Then they go and do that kind of thing. I don't know."

One of the other guards then popped the ammunition clip out of his own pistol and handed Hagey the gun.

"Then he handed me the clip. I was flabbergasted. I had the gun in one hand and the ammunition in the other. I thought briefly about jamming in the clip and blowing them away, but figured I'd probably slip and be dead before I knew what happened." So Hagey examined the pistol, said it was a beautiful gun and handed it back. It was the turning point of his captivity.

"After that, they didn't threaten me or rough me up." They haggled some more and by dawn Hagey had convinced his captors to let him go on the condition that he would go to the bank and meet them that evening with $10,000 cash. "I had a feeling we all knew this was bullshit and just a chance to get this thing over with without them losing face."

Hagey was driven to a taxi rank near the Kuwaiti embassy, where the kidnappers bargained with one of the drivers over the fare. Hagey told them he didn't have any money to pay for the trip home. "No problem, Mr. Steve," one of the gunmen said and proceeded to pay the driver with the cash he had stolen from Hagey.

The next day, when the reporter was safe in London, his kidnappers telephoned UPI's Beirut office. "Where is Mr. Hagey?" the caller asked. "He did not keep his word. He is no gentleman. But we know how to deal with people like this. We have turned this over to our collection agency."

Peter Kilburn, a 60-year-old AUB librarian, fell victim to a more determined band of thugs. A gentle man who spoke often of his love of God, Kilburn disappeared on November 30, 1984. For the next 16 months, his hosts tried to find a buyer for the ailing American, who suffered from heart disease and hypertension. U.S. intelligence sources said the group was demanding "many millions of dollars." Through middlemen, the Reagan administration opened negotiations, but someone else met the price first.[5]

Shortly after the U.S. bombing raid on Libya in March 1986, Col. Qaddafi offered a million dollars for any of the American hostages in Lebanon. Apparently on his behalf, the Palestinian extremist faction headed by Abu Nidal bought Kilburn and promptly executed him in retribution for the attack. With him died two British nationals kidnapped by Abu Nidal's men a few weeks earlier. This was Prime Minister Margaret Thatcher's punishment for allowing the U.S. planes to fly from British bases.

One man who refused to be intimated by the terrorists was Prof. Thomas Sutherland, the dean of agriculture at AUB. A tall, expansive man with a wide grin, Sutherland had arrived in Beirut from Colorado State University just as the Druzes had started shelling the Marines. The fighting hadn't driven him out, nor would the kidnappings.

"I'm not panicked in any way, shape or form," he announced confidently in late spring of 1984 as he sat in the sunny lounge of his home with its commanding views of the campus playing fields and the sea. Gesturing to his smiling wife and fresh-scrubbed teenage daughter, who had come from the States to spend the semester at AUB, Sutherland insisted, "We enjoy life here. I would have to say that."

But he didn't intend to do anything stupid. "Its wise at this time to be cautious and not silly about it. I'm not treating any of those threats lightly." That meant only occasional trips off campus. "Usually we go out two together, or something like that, and don't go out a lot. We go out something like once or twice a week so we don't feel like we're absolute prisoners."

An easygoing man, Sutherland was angry about the embassy's decision to move to East Beirut. "It seems like a kind of capitulation to the scene."

One year later, on June 9, 1985, while he was returning from the airport after a trip to the U.S., Sutherland drove right into Islamic Jihad's arms. The likable teacher from Fort Collins became the ninth American kidnapped since the beginning of 1984.

Alann Steen tried to keep a low profile in Beirut. The journalism professor was part of the small group of American teachers at Beirut University College (BUC). Smaller and less prestigious than AUB, the school lived in the academic shadow of its better-known rival. While AUB might have looked better on their resumes, the relative obscurity of BUC offered certain advantages for the American faculty. While their AUB colleagues were being stalked by the kidnappers, the BUC professors seemed to have been largely forgotten. Still, they were careful.

"The damage that was done by the U.S. involvement here, I think, is going to be indelible," Steen predicted in mid-1984. "I feel, I suppose, a little bit fearful right now."

And while the kidnappers seemed to be ignoring BUC, Steen was under no illusions. "I'm sure my name is on a dossier in somebody's file and I'm sure it's not the U.S. embassy's."

Steen and the BUC crowd would hold on long after most other Americans had fled. Somehow, they continued to remain immune. Until the day in early 1987 when a group of men dressed in Lebanese police uniforms came on campus and summoned the Americans together for a meeting about security. The visitors said they wanted to demonstrate how a real kidnapping took place. As their wives watched, Steen, two other American professors and an Indian with an American residency permit were summoned forward. The Americans laughed and joked as the men locked on handcuffs. They stopped laughing when the men pulled out guns and led them away.

I had a deep and abiding desire not to spend a year chained to a radiator. A little part of the reporter in me did wonder what it would be like to be kidnapped (just as so many reporters secretly hoped to be hijacked).[6] It might make a great story. On the other hand, if you were blindfolded alone in a room 24 hours a day, there wouldn't be an awful lot to say, assuming you eventually got out.

While we endlessly debated the question of whether we, as reporters, still retained a certain immunity (tied with that was the issue of who was behind Levin's abduction), each of us made his or her own personal evaluation of the threat and adjusted his or her life accordingly. In the past, I had usually walked to work. It was a pleasant ten-minute stroll. The aroma of oven-fresh *manouche* (a pizza-like bread eaten at breakfast) wafted from the bakery. Shopkeepers sipping Arabic coffee outside their stores waved good morning, and the guard at the gates of BUC always gave me a smart salute as I cut across the terraced campus to our office at the Commodore. All that stopped. Now, our drivers Bechir or Ayad drove me the few blocks to work each day.

It seemed silly. The neighborhood between the office and my apartment was full of people and cars. But that had not helped Levin or Buckley or Weir. And if all those shopkeepers I waved to knew the route I took each day, it wouldn't be hard for others with a less pleasant greeting to find out.

So each morning when I came down, one of the drivers would be waiting, talking to the Druze militiamen who protected our building (which I had chosen precisely because of their presence, and because it was in a part of town away from my original neighborhood, which I had shared with the kidnapped Americans). "*Mafi Jihad al-Islamia*" (No Islamic Jihad), they would sometimes tease, telling me the coast was clear. It became a joke, but it was comforting to know my enemy was their enemy. I might get grabbed somewhere else, but at least nobody was going to kidnap me in front of my own house with my armed friends standing there.

Still, none of us doubted that if the kidnappers decided they wanted you, they were going to get you. There was no way to prevent it. Some reporters and a few other Americans used that argument as a reason not to alter their lives. If you were doomed in the end, why bother inconveniencing yourself now? I worked on the principal that if I made it difficult for them (whoever "they" were), maybe they would try for somebody else. After all, it wasn't as if I was the U.S. ambassador. Down at my level, we were all pretty interchangeable.

Trying to weigh how much danger we were in, we turned to the people we assumed knew better than we did. Since Ambassador Bartholomew had taken over, the embassy had been reticent about talking to reporters, reticent to the degree that about the only U.S. diplomat who was officially allowed to have much to do with us was the spokesman, Jon Stewart, and he never had anything to say. So when we approached the embassy for a briefing on the security situation in late summer of 1984, it took a while to convince them that we were not looking for a story. Yes, we were reporters, but we were also Americans. As Americans, we wanted to know exactly what our embassy knew about the threat to us.

"I don't want any of this to appear in print in any form," the "senior diplomat" warned as he walked into the room. I suppose I am breaking that agreement now, but only because there is nothing to give away. It is illustrative of how Americans in Beirut were left in the dark.

"If I were an American here and had any choice in the matter, I'd get out," he solemnly advised us. "It's very dangerous here right now for Americans."

Was that so? How enlightening. Perhaps he could give us a few specifics?

"No."

Anything on whether reporters had been targeted?

"No."

Or on who was behind the kidnappings?

"No."

The official *did* emotionally deny any connection between the kidnapped Americans and the 17 men being held in Kuwait, but I knew he was lying. By then, I had been told by several sources that the two were intimately linked. Perhaps the official himself was being lied to – not impossible, but also not likely.

Paranoia about the press might have been what kept him from telling us anything useful, but it wasn't just that. A lot of other Americans in Beirut were complaining about the same thing. At group briefings on the AUB campus and in individual meetings, security officials advised U.S. citizens to vary their routines, to travel to and from work at different times and by different routes, but they said little about the threat itself beyond "it's dangerous in Beirut."

"They've been saying that all along; this is nothing new," complained Prof. Richard Day. "Since I came here in 1980, they've said you've got to be a little concerned about what's going on in Lebanon. They warn us there are obvious dangers. I think you have to be slightly stupid not to see those dangers, but it's the same concern. It would help if we had good information."

"I have heard nothing useful from the embassy," Joe Curtin concurred.

The bottom line on the embassy briefings: "You're on your own. Our security can't do anything for you."

The Americans who were left in Beirut may have been expecting too much. They wanted their government to say, 'We know a series of attacks are being planned; you better get out." A general warning about danger was not going to make them leave, as a U.S. travel advisory for Lebanon had been in effect since 1975. They knew that the government couldn't give away specifics that would compromise intelligence gathering, but they did want some evidence that the embassy really knew what it was taking about. The AUB mass kidnapping story had the ring of Phalangist disinformation. They wondered how much more of the embassy's intelligence was the same.

"Some say that because Israel is supported by America we cannot defeat it, yet in the long term we will. No matter what the might is of the superpowers, no matter that some nations are stronger or larger than we, we shall defeat them," the gray-bearded sheikh tells the barefoot young men assembled on the floor before him, raptly intent on the lecturer's every word. A cheap blue curtain hanging from the cement pillars isolates the women out of sight in one corner of the large, square room.

"We must remember what the Islamic revolution put as a plan: Do not be with the East or with the West. Be with Allah." A black shawl worn over gray robes rustles slightly as he gestures toward the water-stained ceiling with its peeling paint. The rhythm is that of gifted preachers the world over. He uses his voice as a tenor might, repeating certain Arabic phrases, raising it an octave each time, weaving a hypnotic spell until reaching a crescendo that prompts a chorus of "Allah Akhbar" ("God is great") from the crowd.

Portraits of Ayatollah Khomeini and the Imam Musa Sadr hang on the chipped concrete wall behind the holy man. A bodyguard stands at his side. Other gunmen wait at the door, collecting weapons along with the shoes.

Against the wall, an ancient sheikh, too old now to lecture, squints through fading eyes as he strains to hear the words that have been repeated a thousand times in hundreds of similarly nondescript halls across Lebanon and the Middle East. The green flag of Islam and the black flag of the Shi'ites fly from the roof outside, but this is no mosque. It is called a Husseiniyeh, an institution named for the Prophet Muhammed's martyred grandson, whom the Shi'ites revere.

In its strictest sense, a Husseiniyeh was a religious school where clerics lectured on the meaning of Muhammed's teachings. In Lebanon, the Husseiniyehs had become centers for the spread of radical politics influenced by Iran. There, fundamentalist clerics stoked the fires fueled by U.S. and Israeli policy. Some of the shadows that were chasing the Americans dwelled in these religious schools.

Each teacher had his flock. Because the war had destroyed the economy, most of the students were young men without jobs. Because the war had taught them about violence, most knew how to fight. Imbued with a hatred inspired by their teachers, killing the enemies of the Shi'ites was the logical next step. Sometimes, the clerics knew about and helped plot the attacks. In other cases, the young men carried out on their own what they interpreted to be the wishes of their teacher.

It was in the Husseiniyehs that Hizbullah had its roots. In the early days, it was not so much an organization as a trend, inspired by a grouping of the same name that had grown up during the revolution in Iran. Literally translated as "The Party of God," the name was derived from a verse in the Qur'an: "And whoso taketh Allah and His messenger and those who believe for [a] friend (will know that), lo! The Party of God [Hizbullah], they are the victorious."[7]

In Lebanon, Hizbullah first surfaced in the Bekaa Valley, where Shi'ite clerics in close touch with the Iranian Revolutionary Guards in Baalbek began to proselytize on behalf of Khomeini's revolution. Initially, according to Amal officials and Western diplomats, Hussein Musawi's Islamic Amal organization acted as the clerics' military arm. Eventually, however, the religious men began to develop armed cadres of their own. As the Israeli occupation and the U.S. military presence radicalized clerics elsewhere in Lebanon, they, too, began to espouse the extremist politics of Hizbullah.

An Amal official described the genesis of Hizbullah this way: "One sheikh obtains a financier, then he gets money, then he hires people. Sometimes Hizbullah is a huge organization, sometimes it is not. It depends on the flow of money."

Money buys muscle, and not all the people who called themselves Hizbullah were working for Allah's will. One businessman told of a mysterious visitor to his office: "My secretary told me there was an Abu Ali to see me. A large man with a full black beard and dark sunglasses came in and sat down. 'You don't recognize me,' he said. I told him no, I didn't. He took off his sunglasses and smiled. 'It's me, Abu Ali.' Then I realized who he was. The guy used to be a big shot in [a pro-Syrian leftist party]. Now he was Hizbullah with the full beard and the whole thing. I asked him what he was doing. 'I know which way the wind blows,' he told me. 'They've got all the money.'"

Some of the clerics operated under separate banners, like Sheikh Arkadan's Ajama'a Islamia (Islamic Grouping) in Sidon or Sheikh Zuhair Kanj's Tajama'a al-Ulama al-Muslami (the Gathering of Muslims). Others, such as Sheikh Subhi Tofeili in the Bekaa and Sheikh Ibrahim al-Amin in Beirut, actually called the groups they led Hizbullah. Sometimes these groups overlapped (Islamic Amal and Hizbullah shared offices in Baalbek) and sometimes they were at odds with one another. Some of the groups, such as the Musawis and their Mugniyeh kin, were actually extended families, but all of them considered themselves part of the Hizbullah tendency. A statement by Islamic Amal head Hussein Musawi, whose clan had been linked to most of the terrorist acts claimed by Islamic Jihad, illustrates the point: "We belong to the Party of God, which believes in the Islamic line of Imam Khomeini."

Even when Hizbullah began opening offices in Beirut, it appeared to remain more of a movement than an organization as such.

"To say that Hizbullah is doing this or that is wrong," explained an Amal official after one terrorist incident. "You have to identify the group. So when you want to shell Hizbullah in Baalbek in punishment, you are shelling the wrong group."

The gray-bearded cleric lecturing the entranced students at the Husseiniyeh had been called the leader of Hizbullah. He denied that and, in the Western sense of Hizbullah being an organization, it was probably true. He also denied claims that he had been involved in the bombing of the Marine headquarters and that might have been true as well. But there was no doubt that Muhammed Hussein Fadlallah was the spiritual leader of those who "taketh Allah and His messenger and those who believe for [a] friend."

"Hizbullah is a word in the Qur'an. There is a verse in the Qur'an that says the Hizbullah are the blessed," Fadlallah obliquely replied after the lecture, when asked if he was the group's leader. "This represents pure Islam, in an effective and practical and good way."

"We do not approve that such as organization as Hizbullah be turned into a political party or organization. We want to maintain this party free and independent. I represent an independent way of thinking, an independent philosophy," he explained, sitting calmly and erectly in a living room with few decorations aside from a portrait of Khomeini. Born and trained in the Shi'ite holy city of Najaf, Iraq, while his cleric father was studying in the religious schools there, Fadlallah maintained close links with the ayatollah, who spent part of his exile in Iraq.

Followers with pistols sat with him in the room. Before entering the apartment, visitors were frisked by several layers of guards with automatic weapons who sealed off the street on which the cleric lived. The need for the precautions was graphically demonstrated in early 1985, when a car bomb meant for Fadlallah destroyed the adjacent building, killing 85 people. The *Washington Post* reported that CIA-trained Lebanese agents carried out the failed assassination attempt. The CIA claimed the story was false, but that did not ease the outrage of Fadlallah's followers. Beneath a banner that read "Made in the U.S.A.," thousands massed in front of the wrecked building calling for American blood.[8]

One man who had already proved his ability to shed that blood was among those most deeply affected by the failed assassination attempt.

Killed in the blast was a Fadlallah bodyguard named Jihad Mugniyeh, brother of Imad Mugniyeh, the man who had organized the Marine and embassy bombings and was overseeing the kidnapping of Americans. His rage would be felt for years to come.

It was just such a cycle of cause-and-effect that Fadlallah pointed to when, in that interview long before the attempt on his life, he charged that ultimate blame for the attacks on Americans rested with the U.S. "We are not from those who inspire these explosions," he said, glancing at the young men guarding the door. "We do not adopt this style in our work. But we are asking those who denounce the act why they do not think of the causes. People believe the American administration is against their freedom and probably against their existence. If this feeling escalates, they will express themselves in one way or another."

In an interview with a Washington magazine a year later, Fadlallah elaborated on his role: "Yes, I speak with the people about facing American imperialistic plans, [b]ut I do not tell them, I do not specify, for example, 'Blow yourself up.' I call for freedom. If colonialism oppresses a people, the people should fight for it. But to say that I lead people to do violent acts – no."[9]

He did not have to. Tradition taught that the mullahs needed only to provide the broad guidance and their followers would do the rest. Yet even if he *had* explicitly ordered the bombings, there was another tradition that protected Fadlallah. Whereas the doctrine of "plausible deniability" shielded his would-be assassins in the CIA, the ancient Shi'ite art of *taqiyah* allowed Fadlallah to lie about his actions for the greater good.[10]

Others did not bother to obscure their involvement in terror. Opening a February 1985 Hizbullah rally in Beirut, a cleric called Sheikh Gabris boasted that "it was Hizbullah which activated the fighters and expelled the enemy."

In a 48-page manifesto read at the rally by Sheikh Ibrahim al-Amin, the acknowledged head of Hizbullah in Beirut (regularly cited by the Lebanese press as Fadlallah's top aide), the movement defined itself as "the children of the nation whose vanguard in Iran was bestowed with victory." He claimed that Hizbullah had no card-carrying members but promised that "we are headed for dealing with evil at its roots, and the roots are America."

Among Hizbullah's demands: "America, France, and their allies must leave Lebanon once and for all, and any imperial influence in the country must be terminated." It sounded suspiciously like an Islamic Jihad communiqué. With good reason. If the structure of Hizbullah was indistinct, the family tree of Islamic Jihad was a spider's web of intricacy.

There was no Islamic Jihad office; no spokesman reporters could take to lunch. Just the anonymous voices at the other end of the phone. The claims were sometimes contradictory. For example, after Islamic Jihad claimed responsibility for the assassination attempt against the Kuwaiti emir, another caller who said *he* was speaking for the *real* Islamic Jihad said the organization was not involved. The demands varied as well.

Journalists at Western news agencies who fielded the anonymous calls learned to recognize the regulars whom they could trust as genuine. (Islamic Jihad would eventually tell reporters that only statements backed up by pictures of the hostages should be considered authentic.) However, a new voice did not necessarily signal a hoax. All the evidence indicated that Islamic Jihad was not one group but many, all using the name Jihad al-Islami (Islamic Holy War) to create the impression of a Muslim hydra capable of lashing out at its enemies wherever they tried to hide. (Decades later, after al-Qaeda was driven out of Afghanistan, militant Muslim groups around the world would emulate Islamic Jihad's approach.)

"To protect themselves from direct retribution, they tried to mask their activities under the nom de plume 'Islamic Jihad,' which is sort of an umbrella trade name," CIA Director William Casey said in an address to the Fletcher School of Law and Diplomacy in April 1985. The tactic had been employed before, when the PLO had used the cover "Black September" for its terrorist acts in the early 1970s.[11]

Along with the Shi'ite clerics who fell loosely under the Hizbullah banner, other closely allied groups were believed by Lebanese and Western sources to use the name Islamic Jihad for their violent operations. They included such organizations as the Hussein Suicide Commandos, led by Hussein Musawi's cousin, Abu Haidar Musawi (who American intelligence sources claimed provided the trucks, and possibly the men, for the bombings of the Marine and French headquarters); al-Da'wa, which was tied to the Kuwait bombings; the Organization of the Oppressed of the Earth, which would claim credit for some of the kidnappings; and a grab bag of others.[12]

Not all were Shi'ite. Sheikh Said Shabaan's Tawheed (Unity) movement in Tripoli was made up of fundamentalist Sunni Muslims. So were one or two other groups in South Lebanon.

A few leaders, such as Shabaan, received some aid from Yasser Arafat, who was trying to get his foot back in Lebanon's door after twice being expelled, in 1982 and 1983, but the prime conduit, according to Lebanese and Western sources, was Iran. Much of the money was funneled through the Iranian embassy in Damascus. The rest came from the Martyr's Foundation, an organization that provided payments to the families of Iranian soldiers killed in the war with Iraq. The foundation's director,

Hojatoleslam Mahdi Karoubi, traveled openly to Lebanon to meet Shi'ite leaders there. On his first trip to Beirut in 1984, Karoubi arrived carrying $3 million in cash.

The financing was provided on the authority of the Supreme Coordinating Council of the Islamic Revolution and the Islamic Revolutionary Organizations. The council was publicly unveiled in September 1981 and was headed by Ayatollah Hossein Ali Montazeri and Hojatoleslam Muhammed Musawi Khoeni (who had led the 1979 takeover of the U.S. embassy in Tehran). Its task was to oversee the export of the Iranian revolution. Western intelligence officials said members of the council included the commander of the Revolutionary Guards, Mohsen Rafigh-Doust, who had previously served as commander in the Bekaa; Khomeini's defense advisor, Muhammed Mir-Salim; Hojatoleslam Muhammed Bager Hakim, the Iraqi head of al-Da'wa; Mehdi Hashemi, Montazeri's aide and the man in day-to-day charge of terrorist training and operations; and numerous other high-ranking Iranian personalities. Syrian and Libyan intelligence officials were frequently consulted.

Under the governing body in Tehran, according to Arab and Western sources, were regional councils charged with specific areas, including Iraq, the Persian Gulf, Western Europe, the United States, Lebanon, Africa and Asia.

The Iranian embassy in Damascus, according to Western intelligence sources, was the operations center for the Council for Lebanon, which was also responsible for Syria and Jordan. One expert in Damascus called it "the center for terrorism in the Levant." Intelligence sources monitoring activity around the embassy claimed that at least once a month, the council's members gathered in the office of Ambassador Ali Akhbar Mohtashami to plot strategy and plan operations. Among those allegedly present at the meetings were Fadlallah, Hussein Musawi, Abu Haidar Musawi, Sheikh Tofeili, Sheikh Ibrahim al-Amin, representatives of Syrian intelligence and other figures linked to Hizbullah and its companion groups.

There was no governing body of Islamic Jihad, but Western and Arab intelligence sources keeping watch on Iran suspected that the Council for Lebanon and its parent in Tehran were the closest thing to it.

"It is not the only source of Islamic Jihad operations, but it is one of them," said one Western diplomat with access to the intelligence reports. "Fadlallah and the Musawis are not necessarily at every meeting, but they are part of what is going on."

As for Ambassador Mohtashami, one grave-faced U.S. official said, "This man has caused us terrible trouble. He is intimately involved in the Lebanon operations, far overshadowing anyone else."

Ambassador Ali Akhbar Mohtashami had the demeanor of one who was at peace with himself. Sitting beside me on a couch in his embassy office, Mohtashami's face was lit by a beatific smile. More loudly than words, it told of an inner conviction that he was working God's will. I tried to recall where I had seen such a look before. The answer shook me. It was when I had met the pope.

"Iran certainly helps every movement which wants to be free of the domination of the East and West," Mohtashami affirmed in a soft voice. "Naturally, if America comes to our area and does not give attention to the people, it is natural that the people cannot accept the entity that wants to destroy your entity, that wants to kill and destroy everything that you have."

Mohtashami was a hojatoleslam, the religious rank just below that of ayatollah. The robes and turban increased my sense that I should be talking about God, not terror, with this man of the cloth. But it was not long after entering Mohtashami's office on the upper floors of the Iranian embassy that it became apparent there was both religion and violence in his life.

Greeting me, Mohtashami reached out with the mangled remains of his left hand. Only the thumb was intact. The two index fingers ended at the second joint. The other fingers were gone. The right hand was a rubber fake. The detailed work, complete with fingernails and skin creases at the joints, looked so realistic that I was at first deceived.

The disfigurement had been caused by a booby-trapped Qur'an sent to the ambassador several months after the Marine bombing. The gift had blown up in Mohtashami's face when he had opened it. He had spent six months in a German hospital recovering from his wounds. This man of the cloth was a man with enemies.

Mohtashami spoke of the United States as a student who had failed the test administered by his teachers in Vietnam, Iran and Nicaragua. "When it came to Lebanon, we were hoping America had learned from past defeats. We were hoping America was thinking before coming to Lebanon and that now American policy would not commit new faults. We thought that because they made so many mistakes in the past, that in the future America had no capacity to make more," Mohtashami said, as the embassy's first secretary, Mr. Saidi, translated. He was bearded like Mohtashami, but did not wear clerical garb.

The violence that plagued America now, the Iranian ambassador explained, came because the U.S. had taken sides against the Muslims. "America did not come to Lebanon to help the Lebanese. America came to Lebanon to safeguard its own interests and the interests of Israel. America supported Bechir and Amin Gemayel because these two persons were supporting American and Israeli interests," Mohtashami continued, his hands lying motionless in his lap.

The ambassador was reported to be one of the most vehemently anti-American members of Iran's leadership. He blamed the CIA for the bomb that had almost killed him and regularly left the room at diplomatic gatherings if an American entered. Mohtashami said that this was the first time he had spoken to an American journalist, and the encounter developed into more of a dialogue than an interview. He seemed to be picking my brain as much as I was his.[13]

Mohtashami wanted to know whether the United States would ever return to Lebanon. When told that it was unlikely since many Americans perceived the country as a seething cauldron of violence where we could not possibly win, he appeared unconvinced. "America cannot forget Lebanon and also cannot forget Israeli interests and security," he insisted, "and if America leaves Lebanon completely, the interests of Israel will be in danger."

The idea of an American return to the scene of the defeat seemed to obsess him. The Iranian ambassador raised the issue again and again. "I emphasize that the presence of America in Lebanon is very important. America cannot leave it, so America needs to do something that makes its presence in Lebanon acceptable to the Lebanese."

Was he implying, I asked, that Iran and the Shi'ites might be interested in mending their ties with the U.S.? Mohtashami pursed his lips as he framed the answer. When he spoke, the ambassador was at his most animated, waving his mangled hand in the air. "There is a difference between the question in Iran and in Lebanon. We can say that Iran has its conditions and the Lebanese Shi'ites have their conditions.

"We think that as long as America as a superpower looks to Israel in a special way and prefers it to all other countries, and until the U.S. can be nonaligned in the Middle East, there will be difficulties." The Farsi words came out in short, sharp phrases that sounded almost like a chant.

There was a globe and small Iranian flag on the ambassador's desk at the opposite end of the room. A larger, freestanding flag of the Islamic Republic stood behind it, flanking the obligatory portrait of Khomeini in a gilt-edged frame. A silhouette of Jerusalem's al-Aqsa Mosque hung on another wall.

To the right of the desk, the office opened onto a second room containing a long conference table. This, intelligence sources alleged, was where the Council for Lebanon met. According to one informant, Fadlallah had attended the most recent meeting two weeks before.

"The Islamic Republic of Iran has no relations with any specific group. Not in Lebanon or the Islamic world. I think personally that there is not anything named Islamic Jihad," Mohtashami said, shaking his head, when I asked him about Iran's relationship to the shadowy organization. "There is no entity whose name is Islamic Jihad."

He asked me what I thought Islamic Jihad was. I outlined my understanding of the structure and membership of the Supreme Council and the Council for Lebanon. When I said I had been told that he was a key figure behind the attacks against Americans and that the Council for Lebanon met in the room in which we sat, Mohtashami's face split in a wide grin.

He was silent for a few moments, then shifted in his seat, cleared his throat and replied enigmatically, "Sometimes you can tell the news is false by looking to the news itself." He shifted his robes and continued. "Let me tell you clearly that I have 20 years of struggle in Iran and Iraq against the American intervention in our countries. A person like me is not afraid if it is said about him this or that." There was amusement, not anger, on his face.

"This is one of the American faults that America thinks every accident, every activity in every place should be attributed to Iran. We want to say that the people of this area have a political sense. They understand what they want, and they understand their enemies. They can act without us. Naturally, Iran stands ready to help."

When we spoke at the end of May 1985, seven Americans were being held captive by Islamic Jihad. One of them was a friend, Associated Press Middle East correspondent Terry Anderson. Based in Beirut, Anderson and his staff had written extensively on the Israeli occupation of South Lebanon. I pointed out to Mohtashami the irony that a reporter whose work had benefited the Shi'ites was being held captive by them.

"Yes, it is too bad about your friend," Khomeini's man in Damascus said as he walked me to the door. "He is innocent. They are all innocent as individuals. It is a very unfortunate situation. They are suffering for the policy of your government, just as others will suffer until that policy changes."

Two weeks later, TWA flight 847 was hijacked to Beirut.

In the training camps of Iran and the Bekaa, young fighters from around the Middle East were being taught the fundamentals of terror. As far as the foreign experts could determine, some were dispatched on specific missions, some were sent back to their countries to join a pool of men who could be activated on command, and some returned home and carried out operations at the time and place of their own choosing. Iranian Revolutionary Guards and *basiiji* (volunteers) were also deployed as part of the general destabilization campaign. The overall goal was to topple moderate Muslim regimes and replace them with Islamic societies created in the image of Iran. Islamic Jihad was the name most often used when the time came to claim credit.

A sampling of the demands made by some of the bombers and kidnappers gives a hint of their common Iranian parentage:

- A halt in French arms sales to Iraq, Iran's opponent in the Gulf War;
- The cancellation of a French barter deal with Saudi Arabia to trade oil for Mirage fighter jets (the Saudis downed two Iranian jets in a June 1984 dogfight);
- The withdrawal of all Westerners from Lebanon, to clear the way for the establishment of an Islamic state.

At times, even the shield of Islamic Jihad did not put enough distance between Iran and a specific terrorist operation. The 1985 assassination attempt against the emir of Kuwait was a case in point. Shortly after the suicide driver rammed his car into Sheikh Sabah's motorcade, killing four people and slightly injuring the ruler, a caller speaking for Islamic Jihad telephoned a news agency in Beirut. "We hope His Highness has gotten our message," the caller said. "We once again demand the release of the [17] prisoners [in Kuwait]; otherwise all the thrones of the Gulf will be shaken."

The suicide driver was identified as a member of the Iraqi Shi'ite al-Da'wa group, the same Iranian-backed organization of which the Kuwait embassy bombers were said to be members. In the uproar that followed, fingers throughout the Gulf pointed toward Tehran. Someone apparently decided that a bit of public relations damage control was needed. Iranian President Ali Khamene'i sent a message of condolences, claiming that his country "deplores terrorism," and Islamic Jihad made a phone call denying responsibility, charging that the bombing was part of a plot to give it a bad name.

The Kuwaitis had been backing Iraq in the Iran–Iraq war, to the annoyance of Iran. They had been keeping close tabs on Iran's links to 500,000 Shi'ite guest workers in their country, most of them from Iraq, Iran and Lebanon.

"Diplomatic trickery won't justify the reality of Iran's position on the side of the organization that claimed responsibility for the incident," wrote Abdul Aziz al-Masaeed, the outspoken publisher of *al-Ra'i al-Aam*. "Everyone knows that the [Islamic Jihad] organization gets support and blessings from Iran."[14]

If the circumstantial evidence was not enough, the Iranians were not always shy about publicly revealing their ideological and physical links to the terrorists. A pair of writers for a French magazine who claimed to have toured the camps in Lebanon and Iran quoted Muhammed Taki al-Moudarrissa, an Iranian who reputedly headed one suicide unit, as boasting, "I can in one week assemble 500 faithful who are ready to give their lives. No barrier will stop them."[15]

Similarly, Iran's UN delegate, Said Rajaie Khorassani, told the General Assembly six weeks after the Marine bombing that the United States "must prepare itself for further punishment from the Lebanese Muslim masses and further retaliation."[16]

Iranian President Ali Khamene'i concurred. In a sermon marking the fifth anniversary of the takeover of the U.S. embassy in Tehran, he told the assembled faithful that "as long as the U.S. conspires against this nation and against the Islamic Republic, we consider it is our right to retaliate and hit against U.S. interests anywhere in the world."[17]

Iran's hatred of the "Great Satan" stemmed primarily from U.S. backing for the Shah. The Khomeini regime had helped plant the seeds of anti-Americanism among the Lebanese Shi'ites, but that hatred was nurtured by American efforts to prop up Gemayel's Christian regime and U.S. support for the Israelis who were occupying Shi'ite land.

"You cannot go through without a pass," the Israeli lieutenant at the checkpoint on the Awali River politely explained.

"We have passes," we said, proffering our Lebanese government press cards.

The officer, a beefy man with a wild beard, smiled. "I mean an Israeli pass," he said, with emphasis on the "Israeli."

"But this is Lebanon, not Israel and we have Lebanese passes," we insisted, more to make the political point than in hopes of changing his mind.

"It may say that on the map, but these days," he gestured toward the guard tower, "this is Israel."

Sometimes, a conciliatory approached worked best. "Okay, how do we get passes?"

"You must get them from Kfar Fallous," he said, referring to an Israeli military office on the other side of the line.

"How about letting us through to get the passes and bring them back?" I suggested hopefully.

"No."

"How about letting one of us go while the others wait here?"

"No." Firmly. "No one goes through without a pass."

"Could you have someone call your people down there and ask them if they will grant us passes?"

A pause. "Let me ask the captain." A ray of hope.

A few minutes later, he was back with the inevitable news. "The captain says we can do nothing. You must obtain the pass on your own and then you may go through."

"But how can we get passes if we can only pick them up in South Lebanon and you won't let us into South Lebanon without passes?"

The beard parted in a sly smile. "I think that is what is called a Catch-22."

One of his colleagues proposed a solution: "You know how to get there," he teased, holding his hand over the camera lens. "Go back to Beirut, get on a plane to Cyprus, fly to Ben Gurion Airport, then drive up with a military escort."

South Lebanon had become a nation apart. It was a virtual colony of Israel. Israeli troops had been welcomed as liberators by the region's people in the summer of 1982. They had freed South Lebanon from the often-oppressive rule of the PLO. But instead of cultivating the goodwill of the Shi'ites, instead of sending in agricultural advisors and engineers to help the people of the region develop their wrecked infrastructure, instead of acting like a good neighbor beside whom the Shi'ites could happily live, the Israelis acted like the army of occupation that they were. Instead of listening to its own experts on Lebanon who said that Shi'ites who trusted Israel would be a far more effective buffer against the PLO than any army, the government in Jerusalem listened to the generals and sent in more guns.

When the Israelis moved their front line south to the Awali River in September 1983, they further tightened their grip on the vast area of South Lebanon they continued to occupy. Within a few months, the Israelis had firmly established themselves as hated overlords, architects of an occupation viewed by the Muslims as more brutal than anything they had endured before.

Shi'ites who had thrown rice to welcome Israeli forces in 1982 were now throwing grenades. Incited by the fiery sermons of the fundamentalist clergy, they launched almost daily attacks against Israeli troops. Guerrillas fired rockets at passing Israeli convoys and suicide drivers rammed Israeli armored vehicles with explosives-laden cars. The Israelis struck back with a vengeance. Thousands of young Shi'ites were rounded up and imprisoned in the Ansar detention camp, a barbed-wire compound that had been built to house Palestinians when *they* were the primary enemy.

The old man stared suspiciously at the visitors who had invaded his solitude. He slowly raised himself from the ground where he had been lying in the shade against his house and brushed the dust off his dirt-smeared gallibeh (robe).

"*Assalaamu aalaykum*" ("Peace be upon you"), his visitors said in greeting.

"*Waalaykumu issalaam*" ("And upon you peace"), he whispered in reply, through toothless gums. The sight of the empty field had caught our attention. It was a brown scab amid the lush green banana groves that lined the road. At one end, near the house, were piled the gnarled roots of trees. Two bulldozers stood a few yards away. The faint scent of lemon lingered in the air like a memory of the orchard that had flourished there for many years.

At first, the old man would say little for fear that we were Israelis masquerading as reporters. But slowly, as our driver won his confidence, the story came out. It was a common one. The Israelis had uprooted the orchard. There had been an attack on one of their patrols as they passed by on the main road. The guerrillas escaped, so the old farmer took the punishment. He claimed he knew nothing of the attack. How could he stop the young gunmen from using his trees as cover? He may or may not have been telling the truth. It didn't really matter. His trees were bulldozed as a lesson to the locals, to show them what happened to those who helped the guerrillas.

The Israelis taught a lot of lessons to the people of the south. Countless farmers had seen the same thing happen to their fields. When an attack was carried out near a village, Israeli troops or their local allies moved in and rounded up the young men. Guerrillas commonly set up ambushes far from their own villages to save their families from suffering, but that didn't stop the roundups. Some clerics were exiled to Beirut; others were killed. And still the Israelis could not stop the attacks. The guerrillas and the people of the south were one and the same. The minarets of the mosques became the lookout posts. Young men would keep watch for approaching Israeli troops. The loudspeakers that broadcast the call to prayer also broadcast the call to arms. Villagers would pour into the streets, blocking the entrances with burning tires while the gunmen slipped away into the surrounding hills. Frustrated and increasingly jumpy Israeli troops drove through the streets of Sidon spraying cars and sidewalks with machine-gun fire and dumped Lebanese men into the detention camp at Ansar by the truckload. A more silent war was also being fought.

During the summer of 1983, a death list surfaced carrying the names of top Shi'ite political and religious leaders in the south. The assassins usually struck at night. Bands of plainclothes men would roll into a village, assassinate a leading cleric or suspected terrorist and disappear. UN sources reported that the assassins often used cars stolen from local towns. The vehicles would be returned by morning. No one knew who the killers were, but witnesses regularly claimed that they heard Hebrew being spoken during the shootings. That convinced many, including UN officers, that Shin Bet, the Israeli internal security apparatus, was involved. The young Israeli agents in their uniforms of jeans, open-necked shirts, Ray Ban sunglasses and Uzi submachine guns were a common sight cruising South Lebanon's roads in unmarked cars.

Still, Lebanon had plenty of homegrown killers. Muslim leaders opposed to the Israeli occupation charged that much of the dirty work was carried out by Lebanese gunmen of the South Lebanon Army, trained and equipped by Israel. Nazih Bizri, a member of Parliament from Sidon, charged that the militiamen resorted to any means to intimidate Israel's enemies: "Kidnappings, killing, exploding places, stealing cars, imposing taxes. What else can you think of?"

Hatred fed hatred. Attack sparked counterattack. To stem the flow of Israeli blood, Jerusalem inexorably tightened its grip. The Awali River, the Israeli front line in Lebanon, became more difficult to cross than most borders. First, anyone entering the south was screened. Then all Muslims were required to obtain passes issued by the Israelis (Christians had little problem getting through). Finally, all vehicles were banned in both directions. South Lebanon's economy began to wither and die.

When Muslim pressure forced Israel to close down its unofficial embassy outside Beirut, the task of entering the south grew close to impossible. The Israeli liaison office, a remnant of the occupation of Beirut, had issued the passes for the south. Now the only way for Muslims to get across the Israeli lines was to have friends or relatives in South Lebanon go to an Israeli office there and submit the name. If it was cleared, they picked up the pass and brought it to the crossing point where the traveler waited.

"I have been here for two days. I haven't heard from my friends. Isn't there something you can do?" the young Lebanese mother pleaded with us. A child of about four clung to her leg. "Look at all these people. See that woman with the children? She has been here for a week. The Israelis won't talk to us, they tell us to go away."

Hundreds of people were waiting on the northern side of the crossing. Dozens were jammed into a metal-roofed corral awaiting their turn. They were the lucky ones. They had passes. Scores of others milled around, waiting for word from the south. To one side, many had set up camp beneath the gnarled trees of an olive grove. Women nursed infants while older daughters cooked dinner over open fires.

Even having a pass was no guarantee. "The Israeli, he take my pass and rip it." The old man was indignant, confused. "He no tell me why."

"There's a women over there with a French passport. Can you help her?" a Lebanese taxi driver appealed to us. "She came with her husband and children. They had a pass. But the soldiers said she couldn't go because it said it was for a Lebanese family and her passport was foreign. Her husband and children crossed yesterday and she's still here."

Being an American was no advantage. "I just arrived from the States to see my family in the south," explained a naturalized U.S. citizen who was born Lebanese. "My American taxes are helping to pay for their goddamned checkpoint and I still can't get through."

The Red Cross complained that ambulances carrying seriously ill patients to Beirut hospitals were turned back, UN convoys of food and medical supplies for the Palestinian refugee camps in South Lebanon were blocked. In one such confrontation, Israeli officers at the Bater Jezzine crossing even confiscated the UN passport of one official. After promises of a protest "at the highest level," it was handed back.

While occasionally (but only occasionally) the Israelis would give traveling reporters the courtesy of a few words of explanation, the Lebanese were pushed, shouted at and treated with contempt. Israeli troops sometimes fired into the air to force back the crowds of people trying to move around in their own land, although the Israelis were careful to do this only when reporters were not around.

"Sometimes you see a lot of miserable people, miserable stories in front of you," observed a female law student from AUB after she pulled us behind a car out of sight of the Israelis. "But you can't do anything. Just watch and keep your mouth shut and walk."

"You talk to them," pleaded our taxi driver friend on behalf of the woman with the French passport. "We are afraid."

Reporters might have been less intimidated, but they were no more effective. When we tried to intervene, the guard abruptly replied, "That's her affair. Worry about your own business. Now go!"

After their success in driving U.S. and European troops out of Beirut, the Shi'ites directed all their efforts toward doing the same to the Israelis. The top Shi'ite religious leader, Sheikh Mahdi Shamseddine, issued a fatwa (religious order) proclaiming that "comprehensive civil resistance" was the duty of every Muslim. Amal chief Nabih Berri (by then Minister for South Lebanon in Gemayel's reconstituted cabinet) announced that suicide squads were being prepared for new raids, and clergymen in the south delivered fiery sermons demanding jihad.

The Israelis were trapped between the proverbial rock and a hard place. A quick withdrawal would stem the steady attrition that was sapping the country's strength. For a tiny nation that collectively winced each time it lost a man, the regular dirge of death announcements from the military spokesman could not go on indefinitely.

Yet to leave without some assurance that the Syrians and Palestinians would not return to haunt Israel's borders would be to negate the gains of the 1982 invasion. Menachim Begin had promised that never again would rockets fall on the border settlements. He had already been proved wrong.

And so the Israelis hunkered down in fortified positions waiting for the right combination of factors that would let them go home. Huge dirt walls capped with barbed wire and machine guns surrounded them, protection against the implacable threat. It could come from anywhere. Car bombs, truck bombs, suitcase bombs, human bombs. Resistance fighters even rigged a donkey with explosives and sent it against a checkpoint.

More and more patrols were turned over to Israel's proxies in the South Lebanon Army who were being trained to fill the void when the Israelis left. It was their country, let *them* die.

The fiercest resistance came in what the Israelis dubbed the "Iron Triangle," a collection of villages in the hills outside Tyre. This was Jebel Amel. Here the Shia had ancient roots. The region's more recent history was also inextricably entwined with that of Iran. Ties of family, education and, most importantly, religion bound the two. Imam Musa Sadr, the Iranian-born spiritual leader of Lebanon's Shi'ites, had founded a college on Jebel Amel that drew some of the men who would lead Iran's revolution. Khomeini's minister of defense, Mustapha Chamran, had once served as director of the school. Others with names made famous by the revolution, such as Beheshti and Tabatabai, had been frequent visitors to the area around Tyre. Those they taught and came into contact with would one day lead the revolt in South Lebanon. But the travel had not been one way. Many of Jebel Amel's clerics had studied in the religious universities in the Shi'ite holy cities of Qom and Najaf. The philosophy taught there had helped shape the Iranian Revolution. It had shaped the Lebanese as well. So, too, did the Iranian wives they had brought home.

The Shi'ites were at the forefront of the struggle against the Israeli occupation, but with their successes Syrian-backed Lebanese leftist and Palestinian groups joined in.

The Israelis eventually struck back with Operation Iron Fist. Armored columns sealed off villages for days on end. Homes were blown up, mosques said to contain weapons or explosives were destroyed. Muslim villagers claimed that Israeli soldiers desecrated other mosques, sending dogs (considered by Islam to be unclean) inside, tearing up the Qur'an and playing disco music from the loudspeakers used for the call to prayer.

Free-fire zones were established, in which Israeli patrols had orders to shoot at anything that moved. Even outside those areas, nervous soldiers often gunned down innocent people.

The death of innocents in South Lebanon was painfully brought home to us in March 1985 when an Israeli tank fired two shells at a CBS camera crew as they stood with a group of unarmed civilians in the village of Kfar Melki. Cameraman Tewfic Ghrazawi was literally cut in half by the blast. Soundman Behije Mehdi was lifted from the ground and killed instantly. Ayad Harake, the driver, was crippled for life. The Israeli government said the tank crew, driving a Merkava equipped with sophisticated optical devices, thought the camera was a rocket launcher. Many of us found that very hard to swallow.

Jerusalem released pictures showing the similarity between a camera and a rocket launcher when viewed head on. Head on, yes. From the side, not even close. Even an Israeli tank commander questioned privately months later dismissed that claim as "rubbish." There was no way, he insisted, that the tank crew could have made such a mistake if they had bothered to look. In his opinion, the tank crew hadn't fired on the CBS team because they were journalists; they were just shooting at anything that moved. I wasn't convinced.

The incident had followed a concerted effort by the Israelis to keep reporters out of South Lebanon. We had been banned, detained, "deported" back to the north, threatened and had warning shots fired in our direction by Israeli troops. We had been explicitly told that it would be "dangerous" for us if we persisted in trying to slip over the lines. Tewfic, Behije and Ayad discovered just how dangerous.

If they had not been journalists, the fate of the CBS crew would hardly have been noticed in the steadily mounting casualty count. More and more Lebanese were being killed or maimed almost every day. Children were among those that died. Tense confrontations occurred between Israeli units and UN troops as the peacekeepers moved in to try to prevent excesses. There were plenty of wild stories and exaggerations, but there was also plenty of horror.

The Shi'ites' hatred of Israel was building to a fever pitch and they would never forget who provided their enemy with money, weapons and political support.

14
The Unfinished Kitchen

We had adequate warning that there was a threat to our embassy, and we could have done what other embassies did. Either strengthen our security there, or remove our personnel.

—Ronald Reagan in a 1979 debate
with Jimmy Carter, referring to
the Tehran embassy takeover.[1]

In early September 1984, several members of the U.S. embassy security team were sitting in the snack bar of the new embassy in East Beirut (officially called the embassy "annex"). They were discussing the need to step up the pace of construction, when they heard shots fired by the guards outside.

At first, they thought it was a jackhammer manned by one of the work crews. With the second volley, security chief Al Bigler drew his pistol and sprinted for the exit just in time to get hit by the door as it was blown off its hinges. Bigler's face was sliced open. It would take a five-and-a-half-hour operation to put it back together.

The incoming consul general, Patricia Wazer, had just arrived from the airport. As her driver approached the first guard post, she heard shots and her car was rocked by the explosion. Wazer would meet many of her new colleagues for the first time as she visited them in the hospital over the next few days.

Army Chief Warrant Officer Kenneth Welch and Navy Petty Officer Michael Wagner were in the defense attaché's office, which faced the street. Colleagues later speculated that they had run to the window when they heard the shooting. Both men were killed.

Marine Cpl. Larry Gill was on duty at Post One, the guard booth inside the front door, when he heard the squeal of tires "and three or four shots were fired, and my lights went out."

Up on the fourth floor, Ambassador Reginald Bartholomew was meeting with his British counterpart, David Miers, when the roof came down.

Rushing into the office minutes later, Political Officer David Wynn found the British ambassador trying to dig Bartholomew out of the rubble. Miers' tie still hung around his neck, but his clothes had literally been blown off his body. His shirt had been shredded and what was left of his pants amounted to little more than a pair of shorts. He was covered with tiny lacerations from glass and shrapnel and coated with plaster dust.

Fourteen people were dead and dozens more injured. As a *Daily Star* headline put it, America's brand new embassy building had been "Lebanized."

"In the name of God, the Almighty, the Islamic Holy War Organization announces that it is responsible for blowing up a car rigged with explosives which was driven by one of our suicide commandos," the inevitable caller boasted. "The operation goes to prove that we will carry out our previous promise not to allow a single American to remain on Lebanese soil. When we say Lebanese soil, we mean every inch of Lebanese soil."

Standing amid the familiar chaos of the bomb aftermath, staring at the diplomats in blood-soaked clothes, the stretchers with victims being rushed to ambulances, the wreckage of the building, I felt none of the usual emotions triggered by a big story. No adrenaline rush, no excitement, no awe. Just a crushing sense of frustration and disbelief that it had been allowed to happen yet again.

Despite the 1983 embassy bombing, despite the destruction of the Marine headquarters, despite the Kuwait embassy blast, despite the kidnappings of Americans and despite the continued threats, the U.S. ambassador in Beirut had agreed to allow his staff to move into a building that was months away from completion.

Seven weeks after the move, Ambassador Bartholomew's office was comfortably air-conditioned, the carpets, desk and flags were in place, but the most high-risk U.S. embassy in the world still didn't even have a gate. It was a glaring deficiency of which the suicide bomber, and the planners behind him, made good use.

Driving an American van similar to those used by the embassy and equipped with diplomatic plates (stolen from a European embassy in Beirut), the bomber approached the northern end of the street that ran in front of the new embassy annex building. Both ends of the road were blocked by Lebanese guards and dragon's teeth, huge concrete blocks set so that vehicles had to weave between them. The driver had been well briefed. He slowed almost to a stop at the first block, then, as the guards relaxed, he gunned the engine and took off, knocking over the first guard, who banged on the side of the van and shouted for the driver to halt. It was a classic tactic for running roadblocks taught by security professionals. Weaving to the left, he scraped against the second block, smashing in the right front end of the van. Even without the gate, the bomber might have been stopped there, but for two facts. The blocks had been set farther apart than they should have to allow access for cement trucks and other vehicles needed for the renovation of the unfinished embassy; and, because they were going to be moved again later, the blocks had not been anchored in the ground. When the suicide driver rammed the second block, it shifted just enough to allow him to keep going.

Still hesitating because of the diplomatic plates, the guard fired first into the air and then into the back of the van, blowing out one of the rear tires, before his M16 jammed. Clearing the chamber and ramming in a new clip, he opened up again. By that time, a second guard who was walking down the street toward the entrance realized what was happening. As the truck raced past him, Tony Khoury claimed he sprayed the driver's compartment with his weapon on full automatic. After the explosion, a colleague who reached the badly wounded guard actually burned his hand on the red-hot barrel of Khoury's weapon. A third guard, Kasm Atieh, was standing just a few feet from where the bomb eventually exploded. He is also believed to have fired, but was vaporized in the blast.

Credit for stopping the bomber went to the British bodyguards of Ambassador Miers, who were waiting in the parking lot by their boss's motorcade. One of these highly trained and experienced security men claimed he actually saw the driver slump over after he fired, seconds before the van swerved and exploded. Ambassador Bartholomew presented two of the British agents with American flags in gratitude. But investigators later said the only shell casings from the British guns ever located were found much farther down the road, where the two bodyguards later had fired into the air as they rushed the two wounded ambassadors to the hospital. U.S. security officials were bitter that their men, three of whom died in the blast, were never given credit for the role they played.

Regardless of who killed the suicide bomber, someone did. By doing so, he saved scores of lives. The van blew up directly in front of the embassy. If it had gone a few yards farther, it would have turned into a driveway that led to a basement garage. If the bomb had exploded there, the whole building would have come down. Only one guard protected that garage. There was no gate, no barrier.

Planning for the move to East Beirut had begun in May, when Bartholomew went back to Washington. The suggestion that the bulk of the embassy staff be transferred out of West Beirut was welcomed across the board. The Pentagon had been pushing hard to withdraw the remaining 90 marines who were guarding the temporary embassy compound, which the Americans shared with the British. Those 90 marines were tying up a three-ship support flotilla with another 2,000 marines on board. As a result, the Sixth Fleet's entire schedule of maneuvers was being disrupted, all for a couple of dozen diplomats in Beirut. The White House wanted the last marines out of Beirut because they were an election-year liability. The Beirut diplomats, who lived, worked and slept with each other in the crowded apartments of the West Beirut compound, were anxious to escape the prison outside which they rarely ventured.

A fourth factor was the wives. The American dependents had been evacuated in February. Men who were married, including the ambassador, missed their spouses. The Separate Maintenance Allowance, extra money from the government to pay dependents' expenses during an evacuation, was scheduled to decrease after the first six months. Some bitter (and single) diplomats would later claim that this had been a factor in the ambassador's decision on when the move into the unfinished compound would be made.

The site selected for the new diplomatic complex was known as the Baaklini building, an empty apartment block in the Aukar suburb of East Beirut. For political reasons, this would be referred to as the embassy "annex." The Porfine Compound, a former technical school that was being renovated in West Beirut, would be the official U.S. embassy, even though all but a skeleton staff would move to the east. The semantics were designed to maintain the facade that the U.S. was not abandoning West Beirut.

A team from Washington was brought in to approve the purchase of the East Beirut building. Their report stipulated that extensive internal security measures be built in during the renovation. Beirut security chief Bigler also passed muster on the building, reporting in a cable back to Washington that the Baaklini would be adequate once renovation work was complete.

With mounting pressure from the White House and the Pentagon to get the remaining Marine guards out, Bartholomew set a July date for the move. The security staff and several other diplomats were horrified. The building would never be ready in time. In what one participant described as "heated discussions" with the ambassador, several staffers, accepting the political reality that the extra Marine units assigned to protect them had to leave, proposed a range of alternatives to moving into a building with unfinished security. These included a temporary evacuation to Cyprus until the new facility was complete, working from their new apartments in East Beirut, or even staying in the West Beirut compound with the local guard force then being trained. At least the existing compound had barricades in place.

Bartholomew overruled each idea. Eventually he agreed to a ten-day delay, but that was all. The move would go ahead. Even Pentagon officials were reportedly surprised when Bartholomew certified on July 30 that the Lebanese guard force was ready to take over and the Marines could go home.[2]

"It was crazy," said one U.S. diplomat who was stationed in Beirut at the time. "The guys that are paid to stand in harm's way, the guys with the helmets and the flak jackets, those guys the [White House] can't get out quick enough, and they leave us there on our own."

Security chief Bigler was among those arguing for a delay. He and two other diplomats made at least one stab at sending a cable back to Washington registering their concerns, but all cable traffic crossed the ambassador's desk and, in the words of one source privy to the incident, the message was "watered down." Significantly, however, no one in the embassy felt strongly enough to send a dissent cable, an out-of-channel message that did not require the ambassador's signature. (The channel had been created after the Vietnam War as a means for diplomats to protest directly to Washington about a policy pursued by their embassy.)

But the dissenters were in the minority. Most U.S. diplomats in Beirut were champing at the bit to go east.

Not long after the move, in early August, a few reporters were invited to a cocktail party at the new East Beirut apartment of the embassy's cultural attaché. It was a kind of coming out party for the diplomats, who had been cooped up in the West Beirut compound, and a welcome back party for the returning wives and newly arrived staffers.

Sipping gin and tonics on the balcony as a deep orange sun dropped into the sea, the talk was of shopping and restaurants, fashions and visits to the beach. The Americans were giddy with their newfound freedom.

Drink in hand, the new deputy chief of mission, Stephen Lyne, stood telling several of us how safe it was now that the Americans had the Christian Phalangists to protect them. "They never let anything get across the [Green] line," he said authoritatively. Lyne had just arrived from a post in Australia. His wife chatted about how lovely the stores looked. It was just like "back home."

The Beirut veterans were only slightly less enamored of their new surroundings. "It was like moving from Harlem to Long Island," one diplomat said later. "We were in the land of milk and honey. Suddenly we had casinos and cinemas and cookouts."

Like other reporters present, I left the party with the horrible sense that the Americans had let down their guard.

The only diplomats who seemed particularly upset about what was going on were those who still had to spend time in West Beirut. The security team recommended that no Americans work in the new West Beirut compound,[3] which they believed to be extremely vulnerable, and the officers commanding the embassy Marine contingent[4] argued against putting any of their men in the exposed building. The ambassador overruled them all. The U.S. was going to "show the flag." It had been one of Bartholomew's favorite themes.

"We were under a great deal of pressure from him to run around waving the flag at a time when we were under heavy threat," a diplomat recalled of the period.

Bartholomew wanted the visa section open normally and a U.S. Information Service (USIS) officer present in the West Beirut embassy during working hours. Their presence would bolster the story authored in Washington that the West Beirut complex was the "real" embassy and the East Beirut office was just an annex.

"Bartholomew told us that if there were officers over there issuing visas, the Lebanese wouldn't realize the embassy was gone. It was an incredibly patronizing attitude that showed how little he understood about the Lebanese," another diplomat remembered.

Concerned that they were going to be crossing the Green Line at the same time every day, setting precisely the routine that security experts advised against, consular officials suggested that the visa section open at irregular hours. A little inconvenience for the Lebanese who wanted visas to visit the States did not seem an unreasonable sacrifice to ask in return for safeguarding the lives of U.S. diplomats. Bartholomew said no. Instead, the three consular officers would rotate, with two of them present in the West at all times. They would live in the West Beirut compound for two to three weeks, then one would switch with a counterpart in the east.

"I asked them what they would do if fighting broke out and closed the Green Line for a month or two, stranding us over there," one of the trio recounted. "They said they'd try and send a car for us, or maybe a boat!"

In the view of two diplomats, the ambassador was asking too much. Consular Officer Debbie Parks requested reassignment to another job in the embassy. When Bartholomew said that wouldn't be fair to the other consular officers, she and her husband, Political Officer Erik Terzuolo, arranged a transfer out of Beirut.

Refused bodyguards for their daily trips across the Green Line, the USIS team, which had a separate budget, hired their own guards and set their own hours. Ironically, USIS Officer Carol Madison was nervously sitting in the West Beirut embassy the morning its twin in the east was blown up.

When the United States vetoed a UN Security Council resolution calling on Israel to respect the rights of civilians in South Lebanon and allow their free movement, even moderate Lebanese were outraged.

"May this modern civilization that is championed by such cheap values be cursed," Prime Minister Rashid Karami fulminated.

Islamic Jihad issued a statement promising that "very soon we shall strike at one of the vital American installations in the Middle East." We wondered not whether there would be another attack but when and where. Back in July, many of us had done stories about the lack of security at both the East Beirut annex and the new West Beirut embassy compound. We had approached friends in the embassy, expressing our concerns. If we could see glaring deficiencies, so would others with more trained eyes. Our friends, who had the same worries, arranged for several reporters to see the ambassador. Reginald Bartholomew dismissed our concerns out of hand. Any attackers, he confidently asserted, would be cut down by "withering return fire" from the Lebanese guard force.

The security men responsible for those guards had been less convinced. The Lebanese gunmen had been drawn from local militias – 50 Druzes, Shi'ites and Sunnis in the west, 30 Christians in the east – and remained answerable to their former bosses. (The recommendation of those militia chiefs and a quick check with rival groups for any special dirt on the individual was about the only background check possible in the chaos of Beirut.) The decision to use them was a logical outgrowth of the earlier unofficial Druze (and, before that, PLO) protection. They knew the turf and the bad guys, the theory went. Besides, it was better to have them – and, by extension, their militias – with you than against you.

There were also plenty of negatives. Could they be trusted? When push came to shove, whose hide would they protect? Many lived in the area around the respective embassies. In an attack, would they be willing to open fire on gunmen in apartment buildings that might contain their friends or families? Some of the security people thought this was unlikely.

Officials interviewed later agreed to a man that American guards would have been far preferable, despite official rhetoric about the desirability of locals who understood the language and customs, but that possibility was never seriously considered. After all, the whole idea of withdrawing the Marines was to reduce the number of potential targets. "I could just hear Congress if we had gone to them asking for permission to hire 100 U.S. mercenaries to guard our embassy in Beirut," quipped one diplomat.

Faced with orders to provide protection and offered no alternative, the security men had little choice: *their* gunmen became *our* gunmen.

By September 1984, there was little visible improvement in the defenses. Two embassies were being built from scratch in a city where they used diplomats as firewood and, instead of being beefed up, the security detail was down to a minimum. While extra administrative types had been brought in to supervise the actual construction, Bigler and his assistant, Jeremy Zeikel, were left on their own to simultaneously design the defenses for two new compounds on opposite sides of the city. Neither had been properly trained for the job. Zeikel, who had come to Beirut after serving on Secretary of State Schultz's security detail, had not even attended the State Department's ten-week security course.

The pair sat down and sketched out what they thought was necessary. After its May visit, the Washington team had outlined measures for *internal* security. But aside from recommending that only U.S. diplomats be allowed access to the street in front of the annex – a suggestion overruled by the ambassador – the Washington experts left to the local boys the crucial question of how to protect the embassy from the *outside*. "All access points will be controlled by the Post Regional Security Office and designed, implemented and supervised by the RSO [Bigler]," stated their final report.[5]

Bigler and Zeikel already had a plateful. In addition to planning security for the new buildings, they were in charge of selecting and deploying the new 80-man Lebanese guard force, securing and protecting dozens of apartments for the staff in East Beirut, guarding diplomats as they went back and forth across the Green Line, and safely ferrying classified materials out of West Beirut. They were also ultimately responsible for the ambassador's safety. In that, they were assisted by John McKenna and two other Americans who were part of Bartholomew's personal bodyguard detail.

No one person was ever given sole responsibility for the external security of the buildings. They didn't have the people or the time. The security team never asked for extra help, but help was also never offered by Bartholomew or Washington.

"The feeling was always there that we had to watch the budget," according to one of the security men. "Nobody came and said, 'You can have all the people or all the money you want.' We were always wondering where we were going to get the people for this or that, do we need this or that?"

When Zeikel went on vacation in July, Washington did not even bother to send a replacement. His responsibilities were taken over by 36-year-old McKenna, another veteran of Schultz's security detail who, like Zeikel, had been trained in *personal* not *building* security. When Zeikel returned, Bigler, exhausted from months of tension in West Beirut and the frantic prepara-tions for the move, left to visit his family. Again, Washington, despite its hand-wringing after all the other bombings, did not deem it necessary to replace him.

Zeikel and McKenna were left to fend for themselves until Bigler returned the day before the bombing. Two men with little relevant experience had been made responsible for establishing security around the most dangerous set of U.S. diplomatic missions in the world. Zeikel concentrated now on the west (judged to be the more vulnerable) and McKenna took over in the east.

The slowness of the Lebanese contractor has been cited as a major cause of the lack of security, but embassy officials who helped oversee the project point out that while the builder bid on a 90-day contract, the Americans moved in just 45 days later. "People keep pointing a finger at him, and that's wrong," one diplomat said.

In the confusion of trying to work in an unfinished building, everybody wanted his or her office fixed first. "The contractor would be working on a wall and somebody would come along and say, 'Come with me, I need this or that done,'" the diplomat recalled. "The locals did whatever the last Westerner told them. There were too many chiefs trying to run the show."

Security got lumped in with all the rest. Security chief Bigler had been overruled and largely ignored. Zeikel and McKenna, at the bottom of the embassy's food chain, didn't stand a chance.

"You get input from 18 million people and you're a new guy. You've got [General Services Officers] saying the ambassador's air conditioning is not in, political officers shouting about their walls, admin people complaining there's no lights. How do you fight it?" said another diplomat of McKenna's situation.

A Senate investigation of the bombing concluded, "All work seems to have been regarded as having equal priority."[6] Numerous sources involved in the construction of the building rejected that notion.

"Was there a priority? Oh God, I'll say there was," one top embassy official said adamantly. "Finish the ambassador's office. Finish the whole fourth floor."

Another diplomat said that while it was never explicitly stated that the ambassador's office came before the gates, Bartholomew was constantly "breathing down our necks" about completing the job. Those same diplomats reported that the first time they ever heard Bartholomew ask about why the gates weren't in place was *after* the bombing.

Workers were also diverted for such crucial duties as moving a piano into the apartment of one senior diplomat after his wife returned to the country. Still, the security men were not jumping up and down screaming for the gate to be installed. Like everyone else, they were feeling a certain safety just being in East Beirut.

"You've gotta remember, here you are living a normal life, going to the store, swimming, playing bingo, and yet you go to work in a building that's a fortress. It just doesn't jibe," said one of them. "It was a mental state. We relaxed. The gate wasn't up, no, but this was a normal progression. The guards were there, the basics in place. We had a feeling of safety. People ask why we didn't do more right away, but they didn't go through what we did on the west side. They didn't experience the sense of relief when we came over."

Those "basics" of security were little more than the bare necessities. In addition to the guards and the cement blocks at the entrance, a trench had been dug in the field around the exposed side of the building to stop car bombs. But none of the guard towers were in place, the guards' cement huts were only partially built and there wasn't even a sandbag for them to hide behind if attacked.

Inside the building, things were no better. The day the annex was blown up, seven weeks after the diplomats had moved in, shatterproof Mylar tape was still being put on the windows to prevent flying glass, floors were still being reinforced to take the weight of the safes and surveillance-proof communications room, and pulley systems were still being installed on the windows to allow quick escape. Regional security officials said that it would be at least another month before the command post for the Marine guards was outfitted with its standard complement of gear. Until then, there would be no public address system, no sirens, no television camera. The building didn't even have fire extinguishers until someone got fed up waiting for the Washington bureaucracy to move and bought them in Beirut. Security officials were as worried about a fire as a car bomb. "What would have happened if the place went up in flames?" asked one of them. "We would have had to jump out the windows since there was only one door and no fire escapes."

While they were preoccupied with those thoughts, the gates lay on the side of the driveway. Security officials pushed several times for their installation, but they and the contractors kept getting distracted.

Some security men later questioned whether the absence of the gates actually made any difference. These were not steel-reinforced doors that would have sealed off the compound, but rather, flimsy metal poles that could be raised and lowered. "The gates weren't up. So what? They weren't strong enough," one of the security men replied when asked about it later. "They would not have stopped a truck like the one that hit the Marines."

Yet despite the Marine headquarters disaster, no one ever suggested putting in heavier gates. "We just didn't think they were needed," said one of the security men. "We were making it up as we went along and nobody from Washington ever told us we weren't doing enough." The comment carried echoes of Colonel Geraghty's testimony a year before.

Temporary measures to block the street more effectively also could have been taken, but they were not. Crossed steel barricades designed to stop tanks were lined up *along* the side of the street instead of across it. After the BLT bombing, the Marines had used dump trucks and armored vehicles to block all entrances to their compound. The trucks were rolled out of the way when a car had been cleared for entry. Asked why they had not been used at the annex, one security officer replied with disarming candor, "I never thought of it. It's that simple. It never crossed my mind."

Another official who helped oversee the construction of the new building concurred. "We didn't think if it. If we thought of it, we might have done it. I thought the guards would be sufficient for the moment. You can't underestimate what a relief it was for us to get to the east. It was another world."

The security men were also hampered by their lack of access to intelligence. The Senate report on the bombing states that "U.S. intelligence was aware of certain patterns of activity involving the transport of explosives by Iranians operating in Damascus under the shield of diplomat immunity." The CIA station chief and the ambassador might have been aware of that, but if they were, they didn't tell the men in charge of security for their embassy.

It wouldn't have been the first time. The security staff constantly complained that they were not being given the kind of specific information they needed. Part of the reason was that the spooks themselves often didn't have it. The CIA was on its third set of agents since 1983. The first embassy bombing had wiped out most of the agency's Beirut station. The entire Beirut staff had been replaced again after station chief Buckley's kidnapping, for fear he might have revealed their identities under torture. The new team did not want to share what little it did know. The intelligence-sharing problem changed only after the bombing when, in the words of one of the security men, "a bunch of people realized we were protecting their asses."

Bartholomew, too, was known to hold back. Shortly before the move, for example, the security staff found out only by accident that a small bomb had gone off under a car outside the East Beirut apartment of one General Services Administration officer, located just a block away from the new embassy annex. The officer had told the ambassador, who never bothered to advise the men responsible for protecting American lives in Beirut. When he overheard two security men talking about it a few days later, Bartholomew moved them out of earshot of a visiting State Department official and asked not whether his security experts thought the incident had wider implications for the planned move, but instead, "Who told you? How did you find out?"

Still, you did not need to be the CIA station chief to know that the dangers faced by the embassy were awesome. In its phone call after the U.S. veto at the UN, Islamic Jihad had warned, "Our heroes are prepared to sacrifice their lives to destroy an American or Zionist institution, even though it may be small."

Three days before the bombing, the group had a special message for President Reagan: "You, governor of the White House, await a painful blow before your reelection, more painful than our blows against your embassy and your military headquarters in Beirut."

Inside the embassy, these were seen as more of the same general threats the Americans had been living with for so long that they had become meaningless. Since the Marine bombing, there had been a steady stream of reports about car bombs, truck bombs, even model airplane bombs. (After that last report, there were jokes about putting model antiaircraft batteries on the roof.) The embassy had also received more subtle indications that something might be wrong.

A few days before the bombing, one of the Lebanese guards who had been assigned to the ambassador's bodyguard detail went missing for two days. When he showed up for work, he could barely walk. One look at his back revealed that he had been badly whipped. He told a weak story about crossing into West Beirut to visit a friend, being kidnapped and managing to escape. He had obviously been interrogated, but embassy officials never discovered by whom. He was fired two hours before the explosion. After the blast, he came running back into the compound, tearing strips off his shirt to help the wounded.

A few weeks earlier, a man claiming to be a former lieutenant in the Egyptian Army had turned up at the door asking to talk to a CIA agent. He was nervous, sweating, a sleazy piece of work. Questioned by embassy officials, he claimed to have had meetings with someone from the CIA months earlier (before the previous group had been pulled out in the wake of the Buckley kidnapping) and said he had received a signal to "come in." The resident spooks had never heard of him, the Lebanese translators didn't trust him, and security officials had the uncomfortable feeling that he was casing the joint.

The possibility that terrorists might come into the compound and study their defenses worried the security men. It was the main reason they had recommended that the visa section be placed outside the annex perimeter. That suggestion, like so many others, was overruled. The result was a steady stream of Lebanese and other visitors who filed past the guards and stood for hours in line outside the building.

One Phalangist militiaman visited embassy officials shortly before the bombing to tell them he had seen a Hizbullah member standing in the line. The Christian fighter recognized his enemy because they had gone to school together at AUB.

Another incident seemed suspicious only in retrospect. The day before the bombing, two Muslim guards from the West Beirut embassy who had taken a trip to Damascus called in to say that their car had broken down. They would be delayed in the Syrian capital for a day or two. One of the men was a known troublemaker who had once threatened the life of one of the American security men. The Phalangists had warned that he, and several of his colleagues, were informers. Embassy officials wondered later whether their trip, and the delay in coming home, had been more than a coincidence.

As in the case of the Marines before the bombing of their headquarters, a tremendous lack of imagination existed in the Beirut embassy from the ambassador's office on down about the dangers being faced. The same ill-advised complacency contaminated Washington, which seemed to lose interest in Lebanon once the Marines were safely out. Lessons so painfully learned had been forgotten.

One diplomat who was in Beirut at the time summed up the tragedy this way: "It should have been blamed on human frailty. Everybody was burnt out from the west. The RSO [Bigler] was cut out of the decision-making process. The atmosphere in the east made us think we were back in a normal place. The opposition was just a little too clever."

President Reagan, who was elected to office largely on the strength of Jimmy Carter's failure to protect U.S. diplomats in Tehran, dismissed his administration's latest Beirut disaster with a wry aside: "Anyone that's ever had a kitchen done knows that it never gets done as soon as you wish it would."

Ambassador Bartholomew had an even simpler explanation. Bruised and battered after his experience, he fell back on the words U.S. officials in the Middle East had mouthed so many time before: "There isn't anything such as 100 percent security."

15
A Hasty Retreat

[S]lay the idolators wherever you find them, and take them captive and besiege them and lie in wait for them in every ambush.

—Surah IX, 5
Qur'an[1]

Not a single U.S. diplomat remained in the Muslim half of the city and no more than 55 staffers were left in East Beirut. The rest of the diplomats, and all the families, had been choppered out to Cyprus in the immediate aftermath of the bombing. A rough headcount turned up only about 50 native-born U.S. citizens in West Beirut. Half that number were teachers behind the relative safety of the AUB and BUC campus walls. The rest of us were reporters still running around the streets, carrying on a nonstop debate among ourselves about whether we should be there at all.

It would not have taken much at that moment to convince me to leave. Deep down inside I knew I had long overstayed my welcome. Some of my colleagues still clung to their belief in journalistic immunity, but I thought that the armor had worn a little thin. Exactly what was keeping me there, I am not sure to this day. Part of it was probably the newsman in me, reluctant to miss the advertised final act by Islamic Jihad before the election. Then there was the macho war correspondent, unwilling to give in to fear while his colleagues hung on. And, I suppose, there was the adrenaline junkie, refusing to turn his back on the next fix.

As our tolerance level for fighting had risen with the introduction of each new form of warfare, our tolerance level for Islamic Jihad threats kept changing. Although they had said everything short of it, we wanted one of those anonymous voices to state unequivocally that they were after *every single* American in Beirut, *including journalists*. Or maybe one of those faceless individuals could just drop off an engraved invitation for us to leave.

Instead, when the phone rang with a warning, the voice had a face I knew, and it was one I did not trust. "I'm just calling to say that we're worried about you guys over there," U.S. embassy spokesman Jon Stewart said from his latest office in the ambassador's residence inside the presidential compound in East Beirut. "West Beirut isn't a very safe place for Americans these days and, don't forget, you're Americans, too."

"So what else is new?" I asked cynically. "Are you trying to tell me something?"

"It's just a friendly reminder," he said and hung up. I soon discovered that every other American news organization in West Beirut had received the same call. This wasn't just a friendly diplomat touching base. There had to be something more.

"Let's cut through the bullshit," I said when I called him back. "Do you have something specific we should know about?"

"Well," he hesitated, "I just want you to know we're worried about you." How heart warming.

"Why now? It's one thing for you to say that, as Americans, we're in danger. It's quite another to say you have intelligence that there is a specific threat against unofficial Americans or journalists."

Stewart hedged for a bit, then added cryptically, "You notice that I'm calling reporters, not AUB professors." Click.

That knot in my gut tightened, but the cynic in me said something didn't smell right. Other sources at the embassy sniffed something, too. They said the intelligence reports contained nothing to indicate a specific threat against us. Sure, there was an avalanche of information that left little doubt that Shi'ite groups were planning other attacks against American targets before the election. There was reason to believe that enough of the explosives brought in for the annex bombing were left over for another attack. Officials didn't reveal it at the time, but the intelligence included word of a plan to blow up the ambassador's residence, by then functioning as the embassy, and reports of suicide planes being readied. U.S. security men were so worried about a suicide plane crashing into the ambassador's residence that the airspace over the Presidential Palace had been declared a free-fire zone, and guards did open up at least once on a light plane that strayed overhead. All this left little doubt that every American in Beirut was in grave danger.

If you believed that the terrorists were lashing out at any American within reach, our exposed position in West Beirut made us particularly vulnerable. But there was no hard evidence that the bombers were gunning for reporters. The closest thing was a report that Hizbullah had picked up two Israeli agents masquerading as newsmen in the Bekaa.

Nevertheless, the story that someone was gunning for us grew a life of its own. After State Department spokesman John Hughes told of "new information concerning threats across the board to Americans" in Beirut, State Department officials went a step further, whispering off the record that reporters in particular were at risk.

We began to get very nervous, but we also began to suspect that the U.S. government was trying to drive us out of Lebanon. The idea was not as far-fetched as it seemed. With the election less than a month away, the last thing the White House needed was another batch of dead Americans in Beirut. Washington's cables to the Beirut embassy took on an almost hysterical tone. "They were basically telling us not to get ourselves blown up before the election," said a diplomat who read them.

From the administration's standpoint, even if it was only reporters getting killed, it wouldn't look very good. In addition, if there was another attack on the embassy and there were no American reporters left in Beirut to cover it, the incident would have far less impact on the election. The rationale made sense when five or six of us sat together and analyzed the Reagan administration's motives with cool logic and raw cynicism. It was less convincing as I lay awake at night watching slow-motion mental images of the Commodore Hotel going up in a ball of fire.

I was starting to feel hunted. We had sent all the Western crews home and my Lebanese camera team didn't want me in the field with them. The drivers secretly began carrying guns. Arab friends who had always counseled me to stay said I should get the hell out.

The distance between the apartment and the office at the Commodore became my whole world. Sometimes I would test its boundaries by walking a block down to Hamra Street to buy a sandwich or a book, studying each face on the crowded sidewalks, glancing frequently over my shoulder, hugging closer to the shop doors when a car pulled up beside me. Otherwise, the only place I walked alone was across the narrow street that separated the office from the main building of the hotel.

A few months before, when Hizbullah first began to open offices, I debated whether I should go down and introduce myself. In previous years, I would not have thought twice. A reporter in Beirut should know every faction. But if I went to see Hizbullah, I wondered, would I be singling myself out for kidnapping?[2] I had realized then that I had become part of the story; I was no longer functioning purely as an observer. Now it was even worse. Not only was I limited in how I covered the story, but I had become a virtual prisoner.

With the State Department warnings, our bosses at CBS New York became concerned. Executives began calling daily, asking whether Lucy Spiegel and I (the only Americans in the bureau) should leave. Then they started phoning two or three times a day. They faced the classic dilemma of news executives when their employees are in a situation where the danger exceeds the normal "acceptable" limits. They wanted the story covered, but they didn't want their people killed. The bosses made it clear that they were completely behind us if we thought we should pull out; the decision was ours. If we felt we were in danger, we should get on a plane without even bothering to call New York.[3]

We *knew* we were in danger. The question was whether that danger had actually increased or was just being talked about more in Washington. The American press corps in Beirut had remained through civil war, invasions, siege, bombings and kidnappings. We were damned if we were going to be driven out by our own government. Unfortunately, the well-intentioned (but incessant) calls from New York were not helping our faltering efforts to examine our situation dispassionately.

Nerve endings were raw. We stopped thinking about the story and thought only about ourselves. New York had told us to forget doing features or covering anything less than a major attack against the Americans (not that we intended to do otherwise). So we sat waiting for Islamic Jihad to blow up the ambassador's residence – or us.

The diplomats were behind layers of tanks, barbed wire and troops encircling Gemayel's palace. We were so exposed it was almost laughable. All three major American television networks, CNN, the AP and several newspapers had their offices in two buildings directly across from the Commodore, where all visiting Anglo-American reporters and television crews stayed. Cars were permanently parked in front of the Commodore to prevent a suicide bomber from crashing into the lobby. Others blocked the driveway under our building. But the precautions were useless. The narrow street dividing the offices and the hotel was like a cavern. To wipe out the bulk of the Western press corps, all a suicide driver had to do was stop in the middle of the street and press the button.

The office I shared with Lucy was at the back of the bureau, on the side of the building farthest away from the Commodore. I found myself reluctant to walk out into the main reception room, which faced the hotel. When I had to, I inevitably glanced at the street, knowing full well it wouldn't tell me anything. The lane was always backed up with traffic and a car full of explosives doesn't look any different than an empty car. But whenever a van crawled down the street, I mentally braced myself – while carrying on whatever conversation I was involved in – until it had safely passed. When I was on the telex in the hall leading off that vulnerable reception room, I found myself unconsciously leaning to the right, where I was partly shielded by a wall.

Reporters whose offices were elsewhere in town stayed away from the Commodore. The bar was empty at night. I tried to do as much work from home as I could. The strain on all of us was beginning to show. This couldn't go on much longer.

The kidnapping of four Lebanese employees of the Associated Press was the proverbial straw that broke the back of our resistance. The group was grabbed driving to work in a car that had an AP sign in the window. When they were released the next day, we found out the abduction had occurred right around the corner from the Commodore. The kidnappers asked who else worked in the AP office. The four emerged convinced that their captors had been looking for Americans.

With the U.S. presidential election just days away, several news organizations found a sudden need for their Beirut teams to cover stories in Jordan or Africa. A few other reporters realized that they had vacation time due. Several more AUB professors left. The U.S. government, meanwhile, was busy choppering out of Lebanon all but nine diplomats and a dozen people to protect them. Even the ambassador was rumored to have left town. (We found out later that he spent the week before the election in Paris.)

Lucy and I did another headcount: there would be just ten American reporters left in West Beirut. Forget the debate over Washington's motives and the engraved invitation, the odds were getting too slim. When New York ordered us out, we didn't argue.

Cyprus was gray. Rain and wind battered our sea-front hotel. When the storms let up, pale British vacationers huddled on the beach, wrapped in towels against the cold. They had paid good money for a week on the Mediterranean and refused to admit that the brooding sky and icy gale was only slightly more bearable than the foul weather they had left behind.

We stayed locked in our rooms reading or listening to the BBC, pausing only to call Beirut to talk to the Lebanese crew and office staff who had chosen to remain behind. The plan was that if a big story broke, they would cover it and ship the videotape to Cyprus, where I would add the narration. If the election passed without incident, we would fly back.

Two days before the vote, with the American presence in Lebanon down to the barest minimum, a Beirut radio station reported that Islamic Jihad had "threatened to carry out an operation against American interests in the Middle East within the next 48 hours."

Another caller to a Western news agency promised "a painful strike ... very shortly." And he had a special message for President Reagan: "If we were unable to prevent your reelection we will for certain prevent you from continuing your second term in office."

The threats echoed a warning issued by Iran's president a few days before: "As long as the United States government follows a policy of inflicting blows upon the Islamic Republic, we, too, deem it our right to retaliate anywhere throughout the world."

Embassies across the region went on alert. Diplomats in several countries were told to stay at home. The aircraft carriers *Independence* and *Eisenhower* moved into the eastern Mediterranean and the U.S. drew another line in the sand, warning the Islamic Jihad bully that he *really would* get hit if he crossed over it again.

This time, he didn't. Why, we'll never know. Maybe the security finally *was* tight enough to stop him, or maybe he realized that a president on the eve of an election actually *would* strike back. Instead of another attack, there was another faceless voice. As the polls were closing in the U.S. on election day, a late-night caller told a Lebanese newspaper, "We, the Jihad Islami organization, warn on the eve of the reelection of Ronald Reagan to the U.S. presidency, that we shall blow up all American interests in Beirut and elsewhere in Lebanon."

I was just about to head to the airport to fly back to Beirut when the bureau called to tell me of the latest warning. By itself, it was nothing new. But the postscript made me pause: "We address this warning to every American individual residing in Lebanon."

It wasn't an engraved invitation, but it was close enough. I had refused to be driven out of Lebanon by the violence of the war or the machinations of the U.S. government, but I had no hesitation about being banished by Islamic Jihad. If the men driving the suicide trucks were determined to rid Lebanon of every last American, I was not going to stand in their way.

What the Reagan administration refused to admit was obvious from my vantagepoint: the terrorists *had* won.

You needed to look only as far as the concrete barricades around the White House and other government buildings in Washington to see that the terrorists had won.

Soldiers with Stinger antiaircraft missiles stood on the roof of the presidential mansion, the State Department drew up plans for a $4.4 billion program to turn embassies around the world into fortified bunkers, and law enforcement officials cast a worried eye toward the tens of thousands of Lebanese Shi'ites and one million Iranians living in America. Experts warned that Iranian-backed terrorist networks were lying dormant inside the U.S., waiting for the order to strike.

"An incident in the Middle East could cause instantaneous violent reaction in this country," warned FBI Director William Webster.[4] That knowledge hung like a sword of Damocles over the heads of American experts grappling with the issues of whether and how to hit back.

"Terrorism is aggression and, like all aggression, must be forcefully resisted," argued Secretary of State Schultz, who was pushing hard for retaliation.[5]

"The threats by American politicians are empty ones," mocked Iranian President Khamene'i.

"We cannot and will not abstain from forcible action to prevent, preempt or respond to terrorist acts where conditions merit the use of force," National Security Advisor Robert McFarlane insisted.

"We have many times punched the United States in the mouth, and we are ready to do this once again all over the world," replied Tehran Radio.

America's Lebanon policy was dead, but the demons to which it had given birth refused to stop tearing at the corpse. Within a month of Reagan's reelection, a plot was uncovered to blow up the U.S. embassy in Rome. Seven Lebanese Shi'ites were arrested with plans for a truck bombing that, in the Rome police chief's words, "would have been like in Beirut." Swiss police grabbed an accomplice of the group, who was carrying about five pounds of explosives. Those arrests would spark the kidnapping of Italian and Swiss nationals in Beirut.

A few weeks later, Imad Mugniyeh, the man behind so much of the terror, orchestrated the hijacking of a Kuwait Airways jet to Tehran. Two Americans were murdered in cold blood; two others were brutally tortured. "It was 140 hours of hell," said hostage Charles Kaper. "I thought I was going to die every day."

From the beginning, the hijackers singled out the Americans. "The ringleader ... made me lie down on the floor and stood on my back and made a small speech about American imperialism," recalled businessman John Costa, his face marked with cigarette burns, his hair patchy where it had been set on fire.

Kuwaiti nationals had also been targeted. Two of them were roughed up and forced to take part in mock executions, complete with ketchup, in front of Iranian television cameras. The pictures and the screams of the tortured Kuwaiti diplomats broadcast over the plane's radio were designed to force the Kuwait government to give in to the hijackers' demand: the release of the 17 Shi'ites convicted of the U.S. and French embassy bombings.

Kuwait refused to capitulate and eventually, after the drama had dragged on for almost a week, Iranian troops made a show of storming the plane in a rescue denounced by the U.S. as a grand farce. For the hijackers, there was no trial and no imprisonment. For Iran, there was nothing more punishing from Washington than words.

Back in Beirut, five more Americans were kidnapped over the seven months leading up to the most spectacular kidnapping of all, the hijacking of TWA flight 847. It was a scenario that U.S. crisis managers must have imagined only in their worst nightmares. A plane full of American tourists diverted to Beirut, where one of them, a U.S. Navy diver, was shot in cold blood and 39 others disappeared into the Shi'ite slums of the world's terror capital. Their masked captors demanded the release not only of the 17 Shi'ites held in Kuwait and several others scattered around Europe, but also of the more than 700 Muslims arrested in South Lebanon and held in Israel without trial (a violation of the Geneva convention, according to most international law experts). Two of the original hijackers were brothers of detainees in Israel, desperate for a way to free their relatives. The hijacking quickly became a cause célèbre to Shi'ites, who felt the world was ignoring their plight in South Lebanon.

But the operation also bore Mugniyeh's fingerprints, figuratively and literally. FBI experts later found his prints in the plane's rear toilet, and they believed it was he who executed U.S. Navy diver Robert Stethem, who was shot and dumped on the runway in Beirut. Once more, Mugniyeh was venting his hatred of the country that had killed his brother and helped imprison his relatives.

As President Reagan made blustering threats about a blockade of Beirut, a city that had withstood a ten-week Israeli siege and bombardment in 1982, a deal was finally worked out with Iranian and Syrian help. The 39 American passengers would be freed in return for the gradual release of the detainees in Israel over the next few weeks. Washington and Jerusalem denied that there was any link between freedom for the Americans and freedom for the Muslims, but the claim only made the two powers look even more impotent.

The world knew what Washington refused to admit: pro-Iranian Lebanese Shi'ites had once more held America to ransom for Israel's actions.

The fallout from the Reagan administration's Lebanon misadventure and decades of a U.S. Middle East policy that had propped up the Shah of Iran and favored Israel over the Arabs had resulted in another humiliation for the United States.

Meanwhile, yet another lingering embarrassment continued. I was vividly aware of that as I boarded a chartered plane for Cyprus a few days after the TWA drama ended. In an ideal world, I would have stayed in Beirut to cover the dénouement, Israel's release of its Lebanese prisoners. But that would have meant traveling deep into Hizbullah-controlled territory in South Lebanon, the belly of the beast.

The TWA hostages were free, but the threat of kidnapping, which had driven us out of Lebanon the year before, remained as real as ever. Seven Americans were still being held, a fact the White House was doing its best to try to make the country forget.

16
Hostage

The United States is not the frightening giant that it wants
to appear. One can fight the United States, knock it down
and humiliate it into the thing we have turned it into.
                            —Ali-Akhbar Hashemi Rafsanjani
                            Speaker of the Iranian Parliament[1]

The early prisons were in the Bekaa.

For the Reverend Benjamin Weir, the first was an apartment in a military
encampment hard up against the mountains on the western side of the
valley. There, on a stained foam-rubber mattress tossed on a cold tile floor,
he spent the next six months.[2]

He came to know that room better than any other in the world. Every
crack in the pale gray walls, every one of the 33 links of the hardened steel
chain that kept him shackled to the radiator, every one of the 120 slats of
the louvered wooden shutters closed over the glass French doors.

There, Rev. Weir found symbols to remind him daily of his deep religious
faith. In the three wires reaching down from the ceiling, Weir saw the hand
of God; in the hook of a reinforcing rod, His eye; in a stuffed game bird on
a shelf in the corner, the dove Noah sent searching for hope in the chaos.
On one of the nail holes in the wall, he hung the imaginary calendar that
he used to keep track of the passing days.

Even seeing this much was tempting fate. As his kidnappers had
unwrapped the packing tape in which the 63-year-old Protestant pastor
had been mummified for the trip to Beirut, a cloth bandage was tied over
his eyes. Eventually, it was replaced with a ski hat pulled down to block his
vision. He was ordered never to take it off.

A week later, he realized how serious that order was. Twice he had been
caught pulling the mask back on or adjusting it after wiping his eyes. The
third time, Weir felt the barrel of a pistol against his temple and heard the

guard growl, "One more mistake on your part and you're dead. Don't even lift your blindfold again."[3]

Down the hall, CNN reporter Jerry Levin existed in another room much the same. He, too, had a chain and a radiator for company. He, too, played a cat-and-mouse game with the guards over the blindfold. Where the Protestant missionary had faith to support him, Jerry Levin was just discovering his. Born a Jew, Levin would emerge from captivity a strong believer in Christ.

Levin had only been the second American kidnapped. When he was taken on March 7, 1984, abduction had not been very high up on his list of concerns. Locked in his cell months later, he could not know that two other Americans had followed him in quick succession. Deep in the Bekaa at night, he often lay awake wondering why they had taken him.

In the winter, it was cold in the cells – so cold. Cold enough that the hostages could see their own breath. Pajamas and a single blanket barely helped ward it off. The damp, icy wind whipped in through broken windows. The men shivered and shook, chained to radiators that gave off no heat.

In the summer, it was oppressively hot. Stripped to their underwear, the hostages dripped with sweat.

The grinding boredom stayed with them in every season. The single, daily trip to the toilet, the brief visits from the guards. Meals were the only clock. They were Spartan but adequate: bread and cheese or a rare boiled egg for breakfast; a kebab or piece of chicken for lunch; a light snack of bread and jam or soup in the evening.

To maintain his sanity, Weir still slipped the mask up over his eyes, but he was always careful to listen for approaching footsteps. In the other room, Levin more often contented himself with peering out the bottom just enough to confirm that the world was not all dark.

From the odd scrap of newspaper in which his sandwich was sometimes wrapped, Weir, who wrote and spoke fluent Arabic, learned something of the world outside. Once or twice his captors left the French doors of his room open, and by stretching his chain to the limit, he caught a glimpse of the valley and mountains beyond.

Counting his blessings in his constant prayers, the American missionary could be thankful that he had not been physically abused (he did not count the times he was chained in uncomfortable positions that did not allow him to stretch out to sleep). But if he had one major complaint, it was the dirt. The room, the mattress, the pillow were all encrusted with grime. The guards were forever spitting on the floor. His requests for a broom were refused. He was reduced to drying out Kleenex so they could be reused. It was ten days before Weir's first shower and he would have to wait more than a month for another. The first toothbrush arrived somewhere in between the two.

During these long, lonely months, Weir and Levin each realized at least one other captive shared his prison. Around the time of the daily visit to the toilet, they heard other footsteps going down the hall, followed by the sound of the toilet flushing. When tea was served, Weir was certain he heard the tinkling of spoons in more glasses than there were guards. One day when dinner was late, he heard someone banging a dish and he banged back. After his captors forced him to make a videotaped statement about their demands, the missionary heard the murmur of other voices speaking English, and presumed someone else was being forced to do the same.

But something else the same day Weir made the tape convinced him that there was another prisoner nearby. After recording his statement, he was briefly put in another room. Lifting his mask after the door had closed, Weir saw a crude calendar scratched on the wall with some calculations in English. Below were written the words, "111 days." Another human being had endured a third of a year chained in that room. Would he have to do the same? It was a difficult thought to bear. But for Ben Weir, 111 days would be just the beginning.

In early October, the hostages were moved. Their new prison was a building on the northern outskirts of Baalbek. It would prove less than secure. It was from here that Jerry Levin escaped on Valentine's Day 1985. The kidnappers were thrown into an uproar. Within an hour, extra guards poured into the building and the remaining hostages were draped in extra chains. By now, there were three other Americans: Weir, CIA station chief William Buckley and Father Lawrence Martin Jenco, who had only recently arrived in the Bekaa prison. The kidnappers apparently feared Levin would be able to direct a rescue attempt, so that evening the captives were loaded into a truck for a bumpy four-hour drive to an apartment where one of the guards lived with his family. The Americans were allowed to bring their few possessions: a cup and spoon, a water bottle and the plastic container for urinating between daily trips to the toilet. Weir had one additional item he prized above all the rest, an Arabic edition of the Bible. During the journey, Weir and Jenco both felt the presence of other captives.

The following night, there was another ride to another prison. This one was an unfinished building in a small village in the foothills of the mountains. In the previous hiding places, the hostages had been kept in separate rooms. This time, workers were brought in to hastily construct fiberboard partitions to divide a single room into cells.

There was another difference, too. The guards told their captives that the building was "loaded." If the Americans or Syrians tried a rescue attempt, the explosives would be set off and they would all die.

It was here that three of the hostages would finally communicate. The first contact was a whispered exchange through the flimsy divider.[4]

"My name is Ben Weir, a Protestant pastor. Who are you?"

"Lawrence Martin Jenco, Catholic priest."

It was brief, but it was communication with a kindred soul. For Weir, it had been nine months, for Jenco, five weeks.

That afternoon, they met again when the captors ordered Weir to write a letter to be sent to the United States outlining their demands for the release of the 17 prisoners in Kuwait. They then told the clergyman to translate for Jenco, who spoke no Arabic, so he could send one as well. The Americans were allowed no other conversation and they were not allowed to remove their masks, but both were strengthened by the encounter. Each man of the cloth could now take some comfort in the knowledge that there was someone nearby sharing his prayers.

A few days later, they managed one more whispered exchange through the divider. This time their voices were joined by another in a distant stall: "I am Buckley ... William Buckley."[5]

There would be no further contact for five months.

Father Lawrence Martin Jenco squirmed on his mat, trying to find a comfortable position. It was becoming more difficult by the minute. He had been confined in that two-foot by six-foot closet since being brought down from the Bekaa in late February 1985. Weeks had passed. Except when his food was handed in or when he was allowed his daily toilet visit, the folded door was always kept closed.

Jenco was trying to decide which was worse for his bad heart, the damp, drafty unfinished building in the Bekaa that he had shared with Weir and Buckley or the stifling heat of this Beirut closet. In the Bekaa, he had lain awake at night trembling with the cold. Here, he was suffocating in the stagnant air made foul by the stench of the guards' kerosene heaters in the adjacent room. The plastic curtain they had tacked over the closet door kept the stale, oxygen-starved atmosphere trapped inside. And when they caught him slipping his foot under the bottom edge to let in a breath of air, he was struck.

Father Jenco had already concluded that these were violent men. Force was their answer to any transgression. He was hit when they accused him of trying to see their faces. He was hit when he reached for a spoon they claimed he intended to use as a weapon. He was hit whenever he did something they didn't like. His priestly collar was no protection in those early days.

The Servite Order into which Marty Jenco had been ordained in 1959 emphasized respect for the beliefs of others; the fragmented society in which his guards had been reared taught something quite different. They equated Christianity with the Christian Maronites against whom they had been at war for a decade. That priestly collar was another mark against him.

Jenco adjusted the chain with which he had been locked to a series of radiators, pipes and metal rings since January 8, 1985, the day a group of armed men had forced him into a car. The chain made him feel like an animal, but at least a dog could bark. *He* had to remain silent at all times on pain of God only knew what. Jenco wondered again whether he would soon be meeting his God. Only weeks before the kidnapping, he had written to a friend that he doubted his weak heart could survive such an ordeal. He doubted it even more now as the pain in his chest grew. Even if his captors did not purposely execute him, their constant abuse would probably achieve the same result.

The priest said another prayer for the strength to forgive and shifted his attention to the outer room. There were others nearby who also needed his prayers. Through a crack between the panels of the door, he could see a husky man chained to a bed. On and off for several days the stranger had been crying quietly to himself. When the guards questioned him, the American was contemptuous and antagonistic. He repeatedly incurred their wrath.

Jenco's heart went out to his fellow hostage. He wished desperately that there was something he could do to comfort this grieving soul. But he couldn't even help himself.

It would be early July before the priest was allowed to hear the man's confession. By that time, Terry Anderson had shaken off his early depression, rediscovering the Catholic roots that had lain dormant under layers of journalistic cynicism, and through that faith, mentally adjusted to his plight.

In another room in the same apartment, William Buckley lay weak and ill. How long he had been like that, precisely what had brought it on, the world will probably never know for sure. When he was kidnapped on March 16, 1984, Buckley was the CIA's chief of station in Beirut. His head was full of some of the agency's most sensitive secrets about the Middle East, including many of the names. With his abduction, CIA Director William Casey ordered numerous Middle East spy networks dismantled and agents withdrawn. The entire CIA station in Beirut was replaced, setting back efforts to understand and infiltrate terrorist groups there for the second time in less than a year.

Was Buckley kidnapped to be wrung dry by Iran or even the KGB? There were those who insisted that was precisely his fate. Figures involved in the Iran–Contra Affair spoke of a videotape shot by the captors showing Buckley's torture, which the White House, understandably, would not release. Intelligence sources in the United States and Europe gave detailed accounts of Buckley's flight to Tehran, the locations of safehouses where he was held, and the hospitals where he was treated for a series of strokes. Senior politicians on Capitol Hill said Buckley had died in Iran from a massive heart attack brought on by torture in the spring of 1985, while others in Washington placed his death in the autumn.

One aspect of William Buckley's fate is certain. He died in Beirut sometime between ten and eleven o'clock on the evening of June 3, 1985. He had been held in Lebanon at least since the morning in mid-February of that year when he had whispered his name to Weir and Jenco. Where he was in the 11 months between his kidnapping and that day might never be known for sure. He might have been among the other captives both Weir and Levin thought they heard or those sounds might have come only from the Saudi couple or the Kuwaiti who also shared their prison.

Aside from those few words of identification, the CIA station chief was never able to talk with his fellow American captives to clear up the mystery. Nor did they hear any sounds to indicate that he was being tortured while he was with them. They *did* hear him slowly dying.

As the spring of 1985 wore on, Buckley gradually deteriorated. He could be heard coughing and choking with what was probably pneumonia. By late May, the CIA agent was badly dehydrated. He asked for water, but Said, one of the guards, said he remembered his mother telling him liquids were bad for a fever. From his closet cell, Jenco told the guard it was the other way around, but Said was sure he had it right. They brought Buckley food, but without liquids he couldn't swallow.

On May 28, a new captive arrived. He was David Jacobsen, an administrator at AUB Hospital. Blindfolded like the others, he was chained hand and foot to a metal loop in the room Buckley and Anderson shared with the guards. Said did not want to frighten the new American by telling him that one of his fellow captives was dying, so he made believe a guard was sick. "What can we do to help our friend?" he asked. Jacobsen suggested calling a doctor. That wasn't possible, he was told.

By the late afternoon of June 3, Buckley was slipping in and out of consciousness. "I don't know what's happened to my body. It was so strong 30 days ago," he was heard to moan at one point.

Jenco, who had been transferred to the corridor, saw Buckley slumped incoherent on the toilet floor. Hallucinating with fever, he asked for a poached egg on toast. The captives pleaded with the guards to give him water or at least the thin yogurt drink popular in the Middle East. Jacobsen wrote out the name of an antibiotic available without prescription and asked again that a doctor be called. But it was already too late. A few hours later, he heard Bill Buckley exhale for the last time and slump over on the floor.

When the body was carried past Jenco in the corridor, the blindfolded priest asked where Buckley was being taken. "To a hospital," Said replied. When the priest pointed out that there was no sound coming from the body, the guard let slip that Buckley was dead. Jacobsen and Anderson were told that their companion was "in a wonderful place where the sun is shining and the birds are chirping." The guards were describing the Paradise they had read of in the Qur'an.

It was the death William Buckley had feared. A few weeks before his kidnapping, he had talked about the possibility of abduction with a friend in the embassy. "Please," he asked, "if they get me, try not to let the bureaucracy wind its interminable way to the point where I die of ill health or am executed."

Six months after he passed away, Islamic Jihad released a blurred photo of the intelligence agent's remains wrapped in a burial shroud. It announced that he had been "executed" in revenge for an Israeli raid on the PLO headquarters in Tunis. The group first offered to trade the body for 100 Palestinian prisoners held in Israel, then placed it at the "disposal" of the families of the Tunis martyrs.

Buckley's death seemed to have a sobering effect on the guards. A doctor, a Lebanese Jew who was also a prisoner, was quickly brought in to examine Jenco, Jacobsen and Anderson. He apparently told the guards that the filthy conditions and their habit of constantly spitting on the floor had helped kill the American. Brooms and buckets of soapy water were brought out and, in typical Lebanese fashion, the entire apartment was flooded, rinsed down and then mopped with disinfectant.

The guards also became more solicitous, asking if there was anything the captives needed. They had an investment to protect. When Jenco later complained of an upset stomach, they quickly brought him a bottle of Maalox II.

Weir also benefited from this new emphasis on health. He had arrived at the apartment from the Bekaa Valley sometime in late May. After being kept briefly in the corridor where people were constantly stepping over him on their way to and from the toilet, he was moved into an adjacent room where he was unaware of the Buckley drama being played out down the hall. The occasional sound of someone moaning in the distance was his only inkling that something was wrong. So, when people started sloshing soapy water over the floor of his room, a doctor showed up to take his blood pressure and a guard gave him a spoon of cough syrup for a cold that had long since gone, Weir was bemused but pleased.

It was probably the logistics of keeping a group of captives in a small apartment as much as anything else that helped end the grinding isolation of the individual hostages. For months on end, in Weir's case more than a year, they had been alone with their thoughts, the few cheap paperbacks the guards had given them, and the Bible that circulated among them.[6]

In the beginning of July, Ben Weir was woken up late one night and led down the corridor, up a flight of stairs and into a new room. When the door closed behind him, he lifted his mask and saw the bearded face of Marty Jenco.

For the priest, it was an "absolutely glorious" experience. Jenco had never realized how wonderful it was to look into the eyes of another human being. For Weir, this was the answer to a prayer. At first, the clergymen suspected a trick and spoke in whispers. Perhaps, they thought, there was an electronic bug that would record everything they said. Weir pointed to an object on the wall that he thought might be a microphone. But when Jenco reached over and examined it, he found that the object was a solid air freshener. They burst into laughter and the dam of pent-up emotions burst. For hours, they told each other of their lives. They compared experiences in captivity. They laughed, cried and prayed before finally falling asleep, drained and exhausted.

The following morning, as the two clerics prepared to celebrate Mass with a scrap of bread saved from breakfast, Jenco was taken away to hear Terry Anderson's confession. The reporter's religious convictions were being nurtured by reading the Bible aloud to his cellmate, David Jacobsen, who had lost his glasses.

A few days later, Weir and Jenco were joined in their room by yet another kidnapped American, Tom Sutherland, the AUB dean of agriculture. They asked to be allowed to worship with the other two captives. Before the week was out, a Mass for all five was permitted on the condition that they all wore their masks and no one spoke but Jenco, who led the service. The five silently filed in and shook hands for the first time.

After ten days of entreaties for another joint service, the captors gave in. The Americans were led into a room and told they could take off their masks when the door closed. They were on their own. To Ben Weir, it was "a very remarkable change."

Five chained men living in a room ten feet square would be cramped and uncomfortable, but it was a small price to pay for human companionship.

David Jacobsen called Terry Anderson "the Boy Scout" because he created an endless array of useful objects out of nothing. By pulling threads from the worn carpet, he tied rosaries for their daily prayers. With the colored pens they had been given and blank pages torn from the back of their cheap novels and books on religion, he made a set of playing cards. The men broke up into teams and passed many hours engrossed in fierce games of hearts. They kept the deck hidden whenever it wasn't being used, but it was discovered one day and taken away by an angry guard. In a place where the highlight of the day was a trip to the toilet, it was a major loss. The mullahs had declared card playing to be a decadent and forbidden activity, and if the guards couldn't play, neither could the men they were assigned to watch. The Americans would be held to the same strict rules that governed the lives of their Shi'ite fundamentalist captors.

Undeterred, Anderson began collecting scraps of aluminum foil from the wrappers of the processed cheese segments that came with breakfast each day. With these, he proudly fashioned a set of chess pieces. A plastic mat served as the board and a few spirited matches followed. But the chess set quickly went the way of the cards. When it was discovered, the guards asked a mullah to issue a fatwa, a religious ruling, on whether the prisoners should be allowed to play. He decreed that since chess was such a complex game, it used up a great deal of time that could be better devoted to study of the Qur'an or the Bible. However, the mullah decided, the Americans could play Arabic checkers.

One of the guards brought a checkerboard into the cell and challenged Anderson to a game. So the reporter could not see his opponent's face, he had to play blindfolded, peeking out the bottom of his mask only enough to see the bottle caps that served as checkers. Anderson beat the guard in five minutes and the man stormed out, taking his board with him.

Another day, the guards brought in a jigsaw puzzle of the television character Mr. T and boasted that they had put it together in only two days. Anderson took up the implicit dare and had it completed in 45 minutes.

He even engaged in wrestling matches with some of the guards, which he usually won. That was typical of the veteran journalist. He was constantly challenging or questioning his captors.

With the possible exception of Reverend Weir, Anderson knew far more about the reasons for the Shi'ite discontent than any of the other hostages. In the year before his kidnapping, he had reported extensively on the U.S. military involvement in Lebanon and on the Israeli occupation of South Lebanon. Like many American newsmen in Beirut, he had grown appalled by Israel's treatment of the Shi'ites and America's callous disregard for their fate. He also knew personally many of the leaders these young men who now guarded him looked up to. In fact, the day before he was kidnapped, Anderson had interviewed Muhammed Hussein Fadlallah, spiritual leader of Hizbullah. And when other American newspeople decided it was time to leave Lebanon in the face of the kidnapping threat, Anderson steadfastly hung on, arguing that it was the duty of the Western media to stay and report on the plight of the Shi'ites.

While Weir and Jenco debated religion with the guards, Anderson argued politics and justice, challenging the basis of their anti-American ideology. Anderson could be pushy and arrogant. The guards would sometimes grow angry. At least once, they took away the hostages' meager ration of bread for a few days to punish them for one of Anderson's outbursts. Some of the other hostages grew annoyed that they kept suffering for his stubborn streak. On another level, Anderson constantly struggled against the kidnapper's attempts to use him as a puppet. He resisted their efforts to force him to make a videotape until long into his captivity, when he felt abandoned by the U.S. government.

Anderson had been a marine in Vietnam and his captors held that against him. But he was proud of his background and remained defiant even when they attacked the Marine Corps for its role in Lebanon. Yet they came to respect that resolve, and the freed hostages would later insist that Anderson had been treated no worse than the rest.

The kidnappers even learned to indulge the newsman's restive spirit. When he offered one of the young guards a bribe to set them free, Hajj, the leader, came in and reminded Anderson in a joking voice, "My men are little and they're poor, but they have big guns."

The Americans counted about 30 guards in those first two and a half years. As they changed, so did the atmosphere. Some were cold and violent; others were friendly and warm. Some mocked the hostages; others apologized for keeping them chained. This dichotomy was evident at Christmas 1984, when Ben Weir was in his seventh month of captivity. He had been isolated the entire time, cut off from simple human contact, and threatened with death at least once. But on Christmas morning, his guards brought him a chocolate Yule log, a bottle of cologne and a card picturing Christ's manger with the words, "Wishing you a Merry Christmas."[7]

Once the hostages were brought together in Beirut in the summer of 1985, their captors seemed to use any excuse to do something special for them. They celebrated birthdays, name days and even the anniversary of Father Jenco's ordination, since by then the priest's religious background was being viewed as a plus, rather than a detriment.

They also became protective. In June 1985, as the slums in which the Americans were being held became engulfed in fighting between Amal and the PLO, flak jackets were brought to shield the captives from the fragments of shells exploding outside. The guards themselves had no such jackets, but then to the bosses of Islamic Jihad, the Americans were far more valuable than a few hired guns.

The guards had favorites among the captives and would sometimes give them little gifts. When Jenco was released, a guard named Ali presented him with a bouquet of flowers and a handmade crucifix that the priest would long treasure.

Yet they would also walk into the cell unannounced, point a weapon at one of the hostages and pull the trigger. There was never a round in the chamber, but it was an unnerving experience all the same. Or they would frog-march the Americans down the hall, forcing them to chant, "Allah Akhbar." Or they would toy with the hostages, slapping, punching and kicking them at random and without reason. It was all designed to dehumanize the captives and to crush their will to resist.

However, with the exception of Buckley, there never seemed to be a systematic policy of torture or sustained violence toward the captives. Rather, the hostages decided it was more a case of individual initiative, certain little men among the guards showing how macho they were by abusing people who couldn't hit back.

Weir was seriously beaten only once, when he thought the guards had abandoned them in the Bekaa building that had supposedly been wired with explosives. In a panic, he began shouting for help out an open window. After he was discovered by the guards, the missionary was punched and kicked almost senseless by one of the captors, who kept screaming, "I'm going to break your arms and legs." On another occasion when he was caught looking out the window, he suffered a blow that was more symbolic than painful.

Jenco even got away with taking off his blindfold in front of two young guards in the Bekaa. They told him to make sure he put it on quickly if anyone else came. Jenco concluded that he was too naive to be a hostage. He also concluded that he had been lucky. Seeing a guard's face was the quickest way to earn a beating.

Hajj, the boss of the guards, seemed to discourage the kind of senseless taunting, threatening and physical harassment that sometimes went on. When one guard kept bullying the captives during their stay in the Bekaa, Hajj got wind of it and paid a visit to the cells to ask the captives about their treatment. After that, the bully backed off.

Each hostage had his own perspective on the mistreatment, the worst of which had tapered off by the time the group was brought together in July 1985. David Jacobsen was never struck in his first five months of captivity and never saw anyone else hit. For a long time, he thought of Hajj as gentle. He would learn differently, thanks in part to American television.

When Father Jenco was about to be released in July 1986, Jacobsen was ordered to record a videotaped statement for the priest to take to the United States. Along with the kidnappers' message, Jacobsen expressed his condolences to Buckley's widow and daughter on the agent's death.

Some days later, the guards wheeled into the cell a television and video player and proceeded to play for him the tape of an American network newscast. The sound was kept off, but Jacobsen saw his own image come on reading the prepared statement, then watched as a photograph of Buckley appeared in the left corner and the words "Coded Message" were superimposed on the bottom of the screen.

Hajj and his men were seething with anger. They believed that they had been tricked. Jacobsen was ordered to write a letter transcribing exactly what they said. He did as ordered and after a few more days Hajj and another man the hostages called Little Hajj returned angrier than ever, with news that someone on American television had said the letter was grammatically incorrect and had obviously been written under duress.

Jacobsen was brutally beaten with a rubber hose, his genitals were kicked, his toes were forced through the trigger guard of an AK47 while the bottoms of his feet were battered, and hands were clapped over his ears so hard that he literally saw stars. The last technique was a favorite of the captors and would leave Father Jenco with a 20 percent hearing loss.

Jacobsen was then ordered to make yet another tape. This time, the hospital administrator was told that if he made one mistake, one wrong movement, one look to the right or left, *he* would not "have a problem," but Thomas Sutherland would be killed.

It was that fallout from the media that led Jacobsen to lash out at reporters in the White House Rose Garden after his release, appealing, "In the name of God, back off."

Reagan administration officials would seize on that as a warning about the dangers of probing into the then-unfolding Iran–Contra scandal. Jacobsen later insisted that he knew nothing of the arms-for-hostages trade at the time and was referring to irresponsible speculation about the condition and treatment of the hostages. He knew the kidnappers had their own people in America watching and reporting back to them. He had the bruises to prove it.

Jenco, meanwhile, had been humiliated and degraded at the very moment of his release. Again wrapped in packing tape and jammed into the tire well of a truck, he was driven back over the mountains to the Bekaa. The kidnappers had orders from above to release him in Syrian-controlled territory, something they apparently did not want to do.

At the release point, the priest was roughly rolled out onto the ground. Shouting at him, the kidnappers angrily tore the tape from Jenco's body, causing him a great deal of pain, then drove off. Jenco had no idea where he was. He was in shock. One moment he had been a prisoner and the next he was standing in the middle of a field somewhere in the Bekaa. Bits of tape still clung to his face and beard. He began wandering the village roads, distraught, looking for someone to help him, fearing that he would be kidnapped by another group. Finally, exhausted and ill, he slumped on the roadside in tears. A kindly villager discovered the American priest and led him to the Syrian troops. Soon after, he was in the hands of the U.S. embassy in Damascus.

The guards were an assortment of men and boys for whom money was as important as any political or religious commitment. They were the paid guns who formed the bulk of most of Beirut's militias. For $30 or $40 a month, they would take orders from just about anyone. They were almost as anxious for the ordeal to be over as the hostages were. Guards such as Badr and Muhammed talked often of going home to their families.

Among the hostages, Said was the most popular of the guards. He was a barber by trade and spoke excellent English. Said's wife had been killed by a mortar round, lingering on the edge of death for more than a month at AUB Hospital, the facility Jacobsen had helped run.

Sometimes, Said brought his little daughter Fatima to the prison. She had been alive about as long as some of the Americans had been held captive. The first time she saw these strange, pale, bearded men with their long hair, blindfolds and chains, Fatima had screamed bloody murder. She soon grew used to the sight and would race around the prison like a little dynamo. The captives frequently heard her father or Hajj affectionately hugging and kissing her. The presence of this cute little girl with her big, liquid brown eyes was particularly bittersweet for Anderson, who was reminded of the daughter who he had never seen, born after he was taken into captivity.

Ali was another guard who remained with the Americans through most of their time in Beirut. He had studied engineering in the United States, but he wasn't too bright. Once, when he was dictating a statement for the hostages to read, he told them to begin with, "Hi, guys. How are you?" They joked that he must have been taught English by a Californian and proposed a more suitable salutation from captivity. In fact, his grasp of the English language was so limited that the hostages suspected he had probably flunked out of college. The Americans never succeeded in tricking him into saying where he had gone to school, but his knowledge seemed to center in the Midwest. Jacobsen once casually mentioned that Michigan's football team had done poorly the previous season and, without thinking, Ali had responded, "Yeah, the Wolverines had a bad year." He then spent weeks trying to convince the Americans that he had attended school in Florida or Oklahoma.

That connection with America was not unique. One of Ben Weir's early guards had studied physics at Lebanon University and had hoped for a scholarship to the U.S., but the Lebanese government's money had run dry and he had ended up dropping out to join a militia. After Jacobsen was released and returned to the United States, he half expected the phone to ring and hear one of his captors asking for help to get an American residence visa.

The man they all answered to was Hajj. While the guards were low-level paid guns, Hajj represented the force that had ordered the abductions and held final say over the captives' lives. The name Hajj, or *Hajji*, was a common honorific applied to any Muslim who had made the pilgrimage to Mecca. While Hajj had apparently not been to Islam's holiest city, the Americans concluded that he was a junior mullah to whom the guards had given that title out of respect.

He often arrived on Thursdays to check up on the captives. That was the day for discussions. Prayers would follow on Friday and decisions on Saturday. Frequently, others would also come. Among them was a man in metal-tipped cowboy boots to whom Hajj seemed to defer. He was present whenever a major decision was made. He had a hand in Jacobsen's brutal beating. The captives called him Little Hajj. As the Americans reached freedom and spoke with CIA debriefers, the intelligence experts became convinced that Little Hajj was Imad Mugniyeh. To them, he had become the face of the Shi'ites' hate.

Psychologists say that abductees often develop an affinity for their captors. They call it the Stockholm syndrome. In Beirut, to a certain extent, the reverse also appeared to be true. When Jenco was eventually released, Hajj told him to express to Anderson's sister, Peggy Say, his condolences on the deaths of her father and brother, events of which Anderson still had not been told. He also said to tell Weir, who had been released earlier, that they were sorry to hear his daughter had died.

The guards also seemed very worried about the fact that Jenco was celibate. He explained that he would be breaking the rules of his religion to have a wife. They pondered that for a while and found a solution. Islam taught that a man could take new wives in Paradise. They made Father Jenco promise that he would get married after he was dead.

"They really didn't think they were doing anything wrong," Jacobsen insisted after his release. "To us, we were rabbits in a box. To them, we were being treated well. We were getting pretty much the same food they were, living in the same conditions, locked up in the same apartment. They genuinely believed there was nothing wrong with our conditions."

Except that it *was* prison. The shackles bit, the ego rebelled and the spirit rankled. The Americans never saw the light of day, never saw the stars, never saw those they loved. Only those same four walls, those same four faces. Hour after hour, day in and day out, five men in a room ten feet square. At night, when the mattresses were laid out on the floor, there was no place to stand. During the day, when the mattresses were rolled up along the walls, there was no place to go. Even if the door had not been there, the chains would have kept them riveted as firmly in place as the sheet metal over the window.

They lived with threats, they lived with doubt, they lived with despair. They also lived with the knowledge that the people they loved were suffering, too. The few letters and tapes from their families that reached them were consumed more voraciously than any food, but the missives were bittersweet. They were full of news, but often masked even more. For instance, Anderson knew that his Lebanese wife had given birth to a baby girl, but his family did not have the heart to tell him that both his father and brother had died pleading to see him one last time.

As much as they valued the companionship, the hostages couldn't help getting on each other's nerves. The reporter and the hospital administrator went at it the worst. Anderson's incessant jogging in place drove Jacobsen up the wall. But politics caused the most arguments. In that sense, life in a cell was no different than life in the world. A conservative Californian Republican and a liberal newsman who had traveled the globe, chained together for 17 months. There were bound to be sparks.

When Weir got out and told Anderson's sister about life in the cell, she dubbed the group "the odd couple in quintuple." That pretty much summed it up. They darned one another's worn-out socks and ministered to one another's emotional wounds. Day by day, a powerful bond grew. Even the conservative Republican and the liberal newsman grew close. When Terry Anderson presented him with a handmade rosary, David Jacobsen was deeply touched.

Each morning began with Mass. Weir and Jenco took turns leading the service after breakfast. Then the five lonely Americans searched for something to make the time pass. Some days they took imaginary trips together, describing the places they had been and the places they would like to go. Tom Sutherland, the dean of agriculture at AUB, spent many hours advising his companions on the best way to develop a farm. Anderson was particularly interested. He owned a piece of land in New York State that he had plans for one day. The reporter also assiduously studied Arabic under the tutelage of Weir. Sutherland sometimes worked with them. The rest of the time they read, prayed and dreamed of rescue.

It almost happened once. At the beginning of June 1985, a few days after Jacobsen's kidnapping, Amal militiamen who were searching for the missing hospital administrator entered the building. It was before the hostages had been brought together. Jacobsen and Anderson were being held in one room. The guard Said entered and told them what was going on downstairs. He ordered the two Americans to be silent and threw flak jackets over them. Sand-filled barrels were dragged into the room to form a barrier and Said and his men cocked their weapons, preparing to fight it out. But the guards downstairs convinced the visitors that they had seen no Americans and the Amal rescue team went away.

The incident only whet Jacobsen's appetite to find a way out. That and the knowledge that he was serving time in place of another man. In the first hours of his interrogation, it had become clear that the kidnappers had mistaken him for AUB's administrator, Einer Larson. As in the case of Father Jenco, Islamic Jihad had grabbed the wrong American.

All the hostages were exercising to stay healthy, but Jacobsen threw himself into a rigorous program of up to 600 pushups and 600 sit-ups a day. Jacobsen had a goal: He wanted to be strong enough to break a man's neck with his bare hands. His plan was simple. When one of the guards entered the room alone, he would smash his face with a forearm and garrote him. With the guard's rifle, he would shoot the other guard in the hallway, then race downstairs and kill the final man.

"And then?" asked Anderson, who thought the idea was crazy. The newsman had spent a lot of time in the slums around the airport. He predicted that they would never get out of the neighborhood alive. Jacobsen countered that with the guards' guns, they could take over the building and hold off anyone who tried to attack until help arrived.

Anderson shook his head. He would wait to be released or rescued.

Tom Sutherland was the hostage in the most pressing need of rescue. The kidnappers thought he belonged to the CIA.

It was all a misunderstanding. The only trouble was, no one could convince Hajj of that. Sutherland had been kidnapped on the drive in from the airport after a trip back to the States. In his briefcase were some letters acquaintances had given him for friends and family in Lebanon. The group that first grabbed him rifled through the briefcase and opened the letters. When they passed him on to the next group, they tossed all the papers back into the case and closed it, jamming the clasp.

Hajj and his fellow interrogators had to break the lock to force the case open. Inside, they found open letters. Who would read letters from one person addressed to another? In their minds, the answer was obvious: a CIA agent. That conclusion was only bolstered when they discovered a newspaper article about Islam, with a note to the effect, "Tom, you should read this." Why would a legitimate teacher of agriculture carry around such a thing?

The situation took a serious turn when Sutherland was given a copy of Buckley's confession to transcribe. The kidnappers said it was difficult to read and they wanted a clearer version, but Sutherland and the other hostages feared that they actually wanted to make the AUB dean implicate himself by putting into his own handwriting Buckley's admissions of CIA ties. By substituting "Buckley" wherever the CIA agent wrote "I," Sutherland made clear who the real author was.

In the document, Buckley admitted he was the CIA's station chief in Beirut and detailed the duties of his assignment. He explained that his principal task was to act as liaison with the Lebanese government intelligence branch and talked about clerical matters. Apparently to satisfy his interrogators' demand for specifics, Buckley told of some mundane operations, such as the time he warned President Amin Gemayel of an impending assassination attempt. The Lebanese leader, according to Buckley, shrugged it off, saying there had been many before.

Overall, the document was nothing more than a description of the bureaucratic side of spying. What Sutherland couldn't know was how much suffering Buckley had endured to hide the rest or how many more pages there might be.

The guards remained convinced that Sutherland was an agent. Hajj and Said appeared one day and announced that they were taking Sutherland away. Only after Father Jenco burst into tears and pleaded did they relent.

The other hostages even made fun of Sutherland's eccentricities to show the captors that they were wrong about his being a spy. At one point, Sutherland was suffering from hemorrhoids and asked for Preparation H suppositories. The first packet that was brought melted in the heat before he could use them. When the next box arrived, he insisted that it be kept in the freezer.

"Hey, Ali," Jacobsen teased the guard one morning as Sutherland was asking that the box be delivered to him in the toilet, "no way is this guy CIA. You think he could eat live rats? He has to have frozen Preparation H!"

Of all those in the cell, Sutherland probably took captivity the hardest. Aside from his concern about the guards suspecting him of being CIA, the AUB dean tended to worry more than the rest about the world that awaited him outside the prison. How were his wife and daughter? Would he be able to fulfill the balance of his contract with AUB when he was released? If not, where would he teach? The others usually talked him out of these depressions. Jacobsen argued that there was no point dwelling on things that couldn't be controlled. The clergymen, Weir and Jenco, emphasized the positive: he was healthy, his family loved him. They would make a new life.

The Americans grew to hate the French.

The four Frenchmen were being held in another room down the hall. Diplomats Marcel Fontaine and Marcel Carton, Middle East researcher Michel Seurat and journalist Jean-Paul Kaufmann had been abducted in the spring of 1985. The Americans never met the Frenchmen, but they saw and heard evidence of them every day.

One of the constant complaints of the Americans was how little time they were given on the daily trip to the toilet. Ten minutes to wash, brush their teeth, shave and move their bowels. It was never enough. No matter how much they demanded and cajoled, the Americans were rarely given more time. The Frenchmen, however, each had half an hour every day.

To add insult to injury, they left the bathroom a mess. They never cleaned up after themselves and the first American in the toilet each morning burned up valuable minutes just getting the place in shape to use. When the Americans complained about the preferential treatment given the Frenchmen and the filth they left behind, the guards shrugged and asked, "What French?"

In late November 1985, Ellie Hallat, the Jewish doctor who had been brought in after Buckley's death, returned. The Americans learned that one of the Frenchmen was very ill. One day, they were moved temporarily to a new cell. In a trash can in the corner they found an empty pink bottle labeled type O blood and the remains of transfusion equipment. After his release, Jean-Paul Kaufmann would report that Michel Seurat had apparently contracted cancer and received several transfusions, including some with blood drawn from the guards.

Just after Christmas, Seurat was separated from his French companions and died soon after. On March 5, Islamic Jihad released a communiqué announcing that Seurat had been executed. As in the case of Buckley, they did not want the world to know he had died from neglect. The group also announced the execution of Dr. Hallet in retaliation for Israeli actions.

Much later, another French hostage, Marcel Coudari, found the conditions of his captivity so unbearable that he asked his guards for a gun with which to commit suicide. He braced himself, put the pistol to his head and pulled the trigger. There were no bullets. The guards laughed.

The hostages grew increasingly frustrated. Their captors allowed selected bits of news to filter through. The five Americans heard about the deal for the TWA hostages and the trade of a Soviet spy for American journalist Nicholas Daniloff. The guards taunted them: they had been abandoned; no one cared about them; the U.S. government was going to let them rot.

On the other side of the world, the families of the Forgotten Seven, as the hostages had come to be known, complained that they were being ignored. They had no liaison officer in Washington, no special telephone number, no friend. "It's gross neglect of the families," Anderson's sister, Peggy Say, complained. Her constant public appeals and television appearances, which the guards allowed the hostages to see, were a major source of emotional support for the men back in Beirut.

Despite outward appearances, Ronald Reagan did care deeply about the fate of the hostages, so deeply that he would embark on another Middle East misadventure that would ultimately undermine the effectiveness of his presidency.

Officially, the administration called it Quiet Diplomacy. The world would come to know it as the Iran–Contra Affair. The broad strokes of the plan were laid out in a draft National Security Decision Directive (NSDD) circulated to select cabinet members by National Security Advisor Robert McFarlane on June 17, 1984. Among other things, the directive called for the United States to encourage friendly countries to "help Iran meet its import requirements ... includ[ing] provision of selected military equipment." Ostensibly, the purpose was to create an opening to Tehran through which the U.S. could ultimately exert its influence in the inevitable struggle for control in a post-Khomeini era.

Secretary of State George Schultz warned that the plan would quickly degenerate into a straight arms-for-hostages trade. Secretary of Defense Casper Weinberger scrawled in the margin of his copy, "This is almost too absurd to comment on. ... It's like asking Qadaffi to Washington for a cozy chat."

For their candor, the two top officials charged with charting America's diplomatic and military policies were cut out of the "information loop" as McFarlane and his team set out to deal with supposed Iranian "moderates" using the same blinkered approach that had started them down the slippery slope to disaster three years before.[8] Again they sought out the guys in the white hats. Again there were none.

By the summer of 1985, arms-for-hostages was well underway.

Shortly before midnight on Saturday, September 14, 1985, Rev. Benjamin Weir was deposited on a dark street near the AUB campus and told he was free. The painful 16-month ordeal had ended.

For Terry Anderson, September 14 was one of the low points of his captivity. The previous week, Hajj had come in the room and sat down on one of the cots. It was likely, he said, that one of the hostages would be released. It would be up to the captives to decide which one. They could choose among Weir, Jenco and Jacobsen. The captors continued to hold Anderson's Marine Corps past against him and were still convinced Sutherland was a spy.[9]

When Hajj left, the Americans talked among themselves. Weir said that since Jenco was in the poorest health (he was suffering badly from his weak heart), he should be the one to go, but the priest immediately took himself out of consideration, pointing out that Weir and Anderson had been held much longer. Jacobsen did the same. Despite Hajj's instructions, they soon decided that Anderson should be the one to go. As a newsman, he was in the best position to plead their case to the world.

The guards were not pleased when they heard the decision, but said nothing. Then, on Saturday evening, Hajj and Said appeared again. They had a short conversation with Weir in Arabic. The others heard the Protestant missionary exclaim, "Oh my, oh my." When Weir turned, it was to tell his fellow prisoners that they had been overruled. He would be leaving that night.

Anderson was shattered. Only after a long conversation in the corner with Father Jenco was he able to compose a letter to his loved ones for Rev.

Weir to take home.

One consolation was the thought of rescue. The building in which they were being held was located at the edge of Beirut airport, somewhere between the two runways. On one runway, they had counted six seconds between the time the planes hit full throttle and were overhead, eight seconds on the other. What more would American intelligence need to pinpoint their location? And with the airfield just a few yards away, they told each other, an airborne paramilitary assault would be a cakewalk. The group often talked of rescue during their discussions in the cell. Jacobsen was its strongest proponent. Weir adamantly opposed the idea of a military operation to free them.

He would maintain that position once he was free. At the hotel outside Norfolk, Virginia, where the government isolated Weir from the press after his release, the Protestant clergyman answered questions about the food and sanitary conditions in the prison, but when his CIA and FBI debriefers asked the location of the apartment and details on the guard force, the gentle missionary, who had spent 35 years trying to help the Lebanese, demurred, "not wanting to encourage military action." Weir was "quite sure it would lead to the death of the other hostages."

Back in Beirut, it was 29 days before the remaining captives were moved to a new hideout. For 29 days they waited for the U.S. commandos to burst through that door. But the only people who ever came were the guards.

From then on, the hostages were moved frequently among numerous hideouts in Beirut and South Lebanon, often hidden in coffins during the trips. Sometimes the Americans were held together, at other times they were separated and mixed with the mounting numbers of captives from other Western countries. French journalist Kaufmann, for example, spent the last six months of his captivity sharing a cell with Anderson.

The kidnappers were playing their version of *Let's Make a Deal*. Even if a hideout was identified, the rescuers could never be sure whom they would find behind that door. No matter that the abduction had been claimed by Islamic Jihad, the Islamic Jihad for the Liberation of Palestine, the Revolutionary Justice Organization, or Iranian-inspired militants operating under some other banner, the victims were shuffled together like a deck of cards.

Ben Weir would have been horrified at the price of his freedom. The day before his release, White House aide Oliver North had arranged for the Israelis to deliver 408 American-built TOW anti-tank missiles from their stockpiles to Iran. It was the second such shipment in a month. The idea for the arms-for-hostages plan had been concocted by Israeli officials and a grab bag of Iranian arms dealers and middlemen who stood to profit from the deal. The proposal was quickly seized upon by the zealous North and his boss McFarlane, who ultimately diverted profits from the arms sales to the Nicaraguan contras.

The man who unwittingly provided cover for the American arms-for-hostages trade was a burly and flamboyant Englishman named Terry Waite. A special emissary for the archbishop of Canterbury, the 47-year-old layman had earned a reputation as a global troubleshooter. In 1981, he had successfully negotiated the release of four Britons held in Iran. Three years later, he had rushed to Libya for tea with Col. Qadaffi when another group of his countrymen were being used as political pawns. They were freed as well.

His shuttle diplomacy on behalf of the Lebanon hostages would earn him the nickname of the Anglican Henry Kissinger. Beginning in late 1985, the six-foot-seven-inch envoy courageously volunteered for a series of meetings with the kidnappers. It appeared to the world that his negotiations helped win the release of Weir and the others that followed. In fact, apparently unknown to Waite, the hostages were being bartered for arms.

In early 1986, the White House ordered that 500 more TOWS, along with Hawk antiaircraft missiles and other spare parts, be delivered directly from U.S. stockpiles. In May, North and McFarlane, bearing a Bible and a chocolate cake that would later become the foil of late night comedians, arrived in Tehran. But despite the two 707s filled with 90 tons of missiles and spare parts that accompanied them, they left empty-handed after three days of talks with senior Iranian officials. Hope seemed to fade.

Then, in late July, Father Jenco was released and the U.S. quickly dispatched more TOWS and Hawks. But then in September, two more Americans, International School Director Frank Reed and AUB Comptroller Joseph Cicippio, were seized on the streets of Beirut. Hizbullah and its Iranian sponsors, it seemed, were drawing a new hand.

Yet another shipment was dispatched in late October, but instead of prompting a new release, yet another American, poet Edward Tracy Austin, was taken. Soon after, CIA Director William Casey told North "this thing is unraveling" and needs to be "cleaned up." North quickly began shredding the paper trail. Within days, the Lebanese newspaper *al-Shiraa* reported that America was trading arms for hostages.

There is "no foundation" for the claim, Reagan told the American people in a televised news conference. "We *did not*, repeat, *did not* trade weapons or anything else for hostages, nor will we."

When the scandal broke, some said Waite must have been cooperating with the CIA. Angry that his credibility had been undermined, the envoy bravely returned to Lebanon in February 1987 for another meeting with the men behind Islamic Jihad. It would be almost five years before he once more saw freedom.

In addition to Weir, both Jenco and Jacobsen would be traded for a combination of missiles, spare parts and sensitive intelligence, but by the time the nationally televised congressional hearings into the scandal began in the spring of 1987, six more Americans had taken their place in the cells. The U.S. had once more been humiliated and all of Ronald Reagan's sermons about standing fast against terrorism were proved to be no more meaningful than the dialogue in his old movies.

As Secretary of State Schultz put it, "[O]ur guys ... they got taken to the cleaners." And they almost went to jail. North, McFarlane and Vice Admiral John Poindexter, who had replaced McFarlane as national security advisor, were all convicted of obstructing Congress and illegally destroying documents to cover their trail. Weinberger and various other officials were charged but pardoned by President George Bush, himself implicated for his role in the affair as vice president.

So humiliated was Robert McFarlane by the fallout from his disastrous encounter with Lebanon that the ex-marine attempted suicide.

When the final report on the Iran–Contra Affair came out a year later criticizing the Reagan administration for "putting all the cards in the terrorists' hands,"[10] Terry Anderson, Tom Sutherland and their new companions were still counting the days.

Section IV

The Seeds Spread

17
Metamorphosis

You have your Lebanon and its dilemma. I have my
Lebanon and its beauty. Your Lebanon is an arena for men
from the West and men from the East. My Lebanon is a
flock of birds fluttering in the early morning...
—Khalil Gibran[1]

If one of the countless victims of Lebanon's twentieth-century wars awoke
from a coma in the early years of the new Millennium, he might have been
forgiven for thinking he was still locked in a dream.

Beirut had emerged as a city reborn. Bikini-clad nymphs once more
frolicked poolside at the St. George Hotel. Stores crowded with Gucci and
St. Lauren lined the stylish shopping malls that had risen from the killing
fields of the Green Line. On Hamra Street, Americans mingled with business
people from around the world, once more drawn by Beirut's mercantile
flair and strict bank secrecy laws.

In South Lebanon, the Israelis had gone the way of so many other foreign
invaders who had fertilized Lebanon's soil with their blood through the
centuries. The once-despised Lebanese Army now stood as a welcome
presence in their place.

But perhaps nothing would be as likely to disorient a Lebanese
reawakening to this strange new world than the scene in Parliament, where,
among the Christian rightists and aging Sunni politicos, sat eleven members
representing the country's most powerful new political party: Hizbullah.

The Party of God, which once denounced Lebanese politics as "rotten to
the core" and "unreformable," had joined the system.

The transition from terrorist cell to what Beirut's *Daily Star* would label
"the least corrupt, most hard-working and most progressive ... political
party Lebanon has ever seen,"[2] had not come overnight. In between,
Hizbullah fought a war – and won.

The clerics, backed by their Iranian and Syrian patrons, had set out to defeat two of the most powerful armies in the world. And they had succeeded in spades.

Long after the Marines had pulled out and most U.S. civilians had fled, a tiny contingent of Americans assigned to the UN observer group in South Lebanon had hung on. Then, early in 1988, one member of the team, Marine Lt. Col. William Higgins, was kidnapped and hanged. (His body, along with that of former CIA station chief William Buckley, would be dumped on a Beirut street a few weeks after the release of the final, and longest-serving, American hostage, Terry Anderson. The Associated Press bureau chief, who put his life at risk to report on the plight of the Shi'ites, had endured 2,454 days in captivity in Shi'ite hands.)[3]

On December 2, 1988, Washington announced that the remainder of the Americans in the UN team had been withdrawn "for their own safety."[4]

Islamic Jihad had promised it would not rest until "not one American ... will remain in this country." The goal had now been achieved.

It took longer to expel the Israelis, but the victory was no less complete. By mid-1985, the battered IDF had redeployed to a new nine-mile-wide "security zone" north of the Israeli border, but the move did nothing to slow its brutal war of attrition with the Shi'ites.

"The oppressed countries have become the struggle's bone of contention and the oppressed people have become its fuel," Hizbullah wrote in its *Open Letter to the Downtrodden in Lebanon and in the World*, released one month after the redeployment.[5]

America and its proxy Israel stood chief among the oppressors, in this enunciation of the party's worldview. Hizbullah had been born out of the terror war against the U.S. presence in Lebanon. In those days, the various sheikhs and Amal defectors had operated semi-independently under banners such as Islamic Amal, Islamic Jihad, al-Da'wa, the Association of Muslim Ulema of Lebanon, and the Association of Muslim Students. It was the subsequent "resistance struggle" against the Israeli occupation that was responsible for those disparate groups coalescing into a cohesive alliance and, ultimately, a political party.

"Had the enemy not taken this step [invading], I do not know whether something called Hizbullah would have been born," then-Secretary-General Hasan Nasrullah told the party's newspaper *Al-Ahd* in 1997. "I doubt it."[6]

This Hizbullah alliance now took center stage in the "liberation" of the South (with help from fellow Shi'ites of the rival Amal militia, with which it simultaneously fought a bloody conflict between 1985 and 1989). The Islamic Resistance embarked on a devastating campaign of suicide attacks, roadside bombings and conventional guerrilla assaults against Israeli troops and their South Lebanon Army allies.

Years later, after the occupation had ended, South Lebanon's roads would be dotted with historical markers celebrating individual clashes, akin to those found on Revolutionary War or Civil War battlefields in the U.S. One such placard, in both Arabic and broken English, was sighted by a reporter from the *New Yorker* in 2002:

"On Oct. 19, 1988, at 1:25 p.m., a martyr car that was body trapped [sic] with 500 kilogram of highly exploding materials transformed two Israeli troops into masses of fire and limbs, in one of the severe kicks that the Israeli army had received in Lebanon."[7]

As they had earlier done with the PLO and would later repeat on the West Bank, the Israelis ruthlessly retaliated against both military targets and civilians. They adopted a policy of assassinating key Hizbullah leaders, such as Secretary-General Abbas Musawi, who was killed by a missile fired at his car by an Israeli jet in 1992.

A year later, when Israel killed a top Hizbullah military commander, the organization – which, unlike the PLO in Lebanon, had largely confined its attacks to Israeli troops inside Lebanon – unleashed a hail of Katushya rockets on settlements in northern Israel, even as its guerrillas, together with those of the Popular Front for the Liberation of Palestine – General Command (PFLP-GC), killed five Israeli soldiers in a series of attacks inside Lebanon.

For a frustrated and bleeding IDF, it was the last straw. Shi'ite towns and villages were systematically pounded in an eight-week campaign, known as Operation Accountability, that saw the heaviest air attacks since the 1982 invasion. Along with attempting to crush the military capabilities of the Resistance, it quickly became apparent that a key Israeli motive was to turn the civilian population of South Lebanon against Hizbullah. A U.S.-brokered cease-fire eventually produced a verbal agreement between the two sides: Israel would refrain from attacking civilian targets if Hizbullah halted missile attacks on northern Israel. The deal marked another step in the transformation of the Party of God from a loose terrorist alliance into a conventional guerrilla army.

That transformation was also being played out on the ground, where carefully planned guerrilla attacks had become as common as the suicide bombings for which Hizbullah was famous. The fighters often videotaped their attacks against Israeli troops. Footage of these deadly operations would sometimes appear on Hizbullah's television station *Al Manar* – whose signal could be seen inside Israel – even before the Israeli army had notified the families of the dead.

"These videos had a huge psychological effect, not just on Israeli soldiers, but also on Israeli civilians," Hassan Ezzieddine, the head of Hizbullah's media relations department, told the *Christian Science Monitor* years later. "They helped create a climate in Israel for demanding a withdrawal from South Lebanon."[8]

For three years the unwritten agreement held, leading to a surreal scenario in which Israeli government officials spoke of the killings of Israeli soldiers as being "within the rules," and Hizbullah spokesmen actually apologized when unauthorized Katushyas were fired across the border.

All the time, the two sides were locked in a vicious cycle of death. One Israeli think tank estimated that Israeli troops in Lebanon were subject to some 1,000 "incidents" a year.[9] It was a war of attrition pitting an organization whose members ached for martyrdom against a country for which each soldier's death was a body blow.

By the eve of the 1996 Israeli elections, the two sides were once more targeting civilians. A new Katushya attack on northern Israel sparked an intense 16-day Israeli assault, which the IDF dubbed Operation Grapes of Wrath. Israeli jets took out Hizbullah's South Lebanon headquarters, training camps, arms stockpiles and the homes of Hizbullah leaders. Three power plants were also destroyed, sending a message to the government in Beirut that it would be held responsible for Hizbullah's actions in the south.

In the midst of the assault, Israeli shells fell on a UN outpost at Qana, killing four UN observers and 100 Lebanese civilians who had sought safety there. International reaction was swift. Within days, the government of Shimon Peres – who would lose the election – agreed to a new cease-fire. The terms were the same: you leave our civilians alone and we will do the same for yours. But this time the agreement was committed to writing (though unsigned) and a monitoring committee, made up of representatives from the U.S., Syria, Israel and Lebanon, was established. Hizbullah, once just an elusive "trend," was now negotiating treaties.

The two sides settled back into their struggle on the ground. Using Vietnam as a model, Hizbullah officials boasted that the more body bags that were sent back to Israel, the greater would become the opposition to the war. And so it was.

The year 1997 began with news that stunned the Israeli national psyche: 73 soldiers en route to Lebanon had been killed in a helicopter collision. Meanwhile, the death toll from Hizbullah attacks mounted: 39 more dead in 1997, 23 in 1998. Even more upsetting to military strategists was the death ratio. In 1995, five Lebanese guerrillas were being killed for every Israeli soldier that died. By the late nineties, that ratio was approaching one-to-one.[10]

As the military pressure on the IDF increased, so too did the political pressure at home. Just days after twelve members of an elite Israeli commando team were killed in an ambush by Amal and the Lebanese Army, antiwar protesters demonstrated outside the home of Prime Minister Benjamin Netanyahu and Israeli television reported 52 percent of those surveyed wanted the IDF out of Lebanon.[11]

The Israeli government was coming to the conclusion that it wanted the same. Netanyahu floated a proposal: Israel would withdraw from Lebanon as part of a comprehensive deal that included a resolution of the Golan Heights dispute with Syria. Even Ariel Sharon concurred.

The Arabs rejected the idea, calling for an immediate and unconditional withdrawal according to UN resolution 245, which required Israel to pull back across the border. Hizbullah read the obvious message between the lines. Israel's offer "tells much about its plight," observed Hizbullah spokesman Ibrahim Musawi. "We believe that Israel is fed up with casualties. This tells Hizbullah and Lebanon that years of negotiation did nothing, but that resistance made this happen."[12]

Lebanon's foreign minister said the South had become Israel's Vietnam. Many top officers in the IDF quietly agreed.

In a strategy session at the office of the defense minister in late 1997, the commander of the security zone, Major General Amiram Levine, told his bosses that the status quo in South Lebanon, "where Hizbullah is drawing blood and we just bear it, cannot go on." Levine, who would be appointed deputy head of Mossad the following year, proposed a new round of "aggressive actions" to put Hizbullah and it's Amal allies on the defensive. "But," he added, "if you think that what I propose cannot be done, then the alternative is a unilateral withdrawal from Lebanon without waiting for an agreement with the Syrians or the Lebanese government."[13]

Both proposals were rejected and the IDF hunkered down, adopting a combination of high tech and highly unconventional tactics to cut its losses. Long-distance video surveillance cameras and thermal imaging devices were set up both around IDF positions and at known Hizbullah transit points, hot air balloons joined unmanned reconnaissance drones, radar systems were set up on off-shore buoys, and, in one of the more bizarre counterterrorism strategies, the Lebanese newspaper *Albilad* reported that the Israelis were using wild pigs to track guerrillas.

"The Israelis attach electronic instruments to collars on the wild pigs, so that as the pigs roam the streambeds between occupied territory and liberated territory, the movements of personnel can be tracked," the paper claimed. "The use of wild pigs derives from the fact that they frequent inaccessible places and from the fact that a wild pig, upon seeing a human, makes a particular noise."[14]

"What we are really doing is introducing technologies that partially substitute for the physical presence of soldiers," Deputy Defense Minister Ephraim Sneh told the *New York Times*. "The bottom line is that it has improved the efficiency of our presence in southern Lebanon. We can stave off the guerrillas from our border with a lower price."[15]

Tours of duty were extended to reduce the risk of exposure during transfers. Patrols became a thing of the past. And Israeli troops pulled back from the field, leaving less than 20 percent of the IDF positions in South Lebanon manned by Israelis. The rest were turned over to the SLA. On one level, the strategy worked. The number of Israeli soldiers killed dropped dramatically to 13 in 1999 (though that included a brigadier general whose convoy was ambushed), but pressure for a withdrawal continued to mount at home, led by groups like Peace Now and Women and Mothers for Peace.

Lebanon had chewed up and spat out a series of Israeli prime ministers, from Begin – who had become a depressed recluse – to Yitzak Shamir and Peres. Now it appeared poised to do the same to Netanyahu. The war became the key issue during the 1999 election campaign. Labor's Ehud Barak – in an echo of Richard Nixon's election promise – pledged to "bring the boys home" within a year.[16] Polls showed 57 percent of Israelis wanted them out immediately. Morale among the troops on the ground plummeted. No one wanted to be the last solider to die in a lost cause.

Meanwhile, Washington scrambled to run with Netanyahu's South Lebanon–Golan proposal. Envoys shuttled between Damascus and Jerusalem seeking a comprehensive deal. For it was Syrian President Hafez al-Assad's fingerprints that Israel saw stamped all over Hizbullah's operations.

While Hizbullah was largely an Iranian creation, with the rival Amal militia serving as Syria's main proxy among the Shi'ites, nothing happened in Lebanon without Syria's acquiescence. Since Israel's withdrawal from the Beirut area, a *Pax Syriana* had governed Lebanon. Damascus called the shots. That was underlined when Amin Gemayel's successor, the combative Gen. Michel Aoun, was literally bombed out of his palace and driven into exile after a six-month, Syrian-led military confrontation, and replaced by a Christian more sensitive to Syrian goals. When militias were disbanded a few years later, Syria ensured that Hizbullah was the only group allowed to retain its weapons. It would serve as a useful tool in Syria's decades-old struggle against Israel.

Lebanon had always been the wild card of Arab–Israeli politics. It was no different now. And Israel was playing with a weak hand. The idea that it could trade a withdrawal from Lebanon in return for an agreement on the Golan presupposed that the Syrian leader was more anxious to get the Golan back than Israel was to get out of Lebanon. In fact, it was the other way around. Israel needed to withdraw. Desperately. And Assad knew it. With each new attack by Hizbullah, Assad was upping the ante.

A chorus of voices in Israel saw the absurdity of the charade.

"I have come to the conclusion that Israeli policy in South Lebanon has failed miserably, and it is our top national priority to cut our losses," wrote former government spokesman Yossi Olmert. "Continuing the futile and costly Israeli presence in South Lebanon plays into Assad's hands."[17]

The debate soon became a moot point when the Syrian leader and President Clinton met at a March, 2000 Geneva summit. The Americans believed Syrian Foreign Minister Farouk al-Sharaa had signaled that his boss was prepared to compromise. Clinton outlined a deal that would leave the shores of Lake Kinnert in Israeli hands but return the balance of the Golan to Syria. Assad – who had come to Geneva because he was convinced the Americans were about to give him back all he had long demanded – firmly shook his head no. For the Syrian strongman, it was just the latest confirmation that his instinctual distrust of the Israelis – and their American patrons – was well placed.

"Assad seems unable to set aside his deep conviction that Israel is not ready for an honorable peace," his biographer, Patrick Seale, had written the year before, "not ready to be simply one player among others in the Middle East system, but conspires instead to hold sway over the whole region ... with the aim of reducing the Arabs to a subject people."[18]

Resupplied with new stockpiles of weapons shipped from Iran via Damascus, Hizbullah quickly renewed its attacks. Using American-made TOW antitank missiles, ironically said to have come from the arms-for-hostages deal, Hizbullah guerrillas began to cripple Merkava tanks, Israel's most powerful weapon on the ground. In response to the deaths of seven IDF soldiers, Israel broke the Grapes of Wrath accord and unleashed a series of attacks on civilian targets, including new air strikes on power plants that blacked out Beirut and one-third of the country. Hizbullah resisted the temptation to respond in kind.

"It is noteworthy that up until the eleventh hour, Israel never challenged Hizbullah's right to attack its soldiers in Lebanon," respected Lebanon scholar Augustus Richard Norton later observed. Only after the seven soldiers were killed, "were the rules of the game vigorously challenged by Israel under the impact of a public that saw its enemies as terrorists and villains. The shock was as much that the 'bad guys' played by the rules as that the IDF was being outplayed."[19]

Those "bad guys" smelled victory. Hizbullah Secretary-General Hasan Nasrallah said Israel had only two options: "Stay and suffer additional losses of human life" or "pull out unconditionally."

Ehud Barak, who had been elected prime minister the previous year, was already on record as saying Israel would withdraw – with or without an agreement with Syria – by summer. The IDF, he added, should have pulled out years before, but the political leaders didn't have "the strength" to "end this tragedy."[20]

A series of incidents in May, including what Israel said was the "accidental" bombing of a village that wounded 14 civilians, prompted Hizbullah to launch a hail of Katushyas on northern Israel, killing an IDF soldier and wounding several civilians. In predictable fashion, Israel unleashed a new air assault on Hizbullah positions and the Lebanese infrastructure.

Temperatures rose. An American message of support for the Israeli attacks prompted a fiery speech by Nasrallah. Israeli Foreign Minister David Levy shot back with a warning in the Knesset that "Lebanon will burn." The IDF, he promised, would repay "blood for blood, soul for soul, child for child."[21]

But it was, quite literally, all over but the shouting. On May 22, as the IDF began its unilateral withdrawal, the South Lebanon Army disintegrated. Fleeing militiamen abandoned their uniforms and Israeli-supplied weapons and equipment, and crowded the Israeli border crossing points, pleading for asylum. "The role of the South Lebanon Army in southern Lebanon is finished," UN spokesman Timur Gokksel told the BBC.[22]

Two days later, Israel's withdrawal was complete. The 22-year military adventure in Lebanon had ended.

Like Ronald Reagan before him, Barak had once promised that Israel would not withdraw from Lebanon "with our tail between our legs."[23] But the final scenes of wounded soldiers being carried home on stretchers broadcast on Israeli television and the scramble for control in the one-time "security zone" sent a very different message.

Hizbullah's Nasrallah proclaimed "the first victory in 50 years of Arab–Israeli conflict."[24] Lebanese Prime Minister Salim al-Hoss declared a national holiday – The Day of the Resistance and Liberation – and said Israel had withdrawn "terrified and defeated, wagging behind him the tails of a crushing defeat."[25]

The Arabs had achieved their first victory against Israel. The implications were not lost on the Israelis themselves.

"A few hundred Hizbullah combatants have defeated the big and strong Israeli army," Israel's *Yediot Ahranot* newspaper said in an editorial. "They defeated it in the most important of battles: that on the internal front. We can only hope that Hizbullah's victory would not push the Palestinians and the Syrians into deducing that they can achieve [their] goals by force."[26]

The Jaffa Center for Strategic Studies quickly produced a study on the long-term damage caused by the shattering of the myth of invincibility. "Deterrent power is a matter of perception," military expert Shai Feldman observed, "and it must therefore be hoped that the difficult and distressing scenes that accompanied Israel's withdrawal from southern Lebanon at the end of May will not influence its ability to fend off basic security threats."[27]

Others, meanwhile, were tallying the cost. More than 1,200 Israeli dead since Operation Peace for Galilee was launched in 1982. Thousands more carrying physical and emotional scars. Some $20 billion in financial expenditures associated with the war. And then there were the Lebanese. The official Lebanese government figure was 5,000 dead, but few believed that even began to approximate the actual toll.

"What did we gain from all those wasted years, from all the needless bloodshed, from the hundreds of lives lost?" asked columnist Doron Rosenblum in the daily *Ha'aretz*. "Decades of security geniuses have left us, in the final analysis, with a pro-Iranian military organization, Hizbullah, sitting on the very edge of our Northern Highway. They have left us without an ounce of stamina. No one, I think, has the faintest idea what we gained."[28]

The architect of the carnage was unrepentant. Standing beside the border fence through which he had ordered the tanks 20 years before, Sharon declared: "We must launch strikes against Lebanon's infrastructure. We must do so immediately. We must not wait even one second longer. We must silence them!"[29]

It was not just its ability to confront the mighty Israeli military machine that had won Hizbullah the respect of the Lebanese. It was also its ability to reach out to those in need.

By the early 1990s, Hizbullah had established a vast social infrastructure to meet the needs of a Shi'ite population left desperate by decades of war and occupation. As soon as the Israelis redeployed in 1985, the party moved into "liberated" portions of South Lebanon and the Bekaa, setting up hospitals, pharmacies and schools. Between 1988 and 1991 alone, more than 1,000 homes were repaired; loans were offered to rebuild businesses; scholarships were set up; public utilities like power and water were reestablished and run by Hizbullah committees; and agricultural cooperatives were created, selling seeds, fertilizer and pesticides to poverty-ridden farmers at below-market prices. When areas of the mountains were cut off by snowstorms, it was Hizbullah that rushed in with supplies for those trapped.

And in the process, the organization won the loyalty of the vast majority of Shi'ites and the respect of much of the rest of the country.[30]

As UN spokesman Timor Goksel explained to one researcher, "People are noticing these things. Whenever there is shelling Hizbullah will show up saying, 'What can we do for you?' Then you'll become dependent on them. You feel that you owe them something."[31]

"Hizbullah gives assistance to the Lebanese people, not to Lebanese religious sects, and this is the reason why they have so many backers," added Georges Najem, a Maronite Christian who represented Hizbullah in Parliament.[32]

In short, Hizbullah was doing precisely what Israel could have done in the immediate aftermath of the 1982 invasion: win the hearts and minds of a Shi'ite population then jubilant that it had been freed from the hated overlords of the PLO. Instead, Israel had engaged in a shortsighted policy that resulted in an occupation more brutal than anything the Palestinians had ever wrought.

Rather than using Israel's technological and agricultural prowess to make war-ravaged South Lebanon bloom, and in the process creating a buffer zone populated by a grateful people, Ariel Sharon and his successors had opened a Pandora's Box containing a new style of warfare far more terrifying than anything they had ever faced before.

Yet while Hizbullah was winning a vast following in the South, there were still those in Beirut who argued that the party was usurping the government's role. It seemed a hollow argument after decades of neglect of the Shi'ite population, even under Lebanon's new political order, worked out at a 1988 national reconciliation conference in Taif, Saudi Arabia, under which the Sunni Muslim prime minister wielded substantial power.

"Hizbullah is not stealing the role of the government, the government has disappeared from the south," Talal Salman, publisher of the pro-Syrian *As Safir* newspaper, told the *New York Times*.[33]

With political maturity came organizational change – and with that the growing pains of every maturing movement.

"One sheikh obtains a financier, then he gets money, then he hires people. Sometimes Hizbullah is a huge organization, sometimes it is not," I had been told by a wary Amal official in the early 1980s. "To say Hizbullah is doing this or that is wrong. You have to identify the group."

Opposition to the Western presence in Beirut and the Israeli occupation of the South had largely united those disparate elements in the years that followed. Now, with the common enemy removed from Lebanese soil, the differences in ideology among individual sheikhs began to be felt once more.

The divisions became apparent with the resignation of Hizbullah Secretary-General Sheikh Subhi Tofeili over the decision by the party's *Majlis al-Shura al Qarar* (supreme decision-making council) to take part in the 1992 parliamentary elections. So bitter was Tofeili's opposition that he called for the burning of polling stations in his home village of Brital.

Tofeili wanted to continue in opposition to the despised Christian-led government. Hussain Musawi and other Hizbullah leaders disagreed, arguing that it was not right to "shun an impure system" when participation in Parliament would give Muslims a political voice and thus serve the interests of Islam.[34] A series of factors led this group to conclude that it was expedient, for the time being, to set aside their ultimate goal of establishing in Lebanon an Islamic republic mirroring that of Iran. Key among those factors was the recognition among many in the Hizbullah leadership that, given the huge Christian population of Lebanon, the prospect of creating an Islamic republic in the country was unlikely even in the distant future.

"We don't seek the application of Islam by force or violence but by peaceful political action, which gives the opportunity for the majority in any society to adopt or reject it. If Islam becomes the choice of the majority then we will apply it, if not, we will continue and discuss till we reach correct beliefs," the party explained in its "Statement of Purpose."[35]

The pragmatic recognition of Lebanese political realities was based in part on the party's adherence to the Qur'anic injunction that, "Islam cannot be forced upon followers of others faiths" (II:256). The assurance that Islamic rule would not be imposed on the country had been repeated by various Hizbullah leaders through the years, leading to a policy that insisted that only after the arrival of the Shi'ite messiah, the Twelfth Imam, would Lebanon – along with the rest of the region – be subject to Islamic rule. To impose Islamic rule through force of arms, according to Hussein Musawi, would be inherently "unjust."[36]

Along with the party's belief that under *Shar'ia* (Islamic law), rebellion against secular states was considered unacceptable, there was yet another pragmatic consideration: rebellion produced chaos, and chaos allowed external enemies to penetrate the society. Though it had Israel in mind, Hizbullah's very existence demonstrated the truth of the maxim.

For unlike Osama bin Laden, who would be inspired in part by Hizbullah's brand of terrorism, the majority of ideologues within Hizbullah were Lebanese nationalists first and Islamists second. That was reflected in the fact that Christians were included in both Hizbullah's parliamentary delegation and the ranks of its resistance fighters. Fadlallah himself repeatedly and consistently called for a dialogue with Christians on their shared religious values and the creation of a multi-confessional state.

Hizbullah was engaged in a "civilizational" struggle, but, as Hizbullah Planning Council member Ali Fayyah told Lebanese Shi'ite political science professor Amal Saad-Ghorayeb, "while religion is one aspect of civilization, it need not be the only aspect. Ethnicity can also provide the basis for civilization."[37]

A third factor in the decision to engage in Lebanese politics was Iranian President Hashemi Rafsanjani's call for a "relaxation" of Iran's relations with the West. To those who received their support from the Iranian "moderates," the time for a hard line had – at least for the moment – passed. For, as Lebanese scholar Nizar Hamzeh has written, "the struggles for power among Iran's top leaders were mirrored in Hizbullah's leadership."[38]

While experts disagreed on the specifics of the alliances, there were three general (though constantly shifting and overlapping) lines of support tracing back to Iran from Hizbullah's various factions. One group primarily owed their allegiance to Rafsanjani; a second to Iran's former ambassador to Syria, Ali Akhbar Mohtashami, who had served in various senior capacities since returning to Iran; and a third group was closely allied with the *Pasardan* (Revolutionary Guards), which had retained a foothold in Lebanon.

And therein lay the key to the perennial conflict between U.S. officials who claimed Hizbullah was engaged in ongoing anti-American terrorism and Hizbullah officials who insisted that it was not.

While, on one level, the Hizbullah supreme council oversaw a highly organized political, military and humanitarian infrastructure and made unified decisions, on another level Hizbullah remained a philosophical alliance bringing together a constellation of clerics and militants with a variety of shifting agendas, some of whom identified themselves as members of Hizbullah, others who operated on the fringes.

A prime example was Muhammed Hussein Fadlallah. Both inside Hizbullah and without he was considered the organization's spiritual father. One of the most renowned Shi'ite religious thinkers of his generation, it was Fadlallah's treatises that formed the core of Hizbullah's philosophy. Yet from Hizbullah's earliest days, the cleric had consistently denied he was a member of the organization, describing himself to a reporter from the London-based newspaper *al-Hayat* as a *marji'*, or religio-legal authority, who kept himself above the party framework.[39]

U.S. and Israeli intelligence had repeatedly linked Fadlallah with individual terrorist operations. He had spoken out on many issues related to the party, from participation in elections to activities in the south. Fighters in Hizbullah's ranks looked to him for inspiration. Yet there never emerged any concrete evidence to indicate he either officially held a seat on the supreme council or was a "card-carrying member" of the organization.

In its own way, Hizbullah bore certain parallels to an American political party. Just because an individual member of Congress did something outlandish or introduced a provocative bill did not mean the leadership sanctioned the action, though it may ultimately serve the party's aims to have it happen. The difference with Hizbullah was that its provocative acts killed people.

Was "Hizbullah" as an organization responsible for the violence, or were individuals or groups who shared what I had been told so many years before was a mutual "tendency," acting independently from the party hierarchy? The answer appeared to lie within the very definition of Hizbullah put forth by political scientist Amal Saad-Ghorayeb two decades after Iran first started encouraging action by its Lebanese brethren.

"Hizbullah represents an intellectual and political orientation that governs the lives of those who affiliate themselves with it, irrespective of the organizational framework within which they operate," Saad-Ghorayeb wrote in *Hizbu'llah: Politics and Religion*. "According to one Hizbullah official, 'every Muslim is automatically a member of Hizbullah.'"[40]

While Washington's hard-liners were quick to paint the entire Hizbullah organization with the same brush, those who had tracked the group's various metamorphoses recognized the subtle – and not-so-subtle – shades of difference reemerging in the wake of Israel's withdrawal.

"I don't agree that Hizbullah itself is a terrorist organization," Robert Baer, a former CIA operative in Beirut, told PBS's *Frontline*. "It delivers powdered milk; it takes care of people. It's a social organization; it's a political organization. It fights corruption."[41]

Baer and others who had tracked the group drew an analogy with the relationship between Sinn Fein, the Catholic political party in Northern Ireland, and the IRA, the militant organization from which it sprang. "Under the Hizbullah umbrella [is] the Islamic Jihad, which I call their special security," Baer explained. "You can paint Hizbullah as a terrorist organization. You can do that for political reasons, but strictly speaking, it is many things."

Even the U.S. government acknowledged that. At the end of a visit to Beirut at the end of 2001, William Burns, the assistant secretary of state for Near East affairs, told a news conference: "We recognize that Hizbullah has a number of different dimensions to it: as a political party; as a social welfare organization."[42]

Still, there was little disagreement among Western intelligence agencies as to who was behind the majority of the anti-Western mayhem: Imad

Fayez Mugniyeh, the man the American hostages had known as Little Hajj and who the intelligence experts described as the head of Hizbullah's "special operations" wing.

"Again and again, the lines all trace back to him," said one intelligence official, looking at one of the few extant photographs of Imad Mugniyeh. "He is the man responsible for so much of our pain."

Originally a member of Yasser Arafat's personal security detail, Force 17, Mugniyeh, a Shi'ite born in South Lebanon, stayed behind in Lebanon when the PLO was sent into exile after the 1982 siege of Beirut. He soon became a bodyguard for Fadlallah and linked up with Iran and the nascent Hizbullah movement. American intelligence would eventually tie him to the 1983 U.S. embassy bombing that wiped out the CIA Beirut station and killed the agency's head of Middle East operations; to the devastating suicide bombings of the U.S. Marine Corps and French barracks; and to the kidnappings. Mugniyeh, they claimed, personally tortured CIA Station Chief William Buckley. He would also be indicted by the U.S. for organizing the 1985 hijacking of TWA flight 847 and the murder of U.S. Navy diver Robert Stethem, who was shot and dumped on the tarmac, allegedly by Mugniyeh.

The terror chief was also implicated in both the December 1986 Kuwait Airlines hijacking that ended in Iran and the commandeering of another Kuwait Airlines jet three years later. The passengers of that plane included three members of the Kuwaiti royal family. The hijackings were an extension of his campaign to free his brother-in-law, a cousin and other members of the al-Da'wa cell held for the December 1983 bombing of the U.S. embassy in Kuwait. In a reprise of the Stethem execution, two Kuwaitis were shot and dumped on a Cyprus runway. Mugniyeh ultimately failed to win his relatives' release, but Algerian, PLO and Iranian negotiators arranged safe passage for himself and his comrades.

For his next target, Mugniyeh looked far beyond the confines of the Middle East.

The Triple Frontier region of South America, where Paraguay, Brazil and Argentina come together, was home to a substantial Arab population. The first wave of Lebanese immigrants arrived in that lawless region, where the smuggling of drugs, weapons and assorted pirated goods was commonplace, in the early 1980s. Hizbullah began establishing itself there not long after.

Like West Africa, where an estimated 120,000 Lebanese formed a prosperous merchant class, the Triple Frontier soon became a valuable source of party funds, some from voluntary contributions from local Muslims (compelled by the Qur'an to donate 2.5 percent of their annual income to charity), some from strong-arm tactics. And it wasn't small change. When they raided the offices of one alleged Hizbullah enforcer, Paraguayan officials reportedly found a receipt from Hizbullah acknowledging the transfer of $3.5 million. So important was the area, Paraguayan intelligence officials told the *New Yorker*, that in 1994 Fadlallah himself traveled secretly to the region to bless a new mosque.[43]

By the early 1990s, according to Western intelligence officials, Hizbullah was also running schools where young people were indoctrinated in its ideology, weapons training camps, and clandestine communications switching centers, where calls from around the world would be connected to make them untraceable. Also active in the area were Lebanon's Amal, the Egyptian Muslim Brotherhood and other Islamic groups. The discovery of a map and travel advertisements for the region in al-Qaeda safe houses in Afghanistan and the 2002 arrest of two men whom Paraguayan authorities claimed were al-Qaeda operatives, lent credence to speculation that Osama bin Laden's men might also have links there.

So it was natural that, as he began casting about for new targets, Mugniyeh would seize on the Triple Frontier as a base of operations. On March 17, 1992, Mugniyeh and his operatives launched their most ambitious international operation to date: the bombing of the Israeli embassy in Buenos Aires, which killed 29 and injured more than 250. The attack was allegedly launched in retaliation for Israel's assassination of Hizbullah Secretary-General Abbas Musawi in South Lebanon. Argentine officials would eventually issue an extradition warrant for Mugniyeh. Two years later, Hizbullah struck again in Argentina, killing 87 and injuring more than 100 in the bombing of the Buenos Aires Jewish Community Center.[44] The Israelis quickly retaliated in a replay of the abortive 1985 CIA–Saudi attempt to assassinate Fadlallah, setting off a car bomb outside a Beirut mosque where the Shi'ite clergyman was preaching. Once again, Fadlallah escaped. But just as Mugniyeh's brother Jihad had died in the 1985 attempt on Fadlallah's life, this time the explosion went off directly in front of a shop run by his other brother, Fuad, who died instantly. Precisely who was the target – Fadlallah or Mugniyeh's brother – was never clear. But Israeli sources said they used the brother's funeral to lay a trap for Mugniyeh, who managed to elude them.

His apparent absence from the funeral led to widespread unconfirmed reports that the terrorist leader had undergone plastic surgery.[45] Intelligence agencies soon determined that, with Israel and the U.S. both hot on his trail, Mugniyeh had shifted his base of operations to the Iranian holy city of Qom, where he was said to report to Ghassem Soleimani, head of a unit of the Revolutionary Guards.

In 1995, American officials thought they finally had the elusive terrorist chief when they learned he was on board a plane en route to Saudi Arabia, where he was scheduled to make a flight connection. A snatch team was dispatched and the Saudis were asked to delay the connecting plane. But instead, the Saudis refused the plane on which Mugniyeh was traveling permission to land and Mugniyeh escaped.

The following year, Mugniyeh would be linked to the 1996 truck bombing of Khobar Towers, a U.S. military complex in Saudi Arabia, that left 19 Americans dead and 372 wounded. Thirteen men were named in the indictment, which said they were part of Saudi Hizbullah, "one of a number of related Hizbullah terrorist organizations operating in Saudi Arabia, Lebanon, Kuwait and Bahrain, among other places." A fourteenth "unnamed" member of the Lebanese branch of Hizbullah was also indicted. Sources said that man was Mugniyeh. FBI Director Louis J. Freeh said the indictment offered "a snapshot of the Saudi Hizbullah and its relationship with then-members of the Iranian government," which, the U.S. claimed, provided detailed direction and financial support for the bombers, who were trained in Lebanon.[46]

That Mugniyeh was working from Iran, carrying out at least some of the dictates of Iranian intelligence, while Hizbullah itself was moving toward becoming a mainstream political party, made even murkier the question of whose interests he had closer to heart – those of Hizbullah's supreme council or those of his patrons in Iran – and, ultimately, who was calling the shots in Mugniyeh's operations. To many observers, it appeared he was beginning to follow the pattern established by an earlier generation of Middle East terrorists, such as Abu Nidal and Carlos "The Jackal," each of whom emerged from within an existing militant organization with the financial and logistical support of the intelligence agency of a friendly Arab state. Both men were ultimately alienated from their original allies and became tools of whatever intelligence agencies would bankroll their operations.

But no matter whom Mugniyeh considered his master, one thing was clear: he was the critical link between Islamic terrorism's past and its future.

In the terrorist world, there was no greater accolade: Osama bin Laden "admired" the work of Imad Mugniyeh.

That was the testimony given by the al-Qaeda leader's former security chief at his New York trial in connection with the October, 2000 U.S. embassy bombings in Africa. Ali Mohammed, a former U.S. Army intelligence analyst, told the court that he arranged security for a 1994 meeting between the two men in Sudan to discuss how to "cooperate" against the U.S.

Bin Laden, he testified, was impressed with how Hizbullah's tactics had driven American forces from Lebanon and planned to "use the same method to force the United States out of Saudi Arabia."[47]

The meeting was one of several between officials of the two groups after bin Laden, according to a Grand Jury indictment, told supporters that "al-Qaeda should put aside its differences with Shi'ite Muslim terrorist organizations, including the government of Iran and its affiliated terrorist group Hizbullah, to cooperate."[48]

There was much to put aside. Shi'ite–Sunni animosity stretched back to the dawn of Islam. Even the Assassins – historical precursors to both Hizbullah and al-Qaeda – were created as a tool for the Shi'ite Caliphs to eliminate their Sunni rivals.

In more recent times, the Sunni Muslim al-Qaeda and its Taliban allies had been involved in numerous bloody crackdowns against Shi'ites in Afghanistan and Hizbullah's patron Iran blamed al-Qaeda and the Taliban for attacks on both its diplomats and government outposts inside Iran. And while, for the moment, the two groups shared a common enemy in the U.S., they had very different long-term goals. Bin Laden was a millennialist, dedicated to the supranational goal of creating a new global Islamic order. His brand of Islam considered the Shi'a to be apostates. Hizbullah and its Iranian patrons were Islamic nationalists with more finite aspirations: give Islam a greater voice within existing nation-states such as Lebanon and rid the region of the U.S. and its Israeli client state.

Still, history was littered with stranger marriages of convenience.

"Hizbullah provided explosives training for al-Qaeda and [Egyptian] Islamic Jihad," Mohammed testified in the New York trial. "Iran supplied Egyptian Jihad with weapons. Iran also used Hizbullah to supply explosives that were disguised to look like rocks."[49]

The ties would not end there. After the U.S. invasion of Afghanistan, there were numerous reports that al-Qaeda operatives had taken refuge in Lebanon. Much of the connection came through Usbat al-Ansar (League of Partisans), a Lebanon-based Palestinian Sunni Muslim militia headquartered in the Ain al-Helweh refugee camp near Sidon and the Nahr al-Bared camp in the northern port of Tripoli. Like bin Laden, members of the group were followers of the Wahabi or Salafi strain of Sunni Islam and shared his hatred of Jews and "Crusaders." Many of them had fought in Afghanistan and Chechnya. The group received some funding from al-Qaeda and had been implicated in a terrorist plot in Jordan. After a member of the group who called himself "a martyr for Grozny" fired rocket-propelled grenades at the Russian embassy in Beirut, Lebanese media reports claimed Usbat al-Ansar's leader had ordered retaliation against the Russians for atrocities against Muslims in Chechnya.[50]

Usbat al-Ansar was also linked to the more shadowy Takfir wa al-Hijra (Excommunication and Holy Flight), established by several Lebanese with ties to both bin Laden operatives and Omar Abdul Rahman, the blind Egyptian cleric jailed in New York for the 1993 World Trade Center bombing (one leader of the organization, Kasim Daher, was briefly detained by Canadian authorities in connection with the bombing, but later released). The group's pan-Islamic character was reflected in the fact that the name Takfir wa al-Hijra was originally used by the Egyptian militant group that assassinated former Egyptian President Anwar Sadat.[51]

Among the founders was a former Boston taxi driver, Bassam Ahmed Kanj, who was close friends with another cab driver later indicted by Jordan for a series of attacks planned by an al-Qaeda cell in that country, and whom U.S. authorities tied to two of the September 11 hijackers. The goal of Takfir wa al-Hijra, which launched a failed uprising against the Lebanese government in early 2000, was to establish an Islamic mini-state in northern Lebanon – which would eventually encompass the entire country.

According to Lebanese court documents, Takfir wa al-Hijra received funding from bin Laden associates in Central America, Europe and the Arab world. Much of the money was allegedly used to buy weapons from Sheikh Subhi Tofeili, the former Hizbullah secretary-general who had resigned in protest over Hizbullah's moderate political course.[52]

Also on the radar screen of those tracking al-Qaeda's Lebanon connection was the pro-Saudi Islamic Unification Movement of Sheikh Saeed Shabaan, who once headed the Lebanese branch of the Muslim Brotherhood. Shabaan shared bin Laden's Sunni fundamentalist outlook and had imposed Islamic law on the northern city of Tripoli for several years during the civil war. More recently, Shabaan had also forged an alliance with Iran, which put him at the crossroads of militant Islamic politics.

Stories circulating within intelligence circles spoke of bin Laden associates like Salah Hijir, a Yemeni, visiting Lebanon to explore whether it might offer al-Qaeda a new refuge. There were also whispers that Mugniyeh's wing of Hizbullah was providing "back office" and "logistical" support for al-Qaeda operatives who had been cut off from their own networks after fleeing Afghanistan.

Lebanese Defense Minister Khalil Hrawi acknowledged that some al-Qaeda members had infiltrated Lebanon, but insisted "we dealt with their people and operations through coordination with the Americans, France,

Germany, the Arab countries and, of course, Syria." He promised "there won't be any terror attacks or al-Qaeda attacks from Lebanon."[53]

The loudest allegations of an Hizbullah–al-Qaeda alliance came from Israel. In the days after September 11, Israeli intelligence planted stories with the respected British publication Jane's *Foreign Report* and other news outlets claiming that an unholy alliance of Hizbullah, Iraq and al-Qaeda was responsible for the World Trade Center and Pentagon attacks.[54] While the allegation eventually faded from the headlines, variations on the theme of a new global terror alliance were picked up by the media and pro-Israeli politicians in the U.S., who began equating the threat from Hizbullah with that posed by al-Qaeda. The chairman of the Senate intelligence committee, Sen. Bob Graham (D-FL), went so far as to label Hizbullah "the A-team of terrorism," more dangerous even than al-Qaeda.[55]

Based on that premise, it was not much of a leap to conclude Israel and the U.S. were partners in the same fight.

"Israeli and American officials believe," the *New York Times* wrote in March, 2002, "that the 18-year struggle by Hizbullah in Lebanon, backed by tens of millions of dollars worth of arms from Iran, provided a model for what Tehran would like to recreate on the West Bank and the Gaza Strip."[56] Mugniyeh himself, the paper reported, was said to have slipped into the West Bank in the early days of the al-Aqsa Intifada.

Iran emphatically denied the charges and other U.S. intelligence officials insisted that, while the potential for more formal cooperation between Hizbullah and al-Qaeda existed, operational cooperation remained limited and tenuous.

"Are the waters being tested?" asked one intelligence official in the summer of 2002. "Sure. Did bin Laden get some of his inspiration from Hizbullah? Absolutely. Has a new terrorist monolith emerged? Absolutely not. These are very temporary marriages of convenience between very suspicious people."

For Israeli Prime Minister Ariel Sharon, there was huge currency in getting Washington to buy into the notion that Israel and the U.S. faced the same terrorist onslaught. Sharon was once more at war on the West Bank. It was a war he had personally started just as surely as he launched the invasion of Lebanon. With the previous government of Ehud Barak closer to an agreement with Yasser Arafat than at any time in history, Sharon, accompanied by armed bodyguards, had cynically broken the unspoken ban on visits by Israeli officials to the site of al-Aqsa Mosque, one of the most sacred places in Islam, known to Jews as the Temple Mount. Predictably, that provocative act set off stone throwing by Palestinian youths, which sparked an armed response from Israeli troops, and quickly spiraled out of control. The result: riots that unleashed a new round of warfare that would come to be known as the al-Aqsa Intifada, which would set the West Bank alight, kill the peace process, cripple the Barak government, and vault the man Arabs called the Butcher of Beirut into the prime minister's chair.

Now, post-September 11, Sharon systematically set to work aligning his battle with Washington's global war. Adopting President Bush's "If you're not with us, you're against us" rhetoric, Sharon quickly labeled Arafat a Palestinian bin Laden and equated Palestinian violence with the acts of the men who flew planes into the World Trade Center. "Our" terrorists, Sharon was telling the White House, are "your" terrorists.

At first, cooler heads in Washington prevailed. The Palestinian cause, Middle East experts in the administration understood, was a limited struggle with finite goals. This was not the open-ended, millennial battle of bin Laden, but a war for territory. A people that had lost its homeland wanted it (or some portion of it) back. While the Palestinians and al-Qaeda shared certain tactics – the suicide bombings Hizbullah had pioneered – the comparison ended there. Once a Palestinian homeland was established, the vast majority of Palestinians would put aside their weapons. Not so the movement inspired by bin Laden.

"It is obvious that the Israelis are interested in mixing up the past and the present, the false and the truth, the dark and the clear, in order to direct suspicion toward the Palestinians," wrote Arab journalist Hichem Karoui.[57]

The contrast between the goals of the Palestinians (and Hizbullah's mainstream) with the motives of millennialists like bin Laden was summed up by Pakistani journalist Ahmed Rashid. "These new Islamic fundamentalists are not interested in transforming a corrupt society into a just one, nor do they care about providing jobs, education or social benefits to their followers or creating harmony between the various ethnic groups that inhabit many Muslim countries," he wrote in *Jihad: The Rise of Militant Islam in Central Asia*. "The new *jihadi* groups have no economic manifesto, no plan for better governance and the building of political institutions, and no blueprint for creating democratic participation in the decision-making process of their future Islamic states."[58]

Equally important, from the standpoint of the Middle East experts in Washington and U.S. diplomats in the Arab world, the Palestinian cause had vast support across the Islamic world. That had only grown more intense in recent years as the pan-Arab television station al-Jazeera broadcast bloody scenes from the West Bank to a new generation of Muslims. To equate what Muslims perceived as Israel's persecution of the Palestinians with America's war on terror would instantly undermine U.S. efforts to build a broad coalition and would endanger America's Muslim allies. Which was precisely why bin Laden had cynically seized on the Palestinian cause and made it his own.

Bin Laden himself was a manageable threat. It would not be easy, but his infrastructure and top lieutenants could be rooted out and destroyed. The real danger lay in his potential to inspire a socioeconomic revolution driven by religion and fueled by hatred and hopelessness. In slums and overcrowded refugee camps from Jerusalem to Jakarta there existed a vast pool of potential recruits who saw the West as the great exploiter and Israel as its tool. And while they were divided by geography, ethnicity and their particular interpretation of Islam, Muslims the world over – whether in parlors of the well-to-do in Cairo or Malaysia's Islamic boarding schools – were united around one cause: a Palestinian homeland.

"In the Arab and Muslim worlds," observed analyst Michael Eisenstadt of the Washington Institute for Near East Policy, "the 'al-Aqsa Intifada' has reinforced perceptions of Israeli weakness, hardened popular attitudes toward Israel, recast the Arab–Israeli struggle in religious terms, returned the 'question of Palestine' to the center of Arab politics, and led extremists – from Hizbullah to Saddam Hussein – to call for the 'liberation' of Palestine by force."[59]

George W. Bush had already struck a thousand-year-old Muslim nerve when, in the wake of September 11, he had used the word "Crusade" in launching the war on terror. Now, he was again playing directly into bin Laden's hands by allowing Ariel Sharon to co-opt America's battle against terrorism, which even many in the Islamic world supported, and turn it into precisely what even sympathetic moderate Muslims feared: an anti-Islamic Crusade by an alliance of Christians and Jews. What more evidence was needed that *al-hurub al-salibiyya*, the Wars of the Cross, still raged?

"The United States ... wants to besiege and abort the blessed Intifada in Palestine to serve the Jews," declared Hashem Minqara, the leader of one Lebanese Islamic faction, reflecting a view echoing across the Islamic world. "The United States has declared war on Muslims. Its president talked about a crusade. That was not a slip of the tongue. This is the essence of the American–Jewish–colonialist objective."[60]

"We might as well be printing recruiting posters for bin Laden," said one disheartened State Department official.

Yet like Ronald Reagan before him, Bush saw the world in black and white. While his so-called "experts" were trying to make him distinguish between shades of gray, Ariel Sharon pointed to the explosives-wrapped Palestinians blowing themselves up in Israeli cafes and said, "See?"

Ariel Sharon was the expansionist general whose actions had dragged the U.S. into Lebanon. He was the commanding officer directly responsible for laying the seeds that spawned this new, vicious face of Islamic terror. He was the politician who had cynically provoked the latest, most bloody round of Palestinian–Israeli violence to satisfy his own ambitions.

Again and again, this would-be U.S. ally had sacrificed America's interests for his own. Sharon proved that again just days after President Bush announced his global war on terror, when he equated U.S. coalition-building with Chamberlain's appeasement of Hitler in 1938.[61]

But it didn't take long for George W. Bush to swallow Sharon's bait, hook, line and sinker. At a time when the U.S. desperately needed to reach out to Muslim moderates, the President stood on the White House lawn praising the most hated man in the Arab world, spouting Sharonisms like "homicide bombers," and calling for Yasser Arafat to be replaced.

Bush's support would continue despite Sharon's decision to unleash one of Israel's bloodiest military assaults on the Occupied Territories at a critical moment for American diplomacy in the Islamic world.

"The President believes Ariel Sharon is a man of peace," White House spokesman Ari Fleisher told reporters in April, 2002, even as Sharon continued to defy Bush's demand for an end to the massive incursion that would claim hundreds of Palestinian lives.[62]

In late 2002, Sharon told *The Times* of London that the Tehran regime and its surrogates in Hizbullah posed a direct threat to Israel and said he would push Washington to add Iran to the top of the "to do list" once Saddam Hussein was dealt with.[63]

A year later, as the U.S. geared up for the invasion of Iraq, the Pentagon released its long-term strategic plan for the war on terror. Building on the Bush Doctrine of preemptive attack (modeled on Israel's own long-term policy), the plan called for the use of military force against countries suspected of supporting terrorism. Administration officials quickly singled out Iran and Syria – Israel's chief adversaries – as potential targets, telling the *New York Times* that the war against Iraq could send a strong message to the Tehran and Damascus regimes to stop backing Hizbullah.[64]

The two Muslim countries flanked Iraq. To single them out at such a critical time risked complicating the war and adding fuel to the fires of suspicion in the Islamic world.

It was hard not to wonder just whose interests were being served.

18

Inspiration

When God gave me the land of Egypt, I was sure that he
meant Palestine for me too.

—Saladin (1137–1193)[1]

In the weeks after the outbreak of the al-Aqsa Intifada, observers noticed
a new presence in the crowds of angry young Palestinians as they
confronted Israeli troops. Along with the red, black and green flag of
Palestine and the black and white banner of Hamas, Hizbullah's yellow
and red flag began to appear.

It was another reverberation from Israel's Lebanon defeat. Islam had
vanquished the Israeli military machine once; it could do so again.

"The struggle of Hizbullah, which in Palestinian eyes led to the
termination of the Israeli occupation in Lebanon, was adopted as a model
by many Palestinian youngsters, and not necessarily supporters of Hamas
or the Islamic radicals," observed Reuven Paz of Israel's International Policy
Institute for Counter-Terrorism.[2]

Hizbullah's victory in Lebanon coincided with a surge in support for
Hamas and other Islamic groups in the West Bank and Gaza. There were
many factors involved in the rise of the Islamists – chief among them
frustration with the corruption of the Palestinian Authority and impatience
with the ways of Arafat and the old guard of the PLO. As they sought alternatives, Palestinians who had grown up throwing stones in the first Intifada
could not help but be inspired by the deadly new form of resistance that
Hizbullah had wielded so effectively against Israel in Lebanon.

"Blessed be Beirut who broke the enemy and proved that we can defeat
the superpowers," Faysal al-Husseini, the Palestine Authority's minister for
Jerusalem, told a gathering of lawyers in Lebanon. "Blessed be the resistance
[Hizbullah], which gave us the hope that the future is in our hands. The
Lebanese victory is the greatest and most important example of the reality
in which the Israeli enemy is living."[3]

But the Palestinians would receive much more than just inspiration from their Lebanese brothers. Israel itself inadvertently saw to that.

Links between Hizbullah and the Palestinian resistance in the Occupied Territories dated at least back to 1993, when Israel expelled some 400 radicals into southern Lebanon. These men, primarily from Hamas and a Palestinian group that also used the name Islamic Jihad, quickly forged ties with Hizbullah, thus laying the groundwork for ongoing training and operational support. In the years that followed, several dozen Hamas members were sent to Iran, while the Revolutionary Guards, in part through their Hizbullah proxy, stepped up support for the Palestinian branch of Islamic Jihad.

The watershed came in 1998, when Israel allowed jailed Hamas founder Sheikh Ahmad Yassin to travel to Saudi Arabia for medical treatment. From there he toured the Arab world raising, by some accounts, hundreds of millions of dollars. Yassin then went on to Iran, where he was greeted with open arms and established a permanent Hamas office.

The decision to allow Yassin to travel was part of an Israeli divide-and-rule strategy. Israeli officials believed that by allowing the Hamas leader to bolster his position, PLO leader Yasser Arafat would be weakened.[4] Then-Prime Minister Ehud Barak predicted that when Yassin returned to the West Bank, he would serve as a "ticking time bomb at Arafat's doorstep."[5]

History would prove that an ironic choice of words. The trip built a deadly new bridge from Israel's violent past to its bloody future, creating a seamless connection between the disastrous war in Lebanon and the struggle for the West Bank. It also gave Hizbullah's sponsor, Iran, entrée into the Palestinian conflict at a major new level – creating formal synergy between Shi'ite and Sunni militants.

Both the Palestinian Islamic Jihad and Hamas had begun as offshoots of the Palestinian branch of the Muslim Brotherhood. Islamic Jihad had its start as a loose alliance of Islamic activists with ties to Arafat's Fatah. The group, which was instrumental in provoking the first Intifada in the 1980s and pioneered the concept of suicide car bombs in the Occupied Territories, had openly supported the Iranian Revolution and long maintained close ties with Tehran. The much larger Hamas was a creature of the House of Saud, which had given the Saudi Muslim Brotherhood carte blanche to funnel Saudi money to their Palestinian Islamic brethren in return for a promise not to conduct militant activities inside the kingdom. Another Saudi motive, according to French Islam expert Olivier Roy, was to prevent Iran from dominating militant Islamic movements and thus threatening Saudi Arabia itself.[6] Now, the two countries were working for the same cause.

Not long after Yassin's trip, Hamas officials began talking of the "Lebanonization" of the Occupied Territories. Barak's prediction would come true, but not in the way he ever imagined. The "ticking time bomb" of Hamas would pose a political challenge for Arafat, but it was on Israel's doorstep that the human bombs sent by Hamas would explode.

In the decades during which the Palestinians had controlled South Lebanon, Israelis and Lebanese alike knew it as Fatahland, named for Arafat's wing of the PLO. Now Fatahland had become Hizbullahistan and Arafat had taken up residence in Israel. The irony was not lost on some Israeli observers.

"History had a good laugh at Israel's expense during the Lebanon War and its aftermath," wrote military analyst Zeev Shiff. "We expelled Yasser Arafat and his army from Lebanon partly in order to deliver an indirect blow to the Palestinians in the territories. When Arafat tried to return to Lebanon, the Syrians expelled him. Finally, because of the hasty strategy of the Oslo accord, we brought Arafat and his whole army into the Land of Israel and thus began a new round of the 1948 War of Independence."[7]

Lebanon became the rear base for the struggle in the Occupied Territories. While internecine clashes driven by regional politics, religious righteousness and raw ambition continued among the shifting array of Palestinian Islamic and secular factions in Lebanon, the so-called refugee "camps," some of which were now a half-century old, also became a melting pot for militants bent on a common goal, the liberation of Palestine.

Emblematic of the amorphous and shifting alliances of convenience within this constellation of militant groups was the case of Col. Munir Makdah, local commander of Arafat's Fatah movement in Lebanon's Ain al-Helweh camp. He was sentenced to death in absentia by Jordanian officials, who charged that he was part of a group they dismantled in 1999 that had planned a series of attacks on U.S. and Israeli targets in the Jordanian capital, Amman. Jordan claimed the cell had ties to bin Laden, Hizbullah and Palestinian Islamic Jihad. Yet just a few years later, Makdah's pro-Arafat forces were locked in a struggle for control of the camps with several Islamic factions – just as Arafat and Hamas were vying for power in the Occupied Territories – and Makdah announced the expulsion of four Lebanese militants accused of ties with al-Qaeda.

While it was the Palestinians themselves who were primarily involved in the planning that occurred in Lebanon for operations in the Occupied Territories, Hizbullah also took part. The connection should have come as no surprise. Hizbullah had fought side-by-side with the Palestinians in Lebanon's so-called "War of the Camps" against the Syrian-backed Amal

Shi'ite militia in the 1980s, it had led the fight against Israel, and many of Hizbullah's top military commanders – like Mugniyeh – had once served with or been trained by the PLO.

After the Israeli pullout from Lebanon, the Hizbullah hierarchy reigned in its militants, effectively imposing a cease-fire along the Israeli border to enable the organization to concentrate on rebuilding South Lebanon and to give the exhausted Shi'ite population a respite from the violence.[8] But that did not stop the organization from mediating among the various Palestinian factions and helping to facilitate links between Palestinians interested in emulating its tactics in the Occupied Territories, and those – like the Iranians – in a position to make those aspirations real. For pragmatic reasons, Hizbullah might not have shared bin Laden's desire to vanquish the enemies of Islam no matter where they were found, but even its moderates remained deeply committed to at least maintaining the appearance of continuing the battle against what it saw as Israeli oppression of the Palestinians.

"The Palestinian National Covenant remains valid as long as there is a knife in the hands of a Palestinian woman with which to stab a soldier or a settler. The Palestinian National Convention remains valid as long as there are suicide bombers to carry out attack in Jerusalem and Tel Aviv. The Palestinian National Covenant remains valid as long as there is a Palestinian child who hurls a stone at an Israeli solider and whose eyes are fixed on Palestine, from the River to the Sea," Hizbullah leader Nasrallah told a conference in Damascus.[9]

In some ways, Hizbullah was a prisoner of its own rhetoric. Rebuilding Lebanon was now the party's top priority. But its leadership had so loudly and vociferously denounced Israel's occupation of the West Bank and Gaza, so frequently promised to "remain the nightmare of the Zionist enemy," that it had no choice but to offer some level of support to the Palestinian resistance. After all, it had an image to safeguard. The key was to avoid the kind of overt military involvement that would spark Israeli retaliation against the South, thus prompting a backlash against Hizbullah among the Shi'ites who were its prime constituency.

Not all elements of the party agreed with this pragmatic approach. Within the ranks of the resistance fighters who had driven out the Israelis were many who argued that the battle should be carried into Israel itself. It was the classic conflict that had been encountered by maturing guerrilla movements throughout history.

"There are two faces of Hizbullah today," Farid el-Khazen, chairman of the political science department at the American University of Beirut, said in the spring of 2002. "There's the Lebanese political and social-welfare party, and there's the guerrilla group involved in a struggle with Israel. Sometimes, those goals clash."[10]

The most public display of this new-found cooperation among the many factions opposed to Israel's presence in the Occupied Territories came in early 2001, when Iran brought together some 400 participants from across the Islamic world to form a new organization dedicated to "the liberation of Jerusalem and al-Aqsa from the Zionist enemy."[11] Seated side-by-side at the conference were senior Hamas officials, Hizbullah Secretary-General Nasrallah, and the head of the Iranian delegation, Ali Akhbar Mohtashami, the cleric who had bankrolled the birth of modern Islamic terror.

When I had met with Mohtashami at his Damascus office in 1985, he had replied to accusations that he was responsible for much of the terror with a laugh. "Let me tell you clearly that I have 20 years of struggle in Iran and Iraq against American intervention in our countries," Iran's then-ambassador had told me.

More than 15 years later, Mohtashami was still hard at work.

Israeli officials claimed that the tool Iran's terror czar had created so many years before – Imad Mugniyeh's operational wing of Hizbullah – had not only helped train Palestinian militants in suicide tactics, but also directly launched missions in the Occupied Territories. Most of those operations, Israeli intelligence alleged, were conducted in conjunction with Palestinian Islamic Jihad, Hamas or Fatah Tanzim, a militant offshoot of Yasser Arafat's Force 17, the personal bodyguard unit in which Mugniyeh had once served.

Nor, Israeli officials claimed, was the organization loath to send *Hizbullahis* into Lebanon, often carrying Western passports. Mugniyeh, they alleged, was personally involved in at least one such 1996 operation, in which he dispatched a Western-looking former Fadlallah accountant, Hussein Mohammed Mikdad, to blow up an El Al airliner.[12] Traveling on a forged British passport, Mikdad allegedly managed to smuggle military-grade RDX explosives into Israel from Switzerland. But as the self-proclaimed "heroic human flying bomb" attempted to assemble the device in his room at East Jerusalem's Lawrence Hotel, it detonated, ripping off much of the lower portion of his body.[13]

The most spectacular example of the Mugniyeh–Iran–Palestine link came in early 2002 when the Israeli Navy intercepted the *Karin-A*, a freighter carrying 50 tons of weapons and explosives, which had been loaded near the Iranian island of Kish in the Persian Gulf. On board were antitank weapons, long-range missiles and heavy mortars. Israeli officials claimed

Mugniyeh had personally purchased the ship on orders from Iran and placed his top deputy, Haj Bassem, in command for the voyage through the Red Sea to the Mediterranean.

"Mugniyeh was the mastermind of the operation," an Israeli intelligence officer told *The Times* of London. "He made all the preparations."[14] Israeli officials were particularly impressed with Mugniyeh's plan to place the weapons in water-tight containers weighted to remain submerged 16 feet below the water to prevent detection as they were towed to the Gaza coast by Egyptian fishing vessels.

The incident was a major embarrassment for Arafat who, at the time, was trying to present a moderate image to the West as it geared up its war on terrorism. The mission also offered a window on the continued struggle for power in Tehran. Not long before, senior Iranian officials had claimed that Mugniyeh, who was now on the FBI's 20 Most Wanted list with a $25 million bounty on his head, had left Iran and returned to Lebanon. But his involvement in the *Karin-A* affair demonstrated that, while some elements in Tehran were trying to distance themselves from Mugniyeh's activities to prevent a post-September 11 backlash, others remained committed to using the Lebanese operative as a tool in the ongoing battle between the *mustadafeen* (downtrodden) and the *mustakbareen* (arrogant).

Not all the money was coming from Iran. Hamas and Hizbullah were both benefiting from financial support flowing from the U.S. and elsewhere. In the wake of September 11, authorities would close down numerous U.S.-based charities and companies that authorities claimed were supporting not only relief activities, but also terrorist actions. Given the multidimensional nature of both groups, sorting out the difference was not always possible. Arab-American leaders protested that legitimate relief organizations were being damaged by the impression that all Islamic charities were terrorist fronts.

Illegal and quasi-legal business activities were also a key target. In early 2002, authorities smashed an illegal drug operation in the Midwest run by individuals of Middle East descent. "A significant portion of some of the sales are sent to the Middle East to benefit terrorist organizations," claimed Asa Hutchinson, director of the Drug Enforcement Administration.[15] There were allegations that Hizbullah, along with al-Qaeda, was involved in the illicit sale of so-called "blood diamonds" mined by rebels in Sierra Leone. "Even if only 10 percent [of the illegal trade] went to terrorist organizations, you are talking about millions of dollars in virtually untraceable funds every year," a European investigator told the *Washington Post*.[16]

Authorities also went back and picked up some of the threads they had dropped in the years before terrorism became public enemy number one. At year's end, federal authorities shut down a Dallas computer company owned by a top Hamas official and his brothers, which investigators claimed was illegally selling computer equipment to Libya and Syria and funneling the profits to Hamas. The move was part of a flurry of activity designed to sever the financial pipeline for terrorist groups. "The war against terror is a war of accountants and auditors, as well as a war of weaponry and soldiers," Attorney General John Ashcroft told reporters.[17] What he didn't mention was that the Hamas official, who was now safely overseas, had been named a "specially designated terrorist" in 1995 and had once been in U.S. custody. Authorities had failed to come up with enough evidence to convict him and missed the opportunity to tie him to the company or the related Holy Land Foundation for Relief and Development, which Ashcroft now called "the North American front for Hamas."

Much cited in the media, but less compelling as evidence of support for terrorism, was a case in North Carolina. Authorities there convicted a Lebanese man, Mohamad Hammoud, of providing material support to Hizbullah, after he, his American wife, his brother and 15 other Lebanese were arrested for running a cigarette smuggling operation. Given the quantity of money involved – $3,500, which one member of the ring testified Hammoud had asked him to bring to Sheikh Abbas Harake of Hizbullah during a 1999 trip home – it appeared just as likely to be a case of a Lebanese exile wanting to give something back to an organization that had done much for his people. But since the U.S. government had designated Hizbullah to be a terrorist group – without making any distinction between its various wings – any material support was illegal under the 1996 antiterrorism law.

But was Hizbullah the *organization* carrying out acts of terror? The addition of Hizbullah – along with Hamas, Palestinian Islamic Jihad and several other Palestinian groups – to the U.S. State Department's list of terrorist groups came in 2001. Aside from the Khobar Towers bombing orchestrated by Mugniyeh and Iran – in which no other Hizbullah officials were directly implicated – the Party of God had not carried out an attack on U.S. interests in 15 years. What it *had* been doing in the interim was resisting Israel's occupation of South Lebanon and the Palestinian territories.

"What we do now is fight Israel on our land," Hizbullah Deputy Secretary-General Sheikh Na'im Qasim insisted after the U.S. list was released. "We support the Palestinian struggle but in no specific way. We do not fight against the U.S. Even our struggle against Israel never went beyond Lebanon's legitimate border."[18]

The U.S. had long been sensitive to the fragile nature of Lebanon's nascent new democracy in which the maturing Hizbullah was a critical player. While many in Washington – particularly at the Pentagon – could not forgive Hizbullah for the attacks that had killed so many Americans in the 1980s, previous administrations had recognized that geopolitical realities meant the past had to be set aside. As it engaged in a cat-and-mouse game with Lebanese authorities over Mugniyeh and other individuals directly implicated in the terrorist acts, the U.S. government had maintained a hands-off policy toward Hizbullah itself. In fact, its involvement in the 1990s as broker of the agreements between Israel and Hizbullah to avoid targeting civilians meant the U.S. had granted de facto diplomatic recognition to the organization.

"As long as Hizbullah was part of the system, we knew there was a good chance for stability to take hold," said one American diplomat familiar with Lebanon. "But if something drove them out of the process, all bets were off."

Reports in the Lebanese press in the immediate aftermath of September 11 spoke of an understanding between the U.S., Lebanon and Syria: America would avoid targeting Hizbullah in the war on terror and, in turn, the others would ensure Hizbullah would not launch any major cross-border attacks on Israel. The quid pro quo was part of an American effort to prevent an explosion on Lebanon's border that would give Israel an excuse to strike and, in the process, undermine the broader war on terror.

The sudden inclusion of what was now one of Lebanon's most powerful political parties on the list of terrorist organizations "with global reach" had more to do with President Bush's warming relationship with Ariel Sharon than on the war on terrorism itself. These were Sharon's terrorists and he damn well wanted them to be America's, too.

During the same Beirut news conference in which he acknowledged Hizbullah's social welfare role, Assistant Secretary of State William Burns told reporters, "The United States continues to be concerned about Hizbullah's terrorist activities that go well beyond the borders of this country."[19]

In fact, the real concern extended only a few hundred miles south, where George Bush's new friend was fighting a rearguard action.

Sharon needed the political cover that would come from aligning his increasingly desperate conflict against the Palestinians with Bush's war on terrorism. Israel was a nation under siege. Pursuing the same tactics that had proven so counterproductive in South Lebanon – massive military retaliation, the destruction of homes, widespread detentions – Sharon's war in the Occupied Territories had spiraled out of control. Suicide bombings inside the borders of Israel itself had become a numbingly familiar event. And it would only get worse. By the end of 2002, the conflict Ariel Sharon launched the day he set foot on the sacred ground of al-Aqsa had left some 2,000 Palestinians dead and claimed nearly 700 Israeli lives, many of them civilians.[20] Even more chilling, military officials claimed they had intercepted and imprisoned some 140 more would-be suicide bombers.[21] The tactics invented in Beirut and perfected in South Lebanon were once more taking their toll.

By lumping Hizbullah and the most militarily effective of the radical Palestinian groups into the same category as the September 11 bombers, Sharon was paving the way for the same kind of retaliation against them that President Bush planned for al-Qaeda and the Taliban. In the process, Sharon effectively blurred the line between the territorial conflict he was fighting and the civilizational struggle in which the U.S. was engaged.

"Our war on terror begins with al-Qaeda, but it does not end there. It will not end until every terrorist group of global reach has been found, stopped and defeated," President Bush had said in his address to Congress one week after the September 11 attacks.

Not content with the inclusion of Hizbullah and Hamas on the State Department's terrorist list, Sharon pushed hard for Bush to specifically include them among those groups being targeted for "first strike" in the terror war. A few months later, Sharon got his wish. President Bush, the *Jerusalem Post* reported, had explicitly told Foreign Minister Shimon Peres that he defined Hizbullah as a terrorist organization of global reach, "making clear for the first time the Iranian-backed group would be targeted in the next phase of the U.S.-led war on terrorism."[22]

Many would-be allies in the terror war were outraged. In a meeting with U.S. Ambassador Vincent Battle, the speaker of Lebanon's Parliament, Amal chief Nabih Berri, accused the U.S. of "adopting the Israeli point of view."[23] Most experts drew the same conclusion.

The decision, said AUB political scientist Nizar Hamzeh, was "a major strategic mistake."[24] With the U.S. in desperate need of Muslim support for its war on terrorism, what was required was a sophisticated sensitivity to the complexities of Islamic politics, not simplistic solutions. Instead of targeting individuals on a one-on-one basis or, at the very least, differentiating between the military and political wings of Hizbullah, the White House was leaving the impression that it was doing the bidding of Israel – as it had so many times before.

That impression was only bolstered by George W. Bush's attitude toward events in the Occupied Territories. He had apparently never heard the old adage that "One man's terrorist is another man's freedom fighter." Tanks, jet fighters and Cobra helicopter gunships were, it seemed, all legitimate weapons in the struggle between "good and evil," whether employed by the U.S. against Taliban militiamen in Afghanistan or by Israel against civilians on the West Bank. But in Bush's world, there could be no justification – no explanation – for men and women so desperate, so angry, so without hope, so bereft of any other weapon, that they would strap explosives around their bodies and walk into a shopping center or crowded cafe.

"They're not martyrs," President Bush said on the White House lawn. "They're murderers." The American president believed deeply that there was no difference between the truck bombers who had driven America out of Beirut, the men who had piloted the planes into the World Trade Center, and the suicide bombers of Palestine.

And in one sense, he was right. Around the world, millions of Muslims considered them *all* to be heroes. And in places like Kuala Lumpur and Peshawar, a whole new generation looked to these self-proclaimed *jihadis* for inspiration.

19

Beirut, Bali and Beyond

"It is foolish to hunt the tiger when there are plenty of sheep around."

—*Hamas training manual*[1]

When a pair of bombs devastated two nightclubs packed with foreign tourists on the Indonesian island of Bali, the message was clear: if the foot soldiers of the jihad could strike innocent tourists in paradise, no one, anywhere was safe.

"Bali is no longer the last paradise," a friend who lived on that tropical island emailed me a few days after the blast in late 2002. Almost 190 people were dead, many of them Australians on cheap package holidays, scores more lay burned and bleeding in the hallways and parking lots of Bali's underequipped and overburdened hospital.

One of those later arrested in connection with the plot would tell investigators his team had made a mistake: they wanted to "kill as many Americans as possible,"[2] and thought the club was an American hangout. But in the end, it didn't really matter. Their spiritual leaders had called for the killing of *kafir* (infidels), *boule* (Westerners) and Jews, and they had done just that.[3]

The tactic used by these home grown Indonesian *jihadis* had been pioneered on the streets of Beirut. First, a lone suicide bomber wearing a black vest packed with explosives walked into a bar called Paddy's Irish Pub and pressed the detonator. Then, as survivors fled into the street, a white Mitsubishi L-300 van packed with explosives was detonated, devastating those outside, tearing through the nearby Sari Club and engulfing an entire city block in flames.

Bali had once been my home. In the late 1990s as the Indonesian economy collapsed in the great Asian meltdown and the country descended into revolution, my Indonesian wife and I closed down our consulting business in the capital, Jakarta, and moved our children to the safety of that legendary tropical island. It was a place infused with spirituality, where offerings were made to the gods three times a day and the tinkle of bamboo instruments was carried on the wind; home to a gentle people whose Hindu–Buddhist culture was built on a foundation of mutual respect. Our flower-filled thatched roof home overlooking the rice paddies was a world away from the tensions then gripping Jakarta. A universe separated it from the violence of the Middle East.

Or so it had seemed.

But if I had been at my Bali home, less than two miles from the Sari Club, on that fateful October weekend, the explosions would have rocked my bed, just as another series of deadly bombs on another October weekend had shaken me awake 19 years before. Those earlier blasts had left hundreds of U.S. marines and French troops dead and signaled the birth of an unimaginable new kind of war. These new bombs in paradise had stripped away the final layer of innocence. There truly was, the flames seemed to shout, nowhere to hide.

In the wake of the U.S. invasion of Afghanistan, a loose network of Islamic extremist groups across Southeast Asia had begun to shift its focus from strictly regional goals to taking on the U.S. and its allies.

"One Muslim to another Muslim is like a single body. If one part is in pain, then the other part will also feel the pain," said the web site of an Indonesian organization calling itself al-Katibatul Maut al-Alamiya (The International Death Battalion), which claimed responsibility for the Bali bombing. "People from your countries will experience death, wherever they are, as long as the International Christians and their friends do not leave Afghanistan."[4]

The statement reflected the intimate ties that existed between the Asian networks and those from the Middle East. The overlapping connections extended through the Islamic boarding schools of Indonesia and Malaysia to the jungles of the southern Philippines, to the mountains of Afghanistan, and to Yemen, where both bin Laden and several key Indonesian clerics had family roots.

The goal of creating *Darul Islamiyah Nusantara*, an Islamic state incorporating Indonesia, Malaysia and portions of the Philippines, could be traced back to the region's colonial days before World War II. But postcolonial regimes had largely co-opted or crushed the pan-Islamists, leaving militant Islam primarily focused on secessionist movements in Indonesia's Aceh region and the Muslim southern islands of the Philippines. It was in the latter, a Catholic country, that Muslims groups from the Middle East made their first Asian inroads, thanks in part to America's decision to train future *jihadis* for the CIA's war against the Soviets in Afghanistan.[5]

In the late 1980s, Osama bin Laden's brother-in-law, Muhammed Jamal Khalifa, took up residence in Manila, set up Southeast Asia's largest Islamic charity, and financed Abu Sayyaf (Bearer of the Sword), a militant Islamic group founded by a Filipino veteran of the war in Afghanistan. Like the larger Moro Islamic Liberation Front (MILF), Abu Sayyaf was fighting for an Islamic state in the southern Philippines. Khalifa also helped facilitate the movement of Filipino rebels to Afghanistan, where many trained at al-Qaeda's Camp Khaldun.

By the 1990s, the Palestinians of Hamas were also actively involved in the Philippines, providing weapons and organizational help to the Islamic rebels. At times, it was difficult to tell where one Middle Eastern group ended and another began. A major Hamas cell was broken up when authorities tried to apprehend Ramzi Yousef, the Pakistani mastermind of the 1993 World Trade Center bombing who was closely connected with Egyptian extremists, and Khalid Sheikh Mohammed, a relative of Yousef who was raised in Kuwait. The pair authored an elaborate plot to assassinate the Pope during his 1995 visit to the Philippines and to hijack eleven airliners and blow them up over the Pacific.

In a glimpse of what was to come, they also considered crashing an airliner into CIA headquarters. A January 1995 Philippines intelligence document summarized the role of the suicide pilot this way: "He will board any American commercial aircraft pretending to be an ordinary passenger. Then he will hijack said aircraft, control its cockpit and dive it at the CIA headquarters. There will be no bomb or any explosive that he will use in its execution. It is simply a suicidal mission that he is very much willing to execute."[6]

The dry run for the main plot came in the form of a bomb set off on a Philippines Airlines jet in December 1994. Abu Sayyaf claimed responsibility but investigators later concluded Yousef was both responsible and personally made the call. The plan, code-named Bojinka (loud bang) was aborted when the chemicals being mixed for the nitroglycerin bombs caught fire, engulfing Yousef's apartment. Philippines authorities seized computers containing details of the plot. A U.S.-trained Pakistani pilot, Abdul Hakim Murad, and a Pakistani Afghan veteran, Wali Khan Amin Shah, were arrested and authorities eventually dismantled a wider network of Islamic militants, that included Hamas operatives.

Meanwhile, Khalifa, who would be implicated in the World Trade Center bombings, traveled to the U.S., where he was detained in late December 1994 by immigration authorities on a warrant from Jordan, which had sentenced him to death for involvement in a bombing plot in that country. Khalifa was extradited to Jordan, which eventually allowed him to return to Saudi Arabia, where he eventually conducted a series of interviews with Western reporters, insisting he ran nothing more than an Islamic charity organization.

Soon after his departure from the Philippines, Khalifa was replaced by Omar al-Faruq, a Kuwaiti al-Qaeda operative who had trained at Camp Khaldun. Al-Faruq spent three years based at the MILF's Camp Abubakar in the southern Philippines, then, in the wake of the 1998 revolution that ousted Indonesian strongman Suharto and threw Indonesia into turmoil, he was ordered to shift his base of operations. He married the daughter of a militant Indonesian cleric and moved into a house in the hill town of Bogor, just outside Jakarta.

Yousef and Mohammed, meanwhile, fled to Pakistan where they bolstered their links to al-Qaeda. The groundwork they did in Pakistan would not go to waste: Mohammed would eventually emerge as bin Laden's operations chief and the key planner of the September 11 attacks.[7]

In many respects, it would have been much easier for post-September 11 U.S. foreign policy if Suharto had never been overthrown. The former general had used a strong hand to hold together his necklace of 17,000 islands and 300 language groups. Any hint of rebellion in the provinces met with a violent response, as the agony of East Timor – where the Indonesian military mounted a bloodbath in the weeks before independence – painfully demonstrated. Political opposition was bought off or silenced. Islamic sentiment was funneled into tame social movements. Clerics who raised the forbidden subject of Islamic rule were jailed or exiled.

In the years after Suharto was forced from office, the threads that bound Indonesia's ethnic quilt quickly began to fray. Provinces at either end of the vast archipelago were in revolt; officials in oil-rich Aceh established religious police to enforce an Islamic dress code; Muslim–Christian clashes erupted; and a series of ineffectual presidents tried and failed to impose a modicum of stability.

The chaos of Lebanon and Afghanistan had provided the perfect environment for Islamic terror to flourish. Now it was Indonesia's turn.

Indonesian Muslims who had fought alongside the Moros in the Philippines began to arrive on the island of Ambon in the Maluku Islands for a jihad against local Christians that would eventually claim 10,000 lives. They were led by Afghan war veterans, among them a handful of Arabs. As the conflict heated up and spread to the Poso region of Sulawesi, others recruits were sent to Camp Abubakar in the Philippines for training. Eventually, dozens of camps were established throughout Indonesia, at some of which there were sightings of foreign trainers.

While Muslim militants were honing their skills in combat with Christians, the leadership of a clandestine network of clerics who remained committed to the concept of *Darul Islamiyah Nusantara* was once more laying plans. The organization, called Jemaah Islamiyah (Islamic Community), had been created by a group of Indonesian exiles in Malaysia. Jemaah Islamiyah had its roots in a network of *pesantren* (Islamic boarding schools) associated with a school called Pondok Ngruki outside the central Javanese city of Solo. Its spiritual leaders were Abdullah Sungkar, who had fought in Afghanistan and died in 1999, and Abu Bakar Ba'asyir, a cleric jailed for many years by Suharto, who had been preaching in Malaysia since his release. Around Ba'asyir was a corps of Asian militants who had served in Afghanistan and were now eager to bring the battle home. Among them was a young Afghan veteran named Riduan Isamuddin, better known as Hambali, who would emerge as Jemaah Islamiyah's director of operations. In many ways, the relationship between Ba'asyir and Hambali mirrored that of Hizbullah's Muhammed Hussein Fadlallah and Imad Mugniyeh. Like Fadlallah, Ba'asyir would consistently deny he was directly involved with terrorism.

"During my stay overseas, I promoted jihad and the honor of dying in defense of one's religious belief," he told the *Jakarta Post* in early 2002, adding of al-Qaeda, "I can only support them with my statements and my prayers, since I have only those."[8]

Meanwhile, with Ba'asyir's blessing, Hambali was planning and coordinating a host of attacks, eventually ending up on the "most wanted" list of a half dozen intelligence agencies in the aftermath of Bali.

It was sadly ironic that Indonesia would emerge as a center of Islamic terror. For at the turn of the twenty-first century, the country also stood as a model for the rise of a moderate brand of political Islam that gave voice to Muslim aspirations as *part of* rather than *in opposition to* the political process. The 1998 Indonesian revolution had succeeded because it brought together all strata of society – from the street beggars to the Mercedes class – but also because it tapped the latent grassroots power of Islam. Indonesian Muslims, most of whom practiced an extremely tolerant brand of Islam, accounted for more than 90 percent of the country's population. Yet under Suharto and his predecessor Sukarno, Islam had never played a direct political role.

The foot soldiers of the anti-Suharto revolt may have come from the universities. The coup de grâce may have been inflicted by the Army's top general. But the field marshals of the revolution were men like Amien Rais and Abdurrahman Wahid, who flexed the newfound political muscles of the mass Muslim movements they headed and helped drive the longtime strongman from office. Suharto's former vice president and successor,

B.J. Habibie, further strengthened the political power of Muslim groups by cultivating them in a failed attempt to win legitimacy.

"When, a few years from now, historians of Muslim politics look back at the end of the twentieth century, Indonesia will probably deserve to be given pride of place on a par with Iran," observed Robert W. Hefner of Boston University, a leading expert on Islamic politics in Indonesia. "Measured according to its intellectual vitality and prospective mass base, Indonesia in the late 1990s was one of the most vibrant centers for new Muslim political thinking that the modern world has seen."[9]

It was his position as head of the Nahdlatul Ulama (NU), or Religious Scholars organization, with a power base of some 30 million Muslims, that propelled Wahid to the presidency after Habibie's brief term. As *reformasi* (political reformation) took root in the wake of Suharto's rule, the nearly blind cleric had formed the National Awakening Party (PKB) to leverage the NU's existing grassroots network. But like Rais, Habibie and other mainstream Muslim leaders, Wahid (popularly known as Gus Dur) steered clear of using the political process as a vehicle for spreading Islamic beliefs.

"If the new parties want Islam to be a moral or educational force in politics, that's OK", he said in 1999, "but if they want to tinker with the laws of this country, then we must resist that."[10]

Just as Hizbullah had built on its grassroots network to become a powerful force in Lebanese politics, so too did Indonesia's emerging Islamic groups. One example of how the structures of Islam were being used as a political base could be found in the rise of the Partai Keadilan (PK), or Justice Party. Formed in July 1998, the PK was a direct extension of the Arab grandfather of all Muslim resistance organizations, the Muslim Brotherhood. The PK sought to add an Islamic spiritual dimension to political activism, but officially stated that it was up to the individual to interpret the religious teachings of Islam. Party cadres were recruited primarily through local mosques, where students as young as twelve years old were organized into Qur'an reading and discussion groups then, after a year of participation, encouraged to form groups of their own. Through this tiered system, the party was building a long-term strategy by tapping youth often ignored by other political groups in a culture where age was revered. The stated goal was "to use power to serve others," not to implement Islamic law.

"We want the party to become a pioneer in upholding Islamic values and we want to do that within the framework of democracy, national unity and integrity," party chairman Hidayat Nur Wahid told an interviewer.[11] "Even if you are Muslim, if you are unjust and oppress non-Muslims, you should be punished. This is how we view *Shar'ia* (Islamic law)."

With seven seats in parliament, the PK's success underlined both the value of such Islamic political organizations if they remained true to their stated mission and their potential threat if the parties, or individuals within them, drew on those infrastructures to plot a more violent course.

It was precisely that internal contradiction which was being played out in Jemaah Islamiyah (JI). Even as Ba'asyir and other activists formed the Majelis Mujahidin Indonesia (MMI), or Indonesian Warriors Council, in order to take part in the post-Suharto political process, Hambali and his JI militants laid plans for a series of ambitious and provocative acts aimed at further undermining Indonesian stability. Targets included the Jakarta Stock exchange, where 15 people were killed, one of the city's largest malls, where 18 died, and the offices of a mainstream Islamic group at Jakarta's main mosque. On Christmas Eve of 2000, the group's operatives delivered bombs to 30 churches and priests in eleven cities across the Indonesian archipelago. After he was captured by Indonesian authorities in June 2002 and turned over to the CIA, al-Qaeda operative Omar al-Faruq reportedly told his interrogators that he had a hand in some of those attacks, as well as an abortive assassination attempt on President Megawati Sukarnoputri.[12] In a nod toward its regional ties, the JI also attempted to assassinate the Philippines ambassador to Indonesia and joined Moro operatives in blowing up a train in Manila, killing 22 people. Malaysia, meanwhile, rounded up more than 60 alleged terrorist recruits and launched a manhunt for Hambali, who it charged with assassinating a Malaysian politician in partnership with the Kumpulan Militan Malaysia (KMM), the Malaysian Militant Group, an Islamic organization seeking the overthrow of that Muslim nation's government.

The operations were a reflection of the growing regionalization of Southeast Asia's Islamic networks. In 1999, Ba'asyir had initiated the creation of a formal alliance of Muslim militants from the Philippines, Malaysia, Thailand, Singapore and Indonesia, called Rabitatul Mujahidin (Holy Warrior Coalition). The goal was the destabilization of Southeast Asian governments to make way for a regional Islamic state.

But the local groups were not working in a vacuum. Even before the World Trade Center bombing or the invasion of Afghanistan, Southeast Asia had become an important crossroads for Islamic militants. Zacarias Moussaoui, the so-called twentieth hijacker in the September 11 attacks, made several visits to Malaysia, where an Islamic banking system, business-friendly environment and lax immigration laws made it a convenient back office for terrorist operations. It was there that Moussaoui obtained the false documents identifying him as a marketing representative for a Malaysian company that allowed him to enter the U.S. During a visit to

Kuala Lumpur in January 2000, U.S. intelligence sources said, Moussaoui, two of the Pentagon hijackers, alleged September 11 coordinator Ramzi Binalshibh, bin Laden lieutenant Khalid Shaikh Mohammed, and Tawfiq bin Atash, a suspect in the bombing of the USS *Cole*, all met with Hambali and a JI contingent that included a former senior officer in the Malaysian armed forces. The meeting, which was monitored by Western intelligence, took place in an upscale apartment on the outskirts of Kuala Lumpur that was owned by Yazid Sufaat, a U.S.-trained biochemist and member of Jemaah Islamiyah.[13] It wasn't the first time such paths had crossed. Years before, Hambali had joined with Wali Khan Amin Shah, by some accounts a "good friend" of bin Laden, to set up a Malaysian front company called Konojaya, which had helped finance both Abu Sayyaf and Ramzi Yousef's Bojinka plot.

Bin Laden's right-hand man, Egyptian doctor Ayman al-Zawaheri, also passed through the region in June 2000, visiting Indonesia for meetings with the leadership of the Islamic secessionist movement in Aceh. During that time, intelligence sources said, al-Zawaheri also conducted several telephone conversations with Hambali.

Not to be left out, the organization that had helped inspire many of these groups, Hizbullah, also extended its reach into the region. In the early 1990s, Hizbullah established a cell in Singapore around a radical Muslim cleric named Ustaz Bandei, who was wanted by Indonesian authorities for the 1995 bombing of the Buddhist Borobudur temple on Java. The *Hizbullahis*, who sources said were led by an Iranian, then recruited five Singaporeans from among those who attended Bandei's religious sermons at private apartments. According to Singapore's Internal Security Department, the five were trained in Singapore and the Malaysian state of Johor, then ordered to conduct surveillance of the U.S. and Israeli embassies and American naval movements in Singapore harbor.[14] The would-be terrorists eventually backed out, Singapore officials claimed, when the Hizbullah operatives tried to get them to ram a small boat filled with explosives into an American ship – just as al-Qaeda would do against the USS *Cole* years later in Yemen.

Jemaah Islamiyah's method of recruiting new members was much like that employed earlier by Hizbullah. Based on its interrogations of detainees, Singapore's security service reported that JI members acted as talent scouts, recommending to friends, relatives and colleagues that they attend religious classes held by the head of JI's Singapore cell, a cleric named Ibrahim Maidin, who would later be arrested. Maidin, who spent 20 days training in Afghanistan after joining JI, peppered his lectures with comments about the plight of Muslims in other parts of Southeast Asia and places like Bosnia and Palestine.[15] Those students who exhibited particular interest in such topics were asked to stay after class for further discussions. Eventually, after some 18 months, promising prospects were invited to join JI with a strong appeal to their egos.

"The members were taught that anyone who left the group was an infidel. On the other hand, those who remained enjoyed a sense of exclusivity and commitment in being in the in-group of a clandestine organization," psychologists who interviewed 31 of the detainees reported. They had found "the true Islam" and were drawn to Maidin and other JI clerics because they wanted "no fuss" on the path to heaven.[16]

A deep strain of indigenous mysticism was woven through Islam in Southeast Asia. And just as "The Old Man of the Mountain" had wrapped his appeal to the eleventh-century Assassins in mystical garb, so, too, did the JI create a mystic bond with its recruits as it sought to prepare them for *istimata*, the Malay term for martyrdom.

> Secrecy, including secrecy over the true knowledge of jihad, helped create a sense of sharing and empowerment vis-à-vis outsiders. Esoteric JI language or "JI-speak" was used as part of the indoctrination process. Code names for instance resulted in a strong sense of "in-group" superiority especially since JI members were said to be closer to Allah as they believed in the "truth" (JI doctrine); even Muslims who did not subscribe to militant jihad were seen as infidels. This dogma convinced many JI members that in the course of jihad, innocent lives (Muslim or non-Muslim) could be sacrificed.[17]

Each new member was also required to take the *bai'ah*, a sacred pledge of obedience to the head of his cell. Breaking the oath would incur divine retribution. To further cement loyalty, the JI used what experts called "psychological contracting," and "escalation of commitment." Following a particularly fiery speech by a cleric, it would hand out surveys to members asking them to commit to specific actions supporting the cause, from contributing money up to and including martyrdom. Once they had signed the survey, they could not back out.

"Hence," the Singaporean psychologists reported, "although a few members had misgivings about their reconnaissance missions, they felt they could not withdraw as they were already 'in too deep.'"[18]

Most troubling to some Singaporean officials was the fact that this was not only a movement of the dispossessed, in the sense of Shi'ite refugees in Lebanon or Palestinian martyrs on the West Bank. While the majority of those involved in the Indonesian networks had either been educated in the *pesantren* or were laborers, migrant workers or unemployed, militants in Malaysia included police, civil servants and military personnel, and many of those arrested in Singapore came from within the ranks of the workforce. "These were not ignorant, destitute or disenfranchised outcasts," investigators discovered to their surprise. "They held normal jobs."[19]

What Singapore's ethnic Chinese-dominated government, obsessed with its campaigns for racial and religious harmony, did not want to acknowledge was that most of those "normal jobs" – driver, butcher, technician – were at the bottom of the economy. Nor did it mention the deep and abiding hatred of the Chinese among many of Southeast Asia's other ethnic groups. Singapore's very existence was the result of a conflict between the Chinese and Malay, which resulted in the creation of the Chinese-dominated enclave. In both Indonesia and Malaysia, the ethnic Chinese controlled much of the economy, just as the Christians had in Lebanon. An uneasy truce between the two groups prevailed in Malaysia, but much of the violence that had broken out during the revolution that ousted Suharto (who was surrounded by Chinese oligarchs) was aimed at the Chinese.

Proof of that antipathy lay in the fact that long before it targeted U.S. interests in the city-state, JI had conducted reconnaissance on a range of purely Singaporean targets, including water pipelines, the mass transit system, the airport and even the Ministry of Defense.

Political disenfranchisement and economic deprivation were at the root of Muslim anger elsewhere in the world. Southeast Asia was no different. The results of interviews by the Singapore government's own psychologists were telling. The detainees named religion as their most important value, but "the second highest value they were concerned with was economic, i.e. having materials comforts and material wealth."[20]

The invasion of Afghanistan, the arrival of U.S. troops to fight Abu Sayyaf in the Philippines, escalating violence in the Occupied Territories of Palestine, and talk of a U.S. war with Iraq galvanized Southeast Asia's militants. After years of concentrating on targets that would further their aim of creating a regional Islamic state, the terrorist networks now brought the U.S. firmly into the cross hairs.

Under Hambali's direction, the JI planned a massive operation in Singapore that it hoped would rival September 11 itself. Seven trucks laden with three tons each of ammonium nitrate would be driven into the embassies of the U.S., Britain, Australia and Israel, as well as other U.S. targets in the city-state.[21] But the plot was foiled when Afghanistan's Northern Alliance captured a Singaporean Muslim who was involved in the plan and U.S. intelligence uncovered videotapes of the potential targets at the Kabul home of al-Qaeda military commander Mohamed Atef. Singapore arrested 13 extremists, authorities in the Philippines grabbed one of the Indonesian coordinators, who was caught with 1.5 tons of TNT and more than a mile of detonating cord, and Malaysia rounded up other militants allegedly involved in arranging the explosives.

Singapore's founding father, Lee Kuan Yew, was adamant about where the blame lay: "Interrogation [of the suspects] disclosed that Abu Bakar Ba'asyir" was the "overall leader of the JI organization" behind the plot. Indonesia, he told the world, had become "a hotbed of terrorism."[22]

Despite the mounting evidence that all roads on the Southeast Asian terrorist trail led to Indonesia and the increasingly shrill demands from Lee, the U.S. and some of Indonesia's Asian neighbors that it crack down on its militants, the government in Jakarta dragged its heels.

In the immediate aftermath of September 11, American architects of the war on terror had every reason to believe Indonesia's interests would coincide with their own. President Megawati Sukarnoputri's father, the nationalist Sukarno, had fought to contain radical Islam, a job completed by the man who ousted him, Suharto. Surely the woman leader of the world's largest Muslim country would do everything possible to prevent al-Qaeda and its Indonesian allies from fostering a fundamentalist resurgence that would oppose her very existence in office.

Megawati had seemed to confirm that when she stood beside President George W. Bush a week after the September 11 attacks and signaled her country's support for the war on terrorism. But behind that façade was another reality: to overtly confront the forces that *could* threaten her was to strengthen the forces that *did* threaten her.

Within days of returning home from Washington, Megawati was adjusting her message in the face of criticism from figures like her own vice president, Hamzah Haz of the Muslim-oriented United Development Party, who claimed the World Trade Center bombing would "cleanse the sins" of the U.S.

"Prolonged military action is not only counterproductive but also can weaken the global coalition's joint effort to combat terrorism," Megawati said in a speech before Parliament.[23]

The turnaround reflected domestic political realities. A Gallup poll of sentiment in the Islamic world in late 2001 revealed that only 27 percent of Indonesians viewed the U.S. favorably, 89 percent said the U.S. military action in Afghanistan was unjustified and 74 percent said they did not believe Arabs carried out the September 11 attacks.[24]

Given those numbers, any government would hesitate to overtly side with the U.S. That was doubly true of a weak president in a shaky coalition government that depended on several Muslim parties for its survival, including a vice president who once opposed the very idea of a woman in the country's highest office.

Further complicating the situation was an historic love–hate relationship between Indonesia and the U.S., viewed through a prism of nationalism, culture and religion – all exploited at various times by the countrys' leaders for their own ends. Suspicion of the West – and the U.S. in particular – colored every aspect of the relationship.

A tendency toward conspiracy theories ran deep in Indonesian society, illustrated by the widespread belief that the devaluation of the *rupiah* in the early 1990s was the result of collusion between financier George Soros and the country's ethnic Chinese businessmen. Many Indonesians believed the West wanted to break up the country or otherwise prevent it from becoming a regional power.

American criticism of Indonesia's human rights record was widely seen as hypocritical in light of a U.S. foreign policy that was perceived as exploitative and biased, particularly when it came to Israel and the Palestinians, a subject that sparked anger at every level of society.

"The majority of Muslims who are moderates are caught in between (1) sympathy for and identification with the Palestinians and anger against the Israelis, and (2) their desire for a peaceful life of growth and progress," Lee Kuan Yew observed.[25]

His Muslim neighbor, Malaysian Prime Minister Mahathir Mohamed, concurred. "We are sure that the principal cause of the terrorism by Muslims is their anger against Israel," said Muhammed, who emerged as a leading moderate Muslim voice in the post-September 11 era. "If terrorism is to be stopped, then the injustice and the oppression of Israel against Palestine and its people must be stopped quickly first."[26]

While there existed a voracious appetite for things Western – from MTV to Coke – there also existed the same kind of cultural backlash that fueled Osama bin Laden's rise, reflected in a spate of attacks on bars in the years after Suharto's overthrow and the increased appearance of Islamic attire even among the upper classes. As Singapore's terrorism report put it: "The last two decades have seen the rise of a more assertive, severe and conservative brand of Islam imported from the Middle East and the Indian sub-continent."

Moderate Muslim leaders – and the vast majority of mainstream Muslims – had almost as much to lose as Megawati by the rise of fundamentalism. Once the threat manifested itself as reality with the Bali bombing – which sent a shockwave through the already moribund economy – the power centers began to close ranks. But in the meantime, Muslim politicians sought to seize every opportunity to exploit public suspicions of the U.S. as a powerful weapon in their maneuvering toward the 2004 presidential elections.

"Everything that gives the impression that Indonesia is serving the American interest in its drive to fight terrorism will be opposed by the [House of Representatives], the press and the public," Lt. Gen. (ret.) Zen A. Maulani, a former intelligence chief, told one reporter. "This means that they will also oppose Megawati if she allows this impression to gain credence."[27]

As always in Indonesia, it was the "impression" – the appearance – which was at issue. Most Indonesian Muslims were willing to look the other way as extremist elements were neutralized, but they didn't want to be seen to be doing so. Indonesians were proud of their role as the world's largest Muslim society. They were not prepared to puncture the illusion of Islamic solidarity.

To expose the reality of their quiet support for the neutralization of extremists would be to cause a loss of face across the breadth of Indonesian society, from the volatile Islamic schools of Central Java to the Presidential Palace. The question was whether Americans could simultaneously understand, deftly utilize and judiciously penetrate the shadow play.

The answer was not long in coming. At a White House news conference at the conclusion of Megawati Sukarnoputri's September 2001 visit, President Bush indelicately stripped the Indonesian president of her veil of deniability as surely as if he had yanked off the Islamic head cover she sometimes wore.

"Some nations will be comfortable supporting covert activities, some nations will only be comfortable with providing information," Bush told reporters. "Others will be helpful and will only be comfortable supporting financial matters, I understand that." He might as well have said: "Don't worry, she'll secretly do my bidding."

The bullying was not lost on the famously passive former housewife. Speaking at a mosque a few weeks after the Bali bombing, she condemned "a superpower that forced the rest of the world to go along with it."

Instead of complying with American requests that she refute the conspiracy theory, then circulating in Indonesia, that the CIA was behind the blast, she told the crowd: "We see how ambition to conquer other nations has led to a situation where there is no more peace unless the whole world is complying with the will of the one with the power and strength."[28]

Hambali was angry. His Singapore and Malaysian networks had been dealt a severe blow by the failure of the Singapore truck-bombing plot. Many were in jail; others were on the run. Haranguing his top deputies at a secret meeting in southern Thailand in early 2002, the JI operations chief ordered a dramatic shift in direction.[29] He wanted results. No longer would the organization concentrate solely on well-guarded political, diplomatic and military facilities. They would now strike at soft targets: bars, restaurants, nightclubs – anywhere Americans were likely to gather.[30]

Nine months later, the Sari Club went up in flames.

The Bali bombing fit perfectly into the two-pronged strategy of Islamic militants the world over: terrorize the West and destabilize weak regimes. The approach was synergistic: terror breeds instability; unstable countries are a breeding ground for terror.

"Innocence Lost," mourned a headline in the *Jakarta Post* after the bombing. But it was much more than innocence that perished in the flames. Along with the lives of almost 200 people, Indonesia's $5 billion a year tourism industry was snuffed out. So, too, was any small chance that the confidence of foreign investors, who had fled in the aftermath of Suharto's overthrow, could be restored.

"We're finished," said Aburizal Bakrie, chairman of the Indonesian Chamber of Commerce and Industry. "Our defense to convince people that doing business in Indonesia is safe is finished."[31]

Bali finally galvanized the Indonesian power centers into action. From the government down to the mosques, recognition of precisely what was at stake spread among mainstream Muslims. The security forces began rounding up militants whom they had long allowed – and sometimes encouraged – to operate with impunity. Ba'asyir himself was eventually taken into custody. Representatives of the CIA and other Western intelligence agencies were even allowed to sit in on interrogations.

A detailed picture of Southeast Asia's terrorist networks began to emerge. And, in some ways, the more details the investigators uncovered, the more disturbing the picture became.

While much of the world had assumed al-Qaeda was giving orders to local terrorist networks and financing their operations, confessions from al-Qaeda's Omar al-Faruq and jailed militants in Indonesia, Singapore, Malaysia and the Philippines revealed that, just as often, it was the other way around. Sometimes, al-Qaeda "borrowed" assets from JI and other groups in order to mount operations. In other cases, it was al-Qaeda that "lent" expertise needed by the locals. And sometimes, they worked hand-in-hand, as in the Singapore bombing plot, where JI did the reconnaissance and obtained the explosives, and al-Qaeda was supposed to send in its own men on the eve of the attacks to actually drive the trucks.[32]

Such an international partnership also appeared to be the case in Bali, which was conceived by a local cleric who had fought in Afghanistan, named Imam Samudra, and his tiny circle of religious students from the small island of Banten. The operation was initially financed through the small-time robbery of a local goldsmith's shop. They had heard the call to strike soft targets and decided to act.[33]

"The Bali bombing plan was fully Imam Samudra's plan," the cleric's lawyer told reporters. "Hambali was only *informed* by my client."[34]

Hambali was not the only senior figure made aware of the plot. During a series of raids, Indonesian investigators discovered a copy of Jemaah Islamiyah's handbook. Chapter 39 stated that all armed operations must be approved by the group's *emir* or supreme commander. Under interrogation, Indonesian police reported, a JI operative known as Muklas, one of three brothers who played key roles in the bombing, confirmed that that emir was Ba'asyir. During a May 2002 meeting in the Central Java city of Solo, Muklas reportedly told investigators, Ba'asyir met with five of the plotters and approved the operation "in principle."[35] But, he added, "The details, how to carry it off, is the role of the field operatives."

In a bizarre news conference in February 2003 at the site of the bombing, Muklas' brother, Ali Imron, staged a reenactment of the attack, strapping on a black vest packed with simulated pipe bombs. He told reporters that the main bomb, which he claimed to have created, consisted of almost a ton of potassium chlorate, 300 pounds of sulfur and 175 pounds of aluminum sulfate packed into filing cabinets, which were then loaded in the Mitsubishi van.

Imron told reporters he was proud of his bomb-making skills, which he had learned in Afghanistan. "Nobody backed us," he boasted. "Our ability is something to be proud of."[36]

But not everyone was convinced. Through Hambali, investigators claimed, the group had linked up with a Yemeni operative named Syafullah, who had fine-tuned the operational plan. Syafullah's name was well known to Western intelligence services. He had been implicated in numerous terrorist attacks in the Middle East, including the bombing of the American Khobar Towers military complex in Saudi Arabia – an operation planned and organized by Hizbullah's Imad Mugniyeh. Like celebrities in some twisted version of the Kevin Bacon parlor game, the actors in the terror drama quickly connected back to the Lebanese pioneer of anti-American terrorism. With Bali, the seeds of hate sewn in Beirut and fertilized by the blood of a thousand martyrs had now come into full bloom half a world away.

"Let it be known that every single drop of Muslim blood, be it from any nationality or whatever place, will be remembered and accounted for," proclaimed the web site of the JI front group that claimed responsibility for Bali.[37]

The message was an echo of threats once issued by Islamic Jihad and the other phantom organizations operating under Hizbullah's umbrella. The difference now was that the sentiment was shared by an amorphous and constantly shifting network of militants and would-be recruits that stretched from the heart of the Middle East to the jungles of South America to the teeming cities of Asia. Two decades after the first truck bomb shed American blood in Beirut, the structure of anti-Western terror had evolved from a top-down organization with orders originating in Tehran to a many-headed hydra ready and willing to strike anywhere at any time, waiting only for inspiration.

That was driven home shortly after the Bali bombing, when the Arab television station al-Jazeera broadcast a new taped message from bin Laden. The al-Qaeda leader praised the "killing [of] the British and Australians in Bali" and other terrorist acts as a "reaction" of "the sons of Islam" who were "fulfilling the orders of their God and their prophet." He went on to condemn "the killing of our children" by the U.S. and Israel.[38]

Within a week, Australian intelligence warned that it had uncovered a plot to bomb the American, British and Australian schools in Jakarta, attended by thousands of Western children each day.[39]

Across Southeast Asia, foreign schools began installing bombproof blast walls, while in the slums outside their gates, more *jihadis* were preparing to die.

I had a strong sense of *déjà vu* as I walked the streets of Manila in late 2002. There were few Western faces to be seen.

U.S. officials had warned Americans in both the Philippines and Indonesia about a rising danger of kidnapping.[40] Several Americans had already been abducted in the southern Philippines. The arrival of a 1,200-member contingent of U.S. troops to help the Philippines military fight Abu Sayyaf had only increased the threat level. Authorities in Singapore said they had found documents showing that JI had developed lists of U.S. companies with an eye toward identifying Western executives. And in the wake of the Bali bombing, intelligence sources worried that the threat of kidnapping now extended to the capitals of Southeast Asia, just as the abduction of Westerners had followed bombings as a natural progression in Lebanon so many years before.

And it didn't end there. Over breakfast that morning, I had read newspaper reports about Malaysia's arrest of JI members involved in yet another attempt to bomb the U.S. embassy in Singapore and a plot to bomb the Manila subway.

The Manila threat followed a series of bombings that had rocked the Philippines in previous months. As in Indonesia, the targets included shopping malls, buses and government buildings. Just days after I left Manila, bomb threats would close both the Australian and Canadian embassies. "They are targeting specific nationalities, they're not just targeting Westerners," Australian Foreign Minister Alexander Downer told reporters. "The threat is rather specific, that is the threat is against the embassy itself, the building itself."

At the Citibank building, where I was involved in two days of meetings, guards downstairs checked briefcases and purses, but the Americans upstairs knew the security was just window-dressing. Aside from the embassy, it was the most high-profile building associated with the U.S. in the city. But unlike the walled embassy compound, only a narrow sidewalk separated it from the street. There was nothing to stop a suicide driver from crashing into the lobby. If there were any doubts about its potential as a target, they had been erased a few weeks before, when someone set off two grenades on the street outside.

"We just have to hope we aren't at the top of the list," said one British HR manager, displaying the fatalism I knew so well from Beirut.

As I moved around inside the building, I found myself surreptitiously glancing out the window of each office I entered to see which way it faced – toward the potential bomb on the street, or away – and checking out the nearest stairwell in case a quick exit was required. Outside, I fell into the old habit of glancing at each car, studying each face, switching on the mental radar whenever someone fell in step behind me or crossed in my direction.

The hotel offered only a modicum more safety; Western hotels were also on a target list uncovered by Philippines intelligence. I was not displeased that my room faced away from the main road.

"I've had enough of this," said one grim-faced executive, who was hoping his replacement would soon be hired so he could return to the safety of his native New Zealand. His country, it seemed, was one of the few havens left. Even Australia, which once prided itself on its isolation from the world's ills, now had heavy security surrounding key buildings, bridges and the Sydney Opera House. The *Sydney Morning Herald* reported that authorities had discovered 20 JI militants had secretly operated a training camp in the Blue Mountains outside Perth.

Tourists once bound for Thailand or Bali were switching to Vietnam, where communism and Buddhism seemed to offer some protection against militant Islam; intelligence experts worried that the killing fields of Cambodia could become al-Qaeda's next refuge; and Chinese officials in Hong Kong arrested suspected terrorists trying to purchase Stinger antiaircraft missiles.

And the litany of horrors continued to mount like elements of a bad novel. A *Wall Street Journal* reporter was kidnapped and decapitated in Pakistan, a suicide bomber devastated the Russian government offices in Chechnya, Algerians were arrested with small amounts of a biological weapon in London.

The seeds of terror planted in Beirut had spread on the winds of hate and taken root around the world. The terrorists had learned their lessons well; the same could not be said for the inhabitants of the White House.

History had repeated itself in Lebanon. Now it was happening again. The mutually exclusive goals of Reagan administration Middle East policy – serve as a non-combatant "neutral" presence in Beirut and support the Christian government of Lebanon; pursue a wider Arab–Israeli peace and serve as Israel's unquestioning patron – had doomed it from the start. As phase one of America's war on terror bogged down and al-Qaeda's network began to regroup outside Afghanistan, another U.S. administration was once more sending mixed messages.

Muslims heard the Bush White House say it was not engaged in a Crusade against Islam, even as it geared up for battle with Iraq. They listened to Washington talk of international cooperation, even as the Pentagon singled out Syria and Iran as potential next targets. They heard the president call for justice for the Palestinian people, even as he embraced Ariel Sharon.

Once more, diplomatic and intelligence experts waved warning flags. Once more, allies balked. Once more, arrogance and personal prejudice substituted for thoughtful analysis and historical perspective.

"We think that as long as America as a superpower looks to Israel in a special way and prefers it to all other countries, and until the U.S. can be nonaligned in the Middle East, there will be difficulties," Iran's architect of terror, Ali Akhbar Mohtashami, had told me in 1985.

Nearly two decades later, Jemaah Islamiyah operative Ibrahim Maidin was repeating almost the exact same words to Singaporean interrogators: "Maidin [said] the U.S. has to change its policy towards the Middle East. He said that as long as the U.S. hits Islam, JI would have to attack the U.S."

Meanwhile at home, Americans were still asking, "Why?"

Acknowledgments

Two men made a contribution to this book that towers above the rest. They didn't supply details, unearth important documents or correct mistakes in the manuscript. Their role was more basic: they kept me alive in Beirut.

The Harake brothers, Bechir and Ayad, were very simply the best drivers in the Middle East. Whether we were racing through an artillery barrage, navigating a mine-filled road or negotiating past a militia checkpoint, I always knew my life was in good hands. There was no place they would not go, no deadline they could not meet. They put up with my ignorance, taught me to understand their country and watched my back. Their commitment to our work ended up costing Ayad his legs, the day an Israeli tank fired on his car. I owe the Harakis more than I can ever repay.

The camera crews, too, deserve my thanks: Sami Awad and Hassan Harake, our primary team; Tewfic Ghrazawi and Behije Mehdi, killed by the Israeli tank shell that crippled Ayad; and all the crews from Europe and the U.S. that passed through Beirut. They served not only as my eyes, but, journalists all, as my ears as well.

There are others to whom I owe a more traditional debt. Without the staff of the Middle East Reporter (MER), the job of every foreign journalist in Beirut would have been a thousand times more difficult. This daily English-language analysis of the Arabic press was required reading at the breakfast table and an invaluable tool as I reconstructed the chronology of events. Rummaging through my piles of old MERs, I often thought of the three people who spent so many sleepless nights putting it together: Ihsan Hijazi, Tewfic Mishlawi and Nora Boustani (now of the *Washington Post*).

Also valuable was *U.S. Marines in Lebanon, 1982–1984* by Benis M. Frank, the official Marine Corps historian. Ben was good enough to provide me with a prepublication manuscript to aid in my research.

Scores of other sources helped me piece together this mosaic. Many are still in government service and cannot be named. During my years abroad, I have learned that the ranks of the State Department and armed forces are filled with brave, knowledgeable and intelligent men and women who, too often, are ignored by the politicians.

The Lebanese who guided me through their confused and tragic country are too numerous to mention. It is gratifying to see that finally, after all these decades, they are beginning to exhibit to each other the warmth they showed me.

A special thanks to Youseff, Fouad, Muhammed and all the rest who made the Commodore home. There will never be another hotel like it.

Notes and References

The material in this book is drawn largely from my own notebooks, experiences, and the scripts of my television and radio reports from Beirut for CBS News, and articles for other news organizations in the years that followed.

Since this is a reporter's notebook-style work, I have not footnoted every quote or reference. It would be tedious both for me and for you, the reader. Indeed, sorting through the scraps of conversations and impressions in the old notebooks, I would be hard-pressed to put a date, or even a name, to every one. If a quotation is not footnoted, it means it comes from my own original reporting.

I have tried to avoid the temptation of reconstructing conversations. When there are quotes around someone's words, it means they were written down at the time, came from the dozens of hours of interviews videotaped during those years, were drawn from other interviews conducted specifically for this book or were quoted from other sources. In cases where it may appear that the speaker was addressing him or herself to me, but was, in fact, speaking to someone else, I try to make that clear in the text or the notes below. Widely reported comments, such as news conferences or speeches, are the exception.

Inevitably, in this kind of book, there are sources who cannot be named. Some still work for the State Department, the Pentagon or CIA and still have careers to protect. Others remain in the Middle East and, if they were named, might lose more than just their jobs. When these people are quoted, I ask you to indulge me with your trust.

A final note about style and usage. A quick scan of articles and books on the Middle East will reveal that there are a number of different ways in which Arabic can be transliterated into English. The word Muslim, or Moslem, is a case in point. Both are technically correct. So, too, are Koran and Qur'an. Particularly problematic is Hizbullah. The Party of God's Arabic name variously appears as Hizballah, Hizbollah, Hezbollah, etc. I have generally opted for the variations most widely used in English-language publications in the Islamic world, hence "Muslim" and "Qur'an." For the Party of God, I have chosen to use "Hizbullah," which is one of two ways the organization itself spells it in its English language publications, and closest to the more sophisticated rendering, Hizbu'llah. To reduce distraction for the reader, I have standardized the spelling in all quotes used in the book, regardless of the way it was spelled in the original publication, but retained the source spelling in all notes.

Preface

1. Josh Meyer, "Hizbullah Vows Anew to Target Americans," *Los Angeles Times*, 17 April 2003, <http://www.latimes.com/news/nationworld/iraq/world/la-warhezbollah17 apr17,1,4681007.story?coll=;a%2Diraq%2Dworld>.

SECTION I: FERTILE GROUND

Chapter 1

1. Don Oberdorfer, "Making of a Diplomatic Debacle," *Washington Post*, 12 February 1984, A1.
2. Col. Charles Churchill, *The Druzes and the Maronites under the Turkish Rule from 1840 to 1860* (London: Bernard Quaritch, 1982), 50.

Chapter 2

1. Khalil Gibran, *Garden of the Prophet* (New York: Knopf, 1995).
2. Syrian tanks moved in support of the PLO, but then-Air Force Commander Hafez al-Assad's decision to withhold fighter cover forced the armor to retreat, humiliating the Damascus regime and paving the way for Assad's coup.
3. *Daily Star* (Beirut), 8 June 1984.
4. Ibid.
5. *Daily Star*, 24 June 1984.
6. *Daily Star*, 3 March 1984.
7. Khalife was the driving force behind a short-lived peace movement that burst onto the scene in the spring of 1984. Its aim was to stage a huge march for peace by Christians and Muslims, culminating in a rally on the Green Line. The night before it was to take place, militias on both sides began blanket shelling across the city to force its cancellation. Depressed and disgusted, Khalife gave up her efforts and the movement died.
8. *Daily Star*, 20 May 1984.

Chapter 3

1. Churchill, *Druzes*, 12.
2. Churchill, *Druzes*, 67.
3. *Daily Star*, 4 June 1984.

Chapter 4

1. *Traveller's Guide to the Middle East* (London: Middle East Insight Publications, 1979).
2. *Daily Star*, 4 June 1984.

SECTION II: PLANTING THE SEEDS

Chapter 5

1. Churchill, *Druzes*, 115–16.
2. A. Eban, *The Beirut Massacre: The Complete Kahan Commission Report* (Princeton/New York: Karz-Cohl Publishing, Inc., 1983), 14.
3. Ibid., 26.
4. In early 2003, the Belgian Supreme Court cleared the way for a war crimes suit against Sharon filed by survivors of the massacre. See Marlise Simons, "Sharon Faces Belgian Trial After Term Ends," *New York Times*, 13 February 2003, <http://www.nytimes.com/2003/02/13/international/europe/13BELG.html>.
5. Ibid., 27.
6. Ibid., 28.
7. Italics added by author.
8. "Reagan Shocked," *New York Times*, 11 October 1982, A8.
9. "Role of U.S. in Mideast Strengthens," *Wall Street Journal*, 5 November 1982, A1.
10. "Failure to Reach Accord," *New York Times*, 5 December 1982, A12.
11. "A More Visible Presence," *Time*, 15 November 1982.
12. Associated Press (5 December 1982).
13. Robert G. Neumann, "Assad and the Future of the Middle East," *Foreign Affairs*, Winter 1983/84: 240.
14. Associated Press and UPI, 3 February 1983.
15. "Over My Dead Body," *Time*, 14 February 1983.
16. J. Michael Kennedy, "Marine Cheerleader," *Los Angeles Times*, 15 February 1983.
17. Associated Press, (24 March 1983).

18. Benis M. Frank, *U.S. Marines in Lebanon, 1982–1984* (Washington, D.C., 1987), 56.
19. "A Sadly Deteriorating Relationship," *Time*, 21 February 1983, 15.
20. "Wider Marine Role Eyed," *Washington Post*, 25 February 1983.
21. The tear gas actually proved to be a problem during the rescue effort because the canisters kept exploding, engulfing emergency workers in the gas.
22. "Reagan Calls Bombing Cowardly," *New York Times*, 19 April 1983.
23. Each of the brigades was permitted to have 40 tanks, 18 155mm artillery pieces, 39 mortars and 30 antitank weapons. Antiaircraft and ground-to-sea missiles, as well as radar that could reach inside Israel, were banned.
24. "Schultz Shuttle," *Wall Street Journal*, 2 May 1983.
25. "The Making of a Diplomatic Debacle," *Washington Post*, 12 February 1984, 18.

Chapter 6

1. Churchill, *Druzes*, 59.
2. *Review of Adequacy of Security Arrangements for Marines in Lebanon and Plans for Improving That Security*, Hearings before the Committee on Armed Services and the Investigations Subcommittee, 98th Congress (House of Representatives Report 1983), 122.
3. Coincidentally, the day Dillon's move was announced was the same day McFarlane flew to Paris for his first meeting with Jumblatt, in effect acknowledging that Dillon's advice to maintain contact with the Druze leader had been correct.
4. Churchill, *Druzes*, 56.
5. Ibid., 82.
6. Frank, *U.S. Marines in Lebanon*, 78.
7. OPREP-1 message from Commander in Chief, U.S. European Command (USINCEUR) to Commander, U.S. Naval Forces Europe (CINCUSNAVEUR), 24 September 1982.

Chapter 7

1. Churchill, *Druzes*, 85.
2. Sami Nasib Makarem, *The Druze Faith* (New York: Caravan Books, 1974), 4.
3. Ibid., 23.

Chapter 8

1. Churchill, *Druzes*, 134.
2. Frank, *U.S. Marines in Lebanon*, 81.
3. Churchill, *Druzes*, 113.
4. Ibid., 158.
5. The *Bowen* was called in because the Druze battery was hidden behind a ridge that blocked Charlie Battery's 155mm guns. The *Bowen* sailed down the coast to a position where it had a clear shot at the Druze emplacement. Perhaps coincidentally, the first naval salvo of the war was ordered shortly after rockets fell about 200 yards from a pair of visiting Marine generals.
6. The military apparently did not share that confidence in Gemayel. Testifying before a congressional committee on behalf of the Pentagon months later, Marine Col. Richard Gannon said only that "some" Palestinians had fought at Souk al-Gharb.
7. Barbara Tuchman, *The March of Folly* (London: Abacus, Sphere Books, Ltd., 1985), 352.
8. Report of the DOD Commission on Beirut Airport Terrorist Act, October 23, 1983 (Washington, DC: U.S. GPO, 1983).
9. Frank, *U.S. Marines in Lebanon*, 89.
10. Los Angeles Times Service, 25 September 1983.
11. Statement before the House Foreign Affairs Committee, 21 September 1983. Transcript from the *Department of State Bulletin*, November 1983, 25.

Chapter 9

1. Churchill, *Druzes*, 154.

Chapter 10

1. *Middle East Reporter* (Beirut), 10 August 1983.
2. Review of Adequacy of Security, 490–1.
3. Frank, *U.S. Marines in Lebanon*, 56.
4. Report of the DOD Commission, 63.
5. Ibid., 130.
6. Ibid., 130.
7. Ibid., 65.
8. *Review of Adequacy of Security*, 267–8.
9. Ibid., 537.
10. Ibid., 282.
11. Ibid., 272.
12. *Report of the DOD Commission*, 40–1.
13. James Reston, Jr., *Warriors of God: Richard the Lionheart and Saladin in the Third Crusade* (New York: Doubleday, 2001), 28.
14. Karen Armstrong, *Holy War: The Crusades and Their Impact on Today's World* (New York: Anchor Books, 2001), 176.
15. August C. Krey, *The First Crusade: The Accounts of Eyewitnesses and Participants* (Gloucester, MA: P. Smith, 1958).
16. Armstrong, *Holy War*, 195.
17. Ibid.
18. Qur'an, Surah XXII: 40–2.
19. *Congressional Quarterly*, 29 October 1983: 2220.
20. "We're Underestimating the Arabs," *Washington Post*, 11 December 1983, C1.
21. Qur'an, Surah XLVII, 4–6. Other passages in the Qur'an and the Hadith (the teachings of the Prophet) promise that virgins are among the sensual delights awaiting martyrs in Paradise. One example is Surah 56, 12–39: "And theirs shall be the dark-eyed houris, chaste as hidden pearls: a *guerdon* for their deeds ..." Interestingly, modern scholars working from some of the oldest extant copies of the Qur'an, maintain that the "virgins" or "houris" are actually "white raisins of crystal clarity." See Alexander Stille, "Radical New Views of Islam and the Origins of the Koran," *New York Times*, 2 March 2002, <http://www.nytimes.com/2002/03/02/arts/02ISLA.html>.
22. Edward Mortimer, *The Politics of Islam* (New York: Vintage Books, 1982), 46.
23. The Assassins, so named by their enemies, were actually members of the Nizari branch of Isma'ilism, today best known for philanthropic activities under its jet-set Imam, the Aga Khan. The name, which first appeared in Crusader texts, is believed to derive from the Arabic word *hashishiyyin*. The common myth is that the killers were so-called because they smoked hashish before their missions, but scholars argue that the word was, in fact, a local Syrian term of abuse.
24. Bernard Lewis, *The Assassins* (London: Al Saqi Books, 1985), 48.
25. Ibid., 130.
26. Description provided by several Middle Eastern sources.
27. Quoted by above sources.

Chapter 11

1. Jean Rostand, *Pensées d'un Biologiste* (1939), quoted in Robert Andrews, Mary Biggs and Michael Seidel, eds., *The Columbia World of Quotations* (New York: Columbia University Press, 1996), <http://www.bartleby.com/66/73/47273.html>.

Chapter 12

1. Churchill, *Druzes*, 249–50.
2. Fouad Ajami, op-ed page article, *New York Times*, 12 February 1984.

SECTION III: WHIRLWIND

Chapter 13

1. Todd Robertson, "Interview with Hussein Assaf," *Daily Star* (Beirut), 17 April 1984.
2. The group's apparent preference for AFP was a mixed blessing for the news agency. After Lebanese government security officials began to wonder aloud about links between the French reporters and the terrorist group, AFP asked other news organizations to report only that the claims were made in "a call to a Western news agency."
3. The vast majority of the 1,500 to 2,000 Americans listed by the embassy were Lebanese who carried U.S. passports. Their situation was far different from that of native-born Americans, who stood out from the crowd.
4. Based on an interview conducted with Hagey in Washington, DC in October 1985.
5. Intelligence sources and *Report of the Congressional Committees Investigating the Iran–Contra Affair* (New York: Random House, 1988).
6. I almost got my wish a year later when Syrian dissidents hijacked the plane on which I was scheduled to fly back to the Middle East from London. I had switched to a different flight at the airport, to the great disappointment of my CBS bosses who were quite excited when they thought I was on the plane.
7. Qur'an, Surah V, 56.
8. In his book, *Veil: The Secret Wars of the CIA* (New York: Simon & Schuster, 1987), 396–8, *Washington Post* editor Bob Woodward reported that the assassination attempt was a joint U.S.–Saudi operation organized by a British mercenary. After it failed, Woodward relates, the Saudis paid Fadlallah $2 million in humanitarian aid for Shi'ite refugees in order to halt attacks against U.S. and Saudi interests.
9. "Interview with Sheikh Muhammed Hussein Fadlallah," *Middle East Insight* (Washington, DC), June/July 1985.
10. There are numerous references to *taqiyah* throughout the literature on the Shi'ites. One mention appears in Amir Taheri's *Holy Terror: Inside the World of Islamic Terrorists* (Bethesda, MD: Adler & Adler, 1987).
11. William Casey, *Vital Speeches of the Day*, May 1985.
12. The information for this section comes from numerous sources on three continents, including various militia officials in Beirut, U.S. and European intelligence contacts and Iranian exiles.
13. At about this time, late May 1985, the first signals were being sent by Tehran via the Israelis that would eventually lead to contacts with the United States and spark the Iran–Contra Affair. In retrospect, it appears possible that I had been granted the interview so that I might act as an additional conduit to make sure the message reached Washington that Iran was ready to talk.
14. *Daily Star*, 28 May 1985, based on news agency dispatches.
15. Mohamed Selhami and Hamza Kaidi, "I Have Met the Men of the Suicide Squads," *Jeune Afrique*, 25 January 1984.
16. *New York Times*, 14 December 1983
17. Reuters, 2 November 1985.

Chapter 14

1. "Memories of 1980," *Washington Post*, 15 October 1984.
2. Senate Foreign Relations Committee, *The Security of American Personnel in Lebanon* (Washington, DC: GPO, 1984), 7.

3. U.S. intelligence, in fact, detected a plot to bomb the West Beirut complex around the time the East Beirut embassy annex was blown up.
4. This was the normal contingent of 10 to 30 Marines who serve in every U.S. embassy, as distinguished from the special 90-man Marine guard force attached to the Sixth Fleet that had been withdrawn. Marines on embassy duty guard only the inside of the building, while the special unit had been responsible for external security.
5. Ibid., 7.
6. Ibid., 10.

Chapter 15

1. *The Holy Qur'an*, M.H. Shakir, translator (Elmhurst, New York: Tahrike Tarsile Qur'an, Inc. 1983).
2. The basis for such concern would be illustrated later. The day before AP correspondent Terry Anderson was kidnapped in March 1985, he interviewed Hussein Fadlallah. The Hizbullah spiritual leader later condemned Anderson's abduction, but even if he was not involved, it was very possible the kidnappers realized that Anderson was still in Beirut only when he turned up on the cleric's doorstep.
3. This was in sharp contrast to an incident a year later when we returned to Beirut for the TWA hijacking. Once the hijacking was over and street fighting broke out in West Beirut, a CBS News vice president who was with us ordered a chartered plane to get himself and a few of his star correspondents out, leaving us to fend for ourselves.
4. *U.S. News and World Report*, 8 July 1985.
5. *State Department Bulletin*, November 1984.

Chapter 16

1. *Middle East Reporter*, 5 November 1983.
2. This picture of life in captivity is based on a series of conversations with freed hostages Jerry Levin, Father Lawrence Martin Jenco, David Jacobsen and Rev. Benjamin Weir, as well as Peggy Say (sister of hostage Terry Anderson), hostage negotiator Terry Waite, and U.S. and Middle East sources, along with Weir's book cited below.
3. Rev. Benjamin Weir, *Hostage Bound, Hostage Freed* (Philadelphia: The Westminster Press, 1987), 54.
4. Ibid., 110.
5. Ibid., 112.
6. Muslims accept the Bible as a precursor to the Qur'an and recognize Christ and other Christian figures as prophets.
7. Ibid., 92–3.
8. Weinberger would ultimately acquiesce to the plan and order the Pentagon to provide the arms, for which he would later be indicted and ultimately pardoned by President George Bush.
9. U.S. government officials claimed that the high profile taken by his sister, Peggy Say, was also responsible. They argued that her frequent media appearances furthered Islamic Jihad's cause and increased Anderson's value as a hostage.
10. *Report of the Congressional Committees Investigating the Iran–Contra Affair* (New York: Random House, 1988), 242.

SECTION IV: THE SEEDS SPREAD

Chapter 17

1. Khali Gibran, *Mirrors of the Soul*, in Martin L. Wolf, Anthony R. Ferris, Andrew Dib Sherfan, eds./translators, *The Treasured Writings of Khalil Gibran*, (Castle Books New Jersey, 1980), 751.

2. *Daily Star*, 19 February 1998.
3. In March 2000, U.S. District Judge Thomas Penfield Jackson ordered Iran to pay Anderson, his wife and daughter $341 million for its "savage and cruel" treatment of the former hostage. In late 2002, the Bush Administration agreed to pay Anderson $41.2 million as part of a deal brokered by the Clinton Administration and Congress to front more than $213 million for families that had won court judgments against Iran. The family of Col. Higgins was slated to receive $55.4 million under the arrangement. In August 1998, Jackson ordered Iran to pay $65 million in damages to three other freed hostages, David Jacobsen, Joseph Cicippio and Frank Reed.
4. Fida Nasrallah, "The US Travel Ban on Lebanon: In No One's Interest," *Middle East International* (London), 28 April 1995.
5. Hizbullah, *Open Letter to the Downtrodden in Lebanon and the World* (1987), 12.
6. Quoted in Amal Saad-Ghorayeb, *Hizbu'llah: Politics and Religon*, edited by Azza Karam and Ziauddin Sardar, Critical Studies on Islam (London and Sterling, VA: Pluto Press, 2002), 11.
7. Jeffrey Goldberg, "In the Party of God," *New Yorker*, 14 and 21 October 2002, 188.
8. Nicholas Blanford, "Hizbullah Sharpens Its Weapons in the Propaganda War," *Christian Science Monitor*, 28 December 2001, <http://www.csmonitor.com/2001/1228/p6s2-wome.html>.
9. Shai Feldman, "Israel's Deterrent Power After Its Withdrawal from Lebanon," *Strategic Assessment* 3, no. 1 (June 2000), <http://www.tau.ac.il/jcss/sa/v3n1p3.html>.
10. Based on official Israeli government figures and news reports in Israel and Lebanon.
11. Agence France Press, "Poll Shows Israelis Want to Withdraw from Lebanon," 5 September 1997.
12. Scott Peterson, "The Long Goodbye," *Christian Science Monitor*, 9 July 1998, <http://csmweb2.emcweb.com/durable/1998/07/09/p6s1.htm>.
13. Wire Services, "Storm Over Debate on Israeli Unilateral Withdrawal from Lebanon," *ArabicNews.Com*, 27 November 1997, <http://www.arabicnews.com/ansub/Daily/Day/971127/1997112724.html>.
14. The International Policy Institute for Counter-Terrorism, "The IDF's Technological War Against Hizballah Through the Eyes of the Lebanese Media," in Spotlight News Updates, The Interdisciplinary Center, Herzliya, <http://www.ict.org.il/spotlight/det.cfm?id=222>, 28 January 1999.
15. Deborah Sontag, "Israel Changes Its Style in South Lebanon," *New York Times*, 7 October 1999, <http://www.angelfire.com/il/FourMothers/nytimes.html>.
16. Gal Luft, "Israel's Security Zone in Lebanon – A Tragedy?" *Middle East Quarterly* VII, no. 3 (September 2000), <http://www.meforum.org/article/70>.
17. Yossi Olmert, "Cut Our Losses," *Jerusalem Post*, 7 December 1998, <http://www.jpost.com/com/Archive/07.Dec.1998/Opinion/Article-1.html>.
18. Leslie Susser, "A Catalogue of Missed Opportunities," *Jerusalem Report*, 3 July 2000, <http://www.jrep.com/Mideast/Article-12.html>.
19. Augustus Richard Norton, "Hizbullah and the Israeli Withdrawal from Southern Lebanon," *Journal of Palestine Studies* 30, no. 1 (Autumn 2000): 22–36.
20. Lee Hockstader, "Israeli Pullout Unlikely to End Lebanon's Misery," *Washington Post*, <http://www.dawn.com/2000/02/28/int1.htm>, 28 February 2000.
21. "Israel Warns Lebanon Against Attacks," Reuters, <http://www.dawn.com/2000/02/24/int1.htm>, 24 February 2000.
22. "Security Zone Scramble," *ABC News*, 22 May 2000, <http://abcnews.go.com/sections/world/DailyNews/lebanon000522.html>.
23. "Barak on Withdrawal," *Jerusalem Post*, 14 February 2000, <http://www.jpost.com/Editions/2000/02/14/News/>.
24. Associated Press, "Israel Withdraws", 24 May 2000.
25. Ibid.
26. "Background on the Withdrawal," *Yediot Ahranot*, 5 March 2000.

27. Feldman, "Israel's Deterrent Power."
28. Doron Rosenblum, "Eating Away Our Innards," *Ha'aretz* (Tel Aviv), 26 May 2000.
29. Ibid.
30. Nizar A. Hamzeh, "Lebanon's Hizbullah: From Islamic Revolution to Parliamentary Accommodation," *Third World Quarterly* 14, no. 2 (1993): 321–7, and contemporary news reports.
31. Mats Warn, "Staying the Course: The 'Lebanonization' of Hizbollah," American University of Beirut, <http://almashriq.hiof.no/lebanon/300/320/324.2/hizballah/warn2/index.html>, May 1999.
32. Yaroslav Trofimov, "Brandishing Weapons and Aid, the Militant Group Hezbollah Tests U.S. Resolve," *Wall Street Journal* (New York), 18 December 2001, 1.
33. Neil MacFarquhar, "To U.S., a Terrorist Group; To Lebanese, a Social Agency," *New York Times*, 28 December 2001, A: 10.
34. Saad-Ghorayeb, *Hizbu'llah*, 24.
35. Hizbullah Press Office *Statement of Purpose*, 20 March 1998, al-Masriq web site (American University of Beirut), <http://almashriq.hiof.no/lebanon/300/320/324/324.2/hizballah/statement01.html>.
36. Saad-Ghorayeb, *Hizbu'llah*, 36.
37. Ibid., 82.
38. Hamzeh, "Lebanon's Hizbullah."
39. Ibid.
40. Saad-Ghorayeb, *Hizbu'llah*, 70.
41. "Interview with Robert Baer," *Frontline*, <http://www.pbs.org/wgbh/pages/frontline/shows/tehran/axis/terror.html>.
42. "U.S. Promises Continued Support for Lebanon's Reforms," U.S. Department of State, <http://www.uspolicy.be/Issues/Foreignpolicy/leba121401.htm>, 14 December 2001.
43. Jeffrey Goldberg, "In the Party of God," *New Yorker*, 28 October 2002, 75–83.
44. Several Hizbullah members were arrested but later released for lack of evidence. Four years later, Argentina expelled six of the seven Iranian diplomats in the country, claiming they were implicated in both attacks. The Argentines also claimed to have telephone intercepts between the Triple Frontier and sleeper cells in Buenos Aires discussing the attacks.
45. A few years later, other unconfirmed reports would claim he had returned to Lebanon and was serving on Hizbullah's ruling council under an assumed name.
46. "Khobar Towers Press Release," U.S. Department of Justice, <http://www.fbi.gov/pressrel/pressrel01/khobar.htm>, 21 June 2001.
47. Wire Services, "Iran–Hezbollah Terror Connection," *Newsmax.Com*, 2 October 2001, <http://www.newsmax.com/archives/articles/2001/10/2/191921.shtml>.
48. United States District Court Southern District of New York, "U.S. Grand Jury Indictment Against Usama Bin Laden," <http://www.globalsecurity.org/intell/library/news/1998/11/98110602_nlt.html>, 6 November 1998.
49. Jim Miklaszewski and Robert Windrem, "Suspected al-Qaida Camp Seen in Iran," *NBC News*, <http://www.msnbc.com/news/813034.asp?0cl=c4>, 26 September 2002.
50. *An Nahar*, 5 January 2000, quoted in Gary C. Gambrill, "Syrian, Lebanese Security Forces Crush Sunni Islamist Opposition," *Middle East Intelligence Bulletin* 2, no. 1 (January 2000), <http://www.meib.org/articles/0001_l1.htm>.
51. Ibid.
52. Ibid.
53. Michael Wines, "Al Qaeda in Lebanon and Gaza, Sharon Says," *New York Times*, 6 December 2002, <http://www.nytimes.com/2002/12/06/international/middleeast/06MIDE.html>.
54. "Who Did It? Foreign Report Presents an Alternative View," *Jane's Foreign Report* 19, 2001, <http://www.janes.com/security/international_security/news/fr/fr010919_1n.shtml>.

55. Kathy Kiely, "Graham: Step up Hunt, Scale Back on Iraq," *USA Today*, 13 May 2002, <http://www.usatoday.com/news/washington/2002/05/14/graham-inside.htm>.

56. "How Iran Entered the 'Axis'," *Frontline*, <http://www.pbs.org/wgbh/pages/frontline/shows/tehran/axis/map.html>.

57. Hichem Karoui, "Hunting the Faceless Man," *Palestine Chronicle*, 1 October 2001, <http://www.hichemkaroui.com/man.htm>.

58. Ahmed Rashid, *Jihad: The Rise of Militant Islam in Central Asia* (New Haven and London: Yale University Press, 2002), 3.

59. Michael Eisenstadt, "The 'Al-Aqsa Intifada' and the Prospects for a Wider Arab–Israeli War," in Policy Watch, The Washington Institute for Near East Policy, <http://www.washingtoninstitute.org/watch/Policywatch/policywatch2001/516.htm>, 5 February 2001.

60. *As-Safir* (Beirut), 8 October 2001, quoted in Gary C. Gambrill, "Lebanon Ambivalent Towards US War on Terror," *Middle East Intelligence Bulletin* 3, no. 10 (October 2001), <http://www.meib.org/articles/0110_12.htm>.

61. Barbara Plett, "Don't Sacrifice Israel, Warns Sharon," BBC, 4 October 2001, <http://news.bbc.co.uk/1/hi/world/middle_east/1580113.stm>.

62. Randall Mikkelsen, "United States Calls Sharon 'Man of Peace'," *Reuters*, 11 April 2002, <http://ca.news.yahoo.com/020411/5/lodf.html>.

63. Stephen Farrell and Robert Thomson, "Interview with Ariel Sharon," *The Times* (London) 5 November 2002, <http://www.thelikud.org/press_%20releases/press_releases_11_5_02.htm>.

64. Eric Schmitt, "Pentagon Draws Up a 20-to-30-Year Anti-Terror Plan," *New York Times*, 16 January 2003, <http://www.nytimes.com/2003/01/17/politics/17STRA.html?tntemail1>.

Chapter 18

1. Quoted in James Reston Jr., *Warriors of God: Richard the Lionheart and Saladin in the Third Crusade* (New York, 2001), 7.

2. Reuven Paz, "Hizballah and Fatah: A New Alliance Against Israel," The Interdisciplinary Center (Herzliya, Israel), <http://www.ict.org.il/articles/articledet.cfm?articleid=134>, 22 October 2000.

3. "Faysal Al-Husseini: Sharon Must Not Get a Chance," in Special Dispatch Series, Middle East Research Institute (Washington, DC), <http://www.memri.org/bin/articles.cgi?Page=archives&Area=sd&ID=SP19701>, 23 March 2001.

4. Similarly, Lebanon's Christian Phalangists had supplied weapons to Hizbullah during its conflict with its fellow Shi'ites of Amal in the 1980s.

5. "Yassin to Return by End of Week," *ArabicNews.Com*, 6 September 1998, <http://www.arabicnews.com/ansub/Daily/Day/980609/1998060919.html>.

6. Olivier Roy, "Changing Patterns Among Radical Islamic Movements," *Journal of World Affairs* VI, no. 1 (Winter/Spring 1999), <http://www.brown.edu/Students/Journal_of_World_Affairs/roy61.pdf>.

7. Ze'ev Schiff, "The Blunders of Lebanon," *Ha'aretz* (Jerusalem), 7 June 2002, <http://www.4mothers.org.il/lebanon/blunders.htm>.

8. The major exception to this involved a small section of disputed territory wedged between the borders of Lebanon, Israel and Syria, called Sheba'a Farms by the Arabs and Mount Dov by the Israelis. Israel, which occupied the area in 1967, considered it part of the Golan Heights, and thus did not withdraw from there when it left South Lebanon. Beirut and Damascus both insisted the territory was part of Lebanon. Hizbullah kidnapped three Israeli soldiers there in October 2000 and periodic clashes erupted between the two sides in subsequent years.

9. Reuven Erlich, "Hizballah Leaders Promise Continued Terrorism Against Israel," International Policy Institute for Counter-Terrorism, <http://www.ict.org.il/articles/articledet.cfm?articleid=62>, 28 December 1998.
10. Mohamad Bazzi, "Hezbollah Takes Aim, Again," *Newsday*, 22 April 2002.
11. Reuven Paz, *From Tehran to Beirut to Jerusalem: Iran and Hizballah in the Palestinian Uprising*, Peace Watch no. 313 (Washington, DC: The Washington Institute for Near East Policy, 26 March 2001), and *ABC News* quoted on Albawaba.com <http://www.albawaba.com/news/index.php3?sid=213812&lang=e&dir=news.
12. "Details of Lawrence Hotel Bomber Released," Ministry of Foreign Affairs (Israel), <http://www.israel-mfa.gov.il/mfa/go.asp?MFAH0cbj0>, 16 May 1996.
13. "Mikdad: A Terrorist's Account," a documentary on his life, includes an interview with the former Hizbullah operative and footage of his interrogation. Excerpts can be viewed at the website of the International Policy Institute for Counter-Terrorism, http://www.ict.org.il/articles/mikdad1.htm.
14. Richard Beeston, "Waite Kidnapper 'Was Behind Arms Cargo'," *The Times* (London), 15 January 2002, <http://www.thetimes.co.uk/article/0,,3-2002023700,00.html>.
15. "Drug Money for Hezbollah?" *Associated Press*, 1 September 2002, <http://www.cbsnews.com/stories/2002/09/01/attack/main520457.shtml>.
16. Douglas Farah, "Al Qaeda Cash Tied to Diamond Trade," *Washington Post*, 2 November 2001, <http://www.globalpolicy.org/security/issues/diamond/2001/1102qaeda.htm>.
17. "Prepared Remarks of Attorney General John Ashcroft News Conference," U.S. Department of Justice, <http://www.bxa.doc.gov/press/2002/InfocomAshcroftRmks.html>, 18 December 2002.
18. Michael Jansen, "Sticks and Stones," *Al Ahram* (Cairo), 12 November 2001, <http://weekly.ahram.org.eg/2001/561/re3.htm>.
19. "U.S. Promises Continued Support for Lebanon's Reforms," U.S. Department of State, transcript of Beirut news conference, 14 December 2001, posted on web site of U.S. Embassy, Brussels, <http://www.uspolicy.be/Issues/Foreignpolicy/leba121401.htm>.
20. Don Radlauer, "The al-Aqsa Intifada – An Engineered Tragedy," The International Policy Institute for Counter-Terrorism, <http://www.ict.org.il/articles/articledet.cfm?articleid=440>, 7 January 2003.
21. "Israel Launches Strike on Gaza City," CNN 5 August 2002, <http://www.cnn.com/2002/WORLD/meast/08/05/mideast/>.
22. Janine Zacharia, "Hizbullah May Be Next in War on Terror," *Jerusalem Post*, 24 October 2001, <www.jpost.com/Editions/2001/10/24/News/News.36823.html>.
23. Zeina Abu Rizk, "New Rift in Alliance," *Al Ahram Weekly*, 12 November 2001, <http://weekly.ahram.org.eg/2001/560/re4.htm>.
24. Jansen, "Sticks and Stones," *Al Ahram*.

Chapter 19

1. Quoted in John Daly, "Suicide Bombing: No Warning, and No Total Solution," *Jane's Terrorism and Security Monitor*, 17 September 2001, <http://www.janes.com/security/international_security/news/jtsm/jtsm010917_1_n.shtml>.
2. Associated Press, "Americans Target of Bali Bombing," 9 November 2002.
3. Sidney Jones, *How the Jemaah Islamiyah Terrorist Network Operates*, Asia Report no. 43 (Jakarta/Brussels: International Crisis Group, 2002), 17.
4. <http://www.istimata.com.id>.
5. The impact of the Afghan war on the spread of terrorism is beyond the scope of this book. For an excellent account, see John Cooley, *Unholy Wars: Afghanistan, America and International Terrorism* (London and Sterling, VA: Pluto Press, 2002).
6. Maria Ressa, " The quest for SE Asia's Islamic 'super' state," CNN, 29 August 2002, <http://edition.cnn.com/2002/WORLD/asiapcf/southeast/07/30/seasia.state/>.

7. Yousef would be captured in a bin Laden safehouse in Pakistan in 1995 (see Associated Press, "First Trade Center Attack 10 Years Ago," <http://www.cbsnews.com/stories/2003/02/12/attack/main540376.shtml>). Mohammed would eventually be seized in Pakistan in March 2003. See Erik Eckholm, "Pakistanis Arrest Qaeda Figure Seen as Planner of 9/11," *New York Times*, 2 March 2003, <http://www.nytimes.com/2003/03/02/international/asia/02STAN.html?tntemail1>.

8. Kartika Bagus, "MMI Has No Links With Osama," *Jakarta Post*, 22 January 2002.

9. Robert W. Hefner, "Indonesian Islam at the Crossroads," *Van Zorge Report*, <http://www.vanzorgereport.com/search/index.cfm?CFID=216668&CFTOKEN=5717 0556>, February 2002.

10. Jonathan Head, "Battle for Indonesia's Islamic Vote," BBC, 4 June 1999, <http://news.bbc.co.uk/1/low/world/asia-pacific/358276.stm>.

11. James Van Zorge, "Power Means Serving Others," *Van Zorge Report*, <http://www.vanzorgereport.com/search/index.cfm?CFID=216300&CFTOKEN=11217857>, March 2002.

12. Romesh Ratnesar, "Confessions of an Al-Qaeda Terrorist," *Time*, no. 23, 23 September 2002, <http://www.time.com/time/covers/1101020923/>.

13. Sally Neighbour and Jo Puccini, "Cause and Effect: Terrorism in the Asia Pacific Region," ABC Australia Pacific, online transcript of 28 October 2002 broadcast, <http://abcasiapacific.com/cause/network/investigation_6.htm>.

14. "Hizbollah Recruited Singaporeans," *Sunday Times* (Singapore), 9 June 2002, 3.

15. Singaporean authorities discovered a letter Maidin wrote after returning from Afghanistan. In it, he told Taliban leader Mullah Omar, "I am glad to inform you that some of our brothers are ready to extend their help in the cause of Islam and the Muslims."

16. Ministry of Home Affairs, Government of Singapore, *The Jemaah Islamiyah Arrests and the Threat of Terrorism* (2003), 17.

17. Ibid, 15–16.

18. Ibid, 16.

19. Ibid, 15.

20. Ibid, 15

21. For context, each of the trucks contained at least as much explosive as was used to destroy the Federal Building in Oklahoma City.

22. Ministry of Information, Government of Singapore, *Address by Senior Minister Lee Kuan Yew at the 1st International Institute for Strategic Studies Asia Security Conference* (2002), 3.

23. Raymond Bonner and James Perlez, "More Attacks on Westerners Are Expected in Indonesia," *New York Times*, 24 November 2002.

24. Gallup Organization, "Poll Results," *USA Today*, 27 February 2002, <http://www.usatoday/news/attack/2002/2/27/usat-pollresults.htm>.

25. Ministry of Information, Government of Singapore, *Speech by Senior Minister Lee Kuan Yew for the 1st Munich Economic Summit* <http://www.gov.sg/singov/announce/120602sm.htm>, 2002.

26. Lawrence Bartlett, "Malaysia's Mahathir Pushes for Palestinian Justice," *Agence France-Press*, 20 June 2002, <http://www.inq7.net/wnw/2002/jun/21/wnw_2-1.htm>.

27. James Van Zorge, "Megawati Should Steer Her Policies Very Cautiously," *Van Zorge Report*, <http://www.vanzorgereport.com/search/index.cfm?CFID=216695&CFTOKEN=19048492>, February 2002.

28. Raymond Bonner and James Perlez, "More Attacks on Westerners Are Expected in Indonesia," *New York Times*, 24 November 2002.

29. Associated Press, "Americans Target."

30. Simon Elegant, "Unmasking Terror," *Time*, 11 November 2002, <http://www.time.com/time/search/article/0,8599,389016,00.html>.

31. Michael Backman, "Bali Bombing Looks Like the Opening of a Second Front," *The Age*, 17 October 2002, <http://www.theage.com.au/articles/2002/10/16/1034561210607.html>.
32. At that point, there was no known case of a Southeast Asian acting as a suicide bomber.
33. Jones, *Jemaah Islamiyah*, 22–4.
34. "Indonesia Police Say Bali 'Suicide Bombing' Probably an Accident," *ABC News Online*, 4 December 2002, <http://abc.net.au/news/2002/12/item20021203233406_1.htm>.
35. Ellen Nakashima and Alan Sipress, "Evidence Against Cleric Mounts," *Washington Post*, 12 February 2003, <http://www.washingtonpost.com/wp-dyn/articles/A59473-2003Feb11.html>.
36. Raymond Bonner, "Suspect in Bali Bomb Attack says Americans Were Target," *New York Times*, 12 February 2003, <http://www.nytimes.com/2003/02/12/international/asia/12BALI.html?tntemail1>.
37. <http://www.istimata.com.id>.
38. Rajiv Chandrasekaram, "Purported Bin Laden Tape Lauds Bali, Moscow Attacks," *Washington Post*, 13 November 2002, <http://www.washingtonpost.com/ac2/wp-dyn?pagename=article&node=&contentId=A45816–2002Nov12&notFound=true>.
39. There were also suspicions that the Western students may have been the real target of the Bali bombers. Many of them were scheduled to be in Bali for a field trip the following weekend, and it was common knowledge that the Sari Club was one of their favorite hangouts.
40. Bonner and Perlez, "More Attacks."

Index

Compiled by Stephanie Johnson

DS 87.53 .P565 2003

Pintak, Larry.

Seeds of hate

State Library OF Ohio

SEO Library Center
40780 SR 821 * Caldwell, OH 43724